Neither Enemies nor Friends

Neither Enemies nor Friends

Latinos, Blacks, Afro-Latinos

Edited by

Anani Dzidzienyo and Suzanne Oboler

WITHDRAWI

NEITHER ENEMIES NOR FRIENDS
© Anani Dzidzienyo and Suzanne Oboler, 2005.

First published in 2005 by
PALGRAVE MACMILLAN™
175 Fifth Avenue, New York, NY 10010 and
Houndmills, Basingstoke, Hampshire, England RG21 6XS
Companies and representatives throughout the world.

PALGRAVE MACMILLAN is the global academic imprint of the Palgrave Macmillan division of St. Martin's Press LLC and of Palgrave Macmillan Ltd. Macmillan® is a registered trademark in the United States, United Kingdom, and other countries. Palgrave is a registered trademark in the European Union and other countries.

ISBN 1–4039–6567–6 hardback
ISBN 1–4039–6568–4 paperback

Library of Congress Cataloging-in-Publication Data

Neither enemies nor friends : Latinos, Blacks, Afro Latinos / edited by Anani Dzidzienyo and Suzanne Oboler.
p.cm.
Includes bibliographical references and index.
ISBN 1–4039–6567–6 (cloth)—ISBN 1–4039–6568–4 (pbk.)
1. America—Race relations. 2. Latin America—Race relations. 3. United States—Race relations. 4. Racism—Political aspects—America. 5. Racism—political aspects—Latin America. 6. Racism—Political aspects—United States. 7. African Americans—Relations with Hispanic Americans. 8. African Americans—Race identity. 9. Hispanic Americans—Race identity. 10. Ethnicity—America. I. Dzidzienyo, Anani, 1941– II. Oboler, Suzanne.

E29.A1N45 2004
308.8'0097—dc22   2004052797

A catalogue record for this book is available from the British Library.

Design by Newgen Imaging Systems (P) Ltd., Chennai, India.

First edition: March 2005
10 9 8 7 6 5 4 3 2 1

Printed in the United States of America.

CONTENTS

PART 1
COMPARATIVE RACIALIZATION IN THE AMERICAS

Chapter 1
Flows and Counterflows: Latinas/os, Blackness, and Racialization in Hemispheric Perspective[1]

Suzanne Oboler and Anani Dzidzienyo

> *In a country of slaves, there are neither political enemies nor friends: there are some wise people who do business and an enormous mass that wants nothing other than to obey. Moreover, there are whites, Blacks, and mulattos who must continue living together. And that, in the final analysis, is this country's only difficulty.*
>
> —Baroness E. de Langsdorff, Brazil, 1842–1843[2]

Who are the Afro–Latin Americans?[3] What historical contributions do they bring to their respective national polities? What is the nature of their identity? What happens to their identities as a result of migration to the United States? What do we know of the experience of the second and subsequent generations of Afro–Latin American immigrants categorized under the current social labels as "Afro Latinas/os" in the United States? What is the impact of their growing presence within Latina/o populations, particularly with respect to the dynamics of race relations in the United States today? And, more generally, what are the possible goals, the prospects, and obstacles for coalition building between and among racial(ized) minorities and other groups in U.S. society today?

These are some of the key questions guiding the articles in this anthology, the purpose of which is twofold: on the one hand, to examine the contemporary construction and meanings attributed to blackness in the Americas, and, on the other, to acknowledge the role of population movements, specifically of Black and other nonwhite peoples such as Native Americans and Asian Americans within the hemisphere, in reshaping the ways we think about color and phenotype, as well as racialization—a term that, as defined by Darder and Torres (2003:315), alludes to "the use of 'race' in structuring social relations" in the United States today.[4]

The following pages provide a brief rationale for this volume and serve to frame the essays we have included in our anthology. We begin by proposing a transnational framework for situating the parallel origins and development of racialization in the hemisphere. Recognizing the impact of the growing circular migration of people of Latin American descent, we briefly outline some of the commonalities and differences of traditional ideologies of "race" and social hierarchy in the hemisphere. *Mestizaje* (racial mixture or miscegenation) raises questions concerning the validity of the continued adherence to traditional racial ideologies—both in terms of understanding the new transnational context of racialization and of addressing the issue of racism in the Americas and, more specifically, in the U.S. context.

We then focus on the contemporary meanings and uses of racializing categories in U.S. society, as a way of introducing some of the key issues related to the social contextualization, experiences, and relations of African Americans and other Blacks, Latinas/os, and Afro-Latinas/os in the United States. In this section, we discuss the reorganization of society in explicitly racializing terms and examine the potential for, and obstacles to, mobilization and alliance building between African Americans/Blacks and Hispanics/Latinas/os. We also center the role of the Afro-Latina/o in the current historical context in which, for the first time, African Americans have been officially outnumbered by Latinas/os, as the nation's largest minority. We conclude with a brief description of the essays in this volume.

Framing the Debate on Blackness and Racialization in the Americas

There is, it is true, a third world within the first world, and a first world within the third world. But shared misfortune is the consolation of fools. What is important is for us to realize that both worlds, first and third, are unified by global economic integration, by a world-wide dissemination of information, and by the growing migratory currents from west to east, but, above all, from south to north. We have entered a co-responsible universe. Will we know how to assume it? Today, the words by the English Labor leader, Clement Attlee, again take on their full import: "We cannot survive if we create a paradise within our borders and tolerate a hell beyond them."

—Carlos Fuentes (1996)

The idea for this anthology on the meanings attributed to blackness and racialization in the Americas originally emerged from our interest in the implications for contemporary race relations in the United States of a twofold concern. On one hand, there are the very real issues raised by the political boundaries between the United States and Latin America. Border controls, national guards, passports, visas, Orwellian proposals for individual fingerprinting of foreigners, immigration laws, propositions, and policies remind us every day of the continuing relevance of the nation-state as the granter and guarantor of citizenship and rights. On the other, there is the fact that neither visas nor border patrols—nor barbed wire fences or cement walls for that matter—can prevent the values, socialization, and cultural forces that immigrant parents bring with them from also shaping and affecting the lives, ways of thinking, political choices, and positions of their U.S.-born and -raised children. Moreover, many migrant-receiving nations such as the United States have proven unable to stem the undocumented flow of people across their borders.

Thus, understanding that the ideology of racism, like the current flow of corporate capital, recognizes no national boundaries and does not respect the sovereignty of the various democracies in the Western Hemisphere, we organized this anthology as a contribution toward reframing and reconceptualizing the relationship between

North and Latin America, specifically as it refers to the flow and counterflow of racial ideas today. This anthology, then, is informed by the current process of globalization, which threatens in very real terms both to deepen the unresolved and enslaving legacies of the past and to exacerbate the ongoing and unmitigated suffering of the many, provoked by the unbridled greed of the few, thus setting the stage for an all-out war of all against all. Indeed, like our new global context, these ideas are grounded in the international exacerbation of the economic and political principles of late-nineteenth-century imperialism and its ongoing consequences in the Americas.

Certainly, the rationale for better understanding the hemisphere's racial ideologies has been rendered more evident by the globalization of national economies. Together with the glaring extremes of poverty and ever-widening population movements throughout the hemisphere, the task of constructing a common paradigm for the societies of the Americas has become all the more urgent. Incidents such as the police beating of Rodney King in Los Angeles in the spring of 1992 and the massive deportation of Haitians from the Dominican Republic during the 1990s are reminders of the unabating violence of racism and provide a glimpse into the shared experience of Blacks and dark-skinned "others" in the two Americas. Indeed, persistent racial and social prejudices and discrimination continue to be the cornerstone for the practical disenfranchisement of the hemisphere's populations.

The visible consequences of neoliberalism—with the concomitant implosion of the nation-state—unambiguously signify the demolition of the "social contract" on which, according to Locke, the security of the commonwealth depends. This phenomenon is exemplified by the growing unemployment, reduced social services, and rampant poverty of significant segments of the populations throughout the Americas, and the accompanying rise in crime and drug and human trafficking. The cumulative effect of these realities leaves little if any doubt as to the existence today of a widening chasm, which Carlos Fuentes (1996) has called "a third world within the first world, and a first world within the third world." Indeed, the lives of the growing numbers of poor and disenfranchised people in the Americas—many of them "nonwhite"—provide a sharp and painful contrast to the wealth, sophisticated technology, and high standards of living of a relatively small segment of the population, comprising a semianonymous transnational economic caste emerging from the elites of the hemisphere's nations.[5] Again, many of the latter elites are lighter-skinned than most of their compatriots.

Whether in the United States or in the societies of Latin America, equality of opportunity, like access to the rule of law, differs according to social class (Guimarães, 2001). In Latin America the rich are above the law, while the poor are victims of the law (Mendez, O'Donnell, and Pinheiro, 1999)—a situation that is not entirely foreign to poor racial minorities in the U.S. context as well. Indeed, whether in the United States or in Latin America, it is increasingly difficult to ignore the growing recourse to what William Greider (1992) has called "hollow laws," the implications of the spiraling numbers of socially and politically excluded populations, the abrupt ossification of channels of political participation, and the disappearance of viable alternative policy solutions. Together, they raise serious and complex questions about the future consequences of relations between and among racial, ethnic, and other social groups, of the decline of traditional representative institutions, and of the strangulation of the public sphere.

"Freedom" has always had a different meaning for Blacks and other "people of color" throughout the Americas when they censure their movements on streets and in areas where people of white-European descent live; when the hemisphere's indigenous populations know they take a chance by leaving their towns, villages, or reservations; or when African Americans, Blacks, Afro-Latinas/os, Afro–Latin Americans, dark-skinned mestizos, and people of Asian descent are discriminated against in terms of employment and denied access to political and other institutions in the societies of the Americas. Seen from the perspective of those without the right to full citizenship, the world, as Hannah Arendt once observed, does indeed become inhuman and inhospitable to human needs.

Struggles for social justice, grounded in demands for political inclusion and equality in spite of difference, are today being waged by the disenfranchised sectors throughout the hemisphere. The latter include many whose racial and ethnic characteristics have long ensured the denial of their right to full citizenship and belonging. In the United States, for example, more than thirty years after the civil rights movements for inclusion, there is growing vocal disagreement about the actual intent of resulting measures and programs, such as affirmative action. Intended as much to ensure the minimal rights of all, as it was to alleviate the suffering of the society's least fortunate members, this program, after all, was designed primarily to overcome racial discrimination and national fragmentation. Similarly, the push to establish bilingual education as a way of incorporating nonnative English speakers into the American educational system drew much of its inspiration from the civil rights movement. It too is under attack today. Contemporary mass mobilizations and nationwide movements and protests such as those following the verdict in the Rodney King case in Los Angeles (1992), the Million Man March (1995), the Latino March on Washington in support of immigrant rights (1996), the Poor People's March (August 2003), and the Immigrant Workers Freedom Ride in the early fall of 2003, all point to the continuing relevance of political initiatives specifically aimed at the inclusion of people of color in U.S. society.

In Latin America, particularly since the 1980s, there has been a marked increase in the mobilization of indigenous populations of various countries. As Rodrigo Montoya Rojas (1998:9–10) observes:

> In Mexico, Guatemala, Nicaragua, Colombia, Ecuador, Brazil, Bolivia, Chile, and Peru, they are winning battles and their presence on the political scene in those countries shows one of the deep limits of the frustrated dream of nation-states with one state, one nation, one language, one culture, one religion. With varying intensity, their multiple voices make the case for the need and the urgency of multinational, multicultural, and multilingual societies: for societies in which their right to difference, their ethnic citizenship, is recognized concomitantly with their national citizenship. (Our translation.)

Indeed, these contemporary national and transnational movements of indigenous people respond to a historical legacy of political marginalization and unanswered demands for social justice, and also attempt to confront the destructive and relentless assault of current neoliberal policies on indigenous communities (Díaz-Polanco, 1999; Collier, 1994; Van Cott, 1994; Brysk, 1994). In so doing, they have demonstrated, once again, that regardless of the triumph of ideologies of national unity and *mestizaje*, or race mixture, racism—the ideology of the inherent superiority of one population group over another[6]—continues to be a major obstacle in the quest for and attainment of social justice and political inclusion throughout the continent. As Ariel Dulitzky correctly notes in his contribution to this volume, "the official notion of mixed race (*mestizaje*) camouflages diversity, denies nonwhites the right to dissent, while making conditions ripe for excluding anyone who falls outside the 'norm' of *mestizo* or mixed."

Similarly, the recent emergence of social movements and organizations created by Afro–Latin Americans and Afro-Caribbean populations has underscored the intersection of the interests of national nongovernmental organizations and transnational donor organizations (see Ariel Dulitzky's discussion in this volume). That these organizations of Afro–Latin Americans have been able to meet and caucus across national boundaries is a major achievement and poses a challenge to traditional nationalist expressions, more often than not through the medium of nongovernmental organizations. The very nature of NGOs dictates that their activities are directed toward the pursuit of specific goals that may or may not impact on the formation or strengthening of broader political programs. Nonetheless, as the specific cases of Brazil, Colombia, and Ecuador attest, such potential limitations do not in any way undermine the significance of these new Afro–Latin American social movements. Since the late 1970s, for example, Brazil has witnessed the unprecedented emergence of large numbers of Afro-Brazilian organizations, which have been increasingly recognized by both federal and local authorities as well as by various sectors of civil society. In Colombia and Ecuador, national constitutional changes in the 1990s resulted in the two states' formally granting the recognition of collective rights to their respective indigenous populations. In other words, in addressing the specificities of the national experience of indigenous peoples, the mere recognition of the rights of citizens, or individual rights, as traditionally sustained through the acknowledgment of liberal birthright citizenship, was formally recognized to be insufficient by the respective states of both of these multicultural Latin American societies. As Héctor Díaz-Polanco (1999: 148) has explained, "While they are generally essential, these rights neither contain nor reflect the whole range of vital needs of these ethnic groups, particularly as collective entities. In some cases, even the ways that civic rights are formulated in basic law can transform them into restrictions against the sociocultural practices of indigenous peoples." Still, as Carlos de la Torre suggests in this volume, these legislative changes have had important spillover effects for the respective African-descended population groups in each country, for they too have benefited both through new entitlements to historically occupied land and the official recognition of their rights (see also Wade, 1997).[7]

The significance of recent legislative and political gains in the Latin American context cannot be underestimated. For contrary to the United States, where "race" has had a long and complicated history of uncompromising belligerence in structuring public identities and private destinies, in Latin America the celebration of the official ideologies of *mestizaje* in most countries (Torres and Whitten, 1998: 7)—except perhaps in the Southern Cone, where the celebration of whiteness has been much more prevalent—has led to the neglect of racial difference as a significant aspect of social experience, emphasizing instead class and gender as the principal and often sole explanatory and analytical categories. This way of thinking has tended to put the burden of upholding national myths of racial harmony on individuals' efforts to whiten and hence "improve" the race, whether through intermarriage or informal interracial sexual unions (Callirgos, 1993)—thus justifying the ongoing political and social marginality of nonwhite populations in the varied national contexts of that continent. Indeed, this discourse of "racial democracy" has long been dominant in countries as different as Brazil, Cuba, Puerto Rico, and Venezuela.

Precisely because the focus of Latin American and Caribbean societies is on national unity (i.e., "we are all Peruvians," "we are all Colombians," "we are all Mexicans," etc.), attempts by Blacks to draw attention to racial discrimination, or to address their issues in those terms, have consistently been met with accusations that they are subverting the nation and going against the national interest, which puts an unfair burden on them. From a political point of view, anytime Blacks in Latin American societies seek to organize, they have to begin with a self-denying statement explaining that in fighting for their rights, they are not against the nation. Indeed, as Roberto Márquez (2000), citing Zenón Cruz, has observed, the most omnipresent datum about anti-Black Latin American racism is the absurdity and obstinacy of the negation of its existence.

From a comparative hemispheric perspective, one of the unintended consequences of Jim Crow and the history of segregation in U.S. society is the existence of much stronger African American institutions and organizations (Marable, 1996: 5–6). Indeed, the history of segregation in U.S. society ensured that African Americans organized under a racial banner. Hence, African Americans have been less subjected to "national condemnation" than Latin America's Black populations, precisely as a result of the history and practice of Jim Crow and the consequent existence of separate institutions, ranging from churches to public institutions of higher learning and civic organizations dedicated to securing full rights of participation unfettered by racial history. The irony lies in the fact that in Latin America, the nonracialized common citizenship in the wake of independence actually became the venue for the foundation of the first political parties by Blacks in the Americas—first in Cuba (Helg, 1995) and later in Brazil, with the founding of the Frente Negra Brasileira in 1937 (Fernandes, 1969; Dzidzienyo, 1979; Hanchard, 1999).

The corollary of this is that national unity, grounded in the unifying myth of racial miscegenation in Latin America, ignores and underplays in certain countries the oppositional initiatives that Blacks have articulated and undertaken while fully aware of the hostile environment in which they are operating (Helg, 1995). From this point of view, a careful examination of the respective historical sociocial records of each Latin American country might prove invaluable for both advocates and opponents of the move to introduce a multiracial category, particularly in the current context of a growing emphasis on nationalist ideologies tinged with xenophobic supremacy in the U.S. political sphere.

Indeed, in view of the current circular or return migration patterns of people of Latin American descent to and from the United States and the potential impact of this demographic phenomenon in redefining racial and ethnic relations in this society, understanding the historical and contemporary racial representations in Latin America, as well as how these are being transplanted and reformulated in the context of U.S. racial ideologies, could prove to be useful for the ongoing discussion of racialization and for the very concepts of multiracialism and multiculturalism in U.S. society today.

Mestizaje: Race Mixture and Multiracialism in the Two Americas

The negative politics that unfortunately debase us emerged out of that social regime, because we ended up without a people. Slavery did not allow us to get organized, and without the people, institutions don't have roots, opinions lack support, the society has no foundations . . . the national will does not exist.

—Joaquim Nabuco[8]

To reformulate our understanding of the societies of the Americas in hemispheric terms is to provide one approach to the ways in which racism transcends national boundaries and, in so doing, transforms specific national histories and cultural differences into hemispheric categories. Indeed, one of the underlying questions of this anthology is: Do Blacks in the Americas have a greater commonality of experience across the hemisphere, resulting primarily from a comparable historical heritage of slavery, than they do with their noncolored compatriots? And if so, to what extent can this be said to be the case?[9]

Certainly, like the genocide of indigenous people, which effectively cleared the terrain for the conquered, slavery, together with other forms of servitude and coerced labor, has been a cornerstone in the historical process of nation building in the hemisphere as a whole. It has long been acknowledged to be the "original sin" that gave birth to racism as we have come to know it in the hemisphere today. Similarly, scholars have long accepted the reality of U.S. dominance and ideological influence in shaping the political economy and cultural developments of the entire hemisphere. Yet, there is resistance to the notion of a shared ideology rooted in racial and social differences in the "two Americas." As a result, studies of the varied societies and national realities continue for the most part to reinforce the questionable commonplace that "race" (rather than class or wealth) is *the* fundamental "American" (i.e., U.S.) paradox or dilemma, to quote Gunnar Myrdal's (1969) classic title, while issues of "class" and poverty—rather than race—are the "real" problems in Latin America.

Indeed, in addressing the question of the contemporary meanings of blackness and racialization in the hemisphere, it is important to note that, unlike the United States, Latin American societies rarely acknowledge "race" per se as an important historical signifier of experience (Guimarães, 2000; 2001:157–185).[10] Instead, in spite of glaring prejudices based on color and phenotype in all the Latin American countries, there is still a distinct preference for focusing on social, "cultural," and class considerations. At the same time, the steadfast adherence to ideologies of progressive "whitening" (*blanqueamiento*) continues to be difficult to overcome. Class-based considerations embedded in such popular euphemisms as "money whitens" have tended to subsume racial considerations in debates on social and political equality and justice in Latin America. Yet, despite each country's historical and sociopolitical specificities, this in no way undermines the extent to which the postcolonial racial hierarchy of the hemisphere continues to contribute toward structuring and limiting access to full citizenship rights of Blacks and indigenous populations throughout the region. As this collection of essays makes clear, important commonalities in the Black experience in the Americas have tended to be obscured by a continuing overemphasis on the race-versus-class binary and by such persistent myths as Latin America's supposedly more "benign" slavery and its consequences.[11] In spite of historical and contemporary evidence to the contrary, these notions have framed discussions in the scholarly literature and in newspaper and journalistic accounts of daily life in both the United States and Latin America.

The fallacy of the continued adherence to these artificial ideological constructs became patently clear in the U.S. context during the summer of 1996, when a series of articles in the *New York Times* discussed the question of interracial marriages and publicized the efforts of the growing movement to include a multiracial category in the U.S. Census for the year 2000. The zeal with which the *New York Times* reported on the movement is noteworthy, particularly because, according to one writer (Marriot, 1996), its success would actually only affect 1.6 percent of the national population.

The various articles on the multiracial movement in the *New York Times* and their readers' letters of response raise questions that, to this day, are important and pertinent for both the movement's participants and the nation's population as a whole (cf. also, Root, 1996; Wright, 1994). What does it mean, for example, "to belong" in the United States, a country where, as the African American experience has long shown, fitting into the racialized idea (white, Anglo-Saxon, Protestant) of *who* is an American—rather than birthright—has historically been the true measure and mark of belonging? After all, as Charles Byrd, editor and publisher of *Interracial Voice,* put it: "People of mixed race in this country haven't belonged anywhere" (Marriot, 1996: 1, 7).[12] Similarly, what does it mean that those who are visibly nonwhite and of non-European descent—large sectors of the Latina/o populations, Asian Americans, or Arab Americans, for example—continue to elicit the question "Where are you from?" in spite of being born in the United States? More specifically, what does it mean that any person of color who is a U.S. citizen and who has ever been asked "Where are you from?" may always have to contend, at some level, with that question's implicit counterpart: "Are you here to stay?"

These questions are not fortuitous, particularly when seen from the comparative perspective of the histories and societies of other countries in this hemisphere. Latin

American elites have long acknowledged and in fact prided themselves on their multiracial composition and their reliance on *mestizaje* to undermine racist attitudes in structuring the continent's respective national identities. As Charles Hale (1996:2) has argued, racial mixture, or *mestizaje*, "has been a remarkably effective ideological tool in the hands of elites in many parts of Latin America, a unifying myth put to the service of state and nation building." Yet national ideals and aspirations cannot be a substitute for societal realities or everyday practices. As a result, miscegenation—which, after all, has as its historical origin in the physical rape of enslaved indigenous and African women by European men and their descendants—has never necessarily ensured political equality in Latin America, nor has it meant either racial integration or social assimilation.[13]

Indeed, Latin America's early history of miscegenation has long been presented as having firmly established the prevalence of social status over race in the cultural attitudes and perceptions of the populations that persist to this day (Morse, 1968: 164–165). A graded system of color prejudices, or pigmentocracy, was interwoven with the perceived social status of different groups, ultimately creating a highly rigid and entrenched castelike hierarchy whose remnants are still clearly visible in Latin American societies today. From early on, this system created what Peter Wade (1985:233–249, 233) defined as "a black-white continuum (as opposed to the North American black-white division) which places Blacks at the bottom of the social scale while allowing light-skin mulattoes to dissociate themselves from Blacks and be accepted as socially distinct, permitting some of them to 'marry up' racially" (1985:233–249).[14] In other places, Indians were confined to the lower end of the social structure, while lighter-skinned mestizos could sometimes pass as "honorary whites" (e.g., *ladinos* in Guatemala, *trigueños* in other countries).

Thus, along with our earlier argument concerning the commonalities across borders created by the experience of blackness, a second assumption of this book is that although the distinct national composition and demographics in some areas have allocated indigenous peoples to a subordinate position relative to Blacks, they have firmly established the idea that the understanding of blackness—like that of Indianness—is also premised on the group's social position in the country-specific social hierarchies, rather than determined solely on the basis of color and ethnic and linguistic cultures and attributes (dos Santos, 1996:219–224; de la Cadena, 1998:143–164). In short, miscegenation is not necessarily incompatible with segregation, although such segregation can assume forms which differ from the rigid Black–white dichotomy that has historically been prevalent in the United States. Moreover, despite the emphasis through the ideology of *mestizaje* on social class and status, the Black–white continuum has ensured that the marginalization of Black Latin Americans in some nations—or alternatively, the search in others for "solutions" to the "Indian question"—has persisted throughout the twentieth century (Graham, 1990; Minority Rights Group, 1995) and appears to have gained a firm foothold into the twenty-first.

Indeed, in contrast to the patterns of segmented nationality and the history of discrimination against Blacks in the United States, the emphasis on the preeminence of shared nationality in Latin America, with equal rights for all citizens, has long been the ideological staple of the respective governments and social institutions alike. National ideologies have long contributed to the undermining of the discussion on the practical significance of race and racism, obscuring customary practices grounded in racial and color hierarchies, which are heavily weighted in favor of "whiteness." Throughout the continent, these practices have shaped identities, determined people's social location, and, ultimately, reinforced substantially the prejudices against people of African descent, as well as other racial minorities within specific countries. Latin Americans with more pronounced African/Negroid features, as Paulo de Carvalho Neto (1978) has demonstrated, continue to bear the brunt of the prejudice and discrimination in their societies. Indeed, while some Latin American countries may have "nationalized blackness,"[15] the work of Carvalho Neto points to the blatant antiblack sentiments present in day-to-day narratives, popular sayings, and folklore. In other words, the fact that there have been less overt legal proscriptions throughout Latin America has not constituted an effective antidote to a veritable array of customary practices whose over-all import has been the "nationalization" and "naturalization" of Black marginalization throughout the hemisphere.

To frame the discussion of comparative racialization (United States versus Latin America) exclusively in terms of legally sanctioned measures or an index of toler-ated public violence (such as lynching) thus misses the point. It is off the mark precisely *because of* the weight of custom as lived daily experience, as against the *possi-bility* of recourse to explicit constitutional legal antidiscrimination provisions, in Latin America as in the United States, in determining individuals' life chances for social incorporation (López, 1992; Da Matta, 1991: 429–442; de Carvalho Neto, 1978).

The Process of Racialization in the U.S. Context

Being labeled "black" in the U.S. carries a heavy burden of stereotypes that many black latinos would rather not deal with. In my view, if police in a store is following you or you're beaten by the police, it doesn't really matter what you check on a census form.
—Delinda Price (Griffith, 1991: A10)

—*"I'm a Negro."*
—*"You ain't no nigger," José said.*
—*"I ain't?"*
—*"No. You're a Puerto Rican. . . . We're Puerto Ricans, and that's different from being moyetos [a Black man]. . . ."*
—*"That's what I've been wanting to believe all along, José," I said. "I've been hanging on to that idea even when I knew it wasn't so. But only pure white Puerto Ricans are white, and you wouldn't even believe that if you ever dug what the paddy said."*
—Piri Thomas (1991 [1967]: 143–144)

That racial identities are not categorically fixed, that they are subject to constant fluctuations in terms of both their meanings and social value, is so commonly accepted today as to obviate any further elaboration, on our part, of conventional discourses (cf. Winant, 1994 and 2002; Frederickson, 2002). As Jean Rahier (1999: 74–75) notes:

> Cultural, ethnic, or "racial" identities must be understood within the always fluctuating political, economic, and social processes and inscribed in particular spatial-temporal contexts, constituted within local, regional, national, and transnational areas. Identities and their representations are constantly imagined and reimagined, acted and reenacted in specific situations and in political and socioeconomic contexts that are always changing and that provide sites for their negotiation and renegotiation, their definition and redefinition.

Nevertheless, particularly when discussing the issue of racialization in U.S. society, we cannot assume that fluidity in matters of identity is open-ended for all individuals at all times, as the exchange between the Afro-Puerto Rican author Piri Thomas and his brother José exemplifies. Instead, the current ethno-racial context has immersed all U.S. citizens and residents in a paradoxical and complex socioracial conundrum, resulting from the unprecedented decision formulated by the Bureau of the Census in 1977 to recategorize the entire U.S. population into five racial or ethnic groups. Indeed, it seems to us that even if the official classifications now in use were to be abandoned, the nation's historical legacy, together with the effects of the now over twenty-five years of these official racializing labels, cannot be so easily dismissed or ignored.

First created through Directive 15 issued by the Office of Management and Budget, these original classifications were revised in the 1990s (Rodríguez, 2000; Forbes, 1992:59–78; see also Fuchs, 1997:24–28). The official racial categories are now American Indian or Alaska Native; Asian; Black or African American; Native Hawaiian or Other Pacific Islander; and White. "Hispanic" or "Latino" is considered an "ethnicity," for Hispanics "can be of any race."[16] At the time, the fundamentally quantitative nature of these categories was deemed to serve an important purpose, not merely for each group, but for the nation as a whole; unfortunately, that purpose seems to have been largely forgotten today. These categories were initially created in response to the need to address the issue of racial inequalities in U.S. society. Indeed, they were intended to measure how well the nation was doing in the struggle against the racism and social exclusion that had initially led to the emergence of the various civil rights movements. In other words, the origins of recent official ethnic and racial labels are to be found in the government's response to the need to provide such social indicators as how many Latinas/os are in fact graduating from high school or college; to measure how many African Americans are getting loans or mortgages; and to track the progress toward desegregating schools and neighborhoods in the major cities around the country. The idea was that this documentation would allow affirmative action to rectify ongoing social inequalities created by the historical legacy of racism in U.S. society (Oboler, 2000b). Measuring, tracking, and empirically documenting the nation's progress toward becoming a society of equals, "that is, toward a fuller realization of the promise of citizenship inherent in the 14th Amendment of 1868," is a far cry from the creation of a "quota system," the term that U.S. conservatives have tagged on to what became known as affirmative action policies.

Indeed, it is well worth recalling that affirmative action emerged as a result of the civil rights movements of the 1950s and 1960s to address the persistence of racially based inequalities and discrimination in the United States (Chafe, 1986: 127–148).[17] As Manning Marable (1996:3) has noted, "Affirmative action per se was never a law, or even a coherently developed set of governmental policies designed to attack institutional racism and societal discrimination." Nevertheless, while there is no official document explicitly defining affirmative action, its clearest articulation as a policy can be found in President Lyndon B. Johnson's 1966 formulation of its principal objective—to establish "equality as a fact and as result" in U.S. society.[18] Later, when affirmative action was challenged in the courts, Justice Harry Blackmun upheld its continuance in the U.S. Supreme Court decision of 1978, bluntly explaining its rationale and ongoing legitimacy in U.S. society: "In order to get beyond racism, we must first take account of race. There is no other way. And in order to treat some persons equally, we must treat them differently. We cannot—we dare not—let the equal protection clause perpetuate racial supremacy" (cited in Frederickson, 2002:143).

Today, in the absence of viable political alternatives, protecting any measure designed to counteract the persistence of racism has become an exigency of citizenship. Indeed, as Kevin Johnson's chapter in this volume on the ongoing racial profiling of minorities suggests, the continued marginalization of racialized populations, like African Americans and Latinas/os, and their exclusion from full access to citizenship remains a central concern in the ongoing debates on the meanings and social value of ethnicity and the persistence of racism in U.S. society.

Elsewhere in the hemisphere we see evidence of the flow of racial ideas. Public discussions in Brazil now focus on issues relating to affirmative action, quotas, the role of the state in righting the wrongs of the past. Fundamental questions are being posed at all levels of government: Is it even appropriate, some ask, to introduce affirmative action in a society that widely embraces its African heritage? In view of extensive miscegenation and myriad definitions of race—all of which complicate the business of applying the correct racial label to individuals—what will determine who should properly benefit from affirmative action? As in the United States, affirmative action has also been conflated with quotas, igniting discussion of possible threats to "standards." Invariably, questions are also being raised concerning the very introduction of these discussions as a function of noxious North Americanization, which, in the name of cultural sovereignty, must be constantly combated—a point that Silvio Torres Saillant eloquently addresses in his provocative essay on U.S. Latinas/os' role in Afro–Latin Americans' struggles for justice.

These developments in Brazil underscore efforts to confront the history of racial and class discrimination and inequality, and the role of the state and the law in enforcing, facilitating, or combating practices—both legal and customary—in a society that has long been perceived to be one of the leading "symbols" of miscegenation and "racial democracy." In Cuba and Puerto Rico, two other societies where these myths have long prevailed, "affirmative action" practices have proven difficult to implement, for different reasons, as Alejandro de la Fuente (2001) has shown.

Whether in Latin America or in the U.S. context, we contend, these debates on affirmative action and racialization will undoubtedly become increasingly fractious, precisely *because* the respective histories and legacies of racism have yet to be fully confronted in institutional and social terms. Moreover, in the new post-9/11 context, it is unlikely that in the United States discussions about racializing diverse populations, like the recently more pronounced practice of "racial profiling," will disappear in the coming years. Instead, we would argue that similar to Latin American societies, as the gap between rich and poor continues to widen in U.S. society (Darder and Torres, 2003), and as social mobility continues to decline and "caste lines" continue to rigidify, it is inevitable that the poverty line will become even more visibly drawn in racial(ized) terms—even as the recommendations of official reports and government task forces created to address socioracial inequities continue to be shelved and forgotten almost as soon as they are released.[19] Indeed, in our post-9/11 world the problem of addressing racial and social inequalities, like the achievement of justice, is increasingly being pushed into the background in the context of the prioritization of the national security doctrine.[20]

Blacks, Latinas/os, and Afro-Latinas/os in U.S. Society

The white man stood and watched for the next two hours as the Blacks worked in their groups and the Mexicans in theirs. . . . At a shift change, the black man walked away, hosed himself down and turned in his knives. Then he let go. . . . "Who that cracker think he is?" the black man wanted to know. . . . "Keep treating me like a Mexican and I'll beat him!"

As for Blacks, she avoided them. She was scared of them. "Blacks don't want to work," Mrs. Fernandez said. . . . "They're lazy."

—Charles LeDuff (2000)

I have to sift through my own feelings and see how I react to an idea as a Latino [sic] or as a person of African descent. I perceive myself as what's obvious first and what's not so obvious second. The Latino part comes later.

Patricia Walker (LeDuff, 2000)

While national ideologies have long ensured that discussions on "race" remain very much taboo throughout Latin America, once in the United States, and regardless of class, race, or national origins, Latin American immigrants are forced to learn, understand, and incorporate into their daily lives the meanings and social value attributed to the officially imposed, pan-ethnic label, Hispanic. In 1997 the OMB also incorporated the term *Latino*, which until then had been a grassroots alternative to the term *Hispanic*. The official imposition of a new—Hispanic or Latina/o—social identity in turn effectively erases their national, political, social, cultural, or ethnic characteristics and hence differences (Oboler, 1995), insofar as the hegemonic classification system only recognizes their common geographic and assumed linguistic background. Hence not only does arrival signify learning the customs and values (including ethnoracial cultural views and perceptions and behaviors of the dominant society), but equally important is that for many Latin Americans arrival in the United States also signals the first time they meet Latin American nationals from other countries presumed automatically to be more like themselves. A Peruvian may never have set eyes on, much less thought about, the anomaly of Puerto Ricans' political status as colonial citizens of the United States; an Afro-Colombian may never have imagined that he or she would come in contact with an Afro–Costa Rican or a Chilean of European descent. Very few Latin Americans, including some Mexican immigrants, are fully aware of the long presence of Mexican Americans or Chicanas/os on what is now United States territory, dating back to the pre-Puritan days, or their history of conquest and colonization in what is today the Southwest.

Paradoxically, however, the need to come to terms with pan-ethnic identifiers in the larger U.S. society can simultaneously bring to light, for Latin American immigrants, the specificities of the racial meanings and values that nationalist ideologies suppress in Latin America, and to which they may not have given much thought. As Bobby Vaughn and others in this volume exemplify, this can invariably exacerbate divisions within specific national groups in the context of U.S. society.

Thus, it is important to focus on the specificity of the life experience of both Afro–Latin Americans and U.S.-born and/or -raised Afro-Latinas/os. After all, as the essays in this anthology suggest, while the stigma of blackness is similar throughout the hemisphere, the *experience* of blackness is heterogeneous depending on historical and cultural characteristics as well as the demographic composition of each country. Regardless of the homogenizing nature of the label *Hispanic* or *Latina/o*, once in the United States, the national and ethnic differences of first-generation immigrants from various nations do not automatically disappear. The case of Afro-Dominicans and the reconfiguration of their relations with Haitians in the U.S. context, for example, will be of a different order than that of Afro-Ecuadorians and their interactions with either Dominicans or Haitians, or indeed other Blacks, within the U.S. urban setting. Afro-Panamanians of Jamaican and other Caribbean descent may shift between their allegiances to a putative pan-Hispanic community and an African American racial identity.

Indeed, as Roberto Márquez (2000) has cogently argued, the Afro-Latina/o population in the United States continues to have a salient and crucial role in the development and emergence of the critique of the more covert and courtly class and racial protocols of Latin American convention. Afro-Latinas/os are, as he points out, strategically located between the two realities and hence are positioned to be at the transnational center of any debate on this issue. Within the United States, besides their meeting and interaction with non-Afro-Latinos from their respective countries of origin, Afro–Latin Americans interact with U.S.-born Latinas/os and Afro-Latinas/os of other national origins, as well as with African Americans and other Blacks from the Caribbean and continental Africa. Not surprisingly, already abundant opportunities for understanding, discovery, and assertion of solidarities, as well as for their direct or indirect negation, may surge, given that in early 2003 the U.S. Census Bureau announced with great fanfare that "Hispanics," at roughly 37 million people, had surpassed the estimated 36.2 million African Americans to become the largest minority in the United States (Darder and Torres, 2003:307).

Increased numbers do not necessarily translate into greater political power. Still, leaving aside the fact that to date, the presence of Afro-Latinas/os among those identified as "Hispanics" has been publicly neglected, that Latinas/os are now the largest statistical minority in the nation is, nevertheless, a significant milestone in U.S. history—given the extent to which U.S. politics, culture, and race relations have all been so indelibly marked and understood in terms of the white-majority/Black-minority paradigm.

This new status of Latinas/os as the "majority minority" does raise different kinds of questions for the future of both Latinas/os and the society as a whole. For one thing, the demographic milestone will undoubtedly help to reverse the traditional invisibility in which the two largest Latina/o historical minorities—Mexican Americans and Puerto Ricans—have historically lived in U.S. politics and society. In so doing, it reinforces awareness of the ongoing historical exclusion of these two national origin groups from full participation in the U.S. polity. Paradoxically, however, it is important to keep in mind that while the term *Latina/o* (or *Hispanic*) makes the presence of Chicanas/os and Puerto Ricans more marked in U.S. society, it simultaneously serves to obscure the specificity of their respective histories and experiences, as well as their colonized relations with the United States (Oboler, 2000b). At the same time, a repositioning of African Americans in the U.S. polity and society is also likely. Moreover, while this demographic change clearly raises concerns for the African American population in the United States,[21] it can also contribute toward reconfiguring discussions on the possibilities of constructing long-term alliances between them and Latinas/os, as well as on the obstacles to their realization (Betancur and Gills, 2000; McClain, 1996).

Public debates and journalistic reports on the changing demographics have focused on the appropriateness and/or types of classifications and labeling of the U.S. population, creating some debate within academic circles about the implications for U.S. society and minorities alike of the persistent exclusion of racial minorities in U.S. society. Still, beyond these discussions, the new officially recognized demographics invariably mirror, as Tatcho Mindiola, Yolanda Flores-Niemann, and Nestor Rodríguez (2002) point out, the much greater visibility of Latinos and African Americans in the daily life of the society, as exemplified by a variety of social settings, ranging from schools and workplaces to social service agencies and neighborhoods. In this respect, the decennial census report brought to light the extent to which Latinos are now immigrating in significant numbers to parts of the country such as Georgia and North Carolina, where African Americans have historically been the predominant minority (Murphy, Blanchard, and Hill 2001; Fink, 2003), forcing those regions to contend with and address racial issues that to date were restricted to other parts of the nation, such as New York or California. Moreover, referring to the African American and Latino populations, Mindiola, Flores-Niemann, and Rodríguez note that "the 2000 census showed that together, these two group of color outnumbered non-Hispanic Whites in the five largest U.S. cities," namely, New York, Los Angeles, Chicago, Houston, and Philadelphia. This too, as the authors point out, "had never happened before in U.S. history."

Even leaving aside the specific problematic of the Afro-Latinas/os, in view of the changing national demographics and the growth of the Latina/o population in the United States, there have been few in-depth studies exploring interminority relations and, more specifically, those between African Americans and Latinas/os in the U.S. context. For the most part, the relatively few published studies have focused on the politics of joint action, as well as the pros and cons of coalition building. Moreover, barring those that center solely on a particular national origin group (e.g., Cruz, 1998; Rivera, 2003; Torres, 1995), Latinas/os are invariably presented as a politically, culturally, and linguistically monolithic group with very little, if any, focus on the practical implications of their national, regional, social, and racial differences. With the notable exception of the recent book by Nicholas De Genova and Ana Ramos-Zayas (2003) and the above-cited study by Mindiola et al. (2002), which focuses primarily on the role of stereotypes in shaping "Black-brown" relations, there has been minimal consideration of the ways that time of arrival and legal status (e.g., whether long-term citizens or recent immigrant) might impact not only on relations between Blacks and Latinas/os but also on intragroup relations, in national, cultural, generational, or, of course, socioracial terms.

Whether in official documents or in academic studies, the racial/color dimension is consistently neglected, such that many scholars and others do not take seriously the caveat repeatedly pointed out by the U.S. census that Latinas/os "can be of any race." This has deprived us of an opportunity to further unravel the changing meanings of Blackness in U.S. politics and sociocultural relations. Similarly, it does not allow scholars to examine the critical role that Afro-Latinas/os might play in shaping discourses and serving as bridges in more effective cooperative actions that could transcend traditional electoral politics. Indeed, it is our contention that any discussion on Black-Latina/o relations and alliances must also invariably problematize the position of Latinas/os who are visibly black—that is, of Afro-Latinas/os—in terms, for example, of their potential impact on contemporary debates on race relations, particularly as these contribute to the changing articulation of the U.S. polity. The specificity of the Afro-Latina/o experience, like the heightened tensions exacerbated by a shrinking economy and labor market, gives credence to the thesis put forth by Roberto Márquez (2000) concerning their potential role as mediators in future coalitions between Blacks and U.S. Latinas/os. At the same time, as Márquez goes on to suggest, their growing presence could also act as a deterrent to any strategies calculated to divide and conquer in racial terms. Moreover, we also support his view that the Afro-Latina/o population has a potentially pivotal role to play as a connecting link between the hemisphere's two realities and will necessarily find itself at the center of any transnational debate on the issue of race.

Further research is needed on the Afro-Latina/o presence among the Latina/o population. In the heavily race-conscious U.S. context, the Afro-Latina/o category (even though it usually goes unofficially recognized) points to the existence of often-overlooked discrepancies not only of national origin, social status, and language but also of race and color, which can deeply differentiate the daily experiences and life chances of Black, nonwhite, mixed (mestizo), and white Latinos. Moreover, members of the same family can be officially classified as members of different races, especially when they "look different" in their phenotype.

Areas of African American–Latina/o coexistence such as Harlem and Spanish Harlem have, of course, long existed in the United States. And, undoubtedly, Black-Latina/o relations have also produced well-known examples of cross-community solidarities and support, visible in such diverse cases as the election of the first African American mayor, Harold Washington, in Chicago during the 1980s and in the Afro–Puerto Rican Arturo Alfonso Schomburg's pioneering efforts to bring the two communities together, which culminated in the establishment in New York City of the leading research center for the study of Black culture (James, 2001). Another example is the emergence of rap music among African American and Puerto Rican youth in the South Bronx during the 1970s and hip hop during the 1990s (Rivera, 2003).

Indeed, to jump to the conclusion that Latina/o–African American relations are doomed or preordained to conflict does not strike us as either self-evident or inevitable (Vaca, 2004).[22] Such a discourse appears to negate any sort of agency on the part of both Latinas/os and African Americans who are predisposed to coalition building in the service of progressive political agendas aimed at attacking the structures of inequality and injustice that disproportionately impact on the two communities. Such contemplation of a progressive political agenda ultimately implies an even broader-based coalition that will include progressive whites and members of other groups concerned about and dedicated to the attainment of social justice. As Antonia Darder and Rodolfo Torres have argued:

> [I]f we are to effectively challenge the horrendous economic impact of globalization on racialized and other marginalized communities, we must recognize that a politics of identity is grossly inept and unsuited for building and sustaining collective political movements for social justice and economic democracy. Instead what we need is to fundamentally reframe the very terrain that gives life to our political understanding of what it means to struggle against widening class differentiation and ever-increasing racialized inequality. (2003:310)

Still, large-scale migrations from Latin America since the mid-1960s have both increased and changed the nature and import of African American–Latina/o coexistence in urban settings, whether Houston, Los Angeles, or New York. The result today is the emergence of negotiated or renegotiated spaces for access to political power and participation, claims to services, and cooperative political initiatives, in response to their shared "disadvantaged" status in the dominant political, economic, and social structures. A concomitant of this possible emergence or intensification of common action is the reality of incipient mutual antagonisms born of both the competition for scarce resources (Bentacur and Gills, 2000) and the need to avoid the scourge of finding oneself on the very bottom rungs of the employment ladder. Much work remains to be done to fully understand such issues as the fragility of African

American–Latina/o relations in electoral politics, as well as in debates on such potentially explosive issues as immigration and language.[23]

Equally important are the often divergent interests and behavioral patterns among the elites of both minorities and the grassroots. In some cases, such as the immigration debates, for example, as Lawrence Fuchs (1990) points out, the elites are more progressive in their positions; in others, such as New York and Chicago, as Betancur notes in this volume, "at the grassroots, Latinos and African Americans work together and with better results in the solution of common problems than their elites. Elites clash more frequently and bitterly around the distribution of institutional power and divisible gains, and often lead their communities against each other as a means to enhance their own interests—even at the expense of their majority poor."

While many might consider African American–Latina/o coalition building as a given, whether based on their common disadvantaged position vis-à-vis whites, or in some cases simply on the processes of racialization in U.S. society, the fragility of the political alliances between these two groups still needs to be better understood. Undoubtedly, George Lipsitz's (2003) caveat is worth recalling: not even the most militant nationalist groups assume that all members of a particular group are the same—considering that both "African Americans" and "Latinas/os," like all racial categories, are statistically created, heterogeneous categories rather than homogenous organized populations (Oboler, 1995). Glossing over internal differences has a double consequence, which can be both positive and negative. Lipsitz also notes that both neoconservatives and neoliberals have seized on the "mixed race trope as a means of representing race in the United States as personal, private, individual and idiosyncratic, rather than institutional, ideological, collective and cumulative." And Charles Hale (1996:172–175) employs the term "strategic essentialism" and "strategic multiplicity" to suggest the political construction for all forms of ethnic discourse emphasizing identity as a potentially liberating strategy that emanates from the margins of power. Our position, then, is that the meaning of blackness is less categorical than it might appear to be (or not be) in either part of the hemisphere. Moreover, focusing on African American–Latina/o relations enables us to explore the interstices of hemispheric differences that do not appear to have produced maximum advantage for social and racial justice. Thus, instead of dwelling on comparative injustices, or on where and under what conditions there is a greater degree of racism, this volume pays renewed attention to joint struggles for overcoming historical and contemporary injustices and discriminations (be they based on social, racial, ethnic, or gender differences), which, we believe, stands a much better chance of enhancing common citizenship in the United States as in other countries of the Americas.

The Contributions to This Volume

I must remind the Garifuna where they come from. One cannot invent oneself according to one's whim or preference. . . . Like all other Hondurans, the Garifuna are mestizos, from the Arawak

Indian and the African black. To pass as just one of these ancestors is to falsify one's identity, to forget the other complementary component, to betray the ancestors which they are trying to erase from their collective historical certificate. To locate one's identity in history is easy but absolutely insufficient.
—Rodolfo Pastor, Honduran minister of culture
(cited in England and Anderson, 1998)

In this anthology, we have invited scholars in the field to discuss the specificities of blackness and the process of racialization in different Latin American contexts.[24] We have brought their views together with others who discuss how people of Latin American descent in the United States are challenging traditional racial paradigms in this society. In so doing, we hope to contribute to providing the groundwork for the ongoing consideration of the ways that political and economic interests, as much as racism, continue to create obstacles in the struggle for social justice in the United States. This is a particularly urgent task that must be undertaken today in the light of the extremely radical re-racialization of politics post-9/11, for 9/11 has undoubtedly changed the inherited context and continues to do so today.

Moreover, we strongly believe that a radical reassessment of the problems of racism, discrimination, and coalition building between African Americans and Latinas/os in U.S. society is also increasingly essential in the light of heightened population movement across the hemisphere in the current context of globalization. Nevertheless, the aim of this anthology is more modest. In spite of the growing numbers of Latinas/os in the United States—including Afro-Latinas/os—there has not been a commensurate increase in available materials and resources that could contribute toward deepening the discussion of the implications of the nation's changing demographics for theorizing and understanding contemporary race relations in this society. Indeed, over the years, in teaching courses on the processes of racialization and the meaning of blackness in the Americas that emphasize a comparative hemispheric perspective, we have often been frustrated by the lack of available texts focusing specifically on the contemporary experience of Blacks, Latinas/os, and Afro–Latin Americans in the hemisphere. With some notable exceptions (Andrews, 2004; Bonilla-Silva, 2003; Conniff and Davis, 1994; Hamilton et al., 2001; Minority Rights Group, 1995; Safa, 1998; Walker, 2001; Torres and Whitten, 1998; Winant, 1994), most texts on blackness in the Americas tend to focus almost exclusively either on slavery or on the immediate post-abolition era. Moreover, while we recognize the relevance and significance of culture and religion to the understanding of the politics of race and ethnicity, we were particularly interested in focusing this anthology specifically in the realm of contemporary politics, relations of power, and the potential for coalition building between African Americans and Latinas/os in the United States.

In addition to introducing and presenting the debates on the meaning of race and blackness in particular national societies of Latin America, the essays in this volume address the current context of U.S. debates on race and ethnicity in two main ways: (1) by exploring the role that population movements of Blacks and other nonwhite peoples within the Americas are playing in reshaping the ways we think about race, color, and phenotype in U.S. society today; and (2) by examining the implications for U.S. race relations of the contemporary construction and meaning(s) of blackness in the various nations of the Western Hemisphere.

The articles in this volume thus both include and move beyond traditional studies based exclusively on national entities and approaches in addressing the historically destructive force of racism. This seemed to us to be a necessary first step toward examining whether racism and, more specifically, the experience of racially based exclusion in various nations of the hemisphere has had the effect—intended or otherwise—of creating transnational commonalities and differences that transcend national borders in the Americas. Ultimately, this approach stems from our observation that, regardless of the particularities of the respective historical and political processes of each North and Latin American country, the racial ideologies of the two continents have had at least one similar outcome: throughout the hemisphere, the populations of the various nations have been symbolically and socially hierarchized in racial terms. Mediated by class, gender, and other social divisions, and once again transformed by the historical and political events of our time, an inevitable consequence of the persistent legacy of slavery through racism continues to militate against full citizenship and rights for all in the nations of the Americas.

Ariel Dulitzky captures the history of both racism and its denial in Latin American countries. By looking at the continent as a whole, he shows that in spite of historical specificities, when it comes to race relations, similar power arrangements and discriminations have been present in each Latin American country. This is essential background for any discussion on African American–Latino relations in the U.S. context. On the one hand, it provides readers with the necessary background to fully understand the complexity of the racial values and perceptions that Latin American immigrants bring with them to the U.S. context. On the other, it suggests that there is more to understanding comparative race relations than merely contemplating official proclamations and policies. By pointing to the complexities and contradictions created by Latin America's legacy of slavery and racism, Dulitzky's essay contributes to reconfiguring intraracial and class relations in the hemisphere as a whole, moving us away from the seduction of the conventional Latin American/U.S. binary paradigm.

Carlos de la Torre introduces a new understanding of the complexities of the Ecuadorian national imaginary and identity, composed principally of indigenous, whites, and mestizos. His article shows the close links between Afro-Ecuadorian struggles for social justice and the larger civil rights struggles by indigenous peoples for recognition and entitlement. Most important, he argues that Ecuadorians arriving in the United States, especially mestizos and white Ecuadorians, bring with them historical anti-Black biases, which are mediated by the emphasis on making individual Blacks exceptions to a presumed stereotypical image of Blacks. This might have positive results in specific cases where Ecuadorians are thrown together with African Americans and other Blacks. Racialization of white and mestizo Ecuadorians in the U.S. context can potentially become an incentive for joining antiracist struggles. The responses of Afro-Ecuadorians become critical tests of the limits of nationality, ethnicity, and racial solidarity once they are in the United States. Darker Ecuadorians might, for example, choose to move in the direction of pan-blackness, while lighter ones might prefer instead a pan-Latina/o path. Either choice has important implications for circular migration.

Suzanne Oboler's essay seeks to unravel the specificity of the dynamic between "race" and power in Lima, Peru. She makes the case that understanding the meaning and social value of racial prejudices and discrimination in and of itself is ultimately only relevant to the extent that it can be seen to affect the nation's political process and socioeconomic development. Since racism is neither a natural category nor a legally sanctioned practice, particularly in Peru, the understanding of how "race" is socially lived, understood, and experienced requires a critical assessment of daily life in Lima. Her study is grounded in qualitative interviews with law students from different socioracial backgrounds and takes as its point of departure the contradiction in her informants' insistence that there is racism in Peru but no racial discrimination. Although focusing on blackness, she examines the multiple racializing labels used in daily life to assess the extent to which it can be argued at all that there is some awareness of racial difference embedded in the social relations and perceptions among Peruvians in Lima. Oboler shows that while Peruvians, like other Latin Americans, may debate the extent of racism in their society, what is at stake are the ways that racism obstructs the process of democratization of rights and citizenship in all spheres of social life.

Whether in Peru and Ecuador, or in Mexico, the large size of the indigenous populations ensures some acknowledgment of their presence, albeit as second-class citizens in their respective countries' official history and polity, even while it simultaneously obscures the long presence of Blacks in those same societies. Bobby Vaughn's essay serves as an important reminder of the historical presence of Blacks in Mexico and their ongoing invisibility in the Mexican polity—a situation that is at least partially due to their geographical concentration in particular regions of the country. Regionalization has partially contributed to Black isolation, for the parts of Mexico in which Blacks live are largely marginalized from the mainstream of Mexican history, culture, and society. Vaughn's discussion of Afro-Mexicans significantly expands the parameters within which Afro–Latin Americans are discussed. How Afro-Mexicans become inserted into Mexican, Latin American, and Latina/o universes in the United States and the complicated negotiations about nationality, ethnicity, and relations with African Americans and other Blacks is a continually evolving phenomenon. Vaughn thus provides a new and challenging twist to the limits and meanings of blackness and racialization.

Mark Anderson's essay focuses on the transnational dimensions of some stereotypes associated with African Americans in the United States in relation to different kinds of stereotypes about Garifuna, the black population in Honduras. He argues that social scientists need to pay much closer attention to the interplay of different "scales" of the production of racial meaning, namely, the "national," "local," and transnational dimensions of racial categorization and stereotyping. The majority of work on race in Latin America treats racial dynamics within nation-states as if they were isolated from racialized meanings elsewhere, perhaps because much of it is oriented toward comparisons with the United States. He notes that surprisingly few scholars strive to understand the circulation and appropriation of racial meanings, including stereotypes, across national borders even though present-day globalization and transmigration have intensified such processes. He discusses the position of Garifuna and "blackness" within constructions of Honduran *mestizaje* and associated denials of racism; the ambivalence of a recent turn on the part of the state to a discourse of "multiculturalism"; and the meaning of categories such as "mestizo," "*indio*," "*moreno*," and "*negro*" in everyday life in Honduras.

In his article Anani Dzidzienyo focuses on Brazil's race relations, Afro-Brazilians, and the persistence of obstacles to their full belonging and citizenship. Nonetheless, the last two and half decades have been characterized by intensified Afro-Brazilian political and cultural activities and the greater prominence of race relations discourses within the public realm. The image of Brazil as a "racial democracy" has been subjected to serious criticism, and the traditional comparison with the United States no longer automatically favors Brazil. An important sector of the Brazilian elites considers initiatives by the state and other institutions to transform historical disadvantages through "affirmative action" as an example of the "de-characterization" and "Americanization" of Brazil. At the same time, Dzidzienyo points out that the prominence of Africanity and its folkloristic celebration by many nationals has not resolved some of the old problems related to inclusion/exclusion of Afro-Brazilians.

In the third part of the book we bring the discussion to the ways that the specificities of Latin America's forms of racism and meanings of blackness can help us to better understand how they might impact on U.S. relations. John J. Betancur provides a thoughtful discussion of the existing literature on Black-Latina/o relations and reminds us that, ultimately, the framework and context within which these relations have taken place, and continue to do so, have been historically delineated by the dominant white society. These relations have not been static nor do they manifest uniform characteristics nationwide. As Betancur notes, specific political and historical dynamics and situations frame how Latinas/os and African Americans deal with each other, such that what has worked in Chicago, for example, may not work elsewhere—a sobering reminder of the exigency of avoiding generalizations.

Racial and class issues both have to be factored into the discussion of African American–Latina/o relations. As Betancur notes, the traditional "Black-White" paradigm has a critical white power dimension. Without implying that whites are a monolithic group, however, he also draws attention to research pointing to the ways that the Asian American "model minority" trope is used to deflect attention from the social and structural constraints that have produced inequality in the United States. Years of white control and accumulated and reified conditions of exclusion have ensured white dominance, which even affirmative action initiatives have not succeeded in transforming. Betancur argues that denial of the ongoing racism in U.S. society has acquired new life in the post–civil rights period, especially among those with greater access to power. The effects of globalization, the availability of low-skilled and unskilled workers, and the shrinking of opportunities further complicate cooperation for structural improvement. A uniting of forces, not as an automatic occurrence but as a result of sustained efforts, promises rewards for both African Americans and Latinas/os.

Jorge Duany's essay picks up some of Ariel Dulitzky's key issues concerning the denial of racism in Latin America, bringing home many of his points through a discussion of "race" in Puerto Rico. His article is insightful given the complex position of Puerto Rico in the hemisphere as a Latin American society that, as a result of over 100 years of U.S. colonization and presence, is increasingly exposed to racial ideas and practices from the United States. Duany shows how the significance of race is consistently underplayed in Puerto Rico—whether in the academic/scholarly literature or in the daily life of Puerto Ricans. Of particular significance is that the history of Puerto Rico includes both Spanish and U.S. colonization—hence exemplifying the hemispheric continuities in issues related to racism and racial prejudices. North Americans themselves were both enchanted and perplexed by the Puerto Rican racial situation, such that their superficial understanding of Puerto Rican society was that there were no racial problems in Puerto Rico—a discourse promoted by many members of the Creole white elite, including intellectuals. The latest census figures suggesting that most Puerto Ricans on the island are white, while those in the continental United States are not, encapsulate the dilemmas of racial identities caught between the Latin American and U.S. models of racial classification.

Grounded in an understanding of the relevance of race, language, sexuality, gender, and memory in shaping transnational relations, Nancy Mirabal's discussion of Afro-Cubans in the United States sheds important light on hemispheric blackness and its Afro-Cuban and African American specificities since the early twentieth century. Afro-Cubans have been simultaneously included in and excluded from the Cuban national imaginary, complicating their positioning within that society and in terms of relations among Cubans in exile. Moreover, as Mirabal shows, their ambiguous position among Cubans both here and at home was reflected in their relations with African Americans, who, however, imagined Cuba almost as a paradise where Blacks appeared to enjoy an enviable life.

Afro-Cubans and African Americans shared musical and political spaces in the 1940s and 1950s, while in the post–World War II period, the civil rights movement, the Cuban Revolution, and the Black Power movement have provided opportunities for second-generation Afro-Cubans to fuse political agendas with African Americans.

The Mariel and post-Mariel migrations into the United States have revealed a greater presence of Afro-Cubans, as well as the fact that some of them are choosing to leave Cuba—a development that is not lost either on the historical and broader Cuban exile community or on African Americans. Given the dualistic manner in which the racial paradigm of U.S. society has traditionally been understood, the homogenizing notion of "nonwhite people" or "people of color" acts today as a unifying category in the popular imagination, and racial minorities—particularly Blacks and Latinas/os—are perceived to be minimally distinct from, if not pitted against, the dominant "white" society. As a result, the potential for coalitions and political alliances between Blacks and Latinos is usually discussed as given. While this anthology seeks to complicate this assumption, the authors are unanimous in recognizing the existence of differences between and among the groups and in their assessment of the need for continuing efforts to enhance intergroup cooperation.

Louis Herns Marcelin's chapter on Haitians in South Florida and the multiple ways in which socioracial hierarchies, identity, and power among Haitians spill over into their relations with other Latin Americans and African Americans is a timely reminder of the role Haiti has played historically within hemispheric American imaginaries about race and blackness. Haitians' presence in Miami and South Florida expands the borders of Black–Latina/o–African American relations, as well as of Afro-Caribbean and Hispanic-Caribbean relations. As Marcelin argues, the racialization of all Haitians as black destabilizes the self-perception of lighter-skinned Haitian elites who emphasize their European language and culture and keep a distance from the "real Haitians"—dark-skinned individuals who, without the option of reinventing themselves and "passing" as anything other than black, emphasize their cultural and linguistic differences from African Americans.

The fault lines are obvious, but so, perhaps, are the opportunities for new explorations and commitment to common citizenship as an antidote to historical marginality. Haitians are critical to the evolving relations with Latin Americans and Latinas/os, African Americans, and other Americans. They push the Latin America/North America binary into other spaces and point to the intersections of history, race, language, and identity in the Americas, demanding a more nuanced analysis of the meaning of blackness.

José Cruz and Kevin Johnson explore the potential and limits of African American–Latina/o coalitions in two different arenas—respectively, congressional politics and the law. José Cruz explores the factors that shape coalition building among minority political elites, in order to better understand under what conditions African American and Latino politicians act together (or not) in a legislative setting. The inherent formality of the setting imposes specific patterns of behavior on both sides. Focusing on this important arena of political activity, Cruz argues that there is no self-evident reason that these two groups should naturally work together. Instead, he argues, for cooperation to be successful there has to be an ongoing effort and interest shown in each other's issues. He also suggests that the desires of the politicians do not necessarily correspond with those of their constituents. Moreover, Cruz warns that while no one has made the case for the undesirability of joint action between African Americans and Latinas/os, working together on an ongoing basis requires, minimally, constant proactive initiatives.

Kevin Johnson focuses on criminal law enforcement, immigration enforcement, and the post-9/11 War on Terror as three examples that point to the extent to which racial profiling embedded in the law adversely impacts on all minorities. He argues that once race penetrates one aspect of law enforcement (e.g., criminal law enforcement), it ends up permeating all aspects of the law (e.g., immigration enforcement). Moreover, Johnson argues, "it is highly unlikely that the consideration of race can be eliminated from enforcement of the laws against Latinas/os while maintaining it against African Americans, or vice versa. Once race enters the realm of legitimate law enforcement, the logic of racial stereotypes makes *all* minority groups subject to profiling." Hence, there is no other "viable alternative" than for African Americans and Latinas/os to recognize that "political realities dictate that alliances are essential to the quest for racial justice in the United States." As Johnson goes on to show, however, while racial profiling assaults the dignity of all minority groups and simultaneously thwarts the democratic principles of U.S. constitutional law and society, the construction of alliances between Blacks and Latinas/os may nevertheless not be so easily achieved.

Mark Sawyer's chapter considers the central problem of Black politics and Latina/o politics in a multiethnic United States in the context of a broader left retreat from the concept of race. It examines how the role of race in civil society, and in American politics more broadly, might be contested in the near future. Sawyer critiques the new preference for "color blindness" among the left and offers strategic alternatives for discussing race in the context of globalization and the rise of "flexible" identities today. Ultimately, he suggests that diaspora-based research, together with the development of coalition politics around specific policy issues, can provide a better understanding of the ways that "new," more complex racial identities structure political life in the United States today.

Reminding us once again of the fact that Latinas/os cannot be reduced to an abstract, ahistorical, or apolitical entity, Silvio Torres-Saillant provides us with a nuanced historically grounded overview that recognizes the possibilities of Black-Latina/o relations throughout the hemisphere. He discusses the role of history and the historical complicity of the ruling classes in Latin America in perpetrating social–racial inequities and injustices in their respective countries and in their ongoing relations with the dominant elites of the United States. Key to his argument is the responsibility of U.S. Latina/o scholars, as public intellectuals, to influence the struggle against discrimination both in the United States and in the various Latin American countries. He argues that this increases the responsibility of Latin American and Caribbean scholars in the United States to confront frontally the past horrors and injustices perpetrated against the less fortunate in their own lands. In so doing, Torres Saillant challenges all scholars to move beyond routinized academic production—to dare to look for answers to problems rather than continuing to reproduce traditional scholarly inquiries—thus showing the links between scholarship and our accountability and responsibility as public intellectuals to make an impact not only on the experience and meaning of blackness in the hemisphere but also more generally on the world in which we live.

Finally, Nelson Peery, an eighty-year-old African American veteran of social struggles throughout the United States, provides a unique perspective to some of the key issues engaging and bringing together African Americans and Latinas/os in the course of the twentieth century. In so doing, his essay is a timely reminder that the issues of ongoing concern to both groups today did not suddenly emerge in the latter part of the last century. Instead, Peery's lived experience and grassroots participation contribute to deepening our understanding of the challenges posed by interracial and transnational efforts at coalition building. At the same time, his essay suggests, that we cannot underestimate the fact that African Americans and Latinas/os have always struggled to construct and maintain political alliances within an often hostile and divisive mainstream context.

Altogether, the contributions to this volume advance the scholarly understanding of blackness and racialization in the Americas in several ways. Perhaps most important, by presenting the differences and particularities in the experiences of blackness in specific national contexts of Latin America, we hope to encourage readers to take note of the multiple meanings and hence complexity of the processes of racialization in the hemisphere. For these inevitably shape the various forms of racism in the Americas and are embedded in any discussion on Black–Latina/o relations both among U.S. Latina/o populations and between them and African Americans.

The increasingly marked presence of Afro–Latin Americans and Afro-Latinas/os in their respective public spheres throughout the hemisphere provides opportunities for a deeper and more focused discussion of comparative studies of blackness and its various meanings in the Americas. In particular, it allows us to transcend the traditionally accepted but now outdated Latin American/U.S. binary paradigm in the study of racism and the understanding of the flow and counterflow of racial ideologies in the hemisphere. Undoubtedly, Afro-Latin Americans and Afro-Latinas/os alike can potentially play a critical role in bridging the divide between African Americans and other Blacks within the United States. As Torres-Saillant lucidly argues in his essay in this volume, the United States is the arena par excellence in the struggle for multicultural inclusion and racial equality. From this perspective, this anthology, ultimately, also demonstrates that the results of the transnational flows of people within the hemisphere underscores not only the corporate, economic, and social exploitation brought on by globalization, which has forced millions to leave their homelands, but also their unintended consequences—the potential for the emergence of new political forms of national and transnational movements dedicated to the struggle for equality, justice, and rights among Blacks and other groups in the Americas.

Notes

1. Many thanks to Elitza Bachvarova, Antonia Darder, Carlos de la Torre, Jorge Duany, and Silvio Torres-Saillant for their always helpful suggestions and incisive comments on this text. We also thank Ramona Alcalá for her research assistance in sections of this chapter.
2. "Em um pais de escravos, não há inimigos nem amigos políticos: ha algumas pessoas sagazes que fazem negócios e uma imensa multidão que nada deseja alem de obedecer. Ademais, há brancos, negros e mulatos que devem seguir juntos. E esta é, em ultima instancia, a única dificuldade deste pais" (de Langsdorff, 1999:157).
3. As Peter Wade (1993:3) has observed, "To talk about 'blacks,' Indians, and 'race' in Latin America, or indeed anywhere else, is in itself problematic. It is generally accepted that 'races' are social constructions, categorical identifications based on a discourse about physical appearance or ancestry." Indeed, the choice of terminology in itself has been a challenge in thinking about the meanings that both Latin Americans and U.S.-born Latinas/os attribute to blackness and racialization throughout the hemisphere. We are fully aware, for example, of the efforts of activist groups throughout the hemisphere to use the term *people of African descent* instead of *Blacks*. While we are aware that the "generic" term *Black* has been criticized both for its lack of flexibility in describing people of partial African descent, and for its excessive emphasis on skin

color, we have nevertheless chosen to use it throughout this text as a convenient way of generically discussing people of African descent throughout the hemisphere. In speaking specifically about Blacks in Latin America, we refer to those born, raised, and living in Latin American countries as Afro–Latin Americans, inserting particular nationalities where appropriate (e.g., Afro-Ecuadorian, Afro-Mexican). Although the term *Afro–Latin American*, like the prefix *Afro* itself, has not been commonly used in daily life by Latin American Blacks, it is increasingly being adopted by movement leaders and participants as well as by some scholars throughout the hemisphere (Dzidzienyo, 1995).

When Afro–Latin Americans migrate to the United States, they both retain their national origin designation (Ecuador, Mexico, etc.) and come under the general description of Afro-Latinas/os (again, this term is used primarily by movement leaders and scholars). The term *Afro-Latinas/os* also includes Latinas/os of African descent who are U.S. citizens, born and/or raised from a young age in the United States. Finally, we only refer to Blacks as African Americans when we specifically discuss non-Latina/o Blacks who are U.S. citizens. We recognize that the above might not be acceptable to all scholars or the general public but believe that these are workable distinctions for the purposes of the themes of this volume.

4. Darder and Torres (2003:315) usefully provide Robert Miles's (1989:75) definition of racialization as "those instances where social relations between people have been structured by the signification of human biological characteristics in such a way as to define and construct differentiated social collectivities . . . the concept therefore refers to a process of categorization, a representational process of defining an Other (usually, but not exclusively) somatically."

Addressing Latino studies scholars in particular, they boldly make the argument for an "analytical transition" to a more dynamic and grounded interpretation of the structural forces of racism. They call for a much needed move beyond the traditional, essentialist, and ossified "language of 'race' to recognizing the centrality of racism and the process of racialization in our understanding of exclusionary practices that give rise to structural inequalities" (2003:315). We acknowledge the significance of Darder and Torres's study in the debates on the political economy of racism in the United States today. We also want to recognize them for bringing Miles's definition of racialization to our attention in our own process of rethinking the structural position of Latinas/os and other racial minorities in the United States.

5. This is not to say that the Latin American elites are anywhere near having the wealth and power of those in the United States; nor that the standards of living of the poorer sectors in this country necessarily match the manifold misery in which large sectors of the Latin American people live.

6. For excellent concise discussions of recent definitions of racism, see Gall, 1999:145–148; and Casaús Arzú (1998).

7. On the implications of these constitutional changes in the Ecuadorian case, see Carlos de la Torre's essay in this volume; on the Colombian case, see Rappaport, 1996. Particularly noteworthy in this new recognition are the implications of the fact that Afro-descended populations are largely based in rural areas, for this raises the possibility of the governments' not having to confront directly the problems of those inhabiting urban areas.

8. "*Deste regime social, nasceu fatalmente a política negativa que nos abate, porque ficamos sem povo. A escravidão não consentiu que nos organizássemos e sem povo as instituições não tem raízes, a opinião nao tem apoio, a sociedade não tem alicerces . . . a vontade nacional não existe.*" Cited in de Alencar, 2002:20.

9. Certainly, this question could also be asked in relation to the commonalities of experiences of other groups such as indigenous populations, women.

10. The fact that the day after abolition Latin American governments invariably declared that everyone was equal and that no special provisions of a corrective or compensatory nature had to be taken by either state or society meant that slaves and their descendants were left in a sociopolitical, educational, and economic dead end. In effect, throughout the continent, the discourse of equality without meaningful action took away any responsibility from the state and society for the condition of Blacks.

11. In the United States debates in the postwar period on the differences between North and Latin American racial ideologies have largely been framed by the pioneering works of Frank Tannenbaum (1946); Stanley Elkins (1959); and Eric Williams (1994). See also Rubin (1957).

12. As recently as December 2003, Ruth la Ferla penned the article "Generation E.A.—Ethnically Ambiguous." Of the nine accompanying photographs presented as proof of the emergence of this new "generation," not one depicted an individual of recognizable blackness. Indeed, the author notes, "We are seeing more of the desire for the exotic, left-of-center beauty that transcends race or class." In other words, as this quote and the photographs suggest, the attenuation of visible blackness is a positive goal for U.S. society to achieve.

13. See Mörner (1967) and Rout (1976). On the critique of *mestizaje*, see also Mallon (1996) and Wade (1993, 1997). The classic example of the extent to which the myth of racial equality coexists with the reality of racial oppression is Cuba—where the "race wars" of 1912 and the brutal genocide of thousands of Afro-Cubans following their attempts to integrate into Cuban polity and society have effectively silenced the black and mulatto Cuban populations to this day; see Helg (1993). Since the Cuban Revolution of 1959, despite attempts to rectify the historical disadvantages of Afro-Cubans, discrimination and issues related to prejudice seem not to have been overcome; see de la Fuente (2001).

14. See also Graham (1990). As Helg (1993) suggests, the Cuban notions of whiteness and "raza de color" are closer to the U.S. binary than are other Latin American designations. Carl Degler (1971) referred to the "mulatto escape hatch" which has subsequently proven not to be such an escape in terms of earnings and incomes, at least in Brazil. Still, the significance of the emphasis on the mulatto transcends income—for it is in effect a way of being "not black" in a racially hierarchized society.

15. As Robin Moore (1997) has shown in the case of Cuba's literature, arts, and music.

16. As originally defined by the census, the term *Hispanic* referred to all the populations of Latin American and Spanish descent living in the United States, regardless of their national origin, ethnicity, race, class, time of arrival, or generation. During the 1980s progressive sectors of the Latina/o population began to shun the government-imposed designator *Hispanic*, replacing it with the term *Latino*, thus seeking to counter the European connotations of the term *Hispanic*, while simultaneously acknowledging the African and indigenous roots of people of Latin American descent and emphasizing the cultural and linguistic commonalities rooted in Latin America's heritage. *Latino/Latina* has since been used by certain sectors, albeit not necessarily the majority of this population—and primarily those living in large urban centers such as Miami, Los Angeles, New York, and Chicago. In 2000 the census recognized the term *Hispanic or Latino* in its questionnaire.

17. For an excellent historically grounded discussion of the key issues, debates, and critiques involved in affirmative action debates, see Marable (1996). For varying perspectives in the debates on affirmative action, see Beckwith and Jones (1997) and Curry (1997).

18. The lack of concrete alternative policies was underscored by the report of the Clinton administration's President's Race Relations Advisory Board (Franklin, 1998). In analyzing the report's conclusions, Steven A. Holmes (1998) noted, "A number of scholars and civil rights advocates said the board had squandered an opportunity to make a bold contribution to stimulating an informed discussion of race that moved beyond the familiar positions of liberals and conservatives."

19. Again, one of the more recent examples in this respect is the now-forgotten presidential task force on race created by the Clinton administration in 1998 (see note 19). The report of this task force indicated that racism continued to be a serious problem in U.S. society and suggested that the emphasis on ethnic categories simultaneously reinforced the belief in the superiority of whiteness and "white privilege" in the U.S. socioracial hierarchy. The conclusions of the task force have yet to result in the necessary official measures to address in a serious and systematic way the growing socioracial inequities across the country (Franklin, 1998).

20. To what extent the present antiterrorist initiatives will resemble the 1960s Latin American doctrine of "the enemy within" should be a closely watched development.

21. Jaynes (2000:2–3) has observed that African Americans may be "the most ambivalent group in America, reflecting a powerful tension between a widespread belief that increased immigration

is detrimental to Blacks' economic well-being and a moral commitment to equality and the rights of dispossessed peoples."

22. In his recent book, Nicolás C. Vaca (2004:186) adopts the opposite perspective. Citing sources drawn primarily from newspaper accounts and anecdotes, he proposes that "a divide exists between Blacks and Latinos that no amount of camouflage can hide. For each analysis that finds that Latinos and Blacks have a 'natural' basis for mutual support because of a common history of suffering and oppression, there are others that find great antipathy between the two groups."

23. See, for example, Mindiola, Flores-Niemann, and Rodríguez (2002:15). For an excellent case study on the racial hierarchies and relations between African Americans and Latinas/os in the workplace, see LeDuff (2000). For the debate on the impact of Latina/o immigration on job availability for African Americans, see Fuchs (1990), Martínez (1998), and Steinberg (1996). For a brief overview of some of the issues that should be taken into account in discussions concerning African Americans and Latinas/os, see the discussion among Torres-Saillant, Hernández, and Dzidzienyo in *Latino Studies* 1, no. 1 (2003).

24. Some of the essays in this volume were initially presented at a conference held at Brown University in February 2000. Other chapters were later added to this anthology. Although primarily for logistical reasons the contributions of some of the conference participants could not be included in this anthology, we do want to both acknowledge them and express our gratitude for their enthusiastic participation, as well as for the important insights they offered during the conference and in the follow-up workshop we held in 2001.

Bibliography

Andrews, George Reid. 2004. *Afro-Latin America, 1800–2000*. New York: Oxford University Press.

Beckwith, Francis J., and Todd E. Jones. 1997. *Affirmative Action: Social Justice or Reverse Discrimination?* New York: Prometheus Books.

Betancur, John J., and Todd E. Jones, eds. 1997. *Affirmative Action: Social Justice or Reverse Discrimination?* Amherst, NY: Prometheus Books.

Betancur, John J., and Douglas C. Gills, eds. 2000. *The Collaborative City: Opportunities and Struggles for Blacks and Latinos in U.S. Cities.* New York and London: Garland.

Bonilla-Silva, Eduardo. 2003. *Racism without Racists: Color-Blind Racism and the Persistence of Racial Inequality in the United States.* Lanham, MD: Rowman & Littlefield.

Brysk, Alison. 1994. Acting globally: Indian rights and international politics in Latin America. In *Indigenous Peoples and Democracy in Latin America*, ed. Donna Lee Van Cott. New York: St. Martin's Press/Inter-American Dialogue.

Callirgos, Juan Carlos. 1993. *El racismo: La cuestión del otro (y de uno).* Lima: Desco.

Casaús Arzú, Marta Elena. 1998. *La metamorfosis del racismo en Guatemala.* Guatemala: Cholsamaj.

Chafe, William H. 1986. The end of one struggle, the beginning of another. In *The Civil Rights Movement in America*, ed. Charles W. Eagles, 127–148. Jackson: University Press of Mississippi.

Collier, George. 1994. *Basta! Land and the Zapatista Rebellion in Chiapas.* Oregon: Institute for Food and Development.

Conniff, Michael L., and Thomas J. Davis. 1994. *Africans in the Americas: A History of the Black Diaspora.* New York: Bedford/St. Martin's Press.

Cruz, José E. 1998. *Identity and Power: Puerto Rican Politics and the Challenge of Ethnicity.* Philadelphia: Temple University Press.

Curry, George, ed. 1997. *The Affirmative Action Debates.* Reading, MA: Addison-Wesley Publishing Co.

Da Matta, Roberto. Do you know who you're talking to? In *Carnivals, Rogues and Heroes: An Anthropology of the Brazilian Dilemma*, 429–442. Notre Dame, IN: University of Notre Dame Press, 1991.

Darder, Antonia, and Rodolfo D. Torres. 2003. Mapping Latino studies: Critical reflections on class and social theory. *Latino Studies* 1 (2):303–324.

de Alencar, José Almino. 2002. *Joaquím Nabuco: O dever da política; radicalizmo e desencanto*. Rio de Janeiro: Edições Casa de Rui Barbosa.

de Carvalho Neto, Paulo. 1977. Folklore of the black struggle in Latin America. *Latin American Perspectives* 17, Spring.

De Genova, Nicholas, and Ana Y. Ramos-Zayas. 2003. *Latino Crossings: Mexicans, Puerto Ricans, and the Politics of Race and Citizenship*. New York: Routledge.

————, eds. 1978. Latino racial formations in the United States. Special issue, *Journal of Latin American Anthropology*, 8(2): 53–58.

Degler, Carl N. 1971. *Neither Black nor White: Slavery and Race Relations in Brazil and the United States*. Madison, WI: University of Wisconsin Press.

de la Cadena, Marisol. 1998. Silent racism and intellectual superiority in Peru. *Bulletin of Latin American Research*, 143–164.

de la Fuente, Alejandro. 2001. *A Nation for All: Race, Inequality, and Politics in Twentieth-Century Cuba*. Chapel Hill: University of North Carolina Press.

de Langsdorff, E. 1999. *Diário de Baronesa E. de Langsdorff relatando sua viagem ao Brasil por ocasião do casamento de S.A.R. o príncipe de Joinville: 1842–1843*. Trans. Patrícia Chittoni Ramos and Marco Antonio Toledo Neder. Florianópolis, S.C.: EDUNISC.

Díaz-Polanco, Héctor. 1999. *Autonomía regional: La autoderminación de los pueblos indios*. 3rd ed. Mexico City: Siglo XXI.

dos Santos, José Rufino. 1996. O negro como lugar. In *Raça, ciência e sociedade*, ed. Marcos Chor Maio and Ricardo Ventura Santos, 219–224. Rio de Janeiro: Editora Fiocruz.

Dzidzienyo, Anani. 1979. Activity and inactivity in the politics of Afro-Latin America. *SECOLAS Annals* 9 (March):48–61.

————. 1995. Conclusion. In *No Longer Invisible: Afro-Latin Americans Today*, Minority Rights Group. London: Minority Rights Group.

————. 2003. Coming to terms with the African connection in Latino studies. *Latino Studies* 1 (1):160–167.

Elkins, Stanley. 1959. *Slavery*. Chicago: University of Chicago Press.

England, Sarah, and Mark Anderson. 1998. Authentic African culture in Honduras? Afro-Central Americans challenge Honduran mestizaje. Paper presented at the 21st LASA International Congress, Chicago, IL, September 24–27. http://afrolatino.org/Afrolatino2002/messages/1182.html.

Fernandes, Florestan. 1969. *The Negro in Brazilian Society*. New York: Columbia University Press.

Fink, Leon. 2003. *The Maya of Morganton: Work and Community in the Nuevo New South*. Chapel Hill: University of North Carolina Press.

Forbes, Jack. 1992. The Hispanic spin: Party politics and governmental manipulation of ethnic identity. *Latin American Perspectives* 75(19):4, 59–78.

Franklin, John Hope et al. 1998. *One America in the 21st Century: Forging a New Future: The Advisory Board's Report to the President*. Washington, D.C.

Frederickson, George M. 2002. *Racism: A Short History*. Princeton, NJ: Princeton University Press.

Fuchs, Lawrence H. 1997. What we should Count and why. *Society* 34, no. 6 (September–October): 24–28.

————. 1990. The reaction of Black Americans to immigration. In *Immigration Reconsidered: History, Sociology, and Politics*, ed. Virginia Yans-McLaughlin, 293–314. New York: Oxford University Press.

Fuentes, Carlos. 1996. Latinoamerica en la cumbre de Copenhague. http://www.personal.umich.edu/~bjuarez/carlosf1.html.

Gall, Olivia. 1998. Los elementos histórico-estructurales del racismo en Chiapas. In *Nación, racismo e identidad*, ed. Alicia Castellanos Guerrero and Juán Manuel Sandoval, 143–191. Mexico: Editorial Nuestro Tiempo.

Graham, Richard, ed. 1990. *The Idea of Race in Latin America, 1870–1940*. Austin: University of Texas Press.

Greider, William. 1992. *Who Will Tell the People*. New York: Simon and Schuster.

Griffith, Stephanie. 1991. Area's Black Hispanics torn between two cultures: Many feel pressure, tug of history. *Washington Post*, October 8, A10.

Guimarães, Antonio Sérgio. 2001. The misadventures of non-racialism in Brazil. In *Beyond Racism: Race and Inequality in Brazil, South Africa, and the United States*, ed. Charles V. Hamilton et al., 157–185. Boulder, CO: Lynne Rienner Publishers.

———. 2000. *Racismo e anti-racismo no Brasil*. São Paulo, Brazil: Editora 34 Ltda.

Hale, Charles R. 1996. Introduction to *"mestizaje."* Special issue, *Journal of Latin American Anthropology* 1(2).

Hamilton, Charles V. et al., eds. 2001. *Beyond Racism: Race and Inequality in Brazil, South Africa, and the United States*. Boulder, CO: Lynne Rienner Publishers.

Hanchard, Michael. 1999. *Racial Politics in Contemporary Brazil*. Durham and London: Duke University Press.

Helg, Aline. 1995. *Our Rightful Share: The Afro-Cuban Struggle for Equality, 1886–1912*. Chapel Hill: University of North Carolina Press.

Hernández, Tanya K. 2003. "Too black to be Latina/o": Blackness and Blacks as *foreigners* in Latino studies. *Latino Studies* 1 (1): 152–159.

Holmes, Steven A. 1998. Clinton panel on race urges variety of modest measures. *New York Times*, September 18, A1.

James, Winston. 2001. The peculiarities of Afro-Hispanic radicalism in the United States: the political trajectories of Arturo Schomburg and Jesús Colón. In *African Roots/American Cultures*, ed. Sheila S. Walker, 195–231. Lanham, MD: Rowman & Littlefield.

Jaynes, Gerald D., ed. 2000. *Immigration and Race: New Challenges to American Democracy*. New Haven and London: Yale University Press.

La Ferla, Ruth. 2003. Generation E.A.—ethnically ambiguous. *New York Times*, sec. 9, December 28.

LeDuff, Charlie. 2000. At a slaughterhouse, some things never die: Who kills, who cuts, who bosses can depend on race. *New York Times*, June 16, A1.

Lipsitz, George. 2003. Noises in the blood: Culture, conflict, and mixed-race identities. In *Crossing Lines: Race and Mixed Race Across the Geohistorical Divide*, ed. Marc Coronado, Rudy P. Guevarra, Jr., Jeffrey Moniz, and Laura Furlan Szanto, 19–44. Santa Barbara: Multiethnic Student Outreach/University of California at Santa Barbara.

López, Ian F. Haney. 1996. *White by Law: The Legal Construction of Race*. New York and London: New York University Press.

Mallon, Florencia. 1996. Constructing mestizaje in Latin America: Authenticity, marginality, and gender in the claiming of ethnic identities. *Journal of Latin American Anthropology* 2 (1): 170–181.

Marable, Manning. 1996. Staying on the path to racial equality. In *The Affirmative Action Debates*, ed. George Curry, 3–16. Reading, MA: Addison-Wesley Publishing Co.

Márquez, Roberto. 2000. Raza, racismo e historia: Are all of my bones from there? *Latino Research Review* 4 (3): 8–22.

Marriot, Michel. 1996. Multiracial Americans ready to claim their own identity. *New York Times*, July 20.

Martínez, Elizabeth. 1998. It's a terrorist war on immigrants, 1995–present. In *De Colores Means All of Us: Latina Views for a Multi-Colored Century*, ed. Elizabeth Martínez. Boston: South End Press.

McClain, Paula. 1996. Coalition and competition: Patterns of Black-Latino relations in urban politics. In *The Politics of Minority Coalition*, ed. Wilbur C. Rich, 53–64. London and Westport, CT: Praeger.

Mendez, Juán E., Guillermo A. O'Donnell, and Paulo Sergio Pinheiro, eds. 1999. *The (Un)Rule of Law and the Underprivileged in Latin America*. Notre Dame, IN: University of Notre Dame Press.

Mindiola, Tatcho, Jr., Yolanda Flores-Niemann, and Néstor Rodríguez. 2002. *Black-Brown Relations and Stereotypes*. Austin: University of Texas Press.

Minority Rights Group. *No Longer Invisible: Blacks in Latin America*. 1995. London: Minority Rights Group.

Mitchell, Michael. 1983. Race, legitimacy, and the state in Brazil. Paper presented at LASA International Congress, Mexico City, September 29–October 1.

Montoya Rojas, Rodrigo. 1998. *Multiculturalidad y política: Derechos indígenas, cuidadanos y humanos*. Lima: Sur. Casa de Estudios del Socialismo.

Moore, Robin. 1997. *Nationalizing Blackness: Afrocubanismo and Artistic Revolution in Havana, 1920–1940.* Pittsburgh: University of Pittsburgh Press.

Mörner, Magnus. 1967. *Race Mixture in the History of Latin America.* Boston: Little Brown.

Morse, Richard. 1968. The heritage of Latin America. In *The Founding of New Societies,* ed. L. Hartz. New York: Harcourt, Brace and World.

Murphy, Arthur D., Colleen Blanchard, and Jennifer A. Hill, eds. 2001. *Latino Workers in the Contemporary South.* Athens: University of Georgia Press.

Myrdal, Gunnar et al. 1969. *An American Dilemma: The Negro Problem and American Democracy.* New York: HarperCollins.

Oboler, Suzanne. 1995. *Ethnic Labels, Latino Lives: Identity and the Politics of (Re)Presentation in the United States.* Minneapolis: University of Minnesota Press.

———. 2000a. "It must be a fake": Racial ideologies, identities, and the question of rights in the Americas. In *Hispanics/Latinos in the United States: Ethnicity, Race, and Rights,* ed. Jorge Gracia. New York and London: Routledge Press.

———. 2000b. Racializing Latinos in the United States: Toward a new research paradigm. In *Identities on the Move: Transnational Processes in North America and the Caribbean Basin,* ed. Liliana R. Goldin, 45–68. Albany and Austin: Institute for Mesoamerican Studies, University of Texas Press.

Omi, Michael, and Howard Winant. 1986. *Racial Formations in the United States: From the 1960s to the 1980s.* New York: Routledge & Kegan Paul.

Rahier, Jean. 1999. Mami, ¿qué será lo que quiere el negro?: Representaciones racistas en la revista *Vistazo*, 1957–1991. In *Ecuador racista: Imágenes e identidades,* ed. Emma Cervone and Fredy Rivera, 73–110. Quito: Flacso-Ecuador.

Rappaport, Joanne, ed. 1996. Ethnicity reconfigured: Indigenous legislators and the Colombian constitution of 1991. Special issue *Journal of Latin American Anthropology* 1 (2).

Rivera, Raquel Z. 2003. *Nuyoricans from the Hip Hop Zone.* New York: Palgrave Press.

Rodríguez, Clara. 2000. *Changing Race: Latinos, the Census, and the History of Ethnicity in the United States.* New York: New York University Press.

Root, Maria P. P., ed. 1996. *The Multiracial Experience: Racial Borders as the New Frontier.* Thousand Oaks, CA: Sage Publications.

Rout, Leslie. 1976. *The African Experience in Spanish America,* 1502 to the Present. New York: Cambridge University Press.

Rubin, Vera, ed. (1957) 1970. *Caribbean Studies: A Symposium.* Seattle: University of Washington Press.

Safa, Helen. 1998. Race and national identity in the Americas. Special issue *Latin American Perspectives* 25 (3).

Steinberg, Stephen. 1996. *Turning Back: The Retreat from Racial Justice in American Thought and Policy.* Boston: Beacon Press.

Tannenbaum, Frank. (1946) 1993. *Slave and Citizen: The Negro in the Americas.* New York: Alfred Knopf.

Thomas, Piri. 1991 (1967). *Down These Mean Streets.* New York: Vintage.

Torres, Andres. 1995. *Between Melting Pot and Mosaic: African Americans and Puerto Ricans in the New York Economy.* Philadelphia: Temple University Press.

Torres, Arlene, and Norman Whitten, Jr., eds. 1998. *Blackness in Latin America and the Caribbean and Cultural Transformations.* 2 vols. Bloomington and Indianapolis: Indiana University Press.

Torres-Saillant, Silvio. 2003. Inventing the race: Latinos and the ethno-racial pentagon. *Latino Studies* 1 (1): 123–151.

Vaca, Nicolás C. 2004. *The Presumed Alliance: The Unspoken Conflict between Latinos and Blacks and What It Means for America.* HarperCollins/Rayo.

Van Cott, Donna Lee. 1994. Indigenous peoples and democracy: Issues for policymakers. In *Indigenous Peoples and Democracy in Latin America,* ed. Donna Lee Van Cott. New York: St. Martin's Press/Inter-American Dialogue.

Wade, Peter. 1985. Race and class: The case of South American Blacks. *Ethnic and Racial Studies* 2 (8): 233–249.

————. 1993. *Blackness and Race Mixture: The Dynamics of Racial Identity in Colombia.* Baltimore and London: Johns Hopkins University Press.

————. 1997. *Race and Ethnicity in Latin America.* London: Pluto Press.

Walker, Sheila S., ed. 2001. *African Roots/American Cultures.* Lanham, MD: Rowman & Littlefield.

Williams, Eric. 1994. *Capitalism and Slavery.* Chapel Hill: University of North Carolina Press.

Winant, Howard. 2002. *The World Is a Ghetto.* New York: Basic Books.

————. 1994. *Racial Conditions: Politics, Theory, Comparisons.* Minneapolis: University of Minnesota Press.

Wright, Lawrence. 1994. One drop of blood. *New Yorker,* July 25, 46–55.

PART 2
THE POLITICS OF RACIALIZATION IN LATIN AMERICA

CHAPTER 2

A REGION IN DENIAL: RACIAL DISCRIMINATION AND RACISM IN LATIN AMERICA

Ariel E. Dulitzky (Translated by David Sperling)

Racism (and racial discrimination) is, to a certain extent, alive and well in every society, country, and region of the world.[1] It can appear in a variety of forms depending on the culture or context in which it occurs and the period of history during which it rears its head. Nonetheless, one common thread that seems to be woven throughout almost every culture, country, and region is that people deny that racism even exists.

In this article we attempt to delve into the different forms of denying the existence of racial discrimination in Latin America. The crux of our argument is that the people of our region are prone to conceal, twist, and cover up the fact that racism and racial discrimination exists in our part of the world. This phenomenon of denial stands in the way of acknowledgment of the problem and, consequently, hampers effective measures that could be taken to eliminate and prevent racial discrimination. In order to identify the best strategies for combating racism, we must first take a close look at the different forms and manifestations of the phenomenon itself.

A kind of presumption of moral superiority vis-à-vis the United States of America is quite widespread throughout our region. Rarely does a conversation on this issue among Latin Americans take place without mentioning the serious incidence of racism and racial discrimination that exists in the land of our neighbors to the north, a claim that is altogether true. As the Brazilian scholar Antonio Sérgio Guimarães (1999.37; 2001) notes, we point out with nationalistic pride that racial segregation of the type that exists in the United States does not exist in our countries. We pompously tout our "racial democracies," "racial melting pots," "racial harmony," complete *mestizaje,* or mixing of races.

Nothing epitomizes Latin Americans' view on this issue as well as the declaration of the presidents and heads of state of South America that was issued in 2000 at a meeting in Brasília. This statement reads: "The Presidents [of South America] view with concern the resurgence of racism and of discriminatory manifestations and expressions in *other parts of the world* and state their commitment to preserve South America from the propagation of said phenomenon."[2] Or as the Mexican government put it: "The government of Mexico opposes any form of discrimination, institutionalized or otherwise, as well as the new forms of discrimination, xenophobia and other forms of intolerance that have emerged in several parts of the world, particularly in the developed countries."[3]

In short, these leaders concur that racism and racial discrimination are practices that take place in other regions and that Latin Americans possess a moral fortitude that cannot and does not allow any discrimination to be practiced in their countries. Moreover, these statements echo the widespread sentiment of the region.

Our aim here is to encourage a debate on what we feel is a widespread and outright misrepresentation of Latin America as a region that is respectful of racial mobility and more tolerant toward racial identities than it really is. These misguided impressions are merely a reflection of the absence of a deep, sincere, and open political debate on the issue of race in our region. With regard to this point, the Mexican government is right when it states, "In Mexico, the indigenous issue is never approached as a problem of racial discrimination but as a matter related to the right to development and to their situation of economic and social marginalization (exclusion)."[4] This same government would also state that racial discrimination "is not even a issue of national debate."[5]

But to point out that this phenomenon is not part of the national debate, or that it is not viewed as racial discrimination, by no means erases or negates the fact that racism and racial discrimination do exist, and that the countries of the region refuse to admit and combat.

In reality, racial discrimination and racism, like the failure to recognize these phenomena and the absence of a debate on these issues in Latin America, are simply part and parcel of what could be dubbed the "democratic deficit" that we are experiencing in the region. Equality, as it relates to race, gender, ethnicity, or anything else, is still far from being viewed in the region as an essential and basic requirement for democracy. Equality cannot exist without democracy; nor can democracy exist without equality. Hence, the struggle to solidify democracy is a fundamental step in the struggle against racism and racial discrimination.

This article is partly based on a study conducted by Stanley Cohen (1996), which looked at different governments' responses to reports denouncing violations of human rights. In this study, three different types of denial are posited: literal denial (nothing has happened); interpretive denial (what is happening is actually something else); and justificatory denial (what's happening is justified).[6] Sometimes these types of denial appear in sequence; when one type is struck down, it is replaced by another type. For example, literal denial may prove ineffective because the facts may simply bear out that the black population is indeed more disadvantaged than the white population. Therefore, strategy shifts toward use of another type of denial such as a legalistic reinterpretation or a political justification (522).

Before delving into the subject at hand, we would first like to make a point of clarification. This article focuses primarily on the plight of the Black or Afro-Latin American population, with very little discussion on racial discrimination against indigenous peoples or other ethnic groups. It is by no means our intent to ignore or fail to recognize that indigenous peoples are victims of racial discrimination as well. We have chosen to center our analysis on this particular social group, for the most part, because Blacks have been the most low-visibility victims of racial discrimination in Latin American society today.

A Look at the Current Situation in the Region

We must first make sure that readers understand what we mean by racism or racial discrimination. Even though it is true that forms, types, or definitions of "racism" or "racial discrimination" may vary widely, for the purposes of this article we use the definition provided by article 1(1) of the International Convention on the Elimination of All Forms of Racial Discrimination (referred to hereinafter as the "Convention against Racism" or the "Convention"):

> In this Convention the expression "racial discrimination" shall denote any distinction, exclusion, restriction or preference based on motives of race, color, lineage or national or ethnic origin whose purpose or result is to nullify or diminish the recognition, enjoyment or exercise, in equal conditions, of human rights and fundamental liberties in the political, economic, social, cultural or any other sphere of public life.

The true state of affairs in Latin American societies, nonetheless, stands in stark contrast with the objectives pursued by the International Convention. Although very few statistics are available on the phenomenon, the small amount of data we have at our disposal shows how racial discrimination permeates each and every realm of life in our region: from the social to the political, education,[7] labor,[8] cultural, and public health sectors.[9] In countries like Colombia, the Afro-Colombian population is disproportionately a victim of political violence.[10] In other countries of Latin America, access to land has eluded the descendents of African peoples.[11] In many countries of the region, judicial (Adorno, 1999:123) and law-enforcement (Oliveira, 1998:50) systems provide less protection to Blacks and, at the same time, punish them more severely.

For example, a recent study by the UN Economic Council for Latin America shows that Afro-Latin Americans have little or no job security, which is proof of racial segregation throughout the region. Racial discrimination in the labor market stems from inequities in the education sector. Consequently, whites have more of a chance of successfully climbing the corporate ladder, so to speak, or making it to positions of power or upper management. Distribution of income in the region is revealed to be even more unfair when it is viewed by ethno-racial origin of the inhabitants. The Black population has a harder time gaining access to education; they are more likely to fall behind in their studies, to fail to make progress, to drop out of school, and to attend schools of inferior quality.[12]

The government of Colombia, one of the few governments that at least has clearly acknowledged, in written documents, the problem of discrimination, has described the plight of the Afro-Colombian population in the following terms:

> They are among the group of Colombians with the highest indices of unmet needs. Their health conditions are precarious, their sanitation conditions are the most deficient in the

entire nation, and coverage of education services is poor. Housing in Afro-Colombian communities, in addition to [having] poor coverage of public utilities, shows problems in the legalization of property and lots, a high rate of overcrowding, and poor quality. It is estimated that the per capita income of [the members of] these communities is $500 per year, less than one-third of the national average. Afro-Colombian women are facing conditions of poverty, high unemployment rates, low-quality jobs, deficient health care, and a high incidence of domestic violence. Afro-Colombian teens do not have optimal guarantees and opportunities to gain access to higher or vocational education, good jobs, and development in keeping with their world vision and with their sociocultural reality. The territorial entities where the Afro-Colombian population creates settlements are characterized by their poor ability to govern, plan, and manage.[13]

This scenario, which is identical to the situation in several countries of Latin America, makes it all the more necessary to take a closer and more honest look at our region in order to be able to adopt the necessary measures to overcome this crisis. Even so, there are still strong currents of thought in political, academic, and social circles, which deny that racial discrimination even exists or try to explain away these differences as a function of other variables, rather than as a function of race or ethnic origin. In the following section we look closely at some of these variables.

"There Is No Racism or Racial Discrimination": Literal Denial

Literal denial is simply to say *"nothing has happened"* or *"nothing is happening."* What is of concern to us here is that this type of denial is synonymous with saying that there has never been any racial discrimination or racism in the past nor is there any at the present time. Over the past few years, different governments of Latin America have made statements to the Committee on the Elimination of Racial Discrimination (CERD) claiming, among other things, that "racial prejudice"[14] does not exist, "in our country problems of discrimination do not exist,"[15] "racial discrimination does not exist,"[16] "today racial problems practically do not exist any longer,"[17] "this phenomenon does not appear in our country,"[18] or "in society at the present time racial prejudices are practically negligible."[19]

This type of discourse is typical not only of governments that have a well-known history of insensitivity to racial issues, but also of governments that have a track record of being committed, at least rhetorically, to racial equality. Paradoxically, these so-called racially sensitive governments are often the ones who most categorically deny the existence of the problem. It would not be entirely farfetched to hear the following argument brandished in discussing the issue with a Latin American: *"Our government would never allow something like that to happen, and therefore it could never have happened."*

A pseudo sophisticated way of denying that racial discrimination exists is to argue that it could not have taken place because discrimination is illegal in the countries of the region and the governments have even ratified every appropriate international instrument related to the subject. This legalistic version of denial of racial discrimination is based on the following specious claim: "Since racial discrimination is prohibited by law, our government would never allow it and, therefore, it could not have ever occurred" (Cohen, 1996:254).

The most syllogistic form of literal denial is the widespread myth that the region boasts a racial democracy because the concept of race has been officially rejected by government institutions. This type of denial has many variations but essentially amounts to saying that if races do not officially exist, then racism cannot exist either. Nevertheless, erasing the concept of race from laws and other official documents has by no means led to the end of race as a key factor in determining how the benefits of society are distributed, nor does it negate the fact that Latin American society is predicated upon a clearly pyramidal structure with Blacks and indigenous people at the bottom and whites at the top.

"What Goes On in Latin America Is Not Racism or Racial Discrimination but Something Else": Interpretive Denial

At this point in time, it is hard, if not ludicrous, to categorically deny that racial discrimination and racism exist in Latin America. This is because groups that have been discriminated against have become more visible and have begun to engage in activism to address their plight. Additionally, a limited but growing number of studies and statistics, which bear out that racism and racial discrimination still exist in Latin America, are now available. Consequently, people resort to slightly more sophisticated explanations. Instead of denying that economic and social indicators show a wide gap between races, they commonly give reasons other than racism to account for the disparities among Blacks, indigenous peoples, and whites. These disparities, attitudes, and prejudices are framed in far less pejorative or stigmatizing theoretical terms than racism or racial discrimination.

The true story of the racial issue in Latin America is doctored in many different ways. In the following section we identify some of the ways in which the facts are distorted such that they do not fit the definition of racism or racial discrimination.

Euphemisms

One of the most common ways of putting a spin on the facts is the use of euphemistic expressions to mask the phenomenon, confer a measure of respectability on the problem, or paint a picture of neutrality in the face of discriminatory practices. A variety of terms are used to negate or cloud the racist side of certain social conduct or government policies: "ethnic minority,"[20] "restrictions on immigration,"[21] "customer screening or selection" (*selección de clientes*),[22] "reservation of rights to refuse admission" (*reserva de admisión*),[23] "proper attire" (*buena presencia*).[24]

Probably the most common euphemism attributes the differences among races to poverty. The syllogism goes something like this: People discriminate against Blacks or indigenous people *not* because they are black or indigenous, but because they are poor.

The government of Haiti, for example, cited economic reasons for the disparities between whites and other groups: "Even though it is true that in the private sphere prejudices related to color are sometimes expressed, in reality its origin lies in the social inequities that exist in Haitian society."[25] Similarly, the government of Peru claimed, "Today practically every Peruvian is of mixed blood and a racial problem no longer exists. Instead, there exists a problem of economic underdevelopment in certain sectors of the population."[26] Mexico has developed the most explicit arguments on this point: The indigenous issue is not "a problem of racial discrimination"; rather it has to do with "forms of discrimination derived from the socioeconomic reality."[27]

The myth of a racial democracy, which is defined as harmony between ethnic and racial groups and, therefore, the absence of racial discrimination, would lead people to believe that any display of racism and discrimination that may occur is usually a result of social and economic rather than racial prejudice. Once again we cite the official version of the Mexican government: "some forms of discrimination are a result of socioeconomic differences more than a distinction between ethnic groups, and they [the differences] have been addressed by means of a variety of government social development programs targeted toward the most vulnerable groups."[28] This way of thinking is so widespread and has endured for so long throughout Latin America that, regardless of a person's race, the population for the most part is unwilling to explain current social disparities among racial groups in terms of racial inequities. Yet, our societies quite readily accept explanations based on economic disparities (Minority Rights Group, 1999:23).

These interpretations are marred by faulty logic. First, they fail to explain why in our region even though not all people of color are poor, almost all poor people are colored.[29] One government did not have any problem acknowledging "a clear correlation between proportion of the indigenous population and poverty and marginalization indices."[30] Second, several statistical studies on economic disparities in Latin America have shown that even when all possible variables are factored out of the equation, including indicators of poverty, one variable, which can only be attributed to a person's race, always carries over.[31] Moreover, according to this specious argument, it would be lawful to discriminate against poor people. As far as we are aware, there is no provision of human rights law currently on the books that legitimizes unequal treatment of persons based on social class or economic status.[32]

Justification of class-based over race-based discrimination, once again, is simply a corollary to the assumption that we live in racial democracies in Latin America. It is also a corollary to the ideological basis for that assumption, which is that societies in the region are monolithically mestizo or mixed raced and, therefore, allegedly free of prejudice and discrimination. If Latin America indeed lives in racial harmony and there is really only one race in our societies (the mestizo race), then it would follow that any disparities between population groups could never be explained by a person's race but rather would have to be explained as a function of poverty, social status, or education.

Legalisms

Most interpretive denials of racism are laced with some sort of legalistic or diplomatic language to negate the existence of discriminatory practices. Many different legal defenses have been used to counter charges of racial discrimination. To take stock of every single one would far exceed the scope of this article, so in this section we offer only a few examples.

One form of legalistic argument is to maintain that racial discrimination is nonexistent in Latin America because the laws in the countries of the region do not establish rules of segregation or apartheid as is the case in certain other parts of the world. The claim is thus put forth that "never in history has any legal text been in effect that establishes racial discrimination even in a veiled way."[33] The implication of this statement is that discrimination can only exist when it is established by law, and not when sectors of the population are discriminated against by deed or when laws are applied or enforced in a discriminatory way.

Nevertheless, international conventions require our countries to do much more than simply erase discriminatory laws from the books. International treaties call for the adoption of specific laws in support of each provision of these conventions, egalitarian and nondiscriminatory enforcement of laws and conventions, and, particularly, the prevention, punishment, and elimination of discrimination in all its forms, whether by law or by deed. The CERD, therefore, has expressly mentioned the obligation of states to repeal any law or *practice* whose effect it is to create or perpetuate racial discrimination.[34]

The Convention against Racial Discrimination requires nations to adopt comprehensive legislation to prevent, eliminate, punish, and remedy racial discrimination. Such legislation does not exist at the present time in Latin American countries, as the CERD has been pointing out over the past two years.[35] Instead, the respective constitutions contain basic provisions that prohibit racial discrimination; yet the appropriate legislative structures to fully enforce those provisions are not in place.[36] Specifically, the Convention requires enactment of certain criminal laws, which prohibit and adequately penalize any act of racial discrimination that may be committed by individuals, organizations, public authorities, or institutions. To date, in many countries of the Americas, such laws are yet to be passed.[37] In other countries, even though legal provisions designed to eliminate unequal treatment based on racial factors may have already been enacted, express provisions making it unlawful to discriminate on the basis of national or ethnic origin have not been written into the laws.[38] Such specificity is necessary because these types of discrimination are the most prevalent forms of intolerance and bigotry in many nations of the region. In many countries in Latin America, there are no laws preventing racial discrimination in the private sector, despite the fact that section d, paragraph 1, of article 2 of the Convention provides that signatories shall prohibit any racial discrimination practiced not only by public authorities or institutions but also by private "groups or organizations."[39] Lastly, in many of our countries legislation currently in force has proven to be inadequate, either because the ban on discrimination does not go hand in hand with the appropriate punishments[40] or because punishments provided for by law are so lenient that they do not serve as an effective means to prevent, prohibit, and eradicate all practice of racial segregation.[41]

Another way people attempt to prove that racial discrimination does not exist in the region is to point to the fact that Latin American courts receive very few complaints of racial discrimination. As the government of Mexico stated, the absence of racial discrimination "can be corroborated by the absence of both domestic and international complaints"[42]—the logic being that an absence of court convictions for racial discrimination means that the phenomenon is non-existent. Nevertheless, this argument ignores important questions such as whether victims of racism are aware of the legal recourse available to them for their defense; whether laws are effective in combating racial discrimination; or whether the courts properly apply antidiscrimination laws. The low number of complaints may very well be attributable to "unawareness of existing legal remedies available for cases of racial discrimination, and to the public in general perhaps not being very aware of the protection against racial discrimination provided for in the Convention."[43] The small number of complaints and, consequently, convictions may also be due to a lack of confidence in law enforcement and judicial authorities.[44] Lastly, the low incidence of racial dis-crimination cases brought before the court may also stem from the fact that judicial or police officers do not rate this type of behavior as a display of racism or discrimination.[45]

In a variation of the argument that the absence of legislation making racial discrimination a crime is in itself proof that racial discrimination does not exist, the government of Venezuela stated: "Even though it is true that very few laws are in force against racial discrimination and any defense or support (*apología*) that may foment it, we can say that there is no practical need to legislate on this subject, given that problems of discrimination or defense thereof do not exist in our country.... [Such a] situation, fortunately unknown in our milieu, would be different if there were violent clashes between ethnic groups or if certain persons were alienated or left out on the basis of physical characteristics, since in explosive situations such as these would be, the Parliament, which cannot turn its back on the social reality, would issue laws on this subject. It has not done so because there has not been a need for it."[46]

In an extreme variation of this argument, governments respond to allegations of racism and racial discrimination by rattling off a long list of domestic laws enacted, international treaties ratified, and a host of legal mechanisms designed to punish those responsible for discrimination and racism. With such prohibitions in place, racial discrimination cannot possibly exist.

Denials of Responsibility

Many times governments deny any type of state responsibility for racism and racial discrimination, although they acknowledge that such acts may indeed take place.

The argument is that even though some acts of racism and racial discrimination have occurred, such acts are events that cannot be attributed to the government, are out of its control, and are the product of deeply rooted social practices or private actors. The Dominican government, for example, has only accepted that "there exists the possibility that individually, someone in the country, with the utmost discretion supports racial discrimination."[47] Or as the government of Haiti has stated, in the event that there are incidents of racial discrimination, these "are in no case the work of the state."[48]

In any case, under the Convention against Racial Discrimination, these arguments are not a valid justification. Every state must guarantee effective application of the Convention. "Inasmuch as the practices of private institutions influence the exercise of rights or the availability of opportunities, the State Party must ensure that the result of these practices does not have as a purpose or effect the creation or perpetuation of racial discrimination."[49]

Just Isolated Incidents

One of the most common ways in which governments respond to charges of racism or racial discrimination is to accept that a specific act has indeed taken place, but to deny that such acts are systematic, routine, or representative of a pattern of behavior. Typical responses in this category include:

> "Such acts arise in an isolated way and are the result of the motivation of individuals or very small groups."[50]
> Incidents of racial discrimination occur only "episodically and selectively."[51]
> "In present-day society racial prejudices are practically negligible and are manifested in the most intimate spheres of life."[52]
> What occurred was an "*isolated incident*"; such events never occurred in the past, and since they have not happened again, it is unfair to brand our government as racist on the basis of this single event.

Justificatory Denial

Justificatory denial has countless variations, which, generally speaking, involve either an attempt to justify the argument that racism does not exist or an attempt to show that in some hypothetical situations, racism or racial discrimination is in fact justifiable. Some of these denials are offered in good faith; others are simply excuses, fabrications, ideological defenses, or attempts to neutralize allegations.

Camouflaging Racism

We focus here on one of the most pernicious forms of denial—blaming the victim for his or her situation or making the victim of racism and racial discrimination invisible.

In perhaps its most extreme form, whole sectors of the population are simply said not to be victims of racism. Witness the popular Argentine saying: "We Argentines are not racist because we don't have any Blacks." The collective conscience in that country of the Southern Cone, however, refuses to ask key questions such as why today there is no Black population in Argentina, whereas in 1850, 30 percent of the population of Buenos Aires was Black.[53]

Governments throughout Latin America have engaged in a campaign to officially do away with any racial identification by claiming that the population is of mixed race (*mestizaje*). This view is evident, for example, in the way censuses are conducted in the countries of the region. The census of almost every country in Latin America does not include any question on racial identity.[54] The exceptions are Brazil and a few other countries, which are halfheartedly beginning to inquire into these distinctions.[55] This practice only serves to camouflage a highly representative sector of Latin American populations. The absence of official statistics on the true makeup of the population has a most serious consequence: it prevents the true plight of sectors that are victims of discrimination from being known. This practice also makes it impossible to implement public policies to overcome these inequities.

This drastic negation of any racial distinctions within the population makes it impossible to question the prevailing norm in Latin America of a person's color being a decisive factor in determining chances and opportunities to succeed in society. In Latin America, the whiter you are, the better and greater your chances are; while the darker you are, the lesser and worse your chances are. The chromatic social scale is blatant throughout Latin America, and social surveys have begun to corroborate these disparities.[56]

While it is true that racial categories in Latin America differ from those of other parts of the world in that they are not exclusively of a dual nature, that is, Black and white,[57] this by no means does away with the disparities among races or with the fact that the darker the skin, the fewer the economic, cultural, educational, employment, and social opportunities. We could say that a "strong pigmentocracy" prevails throughout Latin America, in which a negative value is attached to darker skin color, thus relegating races other than the white race to the lower echelons of society (Casaús Arzú, 1998:138).

The idea that we are all mestizos,[58] we are all café-au-lait-colored, we all have some indigenous or black blood in us, is an obstacle to identifying and developing the concept of specific racial groups. This myth is used to prevent nonwhites from developing their own identity and demands; however, it is not used to attain a higher degree of equality and social integration for these sectors of the population. The official notion of a mixed race (*mestizaje*)[59] camouflages diversity and denies nonwhites the right to dissent, while making conditions ripe for excluding anyone who falls outside the "norm" of mestizo or mixed (Arocha Rodríguez, 1992:28).

Furthermore, the concept of a mixed race also undermines or weakens the political and social struggle against racial discrimination. If we are all mestizos, then there are no racial distinctions, and mere discussion of the racial issue is therefore viewed by many as foreign to the region. By raising such matters in Latin America, the thinking goes, people are only trying to bring problems into the region that belong to other countries.

Moreover, the mixed-race theory covers up the official racist policy of whitening or infusing white blood into society, which has been attempted in almost every single country of Latin America. Many Latin American countries made a concerted effort to bring down the number of Blacks and indigenous people in the population and, as a last resort, to camouflage these racial groups by encouraging miscegenation, or marriage between nonwhites and whites, to make the population whiter. For example, almost every country in the region has developed at one time or another immigration policies that restrict or deny entry to Black people while strongly promoting European immigration.

The mixed-race claim not only serves to camouflage or make the Black or indigenous population invisible but is also used as proof that racism does not exist. Mexico has explained the situation in the following way:

> Additionally, our historical experience and the makeup of the Mexican population— 90 percent mestizo (mixed race), a product of the mix between Spaniards and indigenous people—give rise to an indisputable fact: the denial of either [one of these] origin[s] does not take place in our country, which is why there has been no need to legislate in this regard, unlike what goes on in other countries where the phenomenon of *mestizaje* did not occur.[60]

Mestizaje is also used as proof of harmony among different racial and ethnic groups. In other words, if there are mestizos, it is because there are mixed marriages between whites and Blacks or indigenous people. As the government of Cuba stated, the fact that there are a high number of racially mixed families on the island is a sign of how limited racial prejudice is.[61] Nonetheless, not even the magical force of *mestizaje* has managed to completely do away with racial prejudice when such marriages take place. Furthermore, many people in Latin America try to keep mixed marriages from ever taking place in their families.

The mixed raced/mixed marriage theory, however, is unable to conceal the fact that the Latin American population in general and the Black/indigenous population in particular feel that whitening one's lineage is the only route to improving one's standing on the social scale. This view is at the root of racism in Latin America; this attitude denies the Black or indigenous presence and identity and stresses the "white" side of the mixed race as the essential ingredient to obtain better social, employment, and education opportunities in a white-dominated world (Minority Rights Group, 1995:28). In reality, more than a democratizing force behind society, *mestizaje* constitutes, for the most part, one of the most masterful forms of racism in Latin America. In order to climb the social ladder, one must be as white as possible and the blending of races is the way to attain it.

In Latin America, as has been correctly pointed out, "the white/mestizo [person] forswears or abjures his or her indigenous [and, we add, Black] part and must constantly demonstrate his or her 'superiority,' even when these displays only illustrate that it is impossible for mestizos to accept their white and Indian humanity" [or the Black side of their humanity, we add once again] (de la Torre, 1997:7).

Even though Latin American governments have officially denied or done away with the different racial identities that exist throughout the region, such an action has not done away with informal racial designations, which in fact have a decisive effect on the social structure in Latin America. Even at the risk of making a sweeping generalization, we feel compelled to call attention to a common fact that has persisted throughout Latin America independently of the social, political, historical, and cultural peculiarities of the different countries: there is discrimination based on skin color (Early, 1999).

Another way of saying that nonwhites are not victims of racism in Latin America is to reduce their sphere of action in society. Accordingly, it is socially acceptable to acknowledge that Blacks excel only in sports, music, and dance; indeed Black equates with soccer: to be Black is to be good at soccer or even to be a soccer player. In keeping with this same line of thinking, the victims of racism are excluded from other sectors, for example, the media, in order to "project the image of a racially white country" (Oscátegui, 1998:31). For example, the CERD has stated its "concern for the information that the media provide regarding minority communities, including the consistent popularity of television programs in which stereotypes based on race or ethnic origin are promoted. The Committee states that those stereotypes contribute to reinforcing the cycle of violence and marginalization that has already had serious repercussions on the rights of traditionally disadvantaged communities in Colombia."[62] The labor market is another place where there is a clear demarcation of the types of jobs that nonwhites may gain access to or not. Nonwhite populations in Latin America usually have access to the lowest-level and poorest-paid jobs.[63]

The last form of this type of denial involves turning the story around to pin the blame on the victims. This takes place when a Black or indigenous person denounces racially discriminatory practices. Many times, the person is branded a victim of unfounded complexes, without even the slightest consideration that he or she may instead be the victim of racial discrimination.

Convenient Comparisons
One of the most common ways of attempting to justify the racial situation in Latin America is to compare the region with other countries of the world. Four countries, South Africa, the United States, Rwanda, and Bosnia, are old standbys that are often used for such comparisons. With regard to each instance, respectively, Latin Americans state, "we never had apartheid in our region"; "nor was there ever any legalized racial segregation";[64] and "we never had racially motivated, violent armed conflicts."[65]

In the report submitted by a government to the CERD, the only time the xenophobia, racism, and racial discrimination are mentioned is in reference to the plight of nationals from that country living in the United States.[66] Discrimination always takes place on the other side of the border.

The intellectual and political elite, in many ways, has made the United States the paragon of racial hatred against which all other societies must be measured. The specious claim goes something like this: since the segregationist laws and practices of the country to the north have not been applied in Latin America, there is no need to look at other forms of racial exclusion and alienation.

None of the above-mentioned comparisons are untrue and this ought to be a source of pride for Latin Americans. However, the people of the region, or anyone else for that matter, should not read anything more into these facts than what they say on the face of things. It is true that there has been no apartheid regime in the region; it is true that no racist legislation has ever existed in the region either; and it is also true that no Latin American government has implemented policies of ethnic cleansing.[67] Nonetheless, these are not the only manifestations of racism and racial discrimination. A myriad of phenomena can be found throughout Latin America that fits the definition of racial discrimination and racism.

Conclusion: Is There a Future Without a Past?

A racist way of thinking has endured throughout our region over the years. Today it is not even entirely far-fetched to hear out of the mouths of Latin Americans such statements as: "The only solution for Guatemala is to improve the race, bring in Aryan studs to improve it. I had a German administrator on my farm for many years and for every Indian girl he got pregnant, I'd pay him an extra fifty dollars."[68]

The existence of racial discrimination and racism, however, continues to be denied or ignored by Latin American societies and governments alike. Very few studies have been conducted on the topic to date, very few statistics have been gathered, and no public debate on the issue is taking place. This grim picture constitutes a roadblock to the development of public policies to combat racial discrimination and racism on the national, regional, and international levels.

In recent years, the advent of democratically elected governments in the majority of the countries of Latin America has paved the way for the improvement of the human rights situation of the region in many ways. Most notably, most countries have no policies of serious state-planned violations. Nevertheless, our democracies still have not been successful at fulfilling their implicit promise and the basic tenet of ensuring full, formal, and effective equality for all segments of society. Consequently, the consolidation of democracy is looming over us both as an unavoidable challenge in Latin America and as the path we must follow in order to combat racism and racial discrimination effectively.

The World Conference against Racism, Racial Discrimination, Xenophobia, and Related Forms of Intolerance (WCAR), which was convened by the United Nations in 2001, may yet spur on the inhabitants of the region to deal with an issue that has long been consigned to oblivion.

A regional meeting in preparation for the WCAR was held for the Americas in Santiago, Chile, from December 3 to December 7, 2000. Two parallel meetings were organized: the governmental conference, the Americas Preparatory Conference Against Racism, Racial Discrimination, Xenophobia and Related Forms of Intolerance (Regional PrepCom), and the parallel NGO forum, titled the Conference of Citizens Against Racism, Xenophobia, Intolerance and Discrimination (the Citizens Conference).

There were several positive outcomes from these meetings. The massive presence of civil society organizations should be highlighted. More than 1,700 people participated. There is still some hope that this significant mobilization could give birth to a strong regional movement to fight racism. The Santiago meetings also contributed to enhancing the dialogue among Afro-descendants throughout the region, bringing international attention to the challenges that they face. The Chile meetings represented a unique, and probably the first, opportunity for Afro-Latin Americans to appear as significant actors functioning in regional groups on the international level. Participating with a burgeoning collective identity that demonstrated enormous potential for bringing the fight against racism to the fore, they successfully heightened both their own visibility and that of the problems they face throughout the entire hemisphere.

On the governmental side, and at least in the declaratory documents, the Regional PrepCom allowed decisive actions to be taken to fight racial discrimination in the region. For the first time, all the governments of the Americas accepted that racial discrimination exists throughout the region and that it should be strongly combated. Some themes, which appeared in the Regional PrepCom's Final Declaration, deserve mention as they point to important changes in the official position of many states in the region highlighted through this article. The Final Declaration includes a clear recognition that the history of the hemisphere has often been characterized by racism and racial discrimination, and that these phenomena persist in the region (preamble). Moreover the governments of the region stated that the denial of the existence of racism and racial discrimination on the part of states and societies directly or indirectly contributes to their perpetuation (para. 2). The documents also included a positive call for governments to include ethnic or racial criteria in order to give visibility to diverse sectors of the population (para. 18).

It is important to note that the presidents and heads of state of the thirty-four countries of the hemisphere expressly endorsed this document. Similarly, the Inter-American Democratic Charter, adopted by the OAS General Assembly in Lima, Peru, on September 11, 2001, in its Article 9, established that "The elimination of all forms of discrimination, especially gender, ethnic and race discrimination, as well as diverse forms of intolerance, the promotion and protection of human rights of indigenous peoples and migrants, and respect for ethnic, cultural and religious diversity in the Americas contribute to strengthening democracy and citizen participation."

The WCAR was held shortly after the Regional PrepCom, during the first week of September 2001, in Durban, South Africa. While the objective of the WCAR was to address issues of discrimination and intolerance around the world and formulate recommendations and action-oriented measures to combat these evils in all their forms, most of the discussions focused on two issues: the conflict in the Middle East and the question of reparations. Notwithstanding the diplomatic hurdles, the event allowed Afro-Latin Americans to continue raising the level of public awareness on a number of important issues, thus replicating their Chilean success. For Latin America, the most important development is that the governments of the region did not retract their prior recognition that the region faces important racial discrimination issues.

The mobilization of civil society groups was quite significant, resulting in a number of positive, tangible developments. Beyond highlighting the problems Afro-Latinos confront, the conference also acted as a welcome catalyst to put in motion the long-overdue debate on how to effectively address racial inequality. The progress here lies in the discussion itself. Perhaps for the first time in Latin America, governments and civil society began to debate racial inequality. At last, the debate over race seemed to have moved beyond the discrete circles of academics and activists to find an incipient place in the region's agenda. As an example, the OAS decided to start discussions on the adoption of an Inter-American convention against racism and any other form of discrimination and intolerance. For a region that, as the first part of this article suggests, denies the existence of racism and racial discrimination, this is an important development.

There have also been some promising institutional developments in the last couple of years in terms of creating public institutions charged specifically with addressing allegations of discrimination or helping in the definition and implementation of public policies for the prevention and combating of racial discrimination. Some examples of this trend are the creation of the National Institute against Discrimination, Xenophobia and Racism in Argentina,[69] the National Council for the Prevention of Discrimination in Mexico,[70] the Presidential Commission against Racism and Discrimination against Indigenous People in Guatemala[71] and the Special Secretariat on Policies for the Promotion of Racial Equality in Brazil.[72] The creation of new institutions, in countries that traditionally did not officially address the problems of exclusion and marginalization in terms of discrimination, could signal a departure from some of the positions highlighted earlier in this article.

Perhaps the most important development in recent years is that the Brazilian government has begun imposing racial quotas for government jobs, contracts,[73] and university admissions.[74] As expected, these measures have unleashed an acrimonious debate in a country that has traditionally prided itself on being a "racial democracy." There is also a racial equality statute pending now before Congress that would make racial quotas obligatory at all levels of government and even in casting television programs and commercials. The debate is broad and very complex, covering questions such as the definition of who is black, a puzzling process in a country where more than 300 terms are used to designate skin color. It has also prompted a discussion on national identity where critics of the measures say the government is importing a solution from the United States, a country in which racial defini- tions and relations are very different.[75] Others say that racial quotas are not needed, since racism is not a feature of Brazilian society and conditions for Blacks will improve as poverty is gradually eliminated. The issue probably will be partially settled in the near future when the Brazilian Federal Supreme Court rules on the constitutionality of racial quotas being challenged by white applicants to federal universities. The decision could have an impact in Brazil and also in the rest of Latin America comparable to that of Brown v. Board of Education in the United States (Rohter, 2003).

In order to capitalize on the momentum created by the WCAR, it is indispensable to keep race and racial inequality in the forefront of Latin American political and legal debate. This is not an easy task and the region faces many challenges. While the Latin American governments took a crucial first step by formally acknowledging at the international level the existence of racial discrimination, this is just the beginning rather the end of the struggle. Despite some of the positive changes that have taken place in the last two years, it remains to be seen whether governments will start laying the groundwork for formulation of effective public policies, including legal reforms needed to address racial disparities. There are signs that officials in some Latin American governments are slowly incorporating diplomatic recognition of the exis- tence of racism and racial discrimination into their official domestic discourse. But throughout the region whether Latin American governments will turn their rhetoric into action remains to be seen.

Notes

1. The views expressed in this article are solely those of the author and do not reflect the official position of the Organization of American States or the Inter-American Commission on Human Rights. I wish to express my gratitude to Flavia Modell for her support in researching this article. I would also like to thank James Early and Ruthanne Deutsch for their input in an earlier version of this article.
2. Meeting of the presidents of South America, communiqué, Brazil, September 1, 2000.
3. 10th periodical report that the states parties were required to submit in 1994: Mexico. 30/03/95. CERD/C/260/Add. 1, paragraph 155.
4. 10th periodical report that the states parties were required to submit in 1994: Mexico. 30/03/95. CERD/C/260/Add. 1, paragraph 161.
5. 10th periodical report that the states parties were required to submit in 1994: Mexico. 30/03/95. CERD/C/260/Add. 1, paragraph 157. Nevertheless, there are authors who have begun to conduct studies on the situation of the indigenous peoples from a racial perspective. See Gall (1998 and 2000).
6. The method used in this study is somewhat limited, mainly because it is of a general nature and, therefore, does not cover specific aspects of racism or racial discrimination. The article is not meant to be a complete study of the significance of race in Latin America, the different manifestations of racial discrimination in the hemisphere, or all of the ways that the existence of racism is denied. We use the paper as a preliminary theoretical framework to draw out debate on the persistence of racism in our region.
7. For example, in Uruguay Black people have a lower level of education and a higher school dropout rate. 12th, 13th, and 14th Consolidated Report of Uruguay to the Committee on the Elimination of Racial Discrimination, & 203 et seq.
8. In Brazil, the Black population shows a higher level of unemployment than the white population, earns at least 40% less salary, and holds the lowest-grade and most unstable jobs on the labor market, which also provide the least benefits. See Inter-American Trade Union Institute for Racial Equality (2000).
9. In Nicaragua, for example, even though 32.3% of the nation's population has access to potable water, the percentage drops off sharply to 8.8% for the population living on the Atlantic coast, where the majority of the indigenous and Afro-Caribbean populations in the country are concentrated. See International Human Rights Law Group (2000).
10. See chapter 11 of the English version of Inter-American Commission on Human Rights (1999).
11. As is the case of the remaining survivors of the Quilombos in Brazil, the Garifunas in Honduras, or the Afro-Caribbean peoples in Nicaragua.
12. CEPAL, Etnicidad, Raza y Equidad en América Latina y el Caribe, LC/R. 1967, March 8, 2000, 36 et seq.
13. 9th periodical report that the states parties were required to submit in 1998: Colombia. 17/11/98.CERD/C332/Add. 1 (State Party Report). See on this same topic, Plan Nacional de Desarrollo de la Población Afrocolombiana, Departamento Nacional de Planeación, 1998.
14. CERD/C331/Add. 1, 02/11/99, and 6 (Dominican Republic).
15. 13th periodical report that the signatories were required to submit in 1994: Venezuela. 13/05/96. CERD/C263/Add. 8/Rev 1, 77.
16. 13th periodical report that the signatories were required to submit in 1998: Haiti. 25/05/99. CERD/C/336/Add. 1 and 15 and 17.
17. Summary of the minutes of the 1317th session: Peru. 16/03/99. CERD/C/SR. 1317, 78.
18. 10th periodical report that the signatories were required to submit in 1994: Mexico. 30/03/95. CERD/C/260/Add. 1, paragraph 157.
19. 13th periodical report that the signatories were required to submit in 1997: Cuba. 07/10/97. CERD/C/319/Add. 4 and 16.
20. In order to cover up exclusion of minorities such as indigenous people in Guatemala or the Black population in Brazil.

21. Immigration policies in our region are highly racist. Uruguay, Paraguay, Honduras, Costa Rica, and Panama prohibited people of African origin from immigrating. Venezuela and the Dominican Republic placed restrictions on the immigration of individuals of African extraction. Quoted in Carlos Hasenbalg (1998:168).

22. For example, this was the criterion used by dance clubs or discos in Peru to discriminate. See Law 27049, Un Gesto Político contra la Discriminación Racial, Ideele. Lima, February 1999, no. 115, p. 57.

23. This is the criterion that is used in Uruguay to prevent entry into certain establishments or clubs. See Mundo Afro (1999:12, 35).

24. One of the most widely used devices in Brazil to keep Afro-Brazilians out of the labor market or to make access difficult for them.

25. 13th periodical report that the signatories were required to submit in 1998: Haiti. 25/05/99. CERD/C336/Add. 1.

26. Summary proceedings of the 1317th session: Peru. 16/03/99. CERD/C/SR. 1317, 78.

27. Final Observations of the Committee on the Elimination of Racial Discrimination: Mexico. 22/09/95. A/50/18, paragraphs 353–398.

28. Summary proceedings of the 12306th session: Mexico. 21/10/97. CERD/C/SR.1206, paragraph 5. The following day, the same representative of the government would admit that when certain practices act as an obstacle to the application of Articles 2 to 5 of the Convention, that constitutes ethnic, if not racial, discrimination. Summary proceedings of the 1207th session: Bulgaria, Mexico. 21/10/97. CERD/C/SR.1207, paragraph 3.

29. "In Peru, not every *cholo* (mestizo, mixed race, black, or Indian) is poor, but almost every poor person is *cholo*" (Oscátegui, 1998:31).

30. 10th periodical report that the signatories were required to submit in 1994: Mexico. 20/03/95. CERD/C/260/Add. 1, paragraph 40. In response to this argument, the CERD stated its "particular concern for the fact that the signatory does not seem to realize that the latent discrimination that the 56 indigenous groups that live in Mexico are experiencing is covered by the definition of racial discrimination that appears in Article 1 of the Convention. The description of the difficult situation of those groups as mere unequal participants in socioeconomic development is inadequate." Final Observations of the Committee on the Elimination of Racial Discrimination: Mexico. 22/09/95. A/50/18, paragraphs 353–398.

31. See Telles and Lim (1998:465–474) and Lovell (2000:85), showing how equally qualified Afro-Brazilians who are defined as both Black and brown Brazilians earn less than white Brazilians.

32. The American Convention of Human Rights states: "The States Parties to this Convention pledge to respect the rights and liberties [that are] recognized therein and to guarantee their free and full exercise to any person who may be subject to their jurisdiction, without any discrimination whatsoever due to reasons of origin, social and economic position or any other social condition" (Article 1.1). The International Covenant on Civil and Political Rights states: "Each one of the States Parties to this Covenant pledge to respect and guarantee all individuals who may be found in their territory and may be subject to their jurisdiction, the rights [that are] recognized in this Covenant, without any distinction whatsoever of social origin, economic position, any other social condition" (Article 2.1).

33. 8th periodical report that the signatories were required to submit in 1998. Addition, Dominican Republic, CERD/C/331/Add. 1, 02/11/99 and 27.

34. Compilation of General Recommendations: 11/02/99. CERD/C/365, General Recommendation XIV pertaining to paragraph 1 of Article 1 of the Convention (42nd Period of Sessions. El énfasis no pertenece).

35. See, for example, Final Observations of the Committee on the Elimination of Racial Discrimination: Chile. 20/08/99. A/54/18, paragraphs 365–383.

36. See, for example, Final Observations of the Committee on the Elimination of Racial Discrimination: Colombia. 20/08/99. A/54/18, paragraphs 454–481.

37. See, for example, Final Observations of the Committee on the Elimination of Racial Discrimination: Uruguay. 19/08/99. A/54/18, paragraphs 454–435.

38. See, for example, Final Observations of the Committee on the Elimination of Racial Discrimination: Costa Rica. 07/04/99. CERD/C/304/Add. 71 and CERD/C/SR/1317, (Peru), 03/16/99, paragraph 35.

39. See, for example, Final Observations of the Committee on the Elimination of Racial Discrimination: Costa Rica. 07/04/99. CERD/C/304/Add. 71.

40. Final Observations of the Committee on the Elimination of Racial Discrimination: Peru. 12/04/99. CERD/C/304/Add. 69 (hereafter referred to as CERD, Peru).

41. CERD, Costa Rica.

42. 10th periodical report that the signatories were required to submit in 1994: Mexico. 30/03/95. CERD/C260/Add. 1, paragraph 157.

43. Final Observations of the Committee on the Elimination of Racial Discrimination: Haiti. A/54/18, paragraphs 253–271.

44. A point made in Brazil's report, CERD/C/SR.1157, 10/23/96, paragraph 55.

45. For example, in Brazil most complaints alleging the crime recognized as racism according to the Constitution, as well as Law 7716/89, amended by Law 9459/97, are described as "crimes against honor."

46. 13th periodical report that the signatories were required to submit in 1994: Venezuela. 13/05/96. CERD/C/263/Add. 8/Rev. 1, paragraph 77.

47. 8th periodical report that the signatories were required to submit in 1998: Dominican Republic. 02/11/99. CERD/C331/Add. 1, paragraph 6.

48. 13th periodical report that the signatories were required to submit in 1998: Haiti. 25/05/99. CERD/C/336/Add.1.

49. Compilation of General Recommendations: 11/02/99. CERD/C/365, General Recommendation 20 (48th period of sessions, 1996).

50. 12th, 13th, and 14th Consolidated Report of the Oriental Republic of Uruguay to the Committee on the Elimination of Racial Discrimination, paragraph 56.

51. Ibid., paragraph 34.

52. 13th periodical report that the signatories were required to submit in 1997: Cuba. 07/10/97. CERD/C/319/Add. 4, paragraph 16.

53. Someone once called Afro-Argentines the first "*desaparecidos*" in the history of the country. See Goldberg (2000:36).

54. There is a widespread sentiment that data collection on racial makeup constitutes a form of discrimination. The government of Uruguay, for example, recognized this practice as being discriminatory in its 12th, 13th, and 14th Consolidated Report to the Committee on the Elimination of Racial Discrimination, paragraph 3. To cite examples, Argentina has not included questions on race or color since 1914; Bolivia, since 1900; Peru, since 1961; Ecuador, since 1950; Venezuela, since 1876; Nicaragua, since 1920; Honduras, since 1945; and the Dominican Republic, since 1950. (Quoted in Hasenbalg, 1998:166.)

55. For example, Bolivia.

56. See Telles and Lim (1998) in which the authors look at how *pardos* (brown people) are closer in terms of social status to the *pretos* (Blacks) than to *brancos* (whites) in Brazil.

57. In fact, there are over 100 different categories in Brazil. See an interesting article by Eugene Robinson (1999), recounting the experience of an African American in Brazil in terms of racial identity.

58. For example, an article that appeared in Peru states that "there is a broad spectrum of interpretive possibilities on the origin, function, and destiny of Black people in Peru, but none of them separates their future from the mixed race (*mestizo*) complex that characterizes the nation" (Millones, 1996:16).

59. In this article, we shall not analyze how the origin of *mestizaje* in Latin America hearkens back to the sexual violence perpetrated by the Spanish and Portuguese conquistadors against indigenous women and later by slave traders against women brought from Africa as slaves.

60. 10th periodical report that the signatories were required to submit in 1994: Mexico. 30/03/95. CERD/C/260/Add. 1, paragraph 157.

61. CERD/C/319/Add. 4, 10.07.97, paragraph 16.

62. Final Observations of the Committee on the Elimination of Racial Discrimination: Colombia. 20/08/99. A/54/18, paragraphs 454–481.
63. Santiago Bastos y Manuela Camus, La exclusión y el desafío. Estudios sobre segregación étnica y empleo en la ciudad de Guatemala (1998).
64. "To speak of racism in Venezuela is somewhat complex, since it is not a very accepted topic, especially if we use the forms of racism that exist in the United States, Germany or in the Republic of South Africa as a point of reference" (Mijares, 1996:52).
65. It would be possible to take exception to this statement by considering the cases of the *política de tierra arrasada* (scorched earth policy) in Guatemala or the many policies of extermination that were implemented against indigenous populations in different countries of Latin America.
66. 10th periodical report that the signatories were required to submit in 1996: Mexico. 30/09/96. CERD/C/296/Add. 1, paragraph 73 ("feeling of xenophobia and racial discrimination in some sectors of American society") and paragraph 75 ("at the present time, it is relatively easy to inflame racist and xenophobic sentiments in some sectors of American society against the streams of migrant labor or refugees"). The report only mentioned the indigenous people as constituting one of the most vulnerable groups to violations of human rights (paragraph 5) or migrant workers on the southern border who face the prospects of fear and uncertainty, and on a few occasions it mentioned the situations of violence, corruption, and vulnerability (paragraph 59), but never did it mention discrimination (within its borders).
67. Of course, with the exceptions noted in the footnote above.
68. Response given in a survey conducted in Guatemala among traditional families in that country, in Casaús Arzú (1998:130).
69. Ley creación del INADI Instituto Nacional contra la Discriminación y la Xenofobia y el Racismo, 23.515, promulgada de hecho, July 28, 1995, Ley 24.515.
70. Decreto por el que se expide la Ley Federal para Prevenir y Eliminar la Discriminación, June 11, 2003, Diario Oficial de la Federación.
71. Acuerdo Gubernativo 390–2002 de creación de la Comisión Presidencial contra el Racismo y la Discriminación contra los Pueblos Indígenas.
72. Law 10.678, May 23, 2003, Cria a Secretaria Especial de Políticas de Promoção da Igualdade Racial, da Presidência da República, e dá outras providências.
73. Presidential decree 4.228 of May 13, 2002, establishing a national program of affirmative action.
74. Law 3.708 of Rio de Janeiro, September 11, 2001 (establishes a quota system of 40% of all the admissions slots for "Black and brown" students in the local universities of Rio de Janeiro).
75. See Carneiro (2003), arguing for the examples from the United States that can be helpful for the Brazilian experience.

References

Adorno, Sérgio. 1999. Racial discrimination and criminal justice in São Paulo. In *Race in Contemporary Brazil: From Indifference to Inequality*, ed. Rebecca Reichmann. University Park: Pennsylvania State University Press.

Arocha Rodríguez, Carlos. 1992. Afro-Colombia denied. In *NACLA Report on the Americas: The Black Americas, 1492–1992* 25, no. 4 (February).

Bastos, Santiago, and Manuela Camus. 1998. La exclusión y el desafío: Estudios sobre segregación étnica y empleo en el área metropolitana de Guatemala. *FLACSO* 43.

Carneiro, Sueli. 2003. Amicus curiae. *Correio Braziliense*, January 8.

Casaús Arzú, Marta Elena. 1998. *La metamorfosis del racismo en Guatemala*. Guatemala City: Cholsamaj.

Cohen, Stanley. 1996. Government responses to human rights reports: Claims, denials and counterclaims. *Human Rights Quarterly* 18:3.

de la Torre, Carlos. 1997. La letra con sangre entra: Racismo, escuela y vida cotidiana en Ecuador, Paper presented at the 20th Congress of the Latin American Studies Association.

Early, James. 1999. Reflections on Cuba, race, and politics. *Souls: A Critical Journal of Black Politics, Culture, and Society* 1, no. 2 (Spring).

Economic Commission on Latin America and the Caribbean (ECLAC). 2000. Etnicidad, raza y equidad en América Latina y el Caribe, August.

Gall, Olivia. 1998. Racism, interethnic war and peace in Chiapas. Paper presented at the 21st Congress of the Latin American Studies Association.

———. 2000. Mestizaje-indigenismo and racism in the Mexican state's ideology of national integration. Paper presented at the 23rd Congress of the Latin American Studies Association.

Goldberg, Marta Beatriz. 2000. Nuestros negros, desaparecidos o ignorados? *Todo es Historia* 393 (April).

Guimarães, Antonio Sérgio. 1999. *Racismo e anti-racismo no Brasil.* São Paulo: Editora 34, Ltda.

———. 2001. The misadventures of nonracialism in Brazil. In *Beyond Racism,* ed. Charles V. Hamilton, Lynn Huntley, Neville Alexander, Antonio Sérgio Guimarães, and Wilmot James. Boulder, CO: Lynne Rienner Publishers.

Hasenbalg, Carlos. 1998. Racial inequalities in Brazil and throughout Latin America: Timid responses to disguised racism. In *Constructing Democracy: Human Rights, Citizenship, and Society in Latin America,* ed. Elizabeth Jelin and Eric Hershberg. New York: Perseus Books.

Inter-American Commission on Human Rights. 1999. Third Report on the Human Rights Situation in Colombia. OAS/ser. L/V; II.102, doc. 9, rev. 1, February 26.

Inter-American Trade Union Institute for Racial Equality. 2000. Map of the Black population in the Brazilian labor market.

International Human Rights Law Group. 2000. Submission to the Inter-American Commission on Human Rights, March 3.

Lovell, Peggy A. 2000. Gender, race, and the struggle for social justice in Brazil. *Latin American Perspectives* 27:85–102.

Millones, Luis. 1996–1997. Peruanos de Eban. *Bienvenida Lima*, December–February.

Minority Rights Group. 1995. *No Longer Invisible: Afro-Latin Americans Today.* London: Minority Rights Group.

———. 1999. *Afro-Brazilians: Time for Recognition.* London: Minority Rights Group.

Mijares, María Marta. 1996. *Racismo y endoracismo en Barlovento: Presencia y ausencia en Río Chico: Autoimagen de una población barloventena.* Caracas: Fundación Afroamérica.

Mundo Afro. 1999. *Situación de discriminación y racismo en el Uruguay.*

Oliveira, Barbosa e dos Santos. 1998. *A cor do medo: O medo da cor.*

Oscátegui, José. 1998. Población, crecimiento económico y racismo en el Perú. *Actualidad Económica* (Lima), May.

Robinson, Eugene. 1999. On the beach at Ipanema. *Washington Post Magazine*, August 1.

Rodríguez, Romero Jorge. 2000. La discriminación racial en la epoca de la globalización económica. *Mundo Afro.*

Rohter, Larry. 2003. Racial quotas in Brazil touch off fierce debate. *New York Times*, April 5.

Telles, Edward, and Nelson Lim. 1998. Does it matter who answers the race question?: Racial classification and Income inequality in Brazil. *Demography* 35 (4):465–474.

UNITED NATIONS. 1995. Committee on the Elimination of Racial Discrimination. 10th periodical report that the signatories were required to submit in 1994: Mexico. March 30, CERD/C/260/Add. 1.

———. Committee on the Elimination of Racial Discrimination. 12th, 13th, and 14th Consolidated Report of Uruguay to the Committee on the Elimination of Racial Discrimination.

———. 1998. Committee on the Elimination of Racial Discrimination. 9th periodical report that the signatories were required to submit in 1998: Colombia. November 17, '98. CERD/C332/Add. 1 (State Party Report).

———. 1999. Committee on the Elimination of Racial Discrimination. Dominican Republic CERD/C331/Add. 1, November 3 and 6.

———. 1996. Committee on the Elimination of Racial Discrimination. 13th periodical report that the signatories were required to submit in 1994: Venezuela. May 13, CERD/C263/Add. 8/Rev. 1.

————. 1999. Committee on the Elimination of Racial Discrimination. 13th periodical report that the signatories were required to submit in 1998: Haiti. May 25, CERD/C/336/Add. 1.

————. 1999. Committee on the Elimination of Racial Discrimination Summary of the minutes of the 1317th session: Peru. March 16. CERD/C/SR, 1317, &78.

————. 1997. Committee on the Elimination of Racial Discrimination 13th periodical report that the signatories were required to submit in 1997: Cuba. October 7. CERD/C/319/Add. 4, &16.

————. 1995. Committee on the Elimination of Racial Discrimination. Final observations of the Committee on the Elimination of Racial Discrimination: Mexico. September 22, A/50/18.

————. 1995. Committee on the Elimination of Racial Discrimination. Final observations of the Committee on the Elimination of Racial Discrimination: Mexico. September 22, A/50/18, paragraphs 353–398.

————. 1997. Committee on the Elimination of Racial Discrimination. Summary proceedings of the 12306th session: Mexico. October 21, CERD/C/SR. 1206, paragraph 5.

————. 1997. Committee on the Elimination of Racial Discrimination. Summary proceedings of the 1207th session: Bulgaria, Mexico. October 21, CERD/C/SR.1207, paragraph 3.

————. 1999. Committee on the Elimination of Racial Discrimination. 8th periodical report that the signatories were required to submit in 1998. Addition: Dominican Republic, CERD/C/331/Add. 1, November 2.

————. 1999. Committee on the Elimination of Racial Discrimination. Final observations of the Committee on the Elimination of Racial Discrimination: Chile. August 20, A/54/18.

————. 1999. Committee on the Elimination of Racial Discrimination. Final observations of the Committee on the Elimination of Racial Discrimination: Colombia. August 20, A/54/18.

————. 1999. Committee on the Elimination of Racial Discrimination. Final observations of the Committee on the Elimination of Racial Discrimination: Uruguay. August 19, A/54/18.

————. 1999. Committee on the Elimination of Racial Discrimination. Final observations of the Committee on the Elimination of Racial Discrimination: Costa Rica. April 7, CERD/C/304/Add. 71.

————. 1999. Committee on the Elimination of Racial Discrimination. Final observations of the Committee on the Elimination of Racial Discrimination: Peru. April 12, CERD/C/304/Add. 69.

————. 1999. Committee on the Elimination of Racial Discrimination. Final observations of the Committee on the Elimination of Racial Discrimination: Haiti. A/54/18, paragraphs 253–271.

————. 1999. Committee on the Elimination of Racial Discrimination. Final observations of the Committee on the Elimination of Racial Discrimination: Colombia. August 20, A/54/18.

CHAPTER 3

AFRO-ECUADORIAN RESPONSES TO RACISM: BETWEEN CITIZENSHIP AND CORPORATISM

Carlos de la Torre[1]

This chapter examines Afro-Ecuadorians' responses to racism, and the impact of their strategies on the democratization of society. Unlike in the United States, where African Americans have used their citizenship rights to resist discrimination (Feagin and Sikes, 1994), in Ecuador, as in most Latin American nations, citizenship is weak and common people use strategies based on paternalism and corporatism to negotiate access to resources from which they are excluded. Whereas paternalist relationships protect a group or a family from some of the major injustices, they do not allow actors to conceptualize domination in structural terms. Paternalist arrangements favor individual accommodation over the collective struggle for citizenship. Under corporatism the leaders of subaltern groups are incorporated into the state, becoming intermediaries who transfer resources to their constituencies. Corporatist processes of inclusion allow for the social mobility of the leadership of subaltern groups. However, they do not always result in the reduction of structural inequality between groups. Moreover, unlike the struggle for citizenship that is based on universalistic conceptualizations of rights, corporatist demands are particularistic and can easily be co-opted into a zero-sum struggle for limited state resources.

This is an exploratory research project on a relative unknown topic. With the exception of a recent study of Blacks in Quito (Fernández Rasines, 2001), most works on Afro-Ecuadorians have focused on the northern Esmeraldas Province (Whitten, 1965, 1974), on the highland Chota-Mira Valley (Stutzman, 1974), or on the smaller cities of Ibarra (Stutzman, 1974) and San Lorenzo (Whitten, 1965, 1974; Schubert, 1981). The data for this chapter comes from twenty-two in-depth interviews and seven focus group interviews with approximately forty Afro-Ecuadorians who live in Quito. It is also based on fieldwork with Black organizations in Quito. The data was gathered from January to June 2000. The interviewees included leaders of social movement organizations, professionals, and common folk.

According to the 2001 census,[2] which used racial and ethnic criteria for the first time in the history of modern censuses in Ecuador, 72.42 percent of the population identified itself as mestizo, 10.46 percent as white, 6.83 percent as Indian, 2.74 percent as mulatto, and 2.23 percent as Black. These results differ from estimates widely used by social scientists, which assumed that Blacks were between 5 and 10 percent of the population, and Indians between 9 and 45 percent.

Two very distinct historical experiences differentiate Afro-Ecuadorians. The highland population of the Chota-Mira Valley is of slave descent. After a long manumission process that started with laws enacted in 1821, 1852, and 1854, but which did not abolish slavery until the 1860s (Whitten and Quiroga, 1998:83), the former slaves became peons in haciendas. Up until the 1960s and 1970s, when haciendas were transformed by agrarian reform laws, exploitation in the haciendas was based on a series of personalized obligations on the part of peons and their families: the head of a household and his family were required to work in the fields for a specified number of days; peons worked as domestic servants in the hacienda house and in the city. Laborers were given access to a small plot of land and meager earnings. Part of their wage was paid in the form of gifts and loans that were essential for their sustenance. These were given as personal favors of the hacienda owner. Starting in the late 1950s and 1960s, the strategy of sustaining Black peasant families, who had small plots of land without irrigation, depended on the temporary migration of some of its male members to agro-export plantations and/or on men and women to cities where they worked as domestic servants and in other humble occupations.

Even though there was some slavery in the province of Esmeraldas (Whitten, 1974:41), most Afro-Ecuadorians of this province are descendants of maroon slaves. Notwithstanding that northern Esmeraldas was not linked to the main cities until a railway from Quito to San Lorenzo was completed in 1957 and a road in the late 1990s, this area was linked to the nation during several agro-export cycles (Whitten, 1974). The boom and bust of export products such as ivory nuts, rubber, timber, and other commodities linked Black inhabitants of this area with white entrepreneurs. Norman Whitten (1974) shows how the spread of capitalist modernization and the increasing presence of the state apparatus since the late 1960s have resulted in ever-increasing levels of Black disfranchisement.

This chapter has three sections. The first briefly sketches racial discrimination against Afro-Ecuadorians in Quito. The second analyzes how the leaders of Afro-Ecuadorian organizations negotiate state resources. The last section explores the possibilities of constructing citizenship by analyzing the everyday strategies that Afro-Ecuadorians use to resist and/or to accommodate to racism.

Patterns of Black Exclusion in Quito

This section briefly outlines some patterns of anti-Black discrimination in Quito. It focuses on the criminalization of Afro-Ecuadorians and on their employment opportunities. Whereas men are constructed as dangerous, violent, and potential criminals, women are seen as sexual objects and are criminalized as prostitutes. According to the 2001 census, approximately 64,220 Blacks and mulattos live in Quito out of a total of a million and a half inhabitants. Most Afro-Ecuadorians are employed as maids, security guards, porters, drivers, and in temporary jobs in the informal sector. A few have had access to education and work in white-collar occupations and as professionals (Rahier, 1998:425).

Most Afro-Ecuadorians interviewed for this chapter reported negative encounters with the police. A leader of Quito's Black movement was arrested when he was a high school student. The arresting law enforcement officers told him: "You are under arrest because you are Black, and all Blacks are thieves." Like their counterparts in other parts of the Americas, Quito's police target and label the poor as criminals instead of protecting them (Chevigny, 1999). This stigmatization of the poor as dangerous is magnified in the case of Black people. Not long ago, in 1995, the chief of Quito's police said, "There is a type of race that is drawn to delinquency, to commit horrible acts . . . that is the Black race, which is taking over the urban centers of the country, forming poverty belts that are conducive to delinquency because of their ignorance and their audacity" (Rahier, 1998:424).

The comments of chief of police reproduce a racist truism that labels all Afro-Ecuadorians as criminals. The media, for instance, only points out the race of criminals when they are Black (Rahier, 1998:423). One interviewee argued: "Many say that all Blacks have criminal tendencies, that all Blacks are thieves, that Black people are aggressive. If everybody says so, it must be true." Another interviewee, a college student, recalled the game in which children shout:

> *Who loves the Black Man?*
> *Nobody!*
> *Why?*
> *Because he is Black!*
> *What does he eat?*
> *Meat!*
> *What does he drink?*
> *Blood!*

As she commented, "It is a pity that white and mestizo children are told in their homes that all Black people are thieves, and assassins. They watch it on television, they listen to it on the radio, and when they are a little older they expect to see this 'reality' in everyday life."

Because they are perceived as criminals, Afro-Ecuadorians can be the object of subtle or overt aggressions in their daily lives. A college professor indignantly told me, "In shopping malls I am closely watched by security guards." A male law student asserted, "When we walk in the streets white women cross the street or grab their purses. One feels attacked, as if one stinks; it has a big psychological impact." Afro-Ecuadorian women have to negotiate their dignity in a society that has constructed stereotypes that oversexualize them and that marks them as prostitutes. According to the resolutions of the First Congress of Ecuadorian Black Women of September 1999, "the media only uses us to shake our buttocks. We are seen as sexual objects, not as humans with an intellectual capacity" (Chalá, 2000:20). Many interviewees talked about ingrained racial patterns of sexual harassment. "Whites think that we are only good to go to bed" and "We are seen as sexual instruments" were typical comments. When Black women walk in the streets, white and mestizo males hiss, "The doctor prescribed a Black woman like you for me" or "*Negra*, you have to be good for my kidneys," in clear reference to the sexual act.

The racialization of Blacks as criminals hides the violence against Afro-Ecuadorians. Juan Carlos Ocles, former president of the Federation of Black Organizations and Groups of Pichincha Province (FOGNEP), narrated the following instances of police, white, and mestizo brutality against Black people. These cases were reported by the press, and despite Black mobilization against police brutality, nobody has been sentenced or sanctioned. Patricia Congo was assassinated when she defended herself from three white and mestizo men who sexually molested her (*Hoy* [Quito], February 23, 1996). In December 1996, Mireya del Rocío Congo was killed by a policeman in front of her children (*El Comercio* [Quito], December 17, 1996). Finally, a police officer shot and wounded Edison Cazares and Carlos Espinoza (*Hoy* [Quito], May 19, 1998).[3]

Afro-Ecuadorian men only have easy access to occupations that require physical strength, such as porters certain agricultural jobs, or guardians and protectors of the properties of the rich. In the words of a law student, "Of course, because they fear us, they hire us as their security guards, body guards, or chauffeurs." Most Black women interviewed for this project have been employed as domestic workers during part of their lives or have close relatives who still perform these jobs. According to Olga Méndez, director of the Association of Domestic Workers Aurora de la Libertad, many Black women who work as maids claim to be secretaries. The stigma attached to working as a maid does not allow many Afro-Ecuadorian organizations to focus on the plight of domestic workers. For instance, the First National Congress of Ecuadorian Black Women demanded, in vague terms, that "domestic workers should receive a fair wage with social benefits" (Chalá, 2000:69). The resolutions did not include concrete proposals on how to organize to improve their wages.

Social networks link Black women seeking jobs as domestic workers with prospective white or mestizo employers. By recruiting workers through networks of trusted people, employers can control and regulate the desired qualities of their employees. These women had to fit into their constructions of what are the acceptable characteristics of a good worker. It seems that in spite of its low wages, domestic work is a source of social mobility for first-generation migrants from very poor Black rural areas. For instance, many Black women who work in Quito as domestics are replacing men as *prioste* (stewards of confraternities) of religious celebrations in their towns in the Chota-Mira Valley.

If James Scott (1990:7) is correct in arguing that "perhaps one vital distinction to draw between forms of domination lies in the kinds of indignities the exercise of power routinely produces," domestic work is possibly one of the most humiliating occupations. Ronald Stuztman describes how white upper-middle-class employers addressed domestic workers as children and used "negative evaluations of the servant's intelligence, parenting abilities, or moral virtues" (1974:102). The few women who talked about their experiences as domestic workers resented how upper-class women selectively used notions of hygiene to discriminate against them. "As a domestic worker

I suffered total discrimination. They set apart your dishes, your spoons. You could not use their glasses to drink water. You had a different glass." Another woman recollected that when her sister was a domestic worker, "the lady of the house did not allow her to use the same silverware or the same tableware; the servants were given a different set." The aversion of upper-class women to sharing eating utensils with their servants might be explained by the strong associations of sharing food with equality and intimacy.

Even though domestic employment might help the social mobility of first-generation migrants, the association of Black females with domestic work seems to be an obstacle for women who have a minimal educational background. For instance, Silvia Maldonado could not find a job as a secretary: "As soon as they saw me they thought that a Black woman can only be a prostitute or a domestic worker" (*El Comercio* [Quito], September 2, 1996). Many interviewees argued that when employers are seeking administrative personnel they demand "good appearance and this meant not to be Black." When companies advertise a job, they ask the applicant to include a photo. A Black secretary recalled, "The first time that I applied for a job I sent a photograph, and I did not get an interview. Next time, I did not include my photo. I was given an interview. The receptionist seemed surprised to see me and told me that the person who was resigning had changed her mind." Interestingly enough, she got her current job because the director of a university, a prestigious scholar and politician, recruited her, saying, "I do not have a Black woman working in my university, and I would like you to work with me."

Because of the widespread practices of discrimination against Afro-Ecuadorians, it is interesting to analyze the strategies they adopt so that they can live with racism. The corporatist practices of Black organizations and the everyday strategies of common people are analyzed in the following section.

Afro-Ecuadorians a New Corporatist Group?

The debates on Latin American corporatism (Malloy, 1977; Stepan, 1978) show that corporatism should be analyzed as a series of structures that organize the relationships between civil society and the state. Under corporatism "the state often charters or even creates interest groups, attempts to regulate their number, and gives them the appearance of a quasi-representational monopoly along with special prerogatives" (Stepan, 1978:46). Corporatism has been the institutional mechanism through which the Ecuadorian state has attempted to channel and regulate social protest.

In the 1930s the state organized entrepreneurs into the Chambers of Commerce, Agriculture, and Industry (Conaghan, 1988:85). Different subaltern groups, such as state employees and industrial workers, were also incorporated into the state as special groups with particular privileges and prerogatives. After the last return to democracy, during the governments of Jaime Roldós and Osvaldo Hurtado (1979–1984), the corporatist pact was broadened to incorporate previously excluded groups such as urban dwellers, peasants, women, and indigenous peoples (León, 1994, 1997).

The corporatist practices of the state promote social organization. The state provides incentives for different groups to get organized. It also recognizes their representatives with whom it negotiates the transfer of resources, promoting the social mobility of these leaders when they are incorporated into the state as employees or consultants. By giving incentives to channel social protest through corporatist arrangements, the state tries to regulate contention. Some forms of protest are rewarded with a favorable state response. Other forms of dissent do not have realistic opportunities to be successful and can also be repressed. When leaders become state officials, their demands might coincide more with the state agenda than with the interests of the rank and file (León, 1997:36).

Even though the Ecuadorian state has had an acute fiscal crisis since the 1980s, it has been able to channel funds, from foreign donors, to new groups such as women, indigenous peoples, and Afro-Ecuadorians. In 1998 the World Bank gave $50 million for development projects for indigenous and Black people (van Nieuwkoop and Uquillas, 2000). Some European states such as Denmark, Holland, and Belgium have created development projects for indigenous people (Dandler, 1999:127), and different nongovernmental organizations are also targeting indigenous groups.

Through the National Confederation of Indigenous Nationalities (CONAIE) the indigenous movement has become a new corporatist group that has been incorporated into the state (León, 1994, 1997). Indian organizations demanded a program of literacy in Kichwa and other indigenous languages during the government of Osvaldo Hurtado (1981–1984). CONAIE administered a program for bilingual education during the government of Rodrigo Borja (1988–1992). Indian organizations were able to secure and manage government and international development funds. In 1998 indigenous demands led to a change in the constitution, which acknowledged the nation's multinational identity. Indigenous groups have also challenged racist constructs of their passivity and lack of intelligence. Nowadays an indigenous intelligentsia occupies important administrative positions in the state, and they have become intermediaries between the state and indigenous communities.

Afro-Ecuadorians are a new group that seeks their corporatist inclusion into the state apparatus. In the words of a leader of Quito's Black women's movement: "We Black people are a special group, and we need to have our own representatives to negotiate with the state, just as public employees, workers, Indians, and cabdrivers do." Their demand to become a new corporatist group coincides with the interest of the state and the World Bank in creating a unitary Black movement, so that they can negotiate with a set of representative leaders rather than with an array of individuals who claim to be its leaders.

Many social scientists have argued that the creation of an Afro-Ecuadorian movement is a grassroots phenomenon (Whitten and Quiroga, 1998:95; Halpern and Twine, 2000:20). Their assertions overlook the role of the state in promoting Black organizations. The government of Fabián Alarcón (February 1997–August 1998), through the National Plan of Human Rights in Ecuador, assumed the responsibility to help to "strengthen and to consolidate the Afro-Ecuadorian movement" (Chiriboga Zambrano and Darlic Mardešic, 1999:14). The government of Jamil Mahuad (August 1998–January 2000) sponsored the First National Black Congress. In this meeting organizations from the highlands and the coast formed the National Afro-Ecuadorian Confederation (CNA).

The state has also created institutions to channel resources to Black organizations. After the failure of Abdalá Bucaram's government (August 1996–February 1997) to establish an ethnicity ministry, Alarcón's regime created the Council for the Development of Indian and Black Peoples (CONPLADEIN). This institution, which included indigenous and Afro-Ecuadorian groups, dissolved owing to their rivalries on how to administer World Bank funds. Indigenous people created the Council for the Development of the Nationalities and Peoples of Ecuador (CODEMPE), and Afro-Ecuadorians the Corporation for Afro-Ecuadorian Development (CODAE) (*El Universo* [Guayaquil], May 28, 2000). These institutions transfer state resources to develop the areas of health, nutrition, housing, and ethnic education.

It is interesting that the demand on which Black organizations have placed most significance is the creation of the Gran Comarca del Norte, or Great Black and Indian Territory, in northern Esmeraldas (Consejo de Palenques, 1999, 2000; Halpern and Twine, 2000). The National Human Rights Plan of Ecuador asserts that the state will "promote autonomous forms of Afro-Ecuadorian organization, such as palenques and comarcas" (Chiriboga Zambrano and Darlic Mardešic, 1999:14). It will recognize the property rights of their ancestral territories. According to the documents elaborated by the Consejo de Palenques (1999:6–8), the Great Black and Indian Territory will give these groups "their own territory" to "strengthen ethnic and cultural identity so that they may continue to be culturally different people." It will give them "political and administrative power to be represented in the state" and the right to "administer, manage, and use resources in a sustainable way . . . directly participating in the preparation, execution, and administration of development projects."

As in other South American nations such as Colombia (Wade, 1998), these proposals illustrate a process of "relocation of 'blackness' in structures of alterity in ways that make it look increasingly like 'Indianness' " (Wade, 1997:37). Many Black organizations are presenting their demands to the state as if they were Indians, according to Wade (1997, 1998), because of the relative success of Indian claims to the state in the last two decades. The relatively favorable state response is explained by the historical legacies of how the state fabricated the categories Black and Indian.

Since colonial times the state has constructed indigenous people both as a group who share ancestral territories and different cultures and as a population with particular needs and obligations. Up until 1857 indigenous people had to pay tribute to the state, and state institutions were created to administer Indian populations and to collect this particular tax. In the 1930s and 1940s *indigenista* policies to rescue the "glorious past of Indian civilizations" were implemented. *Indigenista* intellectuals such as Pío Jaramillo Alvarado and Luis Bossano, among others, occupied important and prestigious governmental posts (Clark, 1999:113–114). Anthropologists and sociologists also studied indigenous people as a group with a distinct culture that was expressed in institutions and practices. The legacies of state policies targeted at the indigenous population explain why their claims were recognized by states in a new international agreement that favors Indian rights. In the 1980s and 1990s Indian organizations were able to change constitutions to acknowledge the multicultural composition of their nations. The state recognized their property rights over ancestral lands, created bilingual education programs, and recognized the importance of traditional medicine and traditional ways to resolve conflicts (Dandler, 1999).

In contrast, and with the exceptions of Cuba and Brazil (Wade, 1997:33), the descendants of African slaves did not have special or positive recognition from the state. Either they were seen as other citizens or they became invisible to the nation. Moreover, unlike indigenous people, they were not institutionalized as the "other" who needed specific attention from the state. Given the success of the indigenous movement, some Black Ecuadorian activists are following their strategies to negotiate with the state. They present themselves not as minorities in need of equality, but as a nation that has occupied an ancestral territory, that has an autonomous culture and needs special rights. That is why they demand state recognition and protection of their lands, and resources to rescue and develop their culture. As Halpern and Twine (2000) argue, the Great Black and Indian Territory will allow rural dwellers to resist agro-export and lumber companies that are expropriating their lands. This project also illustrates the corporatist pattern through which subaltern organizations negotiate with the state.

The creation of *palenques* and *comarcas* will allow some Black organizations the management of state and international development funds. The administration of these projects and the creation of particular policies for Afro-Ecuadorians will also allow some Black leaders access to state employment. For instance, the Consejo de Palenques (2000:13) is demanding that the state create a professorship for Afro-Ecuadorian studies. They are also requesting that the "teachers of our children have to be people from our communities, or people totally identified with our social, political, and territorial demands" (2000:25). The social mobility of some leaders will be complemented by their recognition as the spokesmen of all Black people.

As Charles Tilly argues, "leaders of ethnic groups often acquire just such an interest in maintaining the distinctions between dominant classes and their own constituencies; they become stronger advocates of bilingual education, distinctive cultural institutions, and installation of legally protected categories than many members of their constituencies" (1998:61–62). Whether this struggle for distinction will contribute to eradicating or to diminishing social inequality between different ethnic groups is an open question. Given that the region where the Great Black and Indian Territory will be created is extremely poor, it is not clear if this area will become a marginalized zone from which some Black and Indian leaders administer their poverty, or whether the state will provide the resources to develop this region.[4] Moreover, it seems that the relationships between Blacks and Indians in this zone are not idyllic. In his ethnography on this area Norman Whitten (1974:51) wrote that indigenous people were not pleased by the fact that there was an increasing number of Blacks in their communities, nor did they approve when indigenous women became partners of Black males.

Projects creating rural Black *palenques* and *comarcas* continue to reinforce the dominant Ecuadorian stereotypes that associate blackness with the rural areas (Rahier, 1998). Moreover, these projects do not take into consideration the experiences of the increasing number of Afro-Ecuadorians who live in cities and whose experience of racial discrimination and exclusion will not be addressed as long as they are seen as rural folk who happen to be in the city as temporary migrants. It is also interesting that many Black activists argue that their identity is endangered in the city. For instance, two Black activists born in Quito argued, "When we go to the Chota Valley we feel really Black" and "When we want to say that we are Black or to feel Black here we can't, because there are no referents." As long as Afro-Ecuadorian leaders follow the dominant view that blackness belongs to the rural areas, the experiences and realities of Blacks who reside in cities, where most Blacks live, will continue to be invisible.

The search for a true Black culture that will determine the meaning of being Black has authoritarian undertones. Who has the authority to determine the significance of blackness? Who will be included or excluded from true blackness? If being Black means living in a rural Black community, what should be done about the large numbers of Black people who live in cities? Finally, Norman Whitten's ethnographies (1965, 1974) show that the relationships between males and females in the Black communities of northern Esmeraldas are not equal. Is it liberatory to seek traditional forms of solving communal problems and traditional forms of power and authority that relegate women to a subordinate role?

The Rule of Law and Struggles for Equality in Everyday Life

People who have to navigate a racist society have developed a series of quotidian strategies to resist, or to accommodate themselves to, racial discrimination (Feagin and Sikes, 1994). Social actors use a range of practices and discourses to negotiate their dignity, and to access important economic, cultural, and political resources, including, at times, their physical integrity. People use these strategies almost spontaneously because they have learned them by observing the actions of family members and friends or from their previous encounters with racial discrimination.

Analyzing the latest process of democratization in Latin America, Guillermo O'Donnell (1999) argues that in most of these nations there is no rule of law. Whereas political rights are respected, common people do not have civil rights. The legal system does not provide equality under the law, nor does it give stability and regularity to the relationships among citizens and between citizens and the state. While the privileged use the laws to their convenience, the poor and the nonwhite feel the law as a system of oppression. Many laws have been written in such a way as to make it impossible to follow them. As a result many poor people live on the margins of the law, for instance, selling their wares in cities without permits or occupying lands to build their homes. Laws do not guarantee that all citizens are treated equally by state officials. The poor and the nonwhite have to contact powerful or influential members of the community, or have to beg state officials, for access to their constitutional rights such as a bed in a hospital or a place for their children in school.

In conditions of acute inequality in which common people do not have civil rights they rely on personalized relations with members of the dominant class to escape police brutality and to have access to their constitutional rights to education, health care, and even jobs. Most Afro-Ecuadorians have used their networks with members of the dominant group to get jobs. Even though most of them have access to such low-paying occupations, as maids and security guards, with no possibility for mobility, a few have been able to use their networks to gain access to white-collar occupations.

In an influential study on domination and inequality, Mary Jackman (1994) argues that paternalism should not be seen as an archaic system of domination. On the contrary, paternalism is "a powerful ideological mold" (11). Under paternalism the dominant group assumes that it has a superior moral capacity that allows it to define the interests and needs of subordinates. The powerful idealize the qualities of their dependents. If they behave according to the expectations of the members of the dominant group, they are rewarded with their love; on the contrary, they risk being ostracized. "Subordinates are engulfed by the total and softly coercive grip of paternalist institutions. They are trapped by the conditional practice of love into cooperating in their own subordination" (363).

Because most black employees have particularized relations of domination with individual members of the dominant class, it is difficult for most to conceptualize race and class rule in structural terms. Some Afro-Ecuadorians, for instance, see racism as prejudices based on inaccurate generalizations. A leader of Quito's Black movement argued that racism is "the discriminatory act performed by ignorant people who do not know reality." This interpretation of racism as a form of individualized bigotry also became the official version of the Ecuadorian state. In 1998 the state put together the Operative Plan for Human Rights with the support of more than 540 organizations of civil society, including Black and Indian organizations. According to this official document, "the discriminatory practices of those who use pejorative words against a group due to its physical, economic, social, political, religious, or ethnic condition should be punished" (Chiriboga Zambrano and Darlic Mardešic, 1999:117).

Reducing racism to the hostile words and actions of ignorant, ethnocentric, and parochial individuals, a view that was dominant in American sociology until recently, does not take into account power relations. Whites discriminate "to protect their position against possible incursions by subordinates," rather than out of ignorance (Jackman, 1994:39). Insofar as racism is seen as a problem of individual bias, it is not surprising that many confuse racism with racial or ethnic pride. Many interviewees argued, "I am a racist because I am pro-Black." Or to be a racist is "to love your race." These views that start from the premise that all people can be racist trivializes racism. As a result, a system of power created to rationalize relations of inequality between different groups is transformed into a human quality.

Even though paternalism is the most common strategy used to negotiate access to resources, there are occasions in which discourses and practices of citizenship rights are voiced. A professor, for instance, said, I am "looking to be accepted, that we are given the same rights and duties as everybody else. That is all we are demanding. I am claiming these rights not by shouting or crying, but with my work, my sacrifice, and my own efforts." Sonia Viveros of the Black cultural group Azúcar declared to a newspaper reporter, "We are equal to everyone else and we should have the same rights and duties" (*El Comercio* [Quito], June 5, 1998).

Some leaders of Afro-Ecuadorian organizations see their daily actions as occasions to struggle for their citizenship rights. For example, María Alexandra Ocles, leader of the Movement of Black Women of Quito, in a conference at a major university argued that the strategy of the Black movement should be to "liberate territories: wherever we are we will not allow discriminatory practices to occur." This strategy is understood by many as the need to educate individuals who discriminate. A secretary-receptionist educates her coworkers with this advice: "Whenever you speak badly or you discriminate against any Black person, you are offending me because I belong to that group. I am as Black as the person whom you are talking about."

The collective struggle against police brutality is a strategy that prioritizes the human and civil rights of Afro-Ecuadorians. That is why the Federation of Afro-Ecuadorian Organizations and Groups of Pichincha Province have organized rallies in front of governmental offices and demonstrations to denounce police brutality. For instance, the first demonstration of Afro-Ecuadorians in Quito, on January 7, 1997, was organized under the banner, of "justice and equality." One of the organizers, Juan Carlos Ocles, stated, "Our rights are going to be respected" (Centro Cultural Afroecuatoriano, 1997). This collective effort to demand rights, and to give visibility to the plight of Blacks in their relations with the police, allows coalition building with human rights groups. The Movement of Black Women of Quito has also organized protests against what they view as sexist and racist advertisements. In June 2000, together with feminist organizations, they staged a demonstration and successfully removed a billboard featuring a Black woman's naked buttocks in an advertisement for a new brand of rum.

Conclusions

This chapter has analyzed the ambiguities of Afro-Ecuadorian demands for the democratization of society. The collective struggles of Black organizations against racism, and some of the everyday practices of individual Afro-Ecuadorians, have a great democratizing potential. Black organizations have challenged racist images that have been used to degrade them, such as the over sexualization of the Black female body. Formerly despised and stigmatized, Black identities are being redefined. Many Black activists are using discourses that value blackness to challenge official constructs of their inherent inferiority. Finally, for the first time in history, Black intellectuals discuss national problems in the public sphere with state officials, the media, politicians, and other groups from civil society.

However, when Black leaders present their demands in the public sphere, they employ the rhetoric and practices that were successfully used by other subaltern groups in their bid for incorporation into the state apparatus and the political system. State representatives have also favored corporatist strategies because these are the mechanisms through which they have channeled social protest. It is premature to arrive at conclusions on whether the corporatist demands of Black and Indian groups will reduce inequality among different ethnic groups, or if they will only assure the social mobility of a few leaders and intellectuals. In any case, even these limited patterns of social mobility will call into question racist stereotypes that have assigned Blacks to manual labor, excluding them from intellectual occupations.

Given that the rule of law does not allow the poor and the nonwhite to have equal access to their constitutional rights, it should not be surprising that paternalism is the most commonly used strategy to get access to resources. The problem is that paternalist relations hinder the conceptualization of domination as a structure. Paternalism also privileges individual accommodation to a structure of subordination, instead of collective struggle for citizenship rights.

Even though the discourse of citizenship has been historically used to exclude many from its benefits, this discourse is universalistic enough to help the excluded fight for their inclusion as citizens with equal rights and duties (Tilly, 1998:198–199). Will this be the venue through which Black organizations demand their inclusion? Or will the weight of the past privilege practices such as paternalism and corporatism?

The organizers of this volume have asked us to reflect on the implications of our findings for Latina and Latino immigrants in the United States. Obviously, Latinas and Latinos are not racialized the moment they arrive in the United States. They come with racial and ethnic identities that explain how they will negotiate their new identities as Hispanics. White and mestizo Ecuadorians harbor deep anti-Black biases. They see Blacks as lazy, criminal, dangerous, and noisy. Given that many have to work with either African Americans or Black immigrants in low-paying jobs, and compete with a zero-sum mentality for limited resources, the relationship between Blacks and non-Black Latino immigrants could be contentious. However, these relations may be tempered by the acknowledgment, and acceptance, of exceptional Blacks common in Latin America. The racialization of white and mestizo Ecuadorian immigrants as minorities in the U.S. context, and their transformation into possible victims of racist encounters, might also allow them to understand and join antiracist struggles with other nonwhites.

Ecuadorian immigrants come from an overly politicized country where people form groups to demand services and resources from the state. These corporatist traditions might motivate some immigrants to accept the label Hispanic to negotiate resources and special privileges from the state. Because many middle-class immigrants might benefit from becoming brokers between their constituencies and the state (Oboler, 1995), they could become strong advocates of programs aimed at Hispanics as a specific group, celebrating "Hispanic culture," advocating for example bilingual education.

Given that many Black Ecuadorians are very poor, it has been difficult for them to migrate in large numbers. How would immigration alter their identity? For one thing, they would benefit from a legal system that offers the possibility of negotiating better interactions with the police and other members of the society. The binary system of racial classification will be a constant reminder of their blackness and might also allow some of them to reinforce their Black identity (Dzidzienyo, 1995). Like other Afro-Latino immigrants, they might develop pan-African identities and build solidarity with African Americans. Second-generation immigrants might recognize many commonalities with the experiences and struggles of Black Americans with whom they share schools and neighborhoods. Learning from African-American as well as from other Black traditions of antiracist struggles, they will probably influence the strategies of Afro-Ecuadorian organizations.

Others, especially lighter-skinned immigrants of the first generation, might accept their new Hispanic identity as a way of escaping blackness and also as a way of differentiating themselves from African Americans—and in this they are like other Black immigrants. It is an open question whether Hispanics who see themselves as white will accommodate Afro-Latinos and include them as their equals, or whether this process would lead to the development of Black Hispanic identity. Similarly, whether the Ecuadorian community in the United States will change its self-perception as a white and mestizo community, and will acknowledge its multiracial composition, remains to be seen.

Notes

1. This research was funded by the Centro Andino de Acción Popular, Quito-Ecuador.
2. INEC, VI Censo de Población y V. de Vivienda, November, 2001.
3. Many of the victims of the lynching crowds that are today taking justice into their own hands are Black. For example, Manuel Ayoví was lynched and burned alive in a small city in the Napo Province because he was mistaken for a Black professional killer (*Hoy* [Quito], November 3, 1996).
4. These areas have high levels of both poverty, i.e., income is not enough for a family to have access to basic needs, and extreme poverty, i.e., income does not even cover basic nutritional needs. According to a recent study on poverty in Eloy Alfaro Canton of Esmeraldas Province, 72% of the population are poor and 26% extremely poor. In San Lorenzo 78% are poor and 29% extremely poor (Larrea, 1996).

References

Centro Cultural Afroecuatoriano. 1997. *Por un futuro digno y bonito.* Videotape.

Chalá, Catherine. 2000. *Agenda política de mujeres negras del Ecuador.* Quito: Coordinadora Nacional de Mujeres Negras.

Chevigny, Paul. 1999. Defining the role of the police in Latin America. In *The (Un) Rule of Law and the Underprivileged in Latin America,* ed. Juan Méndez, Guillermo O'Donnell, and Paulo Sérgio Pinheiro, 49–71. Notre Dame: University of Notre Dame Press.

Chiriboga Zambrano, Galo, and Vjekoslav, Darlic Mardešic. 1999. *Plan operativo de los derechos humanos: Una propuesta participativa.* Quito: ILDIS.

Clark, Kim. 1999. La medida de la diferencia: Las imágenes indigenistas de los indios serranos en el Ecuador (1920–1940). In *Ecuador racista: Imágenes e identidades,* ed. Emma Cervone and Fredhy Rivera. Quito: FLACSO.

Conaghan, Catherine. 1988. *Restructuring Domination: Industrialists and the State in Ecuador.* Pittsburgh: University of Pittsburgh Press.

Consejo de Palenques. 1999. Propuesta para la creación de una Comarca Territorial de Negros en la Provincia de Esmeraldas.

———. 2000. Derechos colectivos de los pueblos afroecuatorianos.

Dandler, Jorge. 1999. Indigenous peoples and the rule of law in Latin America: do they have a chance. In *The (Un) Rule of Law and the Underprivileged in Latin America*, ed. Juan Méndez, Guillermo O'Donnell, and Paulo Sérgio Pinheiro, 116–152. Notre Dame: University of Notre Dame Press.

Dzidzienyo, Anani. 1995. Conclusions. In *No Longer Invisible: Afro-Latin Americans Today*, ed. Minority Rights Group. London: Minority Rights Publications.

Feagin, Joe, and Melvin Sikes. 1994. *Living with Racism: The Black Middle-Class Experience.* Boston: Beacon Press.

Fernández-Rasines, Paloma. 2001. *Afrodescendencia en el Ecuador: Raza y género desde los tiempos de la colonia.* Quito: Abya-Yala.

Halpern, Adam, and France Winddance Twine. 2000. Antiracist activism in Ecuador: Black-Indian community alliances. *Race and Class* 42, no. 2 (October–December):19–33.

Jackman, Mary. 1994. *The Velvet Glove: Paternalism and Conflict in Gender, Class, and Race Relations.* Berkeley: University of California Press.

Larrea, Carlos, et al. 1996. *La geografía de la pobreza en el Ecuador.* Quito: Secretaría Técnica del Frente Social.

León, Jorge. 1994. *De campesinos a ciudadanos diferentes.* Quito: CEDIME-Abya-Yala.

———. 1997. Entre la propuesta y el corporatismo. *Íconos* 2 (May–July):29–40.

Malloy, James. 1977. *Authoritarianism and Corporatism in Latin America.* Pittsburgh: Pittsburgh University Press.

Oboler, Suzanne. 1995. *Ethnic Labels, Latino Lives: Identity and the Politics of Representation in the United States.* Minneapolis: University of Minnesota Press.

O'Donnell, Guillermo. 1999. Poliarchies and the (un)rule of law in Latin America: A partial conclusion. In *The (Un) Rule of Law and the Underprivileged in Latin America*, ed. Juan Méndez, Guillermo O'Donnell, and Paulo Sérgio Pinheiro, 303–339. Notre Dame: University of Notre Dame Press.

Rahier, Jean Muteba. 1998. Blackness, the "racial" spatial order, migrations, and Miss Ecuador 1995–1996. *American Anthropologist* 100 (2):421–430.

Schubert, Grace. 1981. To be black is offensive: Racist attitudes in San Lorenzo. In *Cultural Transformations and Ethnicity in Modern Ecuador*, ed. Norman Whitten, 563–585. Urbana: University of Illinois Press.

Scott, James. 1990. *Domination and the Arts of Resistance: Hidden Transcripts.* New Haven: Yale University Press.

Stepan, Alfred. 1978. *The State and Society: Peru in Comparative Perspective.* Princeton: Princeton University Press.

Stuztman, Ronald. 1974. Black Highlanders: Racism and ethnic stratification in the Ecuadorian Sierra. Ph.D. diss., Washington University.

Tilly, Charles. 1998. *Durable Inequalities.* Berkeley: University of California Press.

van Nieuwkoop, Martien, and Jorge Uquillas. 2000. Defining ethnodevelopment in operational terms: Lessons from the Ecuador Indigenous and Afro-Ecuadoran People's Project. LCR Sustainable Development Working Paper 6. http://wbln0018.worldbank.org.

Wade, Peter. 1997. *Race and Ethnicity in Latin America.* London: Pluto Press.

———. 1998. The cultural politics of blackness in Colombia. In *Blackness in Latin America and the Caribbean: Social Dynamics and Cultural Transformations*, ed. Norman Whitten and Arlene Torres, 303–339. Bloomington: Indiana University Press.

Whitten, Norman. 1965. *Class, Kinship, and Power in an Ecuadorian Town: The Negroes of San Lorenzo.* Stanford: Stanford University Press.

———. 1974. *Black Frontiersmen: Afro-Hispanic Culture of Ecuador and Colombia.* New York: John Wiley.

Whitten, Norman, and Diego, Quiroga. 1998. "To rescue national dignity": Blackness as a quality of nationalist creativity in Ecuador. In *Blackness in Latin America and the Caribbean: Social Dynamics and Cultural Transformations*, ed. Norman Whitten and Arlene Torres, 75–99. Bloomington: Indiana University Press.

CHAPTER 4

THE FOREIGNNESS OF RACISM: PRIDE AND PREJUDICE AMONG PERU'S LIMEÑOS IN THE 1990S

Suzanne Oboler

Introduction

There is racism here in Lima; I do think there's racism.
—Mariana, Chinese descent

There's no racial discrimination in Peru.
— Gabriel, white

I'm not the type to notice whether I've been discriminated or not. I haven't felt it, I don't know if anyone's done it or not, but I haven't felt it.
—Celinda, very light Black

We're all Peruvians here.
—Dolores, Black

These statements are among those I heard from law students early in my research on racialization and racial discrimination in Peru.[1] I noted, on the one hand, an acknowledgment that racism exists, or at least an ambivalence as to its existence; and on the other, denial of its existence and, in the absence of personal experience of discrimination, an apparent perplexity about its meaning. Coming from the U.S. context where the civil rights movements and resulting antidiscrimination laws have, if anything, heightened the sensitivity of the nation's population about racial discrimination, I understood immediately that terms appropriate to the U.S. model could not be used to frame the discussion of race relations in Peruvian society.

In fact, the most illuminating comment in the first few weeks of my eight-month stay in Lima, left no doubt in my mind that racial discrimination in Peru hardly seems to exist in people's perceptions of their daily lives. It came in an informal conversation I had with an Afro-Peruvian lawyer who works on cases that include the violation of human rights of various groups, particularly Blacks. When I explained the subject of my research, he responded by telling me that the racial question in Peru differed from that in the United States because in Peru "racism is more hidden, more disguised [*solapado*]." He went on to say that he had been invited to go to the United

States, that this would be the first time he had gone there, and that he had requested to go to the southern states of the country. And when I asked him why he chose that region, he answered with much vehemence: "Because when I go to the United States, I want them to discriminate against me. I want to feel what it means to not be allowed to sit somewhere because I'm Black; or to be thrown out of a place. I want *to feel* discrimination: *to know* what it is!"

This lawyer's comment reinforced, in no uncertain terms, the statements I quoted at the beginning of this paper. For example, it reinforced the idea that although there is a "hidden" racism (*racismo solapado*), there is no explicit racial discrimination in Peru. Similarly, it reinforced the notion that one of the main referents used to understand the very concept of racial discrimination in Peru is personal experience. But at the same time it also added at least two new dimensions to my confusion about how to approach the racial question in Lima. The first is that the referent the lawyer used to understand racial discrimination is foreign: in other words, I realized that direct discrimination, as he seemed to understand it, could only be experienced—"felt"—in the United States, not in Peru. And the second is that the meaning he attributed to discrimination was grounded in an outdated stereotype tied to the physical segregation of Blacks sanctioned by the Jim Crow laws of the United States until 1954. In other words, his off-the-cuff remark revealed to me a definition of discrimination rooted in the legal history of segregation in the United States, and a lack of knowledge about the relevance of race and racism in contemporary U.S. history and politics.

Given these and similar ambiguous attitudes, and in view of the lack of discussion and debate on the question of racism and racial discrimination in intellectual circles, in the literature, in the newspapers, and in the society at large, the impression I was left with at the end of my first few months in Lima was that perhaps I had begun to research an issue that had no relevance to Peruvian society. I felt I had no right to dismiss the claim made by those I had talked to that discrimination in Peru is gender- and class-based, and not racial. Yet at the same time I could not neglect the fact that they simultaneously acknowledged that there is racism; nor could I forget my personal experience and memories growing up in Lima during the 1950s and 1960s, or the disdain toward the indigenous Andean populations, which, like the insults against Black and Asian Peruvians, were rarely nuanced. And so I kept wondering how the virulent marks of the conflicts among whites and indigenous people, Blacks, and Asians during the nation's colonial and republican periods, could have disappeared in the relatively short span of the twenty years since I left Peru.

Furthermore, given the history of colonialism and slavery in the West, it seemed to me that to suggest that racially based differentiations and discrimination do not exist in Peru would make the country an anomaly in the world. After all, racism is an ideology that has plagued the modern world, particularly in the twentieth century. It is an ideology that looks for and reinforces biologically and visually, "inherent" manifestations of difference in order to justify socioeconomic inequality. Moreover, like the practice of racial discrimination, race is neither a category of nature nor a given fact of nature; rather, it is solely a social construct. Thus, racism is above all proof of the success of a socially constructed artifice, rooted in nineteenth- and twentieth-century ideological practices that justified the enslavement and discrimination of one group by another. As Howard Winant (1994:2) has cogently argued: "race remains the fundamental organizing principle, a way of knowing and interpreting the social world. . . . In those *milieux* where, historically, race has been foundational—that is in most if not all human societies—its centrality continues, even after the original reasons for invoking it have disappeared."[2]

From a historical and international perspective, then, I want to emphasize that the main purpose of my research on racism, citizenship, and national belonging in the Americas is not to "prove" that racism exists, whether in Peru, Brazil, the United States, or anywhere else. Rather, the main point of a research project such as this one is to show the specificity of its mechanisms in different social and political formations. For, ultimately, what is at stake is the way racism obstructs the process of democratization of rights and citizenship in all spheres of social life of the societies affected by this phenomenon.

Insofar as it is a social phenomenon, "race" is inextricably bound to class, gender, and social status. As such, it is and has always been an eminently political question, which manifests itself in distinct ways in different countries. As the assimilationist melting-pot myths of the United States have shown, wishful color blindness can undermine the nation's social and economic development with equity, and the acknowledgment of people's rights, citizenship, and sense of belonging to the community. Certainly, the assimilationist myths of the United States refer primarily to immigrants and thus differ from the nation-building ideologies so prevalent in Latin American nations today. At the same time, however, it could also be argued that the ideologies of nationalism in Latin America are comparable to U.S. assimilationist myths with respect to racial distinctions and discrimination. For, just as assimilationist narratives have not blunted the historical impact of racial segregation in the United States, it is not self-evident to me that nationalist discourses such as "we are all Peruvian"—reiterated through the insistence that there is no racial discrimination—could wish away the international trauma of slavery and its continued repercussions in this hemisphere.

On the other hand, since the period of slavery, historical processes have differentiated the political spheres of individual nations. In the United States, the civil rights movements have ensured that there are today a relatively significant number of African Americans and Latinos/as in public office throughout the nation. At the same time, however, as a result of discriminatory sentencing practices, the number of these minorities in prison are disproportionate to their size in the overall U.S. population. In Peru, where racial ancestry, language usage, and the time or way of arrival of different racial and ethnic groups have historically been implicitly de-emphasized in the public sphere,[3] an individual of Japanese descent was elected to the presidency of the nation—in spite of attempts by his opposition to discredit him on the basis of "his Japanese origins as well as his lack of knowledge of Peruvian culture, for speaking Spanish badly" (Montoya, 1998:183).

The differences in the political development of nations that once had slavery can also be stated in terms of economic and social arguments. For example, it is clear from the U.S. experience, particularly during the 1960s, that neither antidiscriminatory laws nor economic growth, wealth, or stability necessarily result in a decline of racism, much less in its disappearance. From this perspective it was also apparent that I could rely neither on the end of inflation and of the violence of terrorism, nor on the current discourse of citizenship and national belonging, nor even on the climate of hope that engulfed Lima in the mid-1990s, to counter either the colonial legacy of slavery (Hunefeldt, 1994) or the ethnic and racial prejudices and discrimination against the indigenous Asian and Black populations that have persisted in Peru.

Still, my first months in Peru made it clear to me that focusing on racism does not appear to contribute to the debates on democratizing citizenship and rights in Peru. How, then, to understand the legacy of colonialism and slavery in a context in which the relevance of race in daily life is diminished through the emphasis on gender, socioeconomic, and status considerations, while the unquestionable presence of racism in the political arena, evident in the violent upsurge of attacks against Asian-Peruvians between the first and second rounds of the 1990s election, had, by the mid-1990s, been relegated to a seeming anomaly in the nation's history?[4]

This essay is a first step toward unraveling the specificity of the dynamic between race and power in Peru. There is no question, as Juan Carlos Callirgos (1993) has noted, that racism is clearly detrimental and very painful in personal and individual terms. But I want to emphasize that the importance of understanding the meaning and social value of racial prejudices and discrimination in and of itself is ultimately only relevant to the extent that it can be seen to affect the nation's political process and socioeconomic development. Grounded in the assumption that the question of race in society is today, as always, strictly an issue of power and status and not of biology, I want to focus here on the process of developing a framework that can perhaps provide one approach to the mechanisms through which racism and racial discrimination is understood, constructed, and negotiated in the daily life and politics of Lima. The development of my research project and the basic argument of this paper is as follows.

My point of departure is that since racism is neither a natural category nor a legally sanctioned practice, particularly in Peru and Latin America, the understanding of how "race" is socially lived, understood, and experienced requires a critical assessment of daily life in society. The contradiction in the idea that there is racism but no racial discrimination in Peru, led me to begin by examining the racializing labels used in daily life, to assess the extent to which it can be argued at all that there is some awareness of racial difference embedded in the social relations and perceptions among Peruvians in Lima. Social labels and discourse, like social practices, are particularly useful in this sense, for they reveal, on the one hand, how racism manifests itself in individual lives and, on the other, the ways that the legacy of colonialism has been handed down and transformed in the process of nation building. This approach thus allowed me to research the forms that racial awareness, including racial discrimination, take in everyday life in Lima. In this essay, I argue that this contradiction is rooted in a definition of racial discrimination that is grounded in criteria imported from abroad—specifically from the United States. More specifically, I argue that these foreign ideological criteria are superimposed on and articulated to Latin America's ideology of *blanqueamiento* (whitening), and together explain the way racism is understood and experienced by different groups in Peru. I conclude by suggesting on the one hand that the experience of racial discrimination of each ethnic and racial group changes and varies over time, according to the symbolic and social position each group occupies in the society; and on the other, that since the 1990 election of Alberto Fujimori, the ideology of racism has become a central and explicit component of the way that political representation and participation is experienced by different ethnic and racial groups in Peru.

The data for this essay is drawn from in-depth interviews with twenty law students, whom I found through snowball techniques drawn from the field of anthropology. Most of the students were in the final months of their studies, and many were already also involved in professional internship programs. They were both males and females, ranging from nineteen to thirty-one years old, and studied in public, private, or elite law schools in Lima. Their social backgrounds were varied, as were their ethno-racial backgrounds, which they themselves defined in survey questions as well as in follow-up qualitative interviews. I chose to focus my fieldwork specifically on law students because their chosen professional career ensured their up-to-date knowledge of Peruvian laws, while the fact that they were all raised in Lima guaranteed their famil-iarity with the customs and traditional relations among different racial and ethnic groups. I should note that the group did include first-generation *Limeños* whose parents migrated from the Andes during the late 1960s and 1970s, as well as members of long-established *criollo*[5] families. For purposes of comparison and data checking, I also conducted in-depth interviews with two female-headed black families—one middle class and one working class—which included three generations and their extended families. Finally, I did a life history of one of the first Afro-Peruvian justices of the peace and a lawyer, a woman who is now seventy-five years old and retired. And, of course, during the eight months I spent in Lima, I talked informally with as many people, from all walks of life, as I could engage in conversation on the subject of racism in Lima. At the same time, I read the available bibliography on the subject and spent time doing archival research on the way racial issues have been reported (or not) by the major newspapers since the nationalist military regime of General Velasco (1968–1975), who repoliticized the ethnic question in Peru (Franco, 1993).

The data analysis in this particular paper, however, is primarily based on the interviews with the law students. I want to emphasize that because of time and funding constraints on my research, I did not set out to provide a survey of racial attitudes and behaviors in Lima, much less in the country as a whole. Rather, based on a very specific group of 38 *Limeños*, my aim was to begin to formulate a theoretical frame-work for understanding how the mechanisms of racism are constructed, experienced, and negotiated specifically in the social and political daily life of Lima.[6] Let me begin, then, by first laying out the context I found in Lima, and the way I approached the development of this framework.

Racializing Labels and *El Racismo Solapado* (Disguised Racism) in Lima

When I first arrived in Lima in early June 1995 to begin this research project on race, citizenship, and national belonging, I found that the country, and Lima itself, had undergone many changes over the preceding twenty years. Clearly there had been a substantial growth of the Andean population in the city, and its impact on the tastes, sights, and sounds now permeated daily life in the city. Street vendors were visible throughout Lima, both on the streets downtown and in the city's outskirts, where since the late 1950s, the migrants had built *"pueblo jovenes"* or, as they were now called, *"asentamientos humanos."* Although the emphasis placed on the significance of recent events varied, intellectuals, old friends, and people I spoke to on the streets all pointed to several factors that have impacted on the daily life of the city in the mid-1990s: the end of the nation's twelve years of civil war, terrorism, and hyperinflation; the election of a Peruvian of Japanese descent (*"el chinito"*) to the presidency, which signaled both the decline of traditional political institutions and, for many, the crumbling of the traditional oligarchy's power; the social movements, protests, and civic organizing led primarily by women throughout the 1980s, which had centered on finding ways of surviving the poverty resulting from the government's "economic packages," on ending the destructive presence of the guerrilla Sendero Luminoso in their neighborhoods, and on demanding the right to representation and protection from the state. Since the defeat of Sendero Luminoso in 1992, the possibility that could exacerbate existing racial and ethnic differences had been replaced by an emphasis on the discourse of nationality and an affirmation of citizenship, rights, equality, and the rule of law.[7]

Particularly among sectors of the middle classes, there seemed to be a widespread recognition that although prejudice and discrimination against Peru's Andean population hadn't disappeared, for better or for worse, as several people put it, "it isn't like it used to be." In many ways, the change was also attributed to the growth of the indigenous migrant population in Lima over the past thirty years, to their development and control of the informal market, and to the rise of a "cholo bourgeoisie." Many traced its origins to the Velasco military government and included in their explanations the continued absence of strong social and political institutions, which could incorporate the peasant populations long excluded from the nation's real and imagined community. Certainly a significant informal market, considered to be the largest in Latin America, has emerged and is being run primarily by the now-grown *limeño* children of the migrants and their parents.[8] Moreover, while many pointed to the significant presence of a new generation of *"cholo*-limeños" in the city's public and private universities, schools, institutions, and services, others noted the increased miscegenation of its population as a whole, and the consequent gradual "disappearance" of the Black-*criollo* from the streets of Lima. And although there were also comments about the unprecedented surge of acts of prejudice and discrimination, particularly against the Asian community following the first round of the presidential election between Fujimori and Mario Vargas Llosa in 1990, as I mentioned above, the incident itself seems to have been largely forgotten.[9]

In short, buttressed by the ongoing historical weakness of the state institutions, the changes in Lima over the past ten years were due to a number of coinciding factors, which, as the anthropologist Jurgen Golte explained to me, ultimately stemmed from the closure of the Peruvian economy to foreign investment during the Alan Garcia administration (1985–1990) and Fujimori's construction of a technical and pragmatic service-oriented state to support his laissez-faire economic liberalism. These factors had in turn fostered the emergence of a sui generis capitalism grounded in the small informal businesses that the Andean migrant populations organized in Lima on the basis of kinship and communal ties. In ethnic and racial terms, the combination of these various factors has literally meant the "emancipation" of large contingents of the long-excluded indigenous populations. Historically and from birth, these sectors had had no hope of escaping a rigid hierarchical and regional socioracial caste society grounded not in the rule of law but in the residual traditional norms of the nation's colonial and neocolonial history and customs.[10]

Certainly, contrary to the situation in the United States, one of the main difficulties in mapping out the mechanism of racism and racial discrimination is the absence in this century of a clear institutional or legal referent that might confirm the racial legacy of colonialism in Peru. Individual Peruvians emphasize, instead, the official nation-building discourse, expressed by several of those I interviewed as "We are all Peruvians here." Together with the search for alternatives to the violence of terrorism through growing demand for the acknowledgment of the rule of law, rights, and citizenship, as Hortensia Muñoz has shown,[11] this discourse does not leave much room for explicit acts of racial discrimination. But what it clearly does do is allow for the existence of what the Black lawyer I cited above called "*racismo solapado*." And so, insofar as it *is solapado*, in the early months of my stay, as I mentioned before, I was often at a loss as to how to best approach the subject of my research.

But as I continued reading, doing interviews, walking all over Lima and listening to people from all walks of life—professionals, the middle sectors, taxi drivers, street vendors, workers, and youth—I began to note that derogatory labels, such as *serrano* and *indio*, which were commonly heard and used twenty years ago, have largely, although not entirely, been replaced today by the seemingly more acceptable terms *provinciano* and *indigena*.[12] Moreover, I also began to realize that although things may not be "like they used to be," the meanings and social values that historically cemented the nation's castelike organization and hierarchized the population's cultural and linguistic attributes, skin color, and phenotype have clearly not disappeared. Instead, they persist, albeit in a more attenuated form through the various labels (*cholo, zambo, moreno, chino*)[13] that are still used to symbolically identify and position various groups in the society's daily life.

I began by researching ethnic and racial labels and exploring the persistence and the changing nature of their attributes today. Social labels have a history of their own, and the meanings attributed to them—like the very names themselves—change through time, highlighting the shifts in the social value and position of each group in specific historical conjunctures (Franco, 1993).[14] The use of social labels and values attributed to them is inevitable in any society—and certainly the interviews confirmed that Peru is no exception to this rule. One of the women I interviewed, for example, described her perception of the attributes of some of the racial labels used in Lima in the following way:

> It's like this. You see a white who has money, and you say, he's a drug dealer, because whites with money are drug dealers. Blacks with money are supported by their women, they call them *caficho*—someone supported by a woman. A *cholo* who has money has it because he works, because he's someone who has dedicated himself to his business. You see a person from the Andes [*paisanito*] still red-cheeked because he's just arrived from the mountains, and you see him in a van and people say, "Oh, that boy has bettered himself, he's worked" and it doesn't occur to them that maybe, who knows, he has also been involved in those things. (Dolores, Black)

Thus, as this woman's comment suggests, in contrast to twenty years ago, *cholos* are now considered to be hardworking. Unlike both Blacks and whites, they are no longer so readily perceived to be "involved in those things," such as drugs—although the television and newspaper images and accounts often seem to point to the contrary. In fact, although the derogatory connotations attributed to Andean populations in the 1960s and 1970s have by no means disappeared, the seemingly more "positive" evaluation of *cholos* in this and other interviews reinforced the significance of the current discussions in intellectual circles on the changing social value of the term *cholo* and the debates on the emergence of a new national identity based on what Carlos Franco (1993), among others, has called the "cholificación del Peru."[15]

Indeed, the term *cholo* is perhaps the most complex of all the Peruvian labels. Writing in the mid-1960s, François Bourricaud, for example, observed that the meaning of the word *cholo* had shifted since colonial times (1970:66): "This name is given with a shade of contempt or condescension to those persons whose origins place them in the indigenous class but who possess some social and cultural attributes which enable them to 'better themselves' and attain higher status." Indeed, embedded in the term are notions of ethnic identity, geography, social class, race, and culture, as well intellectual and social values. Indeed, as Cosamalon Aguilar has explained, "The word *cholo* used as an insult, is a type of social discrimination, the most important one for establishing distances and hierarchies in Peru. It is a way of defining the value of people and the way they should be treated" (cited in León, 1998:167 n. 9). Although in its classical definition the term refers to those migrants from the Andean region of Peru who have arrived in Lima and have been assimilated into Lima daily life, shedding their indigenous clothing, culture, and ways, *cholo* also has distinct socioracial connotations. In her study on discrimination in the schools, Elisabeth Acha (1993:320) also provides a glimpse into its complexity, defining the word *cholo* in the following terms: "More than a racially defined type, such as Black Americans in the United States might be considered, for example, the concept *cholo* has, above all, a social and cultural meaning. It alludes not only to particular physical features but also above all to one's belonging to a lower and less prestigious social class." In short, the seemingly more positive evaluation that my informant Dolores, like others, attributed to the *cholo* in relation to other groups suggests that there appears to be an ongoing, albeit gradual, change in the status of the *cholo* and consequently in the social perception of the group, at least among certain sectors of Lima.[16]

By their very usage, then, labels verify the positioning and repositioning of different groups in society. In the case of stigmatizing social labels in particular, their meaning and the social values attributed to them, like their political and social use in the public sphere, reveal the existence of a distinction between full civil rights guaranteed to all and rights as social privileges extended to certain groups and denied to others. Indeed, as I have argued elsewhere, to varying extents racializing labels in all societies can be said to point to the practices of political inclusion or exclusion of a group's members from full participation as first-class citizens in their nation (Oboler, 1995). Thus the fact that all the people I interviewed could—and did—provide me with clearly defined and similar social attributes for the various racial and ethnic groups in Lima suggested that even while it is not always acknowledged, and even while it is still not explicitly a part of the nation's legal discourse, racism and racial discrimination are very much a factor of daily life in the society. And indeed, in one of the interviews, a male student discussed the discrepancy between the absence of institutionalized legal discrimination based on race, class, and gender and the presence of prejudices and discrimination based on socially constituted differences, including race, in everyday life:

> There is a lot of discrimination, it's not made public. People try to cover it up with a lot of hypocrisy. But there is discrimination at all levels, indistinctly from race to race. It's not only whites specifically who reject Blacks or indigenous people. Instead it's that among people of my race, the Black race, there is often a very marked discrimination toward *serranos*, for example. They categorize them as ignorant, dirty, betrayers, people who can't be trusted. . . . [And whites are considered] cultivated, very educated very intelligent—in short, superior. (Gustavo, Black)

Since the existence of clearly articulated prejudices and differentiations among various groups in a given society is, in and of itself, perhaps inevitable and certainly not unique to Peru, the confirmation of the continued persistence of racializing labels that figured so prominently in daily life and relations in Lima during the 1950s and 1960s led me to formulate my next research question: How, in the absence of its institutionalization, could I pinpoint the mechanism through which racism and discrimination are practiced and are articulated to the power positions occupied by different groups in society? More specifically, how could I explain and specify the ways in which the racial practices of daily life affect, or not, the democratization of citizenship and people's sense of representation and participation in the public sphere? But first I would need a more precise definition of racism in the context of Lima—one that would identify its specific mechanisms and perhaps make sense of the puzzling yet recurrent claim that racial discrimination is somehow absent from that characterization.

Racial Ideologies in Lima: National or Foreign?

It could be argued that to raise the question of racism as a key aspect of daily life and politics in Lima once again distorts the understanding of the society's contemporary history and social reality. As witnessed in the nineteenth century, when European ideas were imported to the New World—creating what the Brazilian theorist Roberto Schwartz (1993: 19–32)[17] has called the "ideological comedy"—this approach would appear once again to involve, at the very least, the distorting effects of analysis grounded in the particularities of another society, in this case the United States, a nation whose recent political history exemplifies in no uncertain terms the consequences of the official use of racial politics and the politicizing of "race" in everyday life (Winant, 1994; Gregory and Sanjek, 1994).

Indeed, as the comments introducing this paper suggest, several of the people I interviewed also confirmed the idea that to approach the question of race in Peru through the prism of race and racial categories could distort understanding of Peruvian and Lima society today. And clearly there are significant differences between Peru and the United States in the role of racism in forging nation identity and in the interplay of the history and law. To begin with, race relations in the history and society of the United States developed on the basis of a very explicit legal definition of biological ancestry to characterize and categorize individuals belonging to particular groups. This legal definition was reinforced and popularized in the customs of daily life through what has commonly come to be known as the "one-drop rule"—that is, the assumption that "one drop of Black blood makes you Black." This social artifice served as the basis for the development of an ideology of racial purity of whites and the racializing and racist practices of that nation.[18]

Contrary to the United States, in Peru the very definition of who is white, who is mestizo,[19] who is *chino, cholo, negro,* or *zambo,* seems to have been historically grounded in the inverse symbolic assumption, which could be informally summarized by the phrase "one drop of white blood can make you white." Rooted in ideological distinctions between indigenous people and whites, the emphasis on an ideology of individual "whitening"—*blanqueamiento*[20]—has long made the category of whiteness, like that of mestizo, difficult to pinpoint, primarily because its meaning has historically been fluid and situational. As Fernando Fuenzalida V. (1970:25) noted more than twenty-five years ago:

> The confusion among scholars increases upon discovering that often the particular case does not match our expectations. Light-skinned individuals with European features such as those in the mountains of Cajamarca and of Ayacucho[21] are classified as indigenous; People from the provinces who are of pure Spanish or Portuguese ancestry, and others whose background is clearly Quechua,[22] receive indiscriminately the name of *mestizos;* members of the so-called oligarchy, whose physical features openly denounce multiple miscegenation, are defined as whites. The race of a man does not coincide with his race. Or perhaps we should say "the *races* of a man."[23]

Together with the notion of *mestizaje,* the ideology of *blanqueamiento* has "confused," to use Fuenzalida's term, the issue of Peruvians' racial identification. Juan Carlos Callirgos (1993:181) notes, for example, that *mestizaje* is a "seemingly democratizing discourse, which is used by the elites to deny the racism existing in Peru." Contrary to the United States, then, *mestizaje* blurs the racial distinctions between self and other in such a way that distinguishing between the two has become "almost impossible" in Peru. As a result, Callirgos (196–197) argues, racism in Peru is lived by the individual primarily as "an internal conflict" for, as he explains, "in discriminating against someone for being an 'Indian,' the probable 'Indian' part within oneself—and hence one's own identity—is necessarily denied." Reinforcing this idea, Nelson Manríque (1996:97) goes on to argue that, as a result, "racism becomes a greater form of alienation, for it presupposes the impossibility of identifying with one's own face as it is reflected in the mirror. Hence, a deeply twisted form of racism is created, one that in theoretical terms is difficult to approach."

There is no doubt that the differing legal and social histories of the United States and Peru have ensured that race cannot be approached or understood in the same terms in the two nations. Yet it is important to consider another question not included by Callirgos, among others, in his comparative comments on racism in Peru and the United States. I am referring to the impact that throughout this century the United States appears to have had on Peru in shaping the definition of what does or does not constitute racial discrimination. While it is important to assess the outcome of the ideology of racial whitening and of *mestizaje* in individuals' interpersonal relations and psychology, I would suggest that this outcome, like the question of race relations in Peru, cannot be fully addressed without reference to how Peruvians perceive race in the United States and how those perceptions influence their construction and/or disavowal of racial discrimination in Peru.

More specifically I want to suggest that the ideology of the one-drop rule, which allowed for the implementation of the U.S. laws of segregation between 1896 and 1954, and ensured the facile identification of Blacks in the U.S. context, has since contributed toward the creation of the paradigms of what constitutes the ideological definition of racism and of racial discrimination in the twentieth century, not only in the United States but also in Peru and indeed in the other nations of the Americas.[24] Indeed, it is interesting to note that unlike our easy acceptance of the notion of the penetration of U.S. political, economic, and cultural influence—what particularly during the 1960s was referred to as "U.S. imperialism"—when it comes to the penetration of ideologies of race, we continue to insist that while racism might exist, it is certainly not a major issue in Latin America: as I was often told during my stay in Lima, "that is a problem of the Americans'." Nevertheless, the fact that legal discrimination was revoked by the U.S. courts more than thirty years ago did not prevent the lawyer I quoted earlier from referring to that nation's segregated past—albeit ahistorically—in defining the specificity of Peruvians' racism and race relations. In so doing, he pointed, through contrast, to his conception of racial discrimination and disguised racism in the Peruvian context. He was not alone in adapting the contemporary history of U.S. race relations to understand racism in Lima:

Racism is not as strong here, and it's more covered up. It's more open in the United States. There, you see, there are restaurants where Blacks aren't allowed to go in, and they hang up their signs. (Rosa, Black)

Comments like Rosa's suggested to me that the issue of racism in Lima is difficult to pinpoint not only because of the interpersonal conflicts inherent in the ideology of racial whitening, but also because the defining referents of the term "racial discrimination" do seem to be rooted in the legal history of the United States in the twentieth century. And so I arrived at the conclusion that while physical segregation through the law is clearly one of the imported referents used in defining and understanding the term "racial discrimination" in Peru, another referent is grounded in the relationship between this legal notion of discrimination as it is linked specifically to the social experience and perception of Blacks. As a result, blackness itself became a second referent for me. My next step, then, was to verify these referents in the context of Lima society and specifically to research the meaning and social value of blackness, and the ways in which the situation of Blacks is perceived in the symbolic and social imaginary of *limeños*.

Blacks in the *Criollo* Imaginary

According to José Carlos Luciano (1995:50–58), there are an estimated 1.4 to 2 million Afro-Peruvians, making up 6 to 10 percent of the nation's population. The interviews leave no doubt of the persistence of racial prejudices against Asians, indigenous populations, *cholos*, whites, mestizos, and the like. At the same time, I found that in all the interviews, the clearest negative stereotypes are consistently and unambivalently attributed to Blacks—which contrasts with the clear ambivalence in the attitudes toward the other groups. Indeed, as a group, Afro-Peruvians consistently figure negatively in the social imaginary—regardless of the respondent's gender, race, social background, or type of contact with Blacks:

> They always think that because you're Black you have no money. They always characterize Blacks that way. And if they see a Black in a fancy car, [they ask] "Who did he steal it from?" or else they'll say, "He's the chauffeur." And if they see a well-dressed Black woman: "She must be a prostitute" or "Her husband is white." (Rosa, Black)

> Do you know why people are scared? Because as I was saying, Blacks haven't developed themselves—culturally, physically, morally, not in any aspect. For the most part, they dedicate themselves to crime, to doing bad things. . . . "There goes a Black! And it's night, and it's dark. Oh! He's going to assault me. He's evil, a rapist!" And why? Because, as I was telling you, they haven't developed. You see a Black man, and he's a criminal. (Ximena, mestiza)

Some of the law students pointed out the legal history of Black slavery as the origin of these stereotypes. Insofar as the history of slavery and colonialism are shared throughout the Americas, it is perhaps not surprising that the ways of perceiving Blacks and positioning them in the symbolic social hierarchy in Peru do not differ from the ways they are portrayed in other parts of the hemisphere. It is true that since the independence period Latin American nations similarly formulated constitutional guarantees of equality and national inclusion of all groups, including Blacks. But while the Latin American nations may share the idea that if there is no legal discrimination there cannot be racial discrimination, the meanings and social values attributed to Afro–Latin Americans also ensure, although to varying extents, their exclusion from the public sphere.

This explains why the two referents drawn from the U.S. paradigm—that is, the historical legal exclusion from public positions of power and the negative social value attributed to Blackness—led several of the people I interviewed to focus on the sphere of politics in comparing the position of Blacks with that of other groups in Peruvian society:

> We have many *cholos* in the government: we have *cholos* in the executive; we have *cholos* in the judiciary; we have *cholos* in the legislative branch. They're there—they have a presence there. *Cholos* already have a presence at that level, which Blacks do not. There was a party, an independent political group, which took part in the last parliamentary elections, and as far as I know, no Black got in. Why? I believe one of the reasons may be race. (Gustavo)

At the same time, contrary to the United States, the perceptions of Blacks and their position in society in Peru—like the discussion of racial discrimination itself—have historically been complicated by the multiracial and multiethnic nature of Peruvian society, and particularly by the presence of the much larger indigenous population. As Luis Millones (1973) suggested, in the early 1970s, the presence and impact of the Indian culture still ensured the invisibility of Blacks, and since the colonial period, "the attitudes toward them have remained essentially the same or, if they have developed, have not changed the perceptions that place them at the lowest strata of society."[25]

Clearly Blacks are not the only group that has negative stereotypes associated with it. In fact, in informal conversations many *limeños*, regardless of their racial and social backgrounds, suggested to me that indigenous people have historically had a more negative image than Blacks. Moreover, as Millones (1973:19) notes, the Peruvian indigenous population occupies a much lower rank in the symbolic status hierarchy: some attribute this to the fact that Blacks are not as numerous as indigenous people and hence never posed as serious a threat to the dominant white oligarchy.

According to several historians, Blacks coexisted very closely with whites throughout the nineteenth century, sharing the space, culture, and behavior codes of the dominant *limeño* classes.[26] Unlike indigenous people, Blacks participated in the private lives of whites through child rearing, sexual initiation and miscegenation itself, domestic service, and social and leisure activities such as music and dance. Confronted by the indigenous presence whose territorial belonging affirms their ethnic definition,[27] the ambivalent coexistence between whites and Blacks—both foreigners on Peruvian soil—affirms itself through their mutual acculturation in the shared space of Lima. Grounded in power and domination, the resulting social ambivalence expressed itself through the emergence of the term *criollo*, which, according to Carlos Ivan Degregori (1990), ended up referring primarily to the "upper and middle, mostly white and light-skinned mestizo classes of primarily Spanish origin," thus relegating the Afro-*limeño* to invisibility.[28]

This historically ambivalent coexistence between Blacks and whites, rooted in customary—although not legal—relations of power and domination, also suggested to me why those interviewed acknowledge a universal discrimination primarily against Blacks and simultaneously contrast Peru's race relations favorably to those of the United States. While, on the one hand, the low status of Afro-Peruvians in Lima points to the persistence of racism in Peruvian society, on the other, their presence seems to be a measure of the extent to which the relationship between race and power in Peru is primarily, albeit not entirely, an issue understood and ultimately best resolved in socioeconomic and status—rather than racial—terms:

> In the United States there's a different level of culture, of thinking, and if we ever reach it here, it's because our mental level has accepted and overcome many things. To access power here you need to be more or less mestizo; in other words, a *cholo* who's become bourgeois, or a white. But I've never seen a Black in Congress. *Cholos*, yes, and there's a bunch of *serranos*, but Blacks, no. (Rodrigo, Chinese-Black)

Again, it is interesting to note, as Rodrigo's comment suggests, that racial discrimination refers only to the absence of Blacks in the public sphere. At the same time, he leaves no doubt that race and status go hand in hand in Peruvian society, and thus in order to have access to power, people of color have to become "bourgeois."

As it became clear to me that the people I interviewed defined racism and racial discrimination in terms of referents grounded in the U.S. paradigm of race relations, it was not surprising to find that some would suggest that racism is a subject related primarily to foreigners:

> I think that in Peru we're not as racist maybe as people are in other places, in other countries. . . . If it's true that there are racists here, I think they are primarily foreigners—people who have come here: they are the ones who have the biggest problems with race. (Juan, white)

Still, while racism is perceived to be related to the social application of the law to an entire national community, and as such is deemed a "foreign" problem, the ideology of *blanqueamiento* has reinforced the notion that interpersonal discrimination among Peruvians can be solved through intermarriage, that is, through a practice that in Latin America is commonly referred to as "improving the race"—that is, miscegenation. As a result, contrary to the United States, where race is clearly understood as a social rather than individual problem, in Peru the racial question is understood in personal terms and thus is seen to have an individual—rather than social or political—solution. Not surprisingly, all those interviewed—including those most conscious of racism and discrimination—insisted that Blacks' status in society was self-imposed:

> For the most part, they [Black women] provoke it themselves, through the miniskirts they wear, or their tight pants, or dress. (Gustavo)
>
> *Morenos* feel they are less. Unconsciously they consider themselves lesser. I don't mean by this that they have a guilt complex, but that they would like to be more, but can't overcome their backwardness. . . . Perhaps they themselves let themselves be dragged down, or don't realize that they can be more, that they have a brain. We all have the same amount of brains. (Rodrigo)

There were some, of course, who recognized that the social impediments placed on Blacks do create problems of self-esteem, making them "feel they are less":

> In our workshops we try to help women overcome their problems, the routine that Black women usually suffer through. For the most part, we are marginalized at work, even in the neighborhoods themselves: Blacks are lazy and all that. We prepare identity and self-esteem workshops that consist in helping women to identify themselves as they are, to accept themselves as they are, to not believe themselves to be less than whites or less than others. (Rosa)

But as this not atypical quote suggests, the solution to the obstacles imposed on Blacks by society also continues to be defined in individual terms, which is perhaps not so surprising, given that acknowledgment that the position of Blacks is socially constructed is superimposed onto a definition of discrimination rooted in the individualistic ideology of *blanqueamiento* in daily life. As I mentioned before, this ideology defines discrimination, on the one hand, as a social and foreign problem to be understood and solved abroad in more universal legal terms; and on the other, as an issue related to specific gender and socioeconomic characteristics that allow for individual solutions. Thus, the burden of changing the position and status of Blacks is placed not on the larger community but rather on the group and the individuals themselves. Indeed, comments such as the following exemplify the extent to which race has been internalized as a personal problem in Peruvian society:

> If they decide to, Blacks could overcome. . . . The society imposes a lot of limits, and Blacks allow it. I think that if we were all united in this country and struggled to open up a space for ourselves, for us to be taken into account, and for us to give ourselves opportunities, we would achieve a lot. There are no Blacks in important positions here—not in the government nor in any institution. On television, Blacks only shine in advertisements for Coca-Cola, carbon paper, Black products, chocolate. (Dolores)

In short, despite the many instances of prejudice and discrimination revealed in several interviews, the individualizing ideology of *blanqueamiento*, coupled with definitions of racism and racial discrimination that derive from a historical experience foreign to that of Peru, has ensured that racism is *not* a significant category openly used to understand or to explain the political or social life of the national community as a whole. Notwithstanding the racism witnessed between the first and second rounds of the 1990s election, the presumed foreignness of racial discrimination and its legal remedies has meant that racism in Lima is understood in terms of interpersonal prejudices that warrant individual solutions by those whom it affects, freeing the larger national community from the burden and hence the task of addressing the problem of racism in the society. Consequently, the racial question is virtually absent from political debates on national development and on the distribution of power and economic resources among various sectors of the population. From this perspective, it is not surprising that many will question whether there is racism in Peru:

> Racial discrimination here is minimal. . . . I think if there is any racial discrimination, it is only in very few cases—more than anything for some types of work. (Juan)

Moreover, it also points to one of the reasons why there is an absence of a strong racial group consciousness in contemporary Peruvian society—both among Blacks and among other ethnic groups such as the indigenous and Asian populations. For although the people I interviewed showed themselves to be both wary of the colonial legacy and hierarchy rooted in social and racial differences and highly conscious of physical appearance, Peruvians continue to adhere strongly to the republican constitutional notion—increasingly questioned in other parts of the world—that birthplace is a guarantee of citizenship and national belonging.

Class, Status, and Racial Differences in Lima Society

"We're all Peruvians here" was the statement that, as I said before, was frequently repeated by the law students to emphasize that the constitution guarantees equality to all—regardless of race, ethnicity, class, or gender. Again, this is not to say that they are not aware of the limits imposed on the law by the customs of a society grounded in the absence of the rule of law. The anthropologist Roberto Da Matta (1991:429–442) has said of Brazil that there the rule of law and the constitution remains only a hope, yet to be achieved. Of Peru, and indeed of the rest of Latin America, much the same can be said. In the words of one of the law students:

> The juridical assumptions in our constitution should be complied with, but instead they are violated in various ways. . . . We should all be equal before the law. These juridical assumptions should govern but don't. They are actually utopias that will never be reached, but we have to try, to the extent that we can, to make that be our aim. (Gabriel)

But although many live it as a hope and others as a reality, the emphasis on equality, and on the idea and the rule of law, also does not mean that there is no consciousness of the existence of racial differences in Peruvian society. Unlike in the United States, where there is no strict status correlation between race and class, in Peru, as in much of Latin America, the racial question is clearly tied to status,[29] which in turn provides the grounds for adherence to the ideology that "money whitens." Even many of those law students who, like Celinda (quoted earlier), did not notice whether or not they had been discriminated against, and emphasized that the problem of discrimination was best understood in gender and socioeconomic terms, acknowledged the relevance of race in structuring the nation's social hierarchy:

> The white race is like a privileged race. It's true that we have economic discrimination, at the level of power, of each person. But it's as if at a lower level, the economic aspects influence what race is; and usually whites are taken more seriously. Whites are a little more. It's a pity but that's the way it is. (Celinda)

Yet, while whites are often ranked at the top of the symbolic status hierarchy, the apparent (mis)perception of their declining social power, in the light of the rising power of Asians of Peruvian descent and perhaps also of the *"cholificacion del Peru,"* means that the social value attributed to whiteness today is also increasingly ambivalent and not always positive:

> Generally speaking, a whitish person is not going to work just anywhere. He's going to want to work somewhere where he's given the most comforts. He tries to make himself the wiseguy, he tries to show he's slick, that's all. What happens is that the whites are the ones who have the most money, that's usually what happens; and they've been accustomed to having everything easy. For example, a family that had money and that no longer has that buying power can't satisfy its needs. The white youth isn't going to be able to adjust to the kind of job that he has to get; that isn't the one he wanted but another one—one that just anybody could do. (César)

Several of those interviewed pointed to the fact that the consciousness of racial differences is very much rooted in the changing relations between the laws and customs that have historically structured the social hierarchy and shaped the political and socioeconomic development of the nation.[30] Thus, for example, originally brought to Peru as serfs and "coolies," Peruvians of Asian descent have the reputation of being hardworking and associated with commerce.[31] Given that the president of the nation at the time of my research was of Asian descent—and, as César noted, "most of the Chinese who came to Peru have gone up in life, they have something, a business, they're always working; they are the ones that move the companies, they don't put anyone else in"—it is perhaps not surprising to find that in a society where money and power whiten, many of those interviewed, like César, described Asians ("*los chinos*") as "white people, with slanted eyes, who work hard."

Beyond the visual reclassification in "whitening" terms that this statement expresses, there is no doubt that in Peru the relationship between race, class, and status is much more ambiguous than it is in the United States, where regardless of class and status, people are perceived, above all, in racial terms. People who migrate from the Andes and become Lima's *cholos*, for example, are a case in point. Thus, on the one hand, for example, as one of the students I quoted before said, people from the Andes are categorized as "ignorant," "dirty," "betrayers," "people you can't really trust." Or, as Pastor put it, "In terms of the masses, there's no doubt that one would say: 'That *cholo*? Aj!—he's so ugly!' People think like that." But on the other hand, the image *cholos* have in society is also coupled with the increasing power status of the group. In fact, today it is often associated positively with the hardworking and enterprising image of Peruvians of Asian descent. Referring to the latter and to *cholos*, César stated:

> Both are hardworking. Perhaps because people in the mountains are used to working all day: it's what they do. And here in Lima, they get a job and they go on working the same.

Thus, to the extent that some recognize the existence of a "disguised racism" in Peruvian society, while others openly acknowledge racial attitudes, stereotypes, and discrimination among groups "indistinctly from race to race," and still others link the prejudices against Blacks directly to their lack of power, it could be argued that racial perceptions in Peru today are not static nor are they inherently attributed to biological characteristics. Instead, they are a function—expressed through the constantly chang-ing use and connotations of labels—of the power and status each group achieves in society. Grounded in the whitening notions that attribute racial discrimination to foreigners, these attitudes are also fed by what Mirko Lauer recently characterized as "the tension between poverty and hope."[32] In this sense they include, at least at an ideological level, a belief in the possibility of some social mobility and, as such, a rejection—at least while this belief lasts—of the creation of a racial consciousness or organization. This explains why there are those who, like Gabriet, refuse to admit the notion of racially based discrimination. Arguing that jokes neither reflect the domi-nant perception in Peru, nor have any relevance for understanding Peruvian society, he went on to explain:

> There is no image of Blacks here. It's because our society is made up of Blacks, whites, *cholos*, and indigenous people. Some people think differently, and they express it through their jokes. About Blacks they think that they are lazy, that they don't like to work; about indige-nous people, they think that they are kitsch; they think whites are proud, arrogant. That business about all Blacks being delinquents is a lie. That reminds me of a joke that says whites dressed in white are doctors, Blacks in white are ice-cream vendors; whites running are athletes, Blacks running are thieves. They are just jokes—I don't think we have that way of thinking here. It's the picaresque nature of the Peruvian to make jokes. I don't think Peruvians think that way—at least that's not the way I think. (Gabriel)

By reducing the content of racial jokes to expressions of insignificant prejudices by a naturally "picaresque" people, Gabriel and others who share his view effectively rele-gate to an irrelevant, and forgotten, past the consequences of a lived experience rooted in the history of colonialism and slavery.

The Question of Race and Power in Peru

While the adherence to national belonging, together with the absence of institution-alized racism, reduces the question of racism to crude racial jokes and ahistorical opinions about prejudices, the main question guiding my research remains: Insofar as it is not institutionalized, how can we pinpoint the mechanism through which racism and racial discrimination determine the power positions occupied by different groups in society? More specifically, how do the racial practices of daily life affect, or not, the democratizing of citizenship and the population's sense that they are represented and are participating in the public sphere?

The period of transformation in Peru at the time of my research was propitious for assessing the extent to which racial images expressed through social labels and their attributes correlate directly with the power position different groups occupy in society. The attitudinal ambivalence toward those of Asian descent and toward *cholos* points both to these groups' histories—albeit differentiated—rooted in a rigid castelike hierarchy and reinforced by negative images associated with each in the past, and to the process through which these images are gradually shifting through the increasing visibility of *cholos* and Asian Peruvians in positions of power in the public sphere.

Two weeks before the November 1995 municipal elections in Lima, in which the government's candidate, Jaime Yoshiyama, a Japanese-Peruvian, was running against the white-*criollo* Alberto Andrade, for example, many of those interviewed seemed to have a strong awareness of the racial solidarity between the nation's president and his candidate, which was reinforced by the preelection televised debates. This consciousness influenced their political assessments of the presence of people of Asian descent in the public sphere and their difference from other "Peruvians." As one woman put it:

> Things are really divided. Yoshiyama could win, but with tricks. With tricks because if Fujimori wants to, he'll get him out. But let's see what happens on election day. For now, everyone is with Andrade. . . . Otherwise *nobody is going to govern anymore*. Otherwise everyone is going to be Chinese, Japanese. However much Yoshiyama may be a Huancaino,[33] he's still got slanted eyes, and he's always going to. (Carmen, Black; my emphasis)

And as another commented:

> There is an area near Barrios Altos[34] where everyone is Chinese. And the other day I was in a taxi talking to the driver, and I asked him, "Who are you going to vote for in the elections"—which is the subject everyone is talking about right now—"for Andrade or for Yoshiyama?" And he answered "Oh, no for anyone except Yoshiyama." "Why?" "Because," he said, "the Asians are taking over everything here. If you look at who's in power, there are no *cholos*. They're going to invade us, they're selling all the state companies, they're kicking out the Peruvians and they're giving work to Asians: they're invading us. Because of that, I'm going to vote for anyone but not for an Asian. Asians are exploiters." And he went on to say some other things but I just kept quiet. (Mariana)

At the root of the question of race and power in Lima is the racial conflict as it is lived in daily life, complete with the mutual labeling and stereotyping that hierarchize each group and find expression in the dynamics of power in Peruvian society. For, ultimately, the dynamics of race and power are grounded in the shifting perception of who, in political terms, is an "acceptable Peruvian"—a "true" Peruvian—and hence can truly represent the national and individual identity and interests of the Peruvian citizenry. Indeed, while Fujimori's reelection seems to have pointed to an acceptance of a Peruvian of Asian descent—a "*chinito*"—in power, his very visibility has heightened the racial consciousness inherent in nation building and the democratization of citizenship.

It is important to note that the fact that racism is discussed as individual prejudices does not mean that the law students I interviewed were not aware of the ever-present potential of racial prejudices being transformed into acts of racial discrimination and violence in Peruvian society. This became particularly clear to me when I contrasted their familiarity with racial labels and prejudices with another phenomenon that I found was clearly foreign to them: I'm referring to their understanding and discussion of the most patent example of racism and racial discrimination in the twentieth century: anti-Semitism. When I began to ask about the Jews in Lima, I had the following dialogue with one Black law student who in all our previous conversations had shown herself to be very conscious of the prejudice and racial stereotypes in the labels used in Lima:

> Oh, don't ask me about the Jews!
> *Why not?*
> Because they're horrible!!
> *Horrible? How? What do you mean?*
> They're exploiters, they're tight, they're misers . . .
> *Do you know any Jews?*
> Me? Oh, no! Luckily I don't! (Dolores)

Dolores's remarks betray her unawareness of anti-Semitism as a distinct form of racism. Given the small number of Jews in Peru today, the tenor of her comments is not surprising. The Jewish presence in the daily life of a Dolores, and for that matter Latin Americans as a whole—with the possible exception of Argentineans—is largely an irrelevance. In other parts of the world—in Europe, in the United States—where Jews have a stronger history and presence, such open and casual expression of anti-Semitism would be exceptional. My dialogue with Dolores helped me understand the extent to which the racial prejudices that locate different groups within Peruvians' symbolic imaginary are unconsciously identified with assumed biological and visible distinctions based on color and phenotype.

From this perspective, the debates in Peru during the 1990s[36] on the merits of Fujimori's presence in the public sphere would seem to represent, on the one hand, a collective and, as yet, unarticulated hope that things weren't the way they used to be, that something had indeed changed; and, on the other, the ever-present anxiety that crude jokes could spark violent acts of racial discrimination. In this sense it could be argued that beneath the surface of Lima society there exist both an understanding of racial discrimination and an awareness of its potential explosiveness. The racial and ethnic question, though relatively neglected, is an indicator of the political and social consequences of the democratization of citizenship and national belonging in Peru.

Transnationalizing Peruvians' Racial Perceptions: From Lima to the United States

While Peruvians, like other Latin Americans, may continue to deny the existence of racial discrimination in their society, it is precisely their implicit understanding of the dynamics of racial discrimination and their awareness of its explosive potential that will serve those who leave Peru and must then negotiate the racial ideologies they encounter once in the U.S. context. Research on the impact of U.S. racialization practices on Peruvian immigrants in the U.S. context has yet to be done. Nevertheless, it is possible to speculate that the very notion of racial labeling with all its nuances, implicit or otherwise, will not be entirely foreign to Peruvians once in U.S. society.

One may speculate that the license provided by the custom of explicit labeling in the U.S. context will serve to bring to light Peruvians' own tendency to use racial and ethnic labels and hierarchies. From this point of view, arrival in the United States could reinforce among Peruvians the meanings and social values attributed to the social and racial hierarchy to which labels such as *cholo, indio, moreno* invariably allude.

Given the stigma attached to Blackness in Peru, and the negative stereotypes about the African American population spread by the international media throughout Latin America, it would seem that prejudices toward African Americans, particularly among recently arrived Peruvian immigrants, would be very strong. At the same time, prejudices among some non-Black Peruvians toward Afro-Peruvians could be mitigated by the explicit racialization they themselves will inevitably undergo in the U.S. context.

While white Peruvians may be somewhat surprised to find that money does not "whiten" them here, their decision to "identify" as U.S. "Latinas/os" is not self-evident. On the one hand, Peruvian—and by extension, Latin American—nationalism and a concomitant sense of anti-U.S. (political) sentiment might influence the decision of some progressive members of the middle classes to define themselves as Latinos. For others, however, ideologies of whiteness, together with long-held prejudices against racialized others, will dictate their distancing from other people of Latin American descent.

In this respect, it can be argued that, in addition to racial characteristics, social status, and nationalism, Peruvian immigrants' ongoing relationship to Peru, together with their commitment to remain in U.S. society, will also play a very big role in defining the kind of racial and ethnic allegiances they might forge with various racial groups in the U.S society. It is conceivable, for example, that those who have not yet made that commitment would choose to live as far apart from the rest of the Latina/o population, distancing themselves from the racialized Latina/o other and defining themselves as much as possible in (white) Peruvian, nationalist terms, at least in part to avoid a perceived and/or real stigma of *Latina/o* or *Hispanic*. Among those who have decided to make the United States their homes, however, skin color, phenotype, and such specific conditions as individual economic status and interests could lead to the creation of a Peruvian community, some of whose members, while defining themselves in strictly nationalist terms, might also be willing to emphasize their Latin American roots and hence mark their identity as Latinas/os in U.S. society.

Ultimately, then, for the Peruvian immigrant, the decision to associate with other Latinas/os, as well as with other racialized groups, will be determined by commitment to remain in the United States, nationalistic allegiance, social status, and racial understanding.

Notes

1. This essay is an expanded and much revised version of "Lo ajeno del racismo: orgullo y prejuicio en la sociedad limeña contemporánea," a talk I presented at the Instituto de Estudios Peruanos in lima, January 11, 1996; it was subsequently published under the title *El mundo es racista y ajeno: orgullo y prejuicio en la sociedad limeña contemporanea.* (Lima: Instituto de Estudios Peruanos, Working Papers series, May 1996). I want to thank the Instituto de Estudios Peruanos for providing me with both the opportunity and the resources to undertake this research project between June 1995 and January 1996; the staff of the institute's library for their efficiency

and constant support in my bibliographical searches and research; Patricia Machacuay for her excellent archival assistance; and Ana Collantes for her support with the interview transcriptions.

Many thanks to my research assistants, Marión Figueroa Won and Delia Almeida for their help with my fieldwork and interviews, and for their commitment to and interest in this project; to Patricia Oliart and Luz Elena Ocampo for their knowledge and insights on racism, rights, and the law in contemporary Peruvian society; and to Elitza Bachvarova, Hortensia Muñoz, Marisol de la Cadena, Maria Celia Paoli, and Elena Sabogal for their always stimulating discussions and comments on this and/or earlier drafts of this paper.

2. In addition to the work of Winant, the following are important contributions to the contemporary understanding of the concept of race: Marisol de la Cadena (2000); Steven Gregory and Roger Sanjek (1994); Michael Banton (1987); Michael Omi and Howard Winant (1986); and David Theo Goldberg (1990).

3. Degregori (1990) has noted this historical lack of emphasis in the Peruvian public sphere.

4. On the racial and ethnic dimensions of the election of Fujimori in 1990, see Valentín (1993: 95–114) and Degregori (1990).

5. In Peru, *criollo* is the name given to non-Andean populations whose families' presence in Lima can be traced back for several generations. The term is discussed more fully below.

6. It is important to emphasize that this research project focused solely on racial and ethnic composition in the city of Lima. For a historical discussion of the issues involved in constructing ideas of race/ethnicity in the southern Andean region of Cuzco, see, for example, de la Cadena (2000) and Flores Galindo (1987).

7. The impact of these and other changes in Lima since the 1950s has been analyzed by Franco (1990); Grompone (1994:125–151); Degregori, Blondet, and Lynch (1986); Golte and Adams (1990).

   A number of works discuss the impact of Sendero Luminoso in Peruvian daily life. See, for example, Manrique (1993 and 1990); Degregori (1987 and 1987); Portocarrero (1991); and Palmer (1992).

8. On the popular informal business sector, see Adams and Valdivia (1991); Villarán de la Puente (1990).

9. Only one or two people mentioned the debates on the impact of the presence in the nation's public life of Máximo San Román who, as Fujimori's first vice president during the latter's "auto-golpe" in April 1992, publicly (and unexpectedly) identified himself as a "*cholo*"— notwithstanding the term's historically negative connotations.

10. Conversation with Jurgen Golte, September 1995. For a political history of Peru through the 1970s, which grounds its analysis of contemporary Peru in the continuity of colonial structures, see Cotler (1982). Two recent excellent collections of essays on Peru are Starn, Degregori, and Kirk (1995), which presents an interdisciplinary overview of Peruvian history, culture, society, and daily life; and Panfichi and Portocarrero (1995), which explores various aspects of the social history of Lima until the 1950s.

11. I thank Hortensia Muñoz for clarifying this aspect of the effects of the 1980s terrorism on creating a consciousness about citizenship and rights in Peru in the post–Sendero Luminoso period. See Muñoz (1998).

12. The term *serrano*, once used to denote a person from the Andean region (*Sierra*) and commonly used in a derogatory way in the past, now seems increasingly to be replaced by what is perceived by some to be the more neutral *provinciano*, a term that simultaneously obscures the person's geographical origins and emphasizes instead his/her migrant status in Lima; similarly, the derogatory *indio* is increasingly being replaced by the more neutral term *indigena*.

13. Several alternative euphemisms are used in daily life in Lima for the term *negro*, among them: *zambo* (a lighter black) and *moreno* (a darker person of African descent). Due to the large, mid-nineteenth-century forced migration of Chinese "coolies" to Peru, the term *chino* (literally a person of Chinese descent) is used to refer to all people of Asian descent, regardless of national origin. As Jack Forbes (1993) has noted, the historical specificity of ethnic and racial terminologies in the Americas has long been obscured, creating a misleading understanding of both the histories of and the interrelations among the various ethnic and racial groups in the

Americas. A case in point is the term *cholo*, which Forbes, quoting from the writings of the Inca Garcilaso de la Vega, states was "used for 'the children of mulattoes.' " He notes that the latter term was in turn used to define "the child of a male Negro and a female [native] American." Garcilaso de la Vega also notes that *cholo* was "a Caribbean coastal word used in a derogatory way by the Spaniards."

14. Omi and Winant's (1986) "racial formations" theory is particularly applicable here.

15. See also Degregori. For an opposing perspective, see Nugent (1992). The pioneering work on the position of the *cholo* in Peru is Anibal Quijano's essay "Lo cholo y el conflicto cultural en el Peru" (1964) in Quijano (1980:47–116).

16. In this respect, it is important to emphasize that prejudices against the *cholo* have not disappeared. Rather, as I discuss below, similar to the case of the populations of Asian descent, the apparent changing nature of the way the *cholo* is currently positioned in the discourse on race/ethnic relations in Lima is perhaps best understood in terms of the changing status of some members of this group.

17. For a discussion of the tensions created by the transplanting of European ideas among members of the Peruvian oligarchy at the beginning of this century, see de Trazegnies (1987:99–134). De Trazegnies (1995, vol. 2) expands on the legal interpretations of this phenomenon.

18. On the early roots of racial divisions in the United States, see Roediger (1990), Saxton (1990), and Horseman (1981). A useful compilation on the subject may be found in Yetman (1985) and King (1992). See also Omi and Winant (1986).

19. *Mestizo* is a term used to describe someone of mixed blood. In Peru, until recently, the term was used specifically to identify people of mixed indigenous and European heritage. It seems today gradually to be extended to include a person with any combination of racial backgrounds.

20. The writings of early-twentieth-century Peruvian ideologues are described by Portocarrero (1995). For an analysis of their presence in the daily social life, see Oliart (1995).

21. Cajamarca and Ayacucho are departments in northern and southern Peru, respectively.

22. *Quechua* is the name of the largest indigenous population group in Peru.

23. At the same time, Oliart (1993:75) has shown that notions of blackness, like notions of who was indigenous or Chinese, were rigidly defined in Peruvian society, particularly in the nineteenth century, in terms of particular physical and cultural characteristics. These in turn served to associate particular occupations with each group as a strategy for restricting their social mobility.

    Nevertheless, in the case of Blacks, as in the case of other racial groups, the emphasis on whitening has meant that racial passing has a long history in Peru. In the case of Blacks, for example, Fernando Romero, among others, has pointed both to the problematic nature of the data and the precipitous drop in the Black population during the nineteenth century. Until the early eighteenth century, the coast had more Blacks than whites (and indigenous peoples). Romero notes that the census of 1791 documents that there were nine times the number of Blacks than whites in the province of Cañete, while in Chancay, Blacks outnumbered whites by a ratio of 4 to 1. Other areas document similar relative figures. In the province of Ica, Blacks were 75% of the population; in the *intendencia* of Trujillo, 60%; in the *partido* of Lambayeque, 57%; in Piura, 54%. In Lima the Black population dropped precipitously during the Republican period. While it reached 40% in 1614 and had risen to 60% in 1791, in 1862 it had dropped to 11%, then to 9.3% in 1876 and finally to 4.8% in 1908. Finding it strange that the Black population in Lima had dropped officially by 55.2% in the course of 138 years solely as a consequence of normal *mestizaje*, Romero suggests instead that it was actually due to the fact that "to a large extent, many of the descendents of Africans managed to have themselves classified as mestizos and even as whites." By 1896 Blacks were recorded as 1.95% of the population, while by 1940 they were only 0.44% (Romero, 1980:57–58).

24. This idea was briefly discussed by Rout (1976:317–318).

25. According to Emilio Harth-Terré (1973), indigenous commoners were also owners of Black, African, and mulatto slaves, who undertook domestic and agricultural labor.

26. For a historical account of Black-white relations during the first half of the nineteenth century, see Hunefeldt (1994). For an overview of Blacks in Peruvian history and society, see Luciano

and Pastor (1995:271–286). Cuche (1975) provides a description of Blacks in post-abolition Peruvian society; and Glaves (1995:24–28) provides a brief overview of the importance of Blacks' contribution to forging the national culture of Peru.

27. On the relationship between ethnic identity and territorial belonging, see Silva (1990).
28. Besides the references to the contributions of Afro-Peruvians and white *limeños*, it is important to point out that according to Degregori (1990) "the meaning of the term *criollo*, since the end of the last century" also included "immigrants who arrived from other European countries."
29. In recent years, a number of new works on race in other parts of Spanish America have been published, among them Torres and Whitten (1998); Wade (1997); Minority Rights Group (1995); Graham (1995). The pioneering book on the subject is by Rout (1976).
30. Recent studies focusing on different aspects of the question of race and racism in contemporary Peru include León (1998); Montoya Rojas (1998); Barrig and Henriquez (1995); Oliart (1993); Manríque (1999); Callirgos (1993); Portocarrero (1995); de la Cadena (2000).
31. De Trazegnies (1995) provides a significant contribution to the legal and cultural history of Chinese populations in Peru.
32. Interview with Mirko Lauer by César Hildebrandt on the television program *La Clave*, Channel 13, Lima, December 8, 1995.
33. Huancayo is a department in the Andes.
34. Barrios Altos is a poor, primarily Black neighborhood in Lima.
35. In 1995 a Jewish teacher and scholar at León Pinelo, the Jewish school of Lima, estimated that there were no more than 3,000 Jews in Peru (private communication).
36. It is important to note that my research does not include the post-Fujimori period, and the nature and understanding of racialization during the Toledo campaign and government.

References

Acha, Elisabeth. 1993. Poder en el Aula: el imperativo de convertirse en cholo a la limeña. In *Los nuevos limeños: Sueños, fervores y caminos en el mundo popular*, ed. Gonzalo Portocarrero, pp. 313–334. Lima: Sur.

Adams, Norma, and Néstor Valdivia. 1991. *Los otros empresarios: Etica de migrantes y formación de empresas en Lima*. Lima: Instituto de Estudios Peruanos.

Adrianzén, Alberto, ed. 1987. *Pensamiento político peruano*. Lima: DESCO.

Banton, Michael. 1987. *Racial Theories*. New York: Cambridge University Press.

Bourricaud, François. 1970. *Power and Society in Contemporary Peru*. New York: Praeger.

Barrig, Maruja, and Narda Henriquez, eds. 1995. *Otras pieles: Género, historia y cultura*. Lima: Pontífica Universidad Catolica del Perú.

Callirgos, Juan Carlos. 1993. *El racismo: La cuestión del otro (y de uno)*. Lima: DESCO.

Cotler, Julio. 1982. *Clases, estado y nación en el Peru*. Mexico: Universidad Autónoma de Mexico.

Cuche, Denis. 1975. *Poder blanco y resistencia negra en el Peru*. Lima: Instituto Nacional de Cultura.

Da Matta, Roberto. 1991. Do you know who you're talking to? In *Carnivals, Rogues, and Heroes: An Anthropology of the Brazilian Dilemma*, 429–442. Indiana: University of Notre Dame Press.

de la Cadena, Marisol. 2000. *Indigenous Mestizos: The Politics of Race and Culture, Cuzco, Peru, 1919–1991*. Durham, NC: Duke University Press.

de Trazegnies, Fernando. 1995. *En el pais de las colinas*. Vols. 1, 2. Lima: Fondo Editorial, Pontífica Universidad Católica del Perú.

———. 1987. La genealogía del derecho peruano: los juegos de trueques y prestamos. In *Pensamiento político peruano*, ed. Alberto Adrianzén, 99–134. Lima: DESCO.

Degregori, Carlos Ivan. 1987a. Del mito del Inkarri al mito del progreso: Poblaciones andinas, cultura e identidad nacional. *Socialismo y Participacion* 36.

———. 1987b. El regreso de los pistacos. *La Republica* (Lima), September 27.

———. 1990. El aprendiz de brujo y el curandero chino: Etnicidad, modernidad y ciudadania. In *Elecciones 1990: Demonios y redentores en el nuevo Peru*, ed. C.I. Degregori and R. Grompone, 71–136. Lima: Instituto de Estudios Peruanos, serie minima.

Degregori, Carlos, Cecilia Blondet, and Nicolás Lynch. 1986. *Conquistadores de un nuevo mundo. de invasores a ciudadanos en San Martín de Porres*. Lima: IEP.

Flores Galindo, Alberto. 1987. *Buscando un Inca: Identidad y utopía en los Andes*. 3rd ed. Lima: IAA.

Forbes, Jack D. 1993. *Africans and Native Americans: The Language of Race and the Evolution of Red-Black Peoples*. Chicago: University of Illinois Press.

Franco, Carlos. 1991. *La otra modernidad: Imágenes de la sociedad peruana*. Lima: CEDEP.

———. 1993. El sentido del Velasquismo en la construcción de una comunidad nacional-ciudadana en el Peru. *Socialismo y participación* 63 (November).

Fuenzalida V., Fernando. 1970. Poder, raza y etnia en el Peru contemporaneo. In *El indio y el poder en el Peru*. Lima: IEP.

Glaves, Luis Miguel. 1995. "A ti sí te cumbén": Una historia de lo afroandino en el Peru. *Somos: Revista de El Comercio* 455 (August 26):24–28.

Goldberg, David Theo, ed. 1990. *Anatomy of Racism*. Minneapolis: University of Minnesota Press.

Golte, Jurgen, and Norma Adams. 1990. *Los caballos de troya de los invasores: Estrategias campesinas en la conquista de la gran Lima*. 2nd ed. Lima: IEP.

Graham, Richard. 1995. *The Idea of Race in Latin America, 1870–1940*. Austin: University of Texas Press.

Gregory, Steven, and Roger Sanjek. 1994. *Race*. New Brunswick, NJ: Rutgers University Press.

Grompone, Romeo. 1994. La política en el inicio de una epoca. *Margenes: Encuentro y debate*. 6, no. 12 (November):125–151.

Harth-Terré, Emilio. 1973. *Negros e indios: Un estamento social ignorado del Peru colonial*. Lima: Libreria-editorial Juan Mejia Baca.

Horseman, Reginald. 1981. *Race and Manifest Destiny: The Origins of American Racial Anglo-Saxonism*. Cambridge: Harvard University Press.

Hunefeldt, Christine. 1994. *Paying the Price of Freedom: Family and Labor among Lima's Slaves, 1800–1854*. Berkeley: University of California Press.

King, Richard. 1992. *Civil Rights and the Idea of Freedom*. New York: Oxford University Press.

León, Ramón. 1998. *El país de los extraños: Una encuesta sobre actitudes raciales en universitarios de Lima metropolitana*. Lima: La Parola Editorial.

Luciano, José, and Humberto Rodriguez Pastor. 1995. Peru. In *No Longer Invisible: Blacks in Latin America*, ed. Minority Rights Group, pp. 271–286. London: Minority Rights Group.

Luciano, José Carlos. 1995. Lo negro en el Perú. *Ideele* 81 (November):50–58.

Manríque, Nelson. 1999. *La piel y la pluma: Escritos sobre literatura, etnicidad y racismo*. Lima: Sur Casa de Estudios del Socialismo.

———. 1996. Racismo y violencia política en el Peru. *Pretextos* 8 (February):89–106.

———. 1993. Violencia política, etnicidad y racismo en el Peru del tiempo de la guerra. Paper presented at "La Violencia Política en el Peru," an international seminar jointly sponsored by IEP, CEPES, and the North-South Center of the University of Miami, Lima.

———. 1990. La década de la violencia. *Margenes, encuentro y debate* (Lima), nos. 5, 6.

Millones, Luis. 1973. *Minorias étnicas en el Peru*. Lima: Pontifica Universidad Catolica del Peru.

Minority Rights Group. 1995. *No Longer Invisible: Blacks in Latin America*. London: Minority Rights Group.

Montoya Rojas, Rodrigo. 1998. *Multiculturalidad y política: Derechos indigenas, cuidadanos y humanos*. Lima: Sur Casa de Estudios del Socialismo.

Muñoz, Hortensia. 1998. Human rights and social referents: The construction of new sensibilities. In *Shining and Other Paths: War and Society in Peru, 1980–1995*, ed. Steven J. Stern. Durham, NC: Duke University Press.

Nugent, Jose Guillermo. 1992. *El laberinto de la choledad*. Lima: Fundacion Friedrich Ebert.

Oboler, Suzanne. 1995. *Ethnic Labels, Latino Lives: Identity and the Politics of (Re)Presentation in the United States*. Minnesota: University of Minnesota Press.

Oliart, Patricia. 1993. "Good" serranos vs "bad" criollos: Politics and ethnic conflict in Lima. Mimeo.

———. 1995. Temidos y despreciados: Raza y género en la representación de las clases populares limeñas en la literatura del siglo XIX. In *Otras pieles: Género, historia y cultura*, ed. Maruja Barrig and Narda Henríquez, 73–88. Lima: Pontificia Universidad Católica del Perú.

Omi, Michael, and Howard Winant.1986. *Racial Formation in the United States from the 1960s to the 1980s*. New York: Routledge & Kegan Paul.

Palmer, David S., ed. 1992. *Shining Path of Peru*. New York: St. Martin's Press.

Panfichi H., Aldo, and Felipe Portocarrero S., eds. 1995. *Mundos interiores: Lima 1850–1950.* Lima: Universidad del Pacifico.

Portocarrero, Gonzalo. 1995. El fundamento invisible: Función y lugar de las ideas racistas en la República Aristocrática. In *Mundos interiores: Lima 1850–1950,* ed. Aldo Panfichi and Felipe Portocarrero. Lima: Universidad. del Pacifico.

———. 1991. *Sacaojos y fantasmas coloniales.* Lima: Tarea.

Quijano, Aníbal. 1980. Lo cholo y el conflicto cultural en el Peru (1964). In *Dominación y cultura,* 47–116. Lima: Mosca Azul.

Roediger, David R. 1990. *The Wages of Whiteness.* New York: Verso Books.

Romero, Fernando. 1980. Papel de los descendientes de Africanos en el desarrollo económico-social del Peru. *Revista Histórica* 4 (1): 57–58.

Rout, Leslie. 1976. *The African Experience in Spanish America, 1502 to the Present.* New York: Cambridge University Press.

Saxton, Alexander. 1990. *The Rise and Fall of the White Republic.* New York: Verso Books.

Schwartz, Roberto. 1993. Misplaced ideas: Literature and society in late-nineteenth-century Brazil. In *Misplaced Ideas: Essays on Brazilian Culture,* 19–32. New York: Verso Books.

Silva, Erika. 1990. Ecuador: El dilema de la identidad nacional. In *Cultura y politica en América Latina,* ed. Hugo Zemelman. Mexico: Siglo 21/Universidad de las Naciones Unidas.

Starn, Orin, Carlos Iván Degregori, and Robin Kirk. 1995. *The Peru Reader: History, Culture, and Politics.* Durham: Duke University Press.

Torres, Arlene, and Norman Whitten, Jr., eds. 1998. *Blackness in Latin America and the Caribbean and Cultural Transformations.* 2 vols. Bloomington and Indianapolis: Indiana University Press.

Valentín, Isidro. 1993. Tsunami Fujimori: Una propuesta de interpretacion. In *Tempo: Los nuevos Limeños: Sueños, fervores y caminos en el mundo popular,* ed. Gonzalo Portocarrero, 95–114. Lima: Sur.

Villarán de la Puente, Fernando. 1990. Riqueza popular. Paper presented at DESCO seminar, El Nuevo Significado de lo Popular en América Latina, Lima, October 8–12.

Wade, Peter. 1997. *Race and Ethnicity in Latin America.* London: Pluto Press.

Winant, Howard. 1994. *Racial Conditions: Politics, Theory, Comparisons.* Minnesota: University of Minnesota Press.

Yetman, N. R., ed. 1985. *Majority and Minority: The Dynamics of Race and Ethnicity in American Life.* Boston: Allyn and Bacon.

CHAPTER 5

BAD BOYS AND PEACEFUL GARIFUNA:
TRANSNATIONAL ENCOUNTERS BETWEEN
RACIAL STEREOTYPES OF HONDURAS AND
THE UNITED STATES (AND THEIR IMPLICATIONS
FOR THE STUDY OF RACE IN THE AMERICAS)

Mark Anderson

Stereotypes are one of the currencies of social life. They represent long-established prejudices and exclusions and, like nationalist ideology itself, they use the terms of social life to exclude others on cultural grounds. They render intimate, and sometimes menacing, the abstraction of otherness. They are thus the building blocks of practical nationalism.

—Michael Herzfeld (1992:72)

Like currency, stereotypes circulate within social life and, like currency, they can be put to use for various purposes by social actors. They involve not simply static images and ideas but mobile representations of selves and others, projected onto someone else or embodied by their targets. Herzfeld urges us to think about stereotypes "not as fixed social categories but as rhetorical images forever in use as the representation of restlessly changing political relations" (1992:70). In thinking about stereotypes it is important not just to consider how they operate within the frames of nationalism and national societies but to analyze how they move across nation-states and how their meanings transform as they settle, albeit restlessly, into specific relations and struggles.

This essay explores practices of stereotyping about and among Garifuna in Honduras. Garifuna are a people of African and Amerindian heritage who are interpellated by the dominant, majority mestizo population as "Black," and who tend to identify themselves as Black. The idea for this essay originally emerged from a discovery of a tourist description of the Garifuna community of Sambo Creek, where I lived during ethnographic fieldwork in Honduras. As part of their "Honduran Notebook," two tourists from the United States wrote:

Sambo Creek was originally settled by escaped slaves. It is a poor village, its panorama dominated by mud huts. . . . The beach at Sambo Creek is wonderful. One can watch the fishermen launch dug-outs that have probably not changed much since Pre-Columbian times. There is one hotel in town. It is marginal, with shared bathroom . . . we overheard that there had been recent break-ins at the hotel, and up in the hills a colonel who had been bathing had been robbed at gun point. Our Detroit instincts told us to leave. We did.[1]

For these tourists, the Garifuna community may have elements of a quaint, traditional fishing village but ultimately it signifies something too familiar, a place that is poor, scary, and Black, with the threat of violence lurking in the corners. The abstraction of otherness is clearly rendered menacing.

This representation caught my attention for two reasons. First, within Honduras, Garifuna communities are rarely understood or depicted as violent places. If anything, Garifuna are stereotyped—in different ways by themselves and others—as *pacífico*, as a peaceful, tranquil, and humble people. Second, the tourists appear to traffic in stereotypes of Black communities as areas characterized by criminal violence familiar to them from the United States. Stereotypes that associate Blacks, especially young men, with a propensity to violence resonate loudly in U.S. media representations, everyday discourses, and state practices that invigorate fears of gangs, thugs, and drugs while perpetrating their own excessive terror of racial profiling, police brutality, and death sentences.[2] If the tourists do not actually use the term "Black" to refer to the occupants of the town, their references to "escaped slaves" and their "Detroit instincts" thinly code race.

Yet perhaps the visitors were not simply trading in falsehoods but picking up on something real, not so much in the actual threat of criminal violence but in the local cultivation of racial meanings in the community, in the look and bearing of some of its members. The absence in their representation, the counterpart to an image of traditional fishermen, is the presence in the community of young men who appear a lot like images of inner-city U.S. African Americans, and not by accident. Young Garifuna men self-consciously adopt an aesthetic of what they call "bad boys" in fashion, style, posture, movement, and speech. These goods and practices derive in good measure from the intense transmigration of Garifuna between Honduras and the United States, developed over the past several decades.[3] Our story, then, cannot just ponder the differences between U.S. stereotypes of African Americans and Honduran stereotypes of Garifuna but must take into account how Garifuna engage such stereotypes in their daily lives.

This essay analyzes the multiplicity of meanings and uses of two stereotypes, a set of images and associations I refer to as "peaceful Garifuna" and "bad boys." The notion that Garifuna are a peaceful, humble people derives from the historical particularities of social relations and representations in Honduras. In contrast, ideas and images of "bad boys" that associate Blacks with criminal violence are drawn from transnational encounters among Garifuna, the United States, and representations of a racial geography referenced as "Black America." What is the relationship between these two (contradictory) stereotypes in representations and performances of identities? The following pages argue that Garifuna perform and embody a "bad boy" image in ways that confront and complicate negative associations tied to the stereotype of the "peaceful Garifuna" and the forms of racial discrimination and oppression encouraged by such associations.

Pursuing this analysis requires an attention to the specificity of "race" within local, national, and regional contexts *and* to the traffic in racial meanings across them. Studies of race in the Americas often employ a comparative framework, contrasting the racial dynamics within the region as a whole, or within particular countries such as Brazil, with racial dynamics in the United States.[4] Although such approaches have much to offer, they often falter in their failure to recognize the ways social agents appropriate racial meanings through transnational relations and in their misrecognition of the ways racial meanings from one part of the world help constitute the lived identities and realities of another. At the end of this essay, I return to this theme, suggesting how analyses of the articulation of transnational stereotypes in local contexts challenge approaches to race and ethnicity that assume that racial dynamics are sealed within nation-states.

Garifuna and the Racial Orders of Honduras

Contemporary practices of stereotypes within Honduras operate within a legacy of racial and cultural discrimination currently undergoing scrutiny and confrontation within social movements and everyday life. An outline of the history of Garifuna, with a particular focus on the ways they have been represented and positioned by dominant social formations, will help set the stage for an analysis of the links between current images of race, violence, peacefulness, and gender.

The people today known as Garifuna, once referred to as Black Caribs within anthropological literature, were deported from the island of St. Vincent to Central America by the British in 1797. During the seventeenth and early eighteenth centuries, St. Vincent remained outside the sphere of direct colonial control and provided a haven for African maroons and an indigenous people known by Europeans as Caribs. The populations of African and indigenous origin intermingled, and although the "native" definition of identity categories remains unclear, Europeans identified a group under the term *Black Caribs,* distinguishing them from "pure" Indians who were labeled *Red Caribs* or *Yellow Caribs.* The British acquired colonial dominion over St. Vincent from France in 1763 and engaged in a series of armed struggles with the Black Caribs centered on the control of land. British officials and planters contested the claims of Garifuna to a "native" status within St. Vincent, depicting them as African usurpers of indigenous culture and identity. After securing victory over Garifuna in 1796, the British deported the majority of the population to Central America.[5]

Upon their immediate arrival, the reputation Garifuna had acquired as fierce fighters followed them as they were at first threatened with expulsion and then incorporated into Spanish militia fighting against the British. However, after Central American independence, Garifuna ceased to play a significant role within national armies and gradually lost their notoriety as dangerous warriors. As Garifuna created a series of coastal communities along the relatively isolated Atlantic littoral, they engaged in a variety of productive strategies combining wage labor, horticulture, fishing, and marketing, carving out spheres of local autonomy while participating in regional markets (Gonzalez, 1988:51–73). During the second half of the nineteenth century, powerful figures such as state agents and church officials expressed admiration for the economic industriousness and versatility of Garifuna yet rendered them as inferior "others," representing them in racial terms as "*negros*" and in cultural terms as "backward," in need of acculturation and civilization (Anderson, 2000: 117–124). Along with indigenous groups of the region, Garifuna occupied the lowest rungs of a hierarchy dominated by foreign whites and a national elite.

The Atlantic littoral of Honduras underwent radical transformations during the early decades of the twentieth century as a result of the creation of an enclave economy based on fruit production (Euraque, 1996a). The fruit trade began to develop in Honduras in the 1860s, attracting immigrants from within and beyond the nation. By the early decades of the new century, three U.S.-based fruit companies came to dominate production, contributing to new forms of racial conflict and discrimination on the North Coast. If the development of the fruit industry produced an international image of Honduras as the quintessential banana republic, it also spurred the creation of new forms of nationalism. Dario Euraque (1996b, 1996c) has traced the rise of an ideology of "Indo-Hispanic *mestizaje*" that glorified the mixed indigenous and European heritage of mestizos as the representative racial-cultural "type" of the nation. Like mestizo nationalisms elsewhere in Latin America, this ideology challenged European and U.S. denigrations of racial hybridity yet produced its own exclusions, most notably in the way it rendered the presence of "blackness" a problem. Euraque suggests that Honduran mestizo nationalisms contributed to forms of anti-Black racism primarily directed against West Indians of African descent, many of whom were employed as workers by foreign companies. Garifuna men also found work with fruit companies and came into conflict with mestizo workers who contested their right to employment on racial grounds. Although they were born on Honduran soil, Garifuna were not embraced as equal citizens or full members of the nation (Soluri, 1998:440).

In fact, Garifuna were in many ways treated as second-class citizens throughout the first half of the twentieth century. The banana companies enforced forms of segregation in living and social arrangements among whites, mestizos, and Blacks. Municipal officials and local elites also perpetrated racist practices. In La Ceiba, Garifuna and West Indians were excluded from many hotels, restaurants, and casinos, and were even prohibited from sitting in public parks (Centeno García, 1997; Canelas Diaz, 1999). Elder Garifuna recall the era of the dictatorship of Tiburcio Carias Andino (1932–1948) as a time of terror, when the police would impress Garifuna to clean the street of dead dogs or beat individuals for failing to give way to elite or officials walking on the sidewalks. The woman in whose house I lived in Sambo Creek, who tells us a story later, recalls this era as a time when people would flee at the sight of armed mestizos in their communities. As we see in more detail below, under these kinds of historical conditions and memories, the notion of Garifuna as a "peaceful" people resonates with a legacy of racial oppression.

The most egregious forms of racial segregation and repression were transformed in the era following World War II as a result of a variety of factors that we can only touch on here. These include the emergence, in the late 1940s, of a left-oriented labor movement that, to a limited degree, included Black protagonists and decried racial discrimination; subsequent changes in the Honduran state from a dictatorship under the National Party toward more democratic forms of governance under the Liberal Party, which sought Garifuna support (Euraque, 1999); the brief emergence of antiracist initiatives among Garifuna themselves in the 1950s (Centeno García, 1997); and the integration of Garifuna into national institutions through increased schooling opportunities and migration to urban centers. Although openings for antiracist politics were curtailed by the installation of a new dictatorship in 1963, overt, state-sanctioned repression of Blacks did not return. During the 1970s Garifuna created "ethnic" organizations similar to indigenous organizations that demanded recognition of rights to land, culture, and identity. By the 1990s these organizations had helped reconstitute the position of Garifuna within Honduran society, contributing to the official recognition of Honduras as a multicultural and multiethnic nation (England and Anderson, 1999). Although the state continues to deny the existence of racism in Honduras and to enact policies detrimental to indigenous and Black peoples, ethnic politics represents an important antagonist, asserting rights to cultural difference and autonomy while calling attention to racial and cultural oppression.

Within Garifuna communities such as Sambo Creek, where I conducted fieldwork in 1996 and 1997 (and visited briefly in 1999 and 2000), Garifuna feel the pressures of outside forces—including agribusiness, tourist development, the creation of nature reserves, and mestizo settlement—on their land and livelihood. Sambo Creek has a long history of land appropriation. In the early twentieth century, land used by local residents was seized by force by fruit companies and mestizo elites for banana cultivation and cattle grazing. Garifuna today often assert that land they once used for shifting cultivation has, since the 1960s, been appropriated by mestizo campesinos. Over the course of the past twenty years, the proportion of mestizo residents in the town has risen dramatically, from 10 percent in 1981 (McCommon, 1982:61) to between 30 and 40 percent in 1997. On a daily basis, relations between the two groups are generally friendly, if marked by a distance in forms of social intimacy. Allowing numerous exceptions for local mestizos, especially those with long-term residence, Garifuna members of the community often portray the presence of mestizos in the community as an intrusion. Drawing on experiences, memories, and narratives of racism, Garifuna tend to convey a sense of the impending threat of hostile forces, a threat that needs to be challenged if they are to retain their integrity and way of life, a threat (and response) sometimes articulated through the medium of racial stereotypes.

Peaceful Garifuna and Violent "*Indios*"

If the position of Garifuna within Honduran society has become a subject of mobilization and debate for the state and public institutions, the tendency to associate Garifuna with essential character traits and habits remains pronounced, whether in media imagery or in everyday conversation. Such essentialization need not overtly or intentionally degrade. Indeed, many of the stereotypes associated with Garifuna—as tropical, happy, fun, sexual, athletic, lovers of music and dance—can be articulated with positive or negative evaluations, whether by Garifuna themselves or by others. The stereotype of what I call the "peaceful Garifuna" represents an intriguing case where an ostensibly positive image carries with it problematic associations.

The image of the peaceful Garifuna sits in contrast with a figure I call the "violent *indio*," a stereotype articulated often by Garifuna and sometimes by mestizos as well. *Indio* is a term Garifuna often use to refer to the category of people officially classified as mestizos. Many mestizos refer to themselves by this term, which tends to have connotations of lower-class status but can reference the majority population as a whole. The stereotype of violent *indio*s comes in a variety of guises, from gangs of marauding teenagers in the streets of major cities, to drunken campesinos fighting over of a bottle of *guaro*, to murdering men lustful of power. Whereas in some Garifuna communities they warn you that if you bathe after dark in the river a malignant spirit might attack you, in Sambo Creek they say that an *indio* may rob or rape you. This substitution of the "violent *indio*" for a ghost is telling because the figure has a certain spectral quality, haunting the imagination of those threatened with material and symbolic violence.

Images of violent *indios* and tranquil Garifuna emerged quite transparently in a conversation I had with Valentin, a working-class mestizo who lived down the street from the house where I stayed in Sambo Creek. A marimba musician who had traveled in many parts of Honduras, Valentin told me he had moved to Sambo Creek from La Ceiba several years previously because life in the city had become "too difficult" with its growing numbers of thefts and murders. He went on to praise his Garifuna neighbors with a series of related adjectives—*llevadera* (easy to get along with), *humilde* (humble), sociable, *aceptada* (accepting), good, friendly, respectful, calm, and *sano* (healthy). Responding to a question concerning his opinions on racism in Honduras, Valentin said:

> Sometimes the *indio* has his errors. But is has nothing to do with Garifuna. Maybe he wants to belittle another person because he is humble. And this has no merit because to be humble is a blessing from God. But I don't want to say that he thinks he is superior but that it is manliness [*hombria*]. The *indio* race has been like this since primitive times. "I'm a man. I kill. Here." In the Garifuna race I have never in my fifty-eight years of life known of a Garifuna murderer but in the *indio* race, yes. There are people that have killed a lot of people.

Valentin evokes images of Garifuna humility and *indio* violence, articulating a clear preference for the former. Nonetheless, he takes care to emphasize that the abuse of the humble is a question of sentiments not of racial superiority but of "manliness," and in this sense the stereotypes register a certain ambivalence. In this discourse the *indio* possesses masculinity, a valued characteristic implicitly denied the peaceful and humble Garifuna. The tacit feminization of Garifuna echoes other dominant stereotypes of race and gender that interpret Garifuna women's participation in agricultural labor and marketing as inappropriate and unfeminine and render Garifuna men as lazy and unproductive. Such tropes help explain, even justify, the presence of mestizos in and around Garifuna communities. If Valentin relocated to such a community because it served as refuge from the urban decay identified primarily with *indio* crime, there is a long history of more violent appropriations of Garifuna lands perpetrated by powerful mestizos. The image of humble, peaceful Garifuna has facilitated such appropriations and relocations. In this case, the abstraction of otherness may not be rendered as menacing but nonetheless facilitates racial domination.

Garifuna accounts of their typically "peaceful" character sometimes register a similar ambivalence around issues of submission and resistance, even as they contest its negative implications. This became clear to me during a discussion with Alfonso, a man in his fifties whom I would often consult on issues that puzzled me. The question at hand concerned an interview with a former labor leader who had identified someone as Garifuna by asserting that he was not "*negro*" but "*moreno*." *Moreno* is a term historically used as a "polite" reference to Garifuna and has fallen out of favor among Garifuna themselves, who tend to proudly self-identify with the term *negro*. Alfonso helped fill me in on the historic uses of these terms and asked if the man I had spoken with was mestizo. When I said he was, Alfonso nodded thoughtfully and added, "Sometimes they believed that we are timid, that we are submissive, but it's not like that." He referred to Garifuna as "*pacífico*," noting, "There has always been an accord between Garifunas, between us as Garifunas, this harmony, this peaceful agreement, this peaceful environment among ourselves. Because our grandfathers were perfectly capable of spilling the blood of their neighbors. They weren't accustomed to this." He went on to explain that Garifuna, particularly in the past, preferred to avoid conflict and live apart from mestizos not because they were timid but because they wanted to live "independent of the power of the state."

Alfonso's commentary indexes some of the negative associations tied to the image of "peaceful Garifuna" even as it strives to refute them. For him, the use of the term *moreno* by a mestizo culled forth a perception of a perception, that mestizos perceive Garifuna as "timid." Like many others in the community, Alfonso often contrasted Garifuna character and culture to a negative image of violent *indios*. Nonetheless, he felt compelled to qualify the peacefulness of his people, highlighting their capacity for struggle and resistance within their preference for harmony and autonomy.

Images of violent *indios* and timid Garifuna emerge most powerfully in stories of the past, of an era when, at least according to some community members, Garifuna felt terrorized by mestizos, backed by state power. Luz, the head of the household where I lived and a woman who grew up in Sambo Creek in the 1930s and 1940s, once recalled to me and her teenage grandsons how her grandfather lost his plot of land in a nearby area.

There came a señor name José Matute, from Olancho. When this señor came he asked my grandfather if he would sell him the land. So my grandfather told him that it wasn't for sale. How was he going to sell it when his family depended on it to live. "From this my people live," he told him. The señor told him, "Look, if you're not going to sell the land to me you are going to lose because I'm going to kill you and take the land. . . . So, since the *negro* has always been a coward, he asked, "How much will you give me for it?" Yeah, my grandfather was intimidated. It was a tremendous fear but today he wouldn't have sold because now the men have courage. So the señor said, "How much are you asking?" My grandfather said, "I have never sold land until right now. I'm going to sell it to you to save my life with my children because I'm not ready to lose them. My life, I give to the hands of the Father, not to the life of another man same as me." My grandfather.

Her grandfather appealed to the municipal authorities in La Ceiba but lost his land and his animals. Like other stories of land loss, this narrative depicts an aggressive *indio* intimidating a submissive *negro* and ultimately ends with a refrain that extended the actions of one man into a type: "*El indio es malo.*"

This story does more than simply exemplify "*indio*" violence and criminality; it comments on the character of Garifuna men in the past and in the present and, perhaps less obviously, articulates a sense of racial terror afflicting community members. bell hooks (1992:172), recalling her own memories of growing up in the U.S. South, notes: "To name the whiteness in the black imagination is often a representation of terror: one must face a palimpsest of written histories that erase and deny, that reinvent the past to make the present vision of racial harmony and pluralism more plausible." Although racial conditions are different in Honduras and the United States, we can draw a comparison between the ways the naming of whiteness by Blacks in the United States articulates forms of racial terror and the ways Garifuna associate the *indio* with racial terror, particularly when recalling the past. The story of land loss personifies and dwells on the "tremendous fear" inspired by the powerful and the failure to confront that fear on the part of the oppressed. This perspective challenges the notion that Honduras has always had a "marvelous culture of tolerance," to quote the words of a former president (*La Tribuna*, 1997).[6]

The story also culls forth the negative associations of the peaceful qualities often attributed to Garifuna, where the refusal to fight becomes rendered as a form of cowardice. Luz attributes the actions of her grandfather not to his individual character but to the character of a people—"the *negro* has always been a coward." The details of the story do not necessarily support the contention that her grandfather acted in a cowardly fashion. In fact, his own reported speech explaining a refusal to die senselessly at the hands of another man "the same as him" establishes an assertion of equality caught up in dialogic tension with interpretations of his cowardliness. Nevertheless, for Luz the story of land loss established an appropriate context for noting how, in the past, Garifuna did not struggle against oppression. Embedded in the narrative is a crucial contrast, framed in a gendered idiom: "now the men have courage." For now is a time in which oppression does not go unchallenged, as evidenced in the development of social movements, community efforts to reclaim and protect lands,[7] and assertions of pride in heritage and culture among Garifuna men and women in everyday life. Whether or not the past was really a time of cowardice perhaps remains besides the point, as affirmations of contemporary courage serve as exhortations to struggle in the present, a message surely not lost on Luz's own grandsons.

Bad Boys

In the early days of my fieldwork in Honduras, I began playing basketball in the nearby Garifuna community of Corozal. Although soccer is the national sport of Honduras, by the mid-1990s basketball had become highly popular among Garifuna youth, especially boys and young men. Some of the best players were transmigrants visiting from New York City, whose crisp jerseys and new sneakers marked them off from youth with limited transnational connections. After subjecting an aging, short, white gringo to taunts such as "White man can't jump," several of the regular players became friendly with me and eventually agreed to tape some of their perspectives on identity, style, and racism. One of the more thoughtful young men was Dennis, a twenty-year-old from a family of modest means who had recently been expelled from secondary school for fighting with a mestizo student after the student had yelled in the bathroom: "Who turned out the lights? It's too dark in here. Oh, it must be this *negro*." Knowing he had strong opinions on racism, I asked him an open-ended question concerning changes in racism in recent years, and he responded:

> I think that racism now has diminished, or that it has been moderated to the lower classes. Anybody can discriminate against a child, but me, they're going to think twice because maybe I can respond or I can attack them too. If I go walking on the street and I go with big pants and a big shirt and I go touching my pockets it's not going to be just any *blanco* [mestizo] that's going to say "Eh, *negro*."

Why does Dennis begin with a discussion of the class dimensions of racism and end with an image of himself walking around with big pants and a big shirt? The kinds of clothes he references, the styles preferred among Garifuna youth, have brand names, such as Nike, Tommy Hilfiger, and Hugo Boss, associated with the United States. They serve as markers of status, not just in terms of their high cost, but in terms of the transnational connections they signify. More than that, the manner in which they are worn—long and baggy, with modifications such as the underwear showing or backwards caps—involves a self-conscious imitation of U.S. African Americans, especially figures Garifuna refer to as "bad boys." The quintessential, stereotyped personages here are drug dealers, gang members, and tough guys of the inner-city. Although Dennis occupies, by local standards, a lower-class position, he projects an image of himself that marks a higher status, embodies a "bad boy" aesthetic, and signifies a potential for violence, a performed masculinity imagined as a deterrent to overt acts of racial discrimination and confrontation.

That Garifuna self-consciously draw on images of inner-city U.S. African Americans can be seen in their very use of the English phrase "bad boy." For example, on a concrete wall in Sambo Creek someone once painted "Bad Boyz." In our interview Dennis noted that the most watched movies (on videocassette sent from abroad by transmigrants) "are of Garinagu, ahh, of bad boys, bad Blacks in the street, American movies of Black Americans like *Boyz 'N the Hood*, *New Jack City*." Indeed, the young men in the household where I lived often watched such "ghetto action films" (Watkins, 1998:226), studying the movements, styles, and speech of their characters and adopting some of them—such as handshakes and greetings like "Yo, cuz"—in their street interactions.

Garifuna encounter ideas and images of bad boys and Black America not just through media forms such as cable television, videos, and magazines but through the discourse of transmigrants. Garifuna living in the United States have a complex set of relations with African Americans, in which "rational affiliation and cultural difference collide to create an uneasy relationship" (England, 1999:27). On the one hand, they typically identify themselves as "Black" and support African American political struggles. On the other hand, they also emphasize the differences of their Garifuna, Caribbean, and Afro-Latino identities and often seek to avoid the stigmas associated with U.S. African Americans. Even as they appropriate cultural meanings associated with Black America, Garifuna living in Honduras become aware of tensions between groups in the United States through communication with friends and relatives and the circulation of stories and ideas. For example, several young men told me that African Americans look down on persons from Latin America and deride Blacks that speak Spanish. Moreover, Garifuna often reproduce many of the stereotypes of inner-city African Americans common in the United States, speaking of them as lazy, failing to take advantage of economic opportunities, or as violent, given to theft, drug addiction, and murder. One young man, relating to a group of friends a conversation he had with a cousin in New York, said, "The Blacks from there are like the *indios* from here."

Nonetheless, Black America serves as a site through which Garifuna imagine and improvise meanings of race and identity in Honduras. Livio Sansone claims that "for black people outside of the USA, an orientation towards the mythical 'super blacks' in the United States becomes a way to differentiate themselves from local white people while claiming black participation in 'modernity' and the rituals of mass consumption" (Sansone, 1997:464). Sansone suggests that Blacks in Latin America view U.S. African Americans as figures of unreflexive emulation and admiration. Although Garifuna I know draw on Black America to differentiate themselves from others while participating in practices associated with modernity, they do not view U.S. African Americans as mythical "super blacks" but articulate ambivalent sentiments toward them and the "bad boy" image sometimes cultivated among themselves. Tyson, one of my closest friends and the nephew of the head of the household where I lived, told me that Garifuna like to watch movies about Black Americans because:

> They show us how they live, the system, how they express themselves, the environment in which they live . . . and we take hold of part of the most important parts. But nevertheless in our environment here there are people that take all the bad. For example, there are the Applic and Cairos [two local youth gangs] and all that, they are things from there. So they dress like Black Americans and, you know, they sometimes try to take a little bit of the bad. . . . But nonetheless it is a life that—eh, for us it's pleasing to imitate them. It's not for nothing but something more related to racism that makes it more essential. That is what makes us more engaged to watch the actions of them, of the Black Americans, because they always fight against racism. There, the most important thing is that the people that want to extend racism against us, the *ladinos* [another term that references mestizos], aren't worth

anything there. Because there, eh, a lot of guys go around real quiet. They don't mess around because they know that there Blacks have a lot of power.

Tyson's layered explanation moves from a discussion of the ways Garifuna learn about the lives of Black Americans through film (implicit here is the possibility that they will also one day live in the United States) to a critique of how some youth imitate "bad" elements such as gangs (although at the time of fieldwork these gangs appeared to do nothing worse than spray paint their names all over town), to a sense that part of the attraction concerns racism and a difference in relations between Blacks and mestizos at home and abroad.

What is the relationship between the critique of the "bad" elements of Black America and the perception of an antiracist stance among African Americans? Although Garifuna often cite figures such as Malcolm X and Martin Luther King Jr. as inspirational figures in struggles against racism, the sensibility articulated here concerns a perception of the kinds of intimidation U.S. African Americans inspire. The abstraction of otherness is rendered menacing but is performed as a feature of the self. Like Dennis and his imagined performance of walking the streets with attitude, Tyson links the issue of racism to a stance of defiance, even hostility, on the part of its potential subjects, a stance that reverses the relations of power between purported aggressor and victim, Garifuna and mestizo. For him, part of the attraction of U.S. African American iconography lies in its capacity to symbolically invert the racial order of Honduras. Neither Tyson nor others I know advocate violence or wish to actually become bad boys. Rather, they perform the image with a mix of serious-ness and playfulness, visibly challenging a perception of Garifuna submissiveness and humility even as they continue to draw contrasts between their typically peaceful ways and *indio* violence and U.S. black violence. Thus, the stereotype of the bad boy circulates in dialogue with the stereotype of the peaceful Garifuna, contesting its negative connotations. These reversals, along with the status and cosmopolitanism accrued from brand-name gear, are crucial features of the meaning and appeal of bad boys for young Garifuna men.

Analyzing some of the social logics of the bad-boy stereotype through attending to the perspectives of young Garifuna men does not require celebrating it. After all, the bad boy—like the violent *Indio* and the peaceful Garifuna—is a stereotype that erases the diversity of U.S. African Americans and ignores the structural racism of U.S. society. Moreover, the appropriation of that stereotype renders contests over power as a masculine, patriarchal affair that excludes women. Garifuna women develop their own forms of engagement with Black America that contest and compli-cate forms of racial and gender subordination, drawing on it for "diasporic resources" (Nassy Brown, 1998) to articulate novel forms of Black femininity in Honduras. They also sometimes critique forms of consumption and practice linked to the bad-boy stereotype as inappropriate use of scarce resources and as expressions of male dominance or insecurity. Older generations also fret over the behavior of youth and, as we have seen, young men themselves sometimes critique the bad "influences" of Black America. These caveats serve as a warning that this essay has barely touched on the complex, contested meanings and uses of Black America among Garifuna as they negotiate their identities and positions within Honduras.

Transnational Encounters and Racial Dynamics within Nation-States

What general lessons might we draw from this analysis of the social life of stereotypes, of the ambivalent appropriation of a transnational "bad boy" image in contradistinction to Honduran stereotypes of "violent *Indios*" and "peaceful Garifuna"? On the one hand, this analysis provides another example of the rather well-worn argument that transnational practices become embedded in specific social formations in which nation-states, local relations, and particular histories matter (Guarnizo and Smith, 1998). The bad-boy stereotype acquires its particular meanings of racialized defiance to ethnic submission as it becomes situated within struggles by Garifuna to define their sense of self within a nation-state heretofore dominated by mestizo nationalism. It does not simply reflect "acculturation" but involves complex, ambivalent practices of diasporic identification. Appropriations of transnational stereotypes, like transnational ideologies, can serve not just as the building blocks of practical nationalism, but figure in efforts to assert antiracist stances, ethnic autonomies, and diasporic affiliations.

On the other hand, it suggests that racialized transnational practices, or the practice of racialized transnationalism, have become part of the very fabric of social life and imagination. This essay has barely touched the surface of transnational influences on Garifuna lives or, better said, the transnational character of Garifuna lives and the various meanings of blackness culled especially from the United States but also the Caribbean and Africa. The consumption of things associated with Black America, discourses concerning African Americans, ideas about blackness, racism, and civil rights associated with the United States and images of bad boys inform everyday existence among Garifuna. They form part of Garifuna "culture," even if Garifuna themselves often mark differences between inherited traditions and appropriated modernities.

Briefly comparing the experiences of Garifuna in Honduras and the United States helps underscore the intricacies and ironies of the transnational dimension of their lives. Assertive identifications with the category of "Black" are more pronounced in Honduras than in the United States, even as Black America serves as a key medium for the articulation of those identifications. In the United States, Garifuna find themselves located betwixt and between the ethnoracial categories of African American and Hispanic (England, 1999). Although Garifuna tend to identify in racial terms as Black, they also differentiate themselves from African Americans, in response to: the stereotypes and low status attached to African Americans; negative experiences with African Americans that disparage Spanish; and sentiments of national, ethnic, and cultural difference. Similarly, although Garifuna express a sense of cultural affinity with people from Puerto Rico, the Dominican Republic, Ecuador, and other countries, racial distinctions and discriminations make Hispanic an uneasy category of identification. According to England, Garifuna straddle the ethnoracial categories of the United States, fitting neatly into none while sometimes choosing to identify primarily as Garifuna or Afro-Hispanic. Garifuna identify as Black yet insist on the differences contained within that category, in part because in the United States the category of Black is associated with African Americans.

In contrast, within Honduras the dynamics of racial and cultural identification and differentiation take on distinctive forms. Garifuna constitute the largest group of people racialized as Black in Honduras, and the dominant "other" they confront is the Spanish-speaking mestizo. In the play of differentiation, assertions of Garifuna identity often draw on racialized notions of blackness in ways that momentarily elide the ethnic, cultural, and linguistic differences among different groups of Blacks that, in the United States, are crucial to the shifting and ambivalent identifications with African Americans. Of course, as noted previously, Garifuna in Honduras also articulate differences between themselves and African Americans, yet in practice self-consciously draw styles and images of Black America to assert a racial identity. To perhaps simplify the point, whereas in the United States "ethnic" identifications and the particularity of Garifuna identity tend to complicate racial identifications, in Honduras racial identifications as "Black" tend to support ethnic identifications as Garifuna. A certain irony emerges here. Within the context of Honduras, "Black America"—and stereotyped representations of it such as the bad boy—becomes a resource for fashioning the meaning of what it means to be Garifuna, even if in the United States itself Garifuna emphasize their ethnic, racial, and cultural particularity within the category "Black."

These brief comments comparing the dynamics of identification among Garifuna in the United States suggest that we need to develop modes of comparative analysis of race that take into account the complex character of transnational relations, flows, and identifications. In drawing comparisons between the United States and Latin American societies we cannot assume the existence of a singular, national ethnoracial logic without internal or transnational differentiations. The case examined in this essay suggests that a transnational approach is necessary for understanding forms of racial consciousness and racial "logics" within everyday existence. Ways of thinking and practicing race among Garifuna in Honduras do not arise simply from the ethnoracial dynamics of the nation-state or from the transnational dimensions of Garifuna lives; rather, they originate in the intersections between them.[8] The circulation of the bad-boy stereotype provides only one instance of the processes by which Garifuna, like many other peoples in the Americas, negotiate their identities within nation-states through transnational connections. These processes appear particularly pervasive in Central America and the Caribbean, perhaps due to the intensity of connections and networks among peoples of African descent, the United States, and Black America in the past and present. Nonetheless, as Livio Sansone (2003) has recently demonstrated for Brazil, in other parts of the Americas the proliferation of signs and goods of the Black diaspora marks and shapes new forms of practices and consciousness around race. Rather than perpetuating an obsession with comparing and contrasting racial dynamics in Latin America (as if it were a homogenous region) with those of the United States, analysis of race in the Americas would profit from modes of analysis that do not simply compare countries but analyze the transnational dimensions of racial consciousness, practice, and politics. In the process, perhaps such analysis can come to terms with the intransigent if malleable character of racial meanings in social life as they become mobilized in struggles over dignity, justice, and livelihood in organized movements and everyday life.

Notes

1. This quote was taken from the Website "Honduran Notebook," by Stephen Goodfellow and Lauren Rowland, located at http://www.goodfellow.com/honduras.
2. Stereotypes of U.S. African Americans as violent have a long history. During debates over slavery the image of Blacks as savage brutes often appeared when pro-slavery advocates imagined what would happen when slaves were freed from white paternalism. At the turn of the twentieth century, such images became both fuel and justification for the institutionalized segregation of Jim Crow and the lynching of Black men for their perceived danger to white women (Frederickson, 1971:53–58, 275–282).
3. For an extensive analysis of Garifuna transmigration between Honduras and the United States, see England (2000).
4. Classic works devoted to extensive comparisons include Tannenbaum (1946), Harris (1964), and Hoetink (1973). Much contemporary scholarship, though varying in final conclusions and ideological underpinnings, is framed within a comparative lens (e.g., Andrews [1991], Hanchard [1994], Winant [1994], Winddance Twine [1998], and Sansone [2003]).
5. This brief account of Garifuna history on St. Vincent has been drawn from Gullick (1976), Gonzalez (1988), Craton (1997), and Anderson (1997).
6. These words are from former president Roberto Reina (1994–1998).
7. In August 2001 residents of Sambo Creek mobilized to protect lands claimed by a mestizo lawyer from La Ceiba, leading to a conflict that resulted in violent repression of community members by the police. See *El Tiempo* (2001).
8. This argument applies to the past as well as the present. For example, the "ethnoracial logics" of Honduran society in the twentieth century emerged in relation to forms of hegemony exercised by "outside" forces, in particular U.S. hegemony, whether in the development of a mestizo nationalism articulated in part in response to the power of the U.S. State Department and corporations or in the development of anti-Black segregationist practices in the enclave economy.

References

Anderson, Mark. 1997. The significance of blackness: Representations of Garifuna in St. Vincent and Central America, 1700–1900. *Transforming Anthropology* 6 (1–2):22–35.
———. 2000. Garifuna kids: Blackness, modernity and tradition in Honduras. Ph.D. diss., University of Texas at Austin.
Andrews, George Reid. 1991. *Blacks and Whites in São Paulo Brazil, 1888–1988*. Madison: University of Wisconsin Press.
Canelas Diaz, Antonio. 1999. *La Ceiba, sus raices y su historia (1810–1940)*. La Ceiba: Tipografia Renacimiento.
Centeno García, Santos. 1997. *Historia del movimiento negro hondureño*. Tegucigalpa: Editorial Guaymuras.
Craton, Michael. 1997. *Empire, Enslavement, and Freedom in the Caribbean*. Princeton, NJ: Markus Weiner Publishers.
El Tiempo. 2001. Violento desalojo de garífunasen Sambo Creek, August 21.
England, Sarah. 1999. Negotiating race and place in the Garifuna diaspora: Identity formation and transnational grassroots politics in New York City and Honduras. *Identities* 6 (1):5–54.
———. 2000. Creating a global Garifuna nation? The transnationalization of race, class, and gender politics in the Garifuna diaspora. Ph.D. diss., University of California-Davis.

England, Sarah, and Mark Anderson. 1999. ¿Auténtica cultura africana en Honduras? Los afro-centroamericanos desafían el mestizaje indo-hispánico hondureño. Paper presented at Taller, Proyecto "Memorias del Mestizaje," Tegucigalpa, July 24–25.

Euraque, Darío. 1996a. *Reinterpreting the Banana Republic: Region and State in Honduras, 1870–1972.* Chapel Hill: University of North Carolina Press.

———. 1996b. La creación de la moneda nacional y el enclave bananero en la costa caribeña de Honduras: ¿en busca de una identitidad étnico-racial? *Yakkin* 14 (1–2):138–150.

———. 1996c. *Estado, poder, nacionalidad y raza en la historia de Honduras: Ensayos.* Tegucigalpa: Ediciones Subirana.

———. 1999. El mestizaje y los negros en la historia de Honduras: Apuntes para una próxima investigación. Paper presented at Taller, Proyecto "Memorias del Mestizaje," Tegucigalpa, July 24–25.

Frederickson, George M. 1971. *The Black Image in the White Mind.* New York: Harper & Row.

Gonzalez, Nancie. 1988. *Sojourners of the Caribbean: Ethnogenesis and Ethnohistory of the Garifuna.* Champaign: University of Illinois Press.

Guarnizo, Luis, and Michael Peter Smith. 1998. The Locations of transnationalism. In *Transnationalism from Below,* ed. Michael Peter Smith and Luis Guarnizo, 3–34. New Brunswick, NJ: Transaction, Rutgers University.

Gullick, C.J.M.R. 1976. *Exiled from St. Vincent: The Development of Black Carib Culture in Central America up to 1945.* Malta: Progress Press.

Hanchard, Michael. 1994. *Orpheus and Power: The Movimiento Negro of Rio de Janeiro and São Paulo, Brazil, 1945–1988.* Princeton, NJ: Princeton University Press.

Harris, Marvin. 1964. *Patterns of Race in the Americas.* New York: W. W. Norton.

Herzfeld, Michael. 1992. *The Social Production of Indifference: Exploring the Symbolic Roots of Western Bureaucracy.* Chicago: University of Chicago Press.

Hoetink, Harry. 1973. *Slavery and Race Relations in the Americas: An Inquiry into Their Nature and Nexus.* New York: Harper & Row.

hooks, bell. 1992. *Black Looks: Race and Representation.* Boston: South End Press.

La Tribuna. 1997. Garífunas entregan al presidente su Plan Nacional de Desarrollo, April 14.

McCommon, Carolyn. 1982. Mating as a reproductive strategy: A black Carib example. Ph.D. diss., Pennsylvania State University.

Nassy Brown, Jacqueline. 1998. Black Liverpool, Black America, and the gendering of diasporic space. *Cultural Anthropology* 13 (3):291–325.

Sansone, Livio. 1997. The new Blacks from Bahia: Local and global in Afro-Bahia. *Identities* 3 (4):457–494.

———. 2003. *Blackness Without Ethnicity: Constructing Race in Brazil.* New York: Palgrave Macmillan.

Soluri, John. 1998. Landscape and livelihood: An agroecological history of export banana growing in Honduras, 1870–1975. Ph.D. diss., University of Michigan.

Tannenbaum, Frank. 1946. *Slave à Citizen: The Negro in the Americas.* New York: Vintage Books.

Watkins, S. Craig. 1998. *Representing: Hip Hop Culture and the Production of Black Cinema.* Chicago: University of Chicago Press.

Winant, Howard. 1994. *Racial Conditions.* Minneapolis: University of Minnesota Press.

Winddance Twine, France. 1998. *Racism in a Racial Democracy: The Maintenance of White Supremacy in Brazil.* New Brunswick, NJ: Rutgers University Press.

Chapter 6

Afro-Mexico: Blacks, Indígenas, Politics, and the Greater Diaspora

Bobby Vaughn

Mexican scholarly, political, and popular discourses have grappled with the race question since the inception of the colonial project in 1519. The arrival of European conquistadors in the indigenous continent forced a cultural encounter that has had fundamental and enduring ramifications. Indeed, most Mexican nationalist ideology grapples simultaneously with at least two questions in this regard. First, how should the *indígena* be situated in the narrative of the imagined community's (Anderson, 1991) origin? This is essentially a discourse about the past. Second, the question of the role that contemporary indigenous peoples play in present and future Mexico has been of major concern.

During the colonial era the Spanish sought to regulate the different *races* through the imposition of a system of *castas*. The *castas* created explicit hierarchies based on race and race mixture.[1] Elaborate taxonomies categorized people based on both ancestry and physical characteristics (Wagley, 1968:161), and specific terms corresponded to the various permutations (see León [1924] for elaborate oil paintings depicting the *castas*). The system was designed to confer relative privilege to the Spanish and to persons of predominantly Spanish ancestry. In turn, the darker, more indigenous or Black mixtures were to move only within prescribed spheres of the colonial social order. In practice, however, it is likely that there was a great deal of social movement among the popular classes who rarely interpreted their own *casta* position with the rigidity anticipated by the elite design.[2]

With independence (1810–1821) came the abolition of the Spanish-imposed *castas* system, creating the need for alternative visions of a unified nation. Most of these deliberations seem to have centered on how to build a nation along a European model in a country with such a strong indigenous and mixed-race population. A project of recuperating indigenous civilization thus began. Such recuperation began at least as early as Francisco Javier Clavijero's eighteenth-century protonationalist defense of indigenous religion against the prevailing notion that it was of demonic origin (Brading, 1980:37; Ronan, 1977). They continued with Carlos Maria de Bustamante who, in his nineteenth-century historical works, represented the grandeur of pre-Hispanic civilizations as a source of national pride (Brading, 1980:116–119). And in the twentieth century, in the aftermath of the Mexican Revolution of 1910, José Vasconcelos (1979) introduced his *raza cósmica* (cosmic race) concept that helped solidify the still influential view that Mexico's indigenous and Spanish mixed-race origins are a valuable asset and key to its future. Contemporary with Vasconcelos was the dean of Mexican anthropology, Manuel Gamio, who, while also in accord with Vasconcelos's preoccupation with *mestizaje* (race mixing), emphasized the importance of studying indigenous civilization and customs both as cherished cultural patrimony and as a key to the *progress* of indigenous communities.

Taken as a whole, this intellectual journey has produced in Mexico (1) a hegemonic reverence for the symbols of the indigenous past—monuments, statues, Nahuatl names given to public spaces, and so on; (2) a popular interest in the exotic symbols of present-day indigenous material culture—museums and a tourist industry that promotes the color, exoticism, and *culture* of *indígenas*, especially in the largely indigenous states of Oaxaca and Chiapas; and (3) a continuing chasm between this symbolic embracing of the previous two points and an overall lack of concern for the concrete material conditions of *indígenas*, which accompanies the widespread racism and marginalization experienced by indigenous peoples.[3]

These important discourses of race in Mexico and the policy initiatives to which they give rise have focused almost exclusively on indigenous people, Spaniards, and their mixed-race progeny, the mestizos, to the exclusion of other minority groups. One glaring omission in most of this work is an acknowledgment of both the contemporary experience and historical legacy of Mexicans of African descent as well as the recognition of the significance of African slavery in Mexican history. Mexico (then called New Spain) played a prominent role, particularly in the earliest stages of the slave trade in the sixteenth and seventeenth centuries. In the sixteenth century an estimated 60,000 slaves were brought to Mexico. In the seventeenth century slave imports doubled to about 120,000 and in the eighteenth century the volume of slave imports dropped sharply to about 20,000 (Valdés, 1987:171). The generally accepted view is that over the course of the slave trade some 200,000 slaves reached Mexican shores.

Spain and Portugal were the major powers both during the early part of the trade and throughout the first century of the colonial project in New Spain (1521–1639). Mexico received nearly one out of every two slaves destined for the Spanish New World (Palmer, 1976). Indeed, no other locale in the Americas received more African slaves than Mexico during that period (Carroll, 1991:145). Even Brazil, which received almost 40 percent of the total number of slaves brought to the Americas and was a significant participant in the trade for more than 300 years, was outstripped by Mexico in the sixteenth and early seventeenth centuries (Appiah and Gates, 1999). It was only after the middle of the seventeenth century that most slave imports were diverted from Mexico elsewhere.

Afro-Mexicans of the Costa Chica

At the outset it is necessary to explain the racial/ethnic/color terminology that I use in this article and distinguish it from that which is used in Mexico by both academics and people in the Costa Chica. I use the terms *indígenas* and *indigenous people* somewhat interchangeably as a preference over Indian. This follows Mexican academic and popular conventions. In the Costa Chica most Mexicans of African descent opt for the more distasteful *indio*. With respect to Mexicans of African descent, I generally use the terms *Afro-Mexicans* and *Blacks* interchangeably. Unless specified, my use of the term *Black* is a shorthand for *Afro-Mexican* and is not meant to suggest a particular skin color.[4] *Afro-Mexican*, then, is roughly equivalent to the local term *moreno* in instances where locals refer to the entire ethnic community regardless of color. It is very common, for example, to hear such groupings referred to as *"la gente morena," "la gente blanca,"* and *"los indios."*

My use of *Afro-Mexican* and *Black* differs importantly from the conventions employed by the Mexican academy, where *afromestizo* is the preferred term. As will become clear later, this expression is embedded within a particular ideological context—that of a unifying nationalist *mestizaje* discourse—that is peculiar to Mexico in its power. I, therefore, employ *afromestizo* only when referring to this political project.

The Costa Chica region of southern Mexico is a unique place in which to study race and ethnicity generally and blackness in particular. The 200-mile coastal region (comprising parts of Guerrero and Oaxaca States) is home to some 50,000 Mexicans of African descent who live in immediate proximity to indigenous people as well as mestizos. The Afro-Mexicans are descended from African slaves brought to Mexico in the sixteenth and seventeenth centuries as part of the Spanish effort to meet the labor demands of its American colonies. While the Afro-Mexican population was widespread throughout the colonial Mexican landscape (Martínez Montiel, 1994), the Costa Chica and a small portion of Veracruz[5] are the only regions where Afro-Mexican towns remain. The essay draws on ethnographic research conducted primarily in and around Collantes, a town located in the municipality of Pinotepa Nacional, Oaxaca.

What it means to be Black in Mexico is inextricably linked with what it means to be indigenous and, likewise, with what it means to be mestizo. This essay is an effort to show how the Afro-Mexican experience, while perhaps sharing parallels with other Afro-Latin American communities, is a unique experience whose particularities stem from a range of ethnohistorical and demographic phenomena that give rise to characteristically Mexican racialized discourses. Along with nationalist discourses of *mestizaje*, which pervade Mexican society, *indigenismo*—a generalized preoccupation with the "Indian question"—likewise dominates contemporary contemplations of race in Mexico. This essay thus begins with a treatment of Afro-Mexicans in the Costa Chica that teases out the relationship between these Black people, their indigenous neighbors, and the hegemonic *indigenismo* discourse.

The challenges of political organizing among Afro-Mexicans is then taken up. One of the common characteristics among many contemporary Afro-Latin communities is their tendency to organize in political associations or otherwise collectively resist systems of repression. A kind of universal pattern of Black political mobilization, however, should not be presupposed. Black movements involving Afro-Latin Americans differ in important ways from those of North America while, similarly, such movements differ in important ways among Afro-Latin American communities. I examine the embryonic México Negro movement in the Costa Chica, outlining some of its goals, activities, and obstacles as an example of how local and national racial ideologies shape *political* blackness in Mexico. The essay ends with a brief discussion of Afro-Mexican migration to the United States as a tentative description that may also serve as a call for further research in this area. As Afro-Mexicans come into greater contact with the United States in increasingly transnational relationships, one might reasonably expect challenges to the conventional ways they view their own nationality and their own blackness.

The two major indigenous groups who live in the Costa Chica are the Amuzgo and the coastal Mixtec, followed in smaller numbers by the Tlapaneco and Chatino groups. The Amuzgo live primarily in Guerrero, while the Mixtec are found on the Oaxaca side of the state line. The major Amuzgo towns are Xochistlahuaca and San Pedro Amuzgos. The population of coastal Mixtec is larger than that of the Amuzgo, and the main Mixtec population centers are Pinotepa Nacional, Jamiltepec, Huazolotitlán, and Jicayán. Most Mixtec in the municipality of Pinotepa Nacional speak coastal Mixtec in addition to Spanish, and there are very few monolingual Mixtec speakers.

Turn on the radio during daylight hours and while there are no tunable FM bands, you will find one or maybe two audible stations on the AM dial. The most powerful signal comes from XEJAM, the so-called Voice of the Costa Chica, which is based in Jamiltepec. The station, established in 1994, is operated by the Instituto Nacional Indigenista (INI) and is housed in INI's Centro Coordinador. INI, which was founded in 1948, established Centros Coordinadores to serve in rural areas adjacent to sizable indigenous communities. These Centros Coordinadores serve as bases of operation for the various INI programs, such as the study of indigenous culture and language, and provide services to the *indígenas*. A state-run institution, INI works in concert with nationalist efforts to assimilate the indigenous communities. As XEJAM is an INI station, it should come as no surprise that about 70 percent of the broadcast day is programmed in indigenous languages, with the other third or so aired in Spanish. News, music, and other information, then, is heard in Mixteco, Amuzgo, and Chatino.

The station is less useful to the Spanish-speaking Afro-Mexican community, since so many of the broadcasts are conducted in indigenous languages. Interestingly, even the Spanish-language announcements target indigenous communities:

> Attention, radio audience . . . Señora Catalina Martinez, your daughter will be calling you this Sunday at the telephone in the town of La Tuza at ten a.m. Please be present to receive the call.
>
> Attention, radio audience . . . The town of San Pedro Amuzgos requests your attendance at the annual fiesta of their patron saint this Saturday. There will be a rodeo as well as music provided by the band Grupo Ritmo. All are invited.

One seldom hears mention of an Afro-Mexican town in these announcements. Most Black families hardly listen to the radio, their primary source of entertainment being television and cassette tapes. Some women turn on the radio while doing household chores and will listen to the indigenous music or announcements simply as background noise. Since few Blacks have incorporated the radio into their daily lives, only a scant number of Afro-Mexicans know about the one program that is designed to appeal to them: *Cimarrón: The Voice of the Afromestizos.*

Cimarrón, Spanish for runaway slave, airs every Sunday afternoon for a half hour and is the brainchild of Israel Larrea, a mestizo who has long lived in the Black town of Morelos, Oaxaca. The program includes poetry, music, and news from the Afro-Mexican Costa Chica as well as some material representing the larger African diaspora. Personnel at the radio station indicated to me that they would like to increase the station's coverage related to Black towns, but the then-director of the Centro Coordinador was clear in explaining to me that the station, as well as INI in general, is primarily concerned with the indigenous communities.

Certainly to the extent that INI is concerned with *culture*, most discussions of Blacks tend to shift toward a discourse on *indigenismo*. In Mexico in general as well as in the Costa Chica, *culture* is often understood to be synonymous with *indigenous culture*. It was therefore no surprise that Blacks and non-Blacks alike in the Costa Chica, upon learning that I was an anthropologist, asked if I was looking for indigenous stone figurines like the ones they enthusiastically boasted of having found on their land. It appears, then, that the indigenous-centeredness of commonsense views of what rural development is, as well as what culture and ethnicity are, has pushed Blacks to the margins. Blackness is not considered a topic germane to most discussions of culture, ethnic development, or ethnicity in general.

By contrast, there has been a long tradition in Mexico, since the pioneering sixteenth-century studies by Sahagún, of recognizing that indigenous people possessed particular ways of living, dressing, celebrating, worshiping, and the like. While much of this early interest in indigenous culture suffered from a certain high-civilization bias in favor of the Aztecs, Mexican elites and planners embraced the anthropologist Manuel Gamio's post-Revolution concerns with indigenous culture in the 1940s. Later, the Mexican middle class became interested in the ethnography (or at least the spectacle) of indigenous people as early as the 1950s. The failure of the Costa Chica Afro-Mexicans (or the Veracruz Afro-Mexicans for that matter) to become incorporated into the Mexican "culture discourse" is attributable to the almost entirely indigenous-centeredness of the culture discourse in Mexico.

In Mexico, the culture concept is strongly tied to language and dress. Black Mexicans, all of whom speak only Spanish, dress in typical mestizo clothes. Thus they neither share these typical "ethnic" markers nor do they see themselves as an "ethnic" group (*grupo étnico*) distinct from mestizos. My argument is not that Blacks do not see themselves as ethnically different from *indígenas*. Instead, it is that the difference lies in the Blacks' *lack* of ethnicity, rather than in the *different* ethnicity of Blacks. The *indígenas* are ethnic and the Blacks are not. A certain dichotomy between marked and unmarked ethnicity emerges, in which Afro-Mexicans would locate themselves in the unmarked category.

In the Costa Chica, then, since the Afro-Mexicans are not readily considered to be part of the discourse on *indigenismo*, ethnicity, and culture, they have not been able to tap into the ideological power with which these concepts are imbued in Mexico. At the same time, however, they suffer from the social marginality of which their "blackness" has been a major determinant. So, while Blacks are not ethnically marked, they do not escape the stigmatization of being Black.

The terms *negro* (black) and *moreno* (brown), while concerned primarily with skin color, are not used to refer to persons of indigenous background. The ways *indígenas* are conceived of by Blacks clearly shows that there are perceived differences between those of African descent and those of indigenous background, regardless of skin color. In other words, skin color is not the determining factor when it comes to drawing lines between groups. Many indigenous people in the Costa Chica have skin that is as dark as that of many *morenos* and some *negros*. But these dark-hued indigenous people (Mixtec in this case) are never called *morenos* or *negros*. They are typically called *indios* and very often the pejorative term *indito* is used.

One man in the town of Minitán who self-described as *negro* explained to me the difference between *negros* and dark-skinned indigenous people: "There are some *indios* who are very dark, but their straight hair gives them away . . . *indios* don't have the curly hair that *negros* do, unless either their father or mother was *negro*." Then, to further make his point and add a bit of humor he concluded, "and if you see an *indio* with curly hair, he's probably a *negro* disguised as an *indio*."

Thus, the language used to refer to indigenous people usually does not involve the same calculus of color that is used to talk about Blacks and whites.

As we have seen, the *indígena* in Mexico occupies a somewhat contradictory and complex place in society. On the one hand, indigenous cultures are seen as being in a kind of cultural stagnation and as an impediment to "progress." The very word *indio* is commonly used in derision as is its variant, *naco*, which refers to the urban *indígena* who, try as he might, cannot escape his backward *indígena* nature. *Indígenas* are envisioned as decidedly nonnational in that their "incorporation" into the national mainstream is an enduring preoccupation. Paradoxically, it is this marginalized *indígena* whose past is glorified and upon whose shoulders rests the ideological foundation of Mexico. Museums, murals, and monuments attest to the importance placed on *indígenas* as the historical forebearers of Mexicanness.

Afro-Mexicans engage with this official discourse in several ways. First, they largely agree with the pejorative images of *indígenas*. Second, the *mestizaje* evident in Afro-Mexican communities is not consistent with the common pattern of "mixing with the natives." Third, while Afro-Mexicans see themselves as superior to *indígenas* in terms of a naturalized *civilization* that the *indígena* lacks, a few Blacks express some envy with respect to the *indígenas'* success in "developing" their communities.

Blacks share in the pervasive negative view of *indígenas*. The dominant image of *indígenas* among most Costeños is that of poverty, ignorance, and lack of civilization.[6] While the colonial distinction of *indígenas* as not being *gente de razón*—essentially "civilized" or "rational" people—has fallen out of common usage in almost all of Mexico, in the Costa Chica the distinction is still used frequently.[7] The term is commonly used by Afro-Mexicans and mestizos to distinguish themselves from *indígenas*; implicit in the distinction is the superiority of people *"de razón"* over the *indígenas*.[8]

An Afro-Mexican woman, in the context of a discussion we were having about the indigenous people in the town of Jamiltepec, commented, "They say that they're trying to become more civilized these days, but yeah, they're still *indios*."

While Blacks do not balk at recognizing their own poverty, the *indígenas* are much worse off in their view. I asked a Black campesino to comment on the tendency of most mestizo landowners to prefer *indígena* day labor over Black day labor, presumably because *indígenas* are thought to be harder workers. "I don't have a problem with that," he told me. "Many *indios* don't have anything and they need to work just to eat. We're not that badly off." Another statement illustrative of the Afro-Mexican vision of *indígenas* as impoverished was evoked when a Black *señora* was complaining about not having enough money: "¡Yo no soy *india* para estar comiendo frijoles todos los días!" (I'm not an *india*, to have to be eating beans every single day!).

So, while this element of Black views of *indígenas* is similar to the prevailing view, a difference should be noted. I have found no evidence among Blacks of the dominant Mexican view that indigenous heritage is central to one's own heritage, nor that in some similar way indigenous legacy is something of which Blacks are proud. In other words, Blacks do not seem to accept the now hegemonic principle that indigeneity (albeit imagined in some sort of racially and culturally amalgamated, mixed, or hybrid form) is part and parcel of what it means to be Mexican. For most Mexicans this centrality of an indigenous national identity is largely symbolic and was forged in the aftermath of the Mexican Revolution of 1910 as discussed in this chapter's opening paragraphs.

If mestizos have interpreted an important part of their own heritage as being indigenous, Afro-Mexicans do not share this interpretation.[9] Indeed, the *indígena* does not enjoy any symbolically privileged status among Blacks. Perhaps it is because of the immediacy of Blacks' lived experience with *indígenas*, coupled with the failure of competing nationalistic pro-indigenous discourses to reach the Costeños (or their rejection of such discourses), that symbolic veneration of the *indígena* is lacking. Indeed, I follow Gutiérrez (1999) in understanding the nationalist reverence of *indígenas* to be largely produced for and consumed by urban mestizos. These discourses failed to reach most rural *indígenas*; nor, I would suggest, did they reach Blacks in any significant way. Any state discourse about the grandeur of the indigenous civilizations would not square with the day-to-day reality of Black interaction with poor *inditos*.

While it is generally understood that the overwhelming number of mestizos are the product of a certain degree of Spanish and indigenous interbreeding, the case of the Afro-Mexican is less clear. My reading of race mixture in the Costa Chica is that it has a much larger proportion of Black-mestizo intermixture than of Black-indigenous intermixture. Historically, it seems that there was little significant intermixture between Blacks and any other groups. This would appear consistent with the general settlement patterns in the region, with Blacks inhabiting the coastal lowlands and the *indígenas* living in the foothills. The distinction between indigenous towns and Black towns was (and still is) quite clearly demarcated. However, when mestizos began to settle in the Costa Chica in the later part of the nineteenth century, they settled in indigenous towns as well as in Black towns. Mestizos are thus the only non-Black group that has lived in Black towns.

My interviews as well as the scarce documentary evidence that has something to say about race mixture in the Costa Chica (Aguirre Beltrán, 1989; Basauri, 1943a and 1943b; Flanet, 1977; Tibón, 1981) are consistent in their characterization of Costa Chica towns as being almost entirely Black. In my survey of Collantes I found no Collanteño families who could point to any indigenous ancestry—no ancestor who either spoke an indigenous language, wore traditional indigenous clothing, or was from a town that was other than a Black town. Furthermore, kinship analysis revealed almost no surnames outside the set of the most common Afro-Mexican surnames.[10] My ethnographic findings are consistent with recent historical work by Vinson (2000) who found that Afro-indigenous *mestizaje* was limited during the late eighteenth century. Furthermore, it appears as if most race mixture occurred in these communities within memory of the oldest Costeños, for they recall a Collantes of *"pura gente negra"* (only Black people). Thus, the *mestizaje* of Costa Chica is a recent phenomenon that is much more about Blacks and mestizos than it is about the mestizaje of the popular nationalist narrative in which *indígenas* and whites give birth to the mestizo.[11]

There is another factor that complicates the ways that Afro-Mexicans experience nationalist *indigenismo*. While it is true that Blacks generally deride *indígenas*, Blacks have begun to accord them some respect for having undertaken to better themselves and their communities in ways that Blacks have as yet been unable to match. This sentiment is expressed most often in terms of education. "Look at the *indio*," I was told by a Black Collanteño. "Ya se están civilizando y estudian. Mira que los maestros ya son indios." (They are becoming civilized and they go to school. See how even the teachers are *indios* now.) Such commentaries also often point to the growing number of doctors, engineers, and other professionals of indigenous background.

Nearly all the primary school teachers who are sent to rural communities are from other parts of the states and there are only a handful of Afro-Mexicans among the teachers working in Black towns. Many of the teachers are of indigenous descent. I attended a secondary school graduation ceremony in town, and an Afro-Mexican friend turned to me and lamented the lack of Black teachers assembled. While some Blacks react to this with the customary anti-indigenous contempt—"they may be educated, but they're still *indios*"—there appears to be a growing current that envies the *indígenas'* ability to better themselves and their communities.

People in the Afro-Mexican town of Cuajinicuilapa suggested that I visit the nearby indigenous town of Xochistlahuaca where I would see how the *indígenas* were "progressing." Indeed, the drive up the narrow, winding, gravel road was rewarded by a small, well-planned town with a beautifully landscaped central plaza and more than a few paved streets. The Blacks in Cuajinicuilapa were comparing the "progress" in Xochistlahuaca with the more random town planning and generally less well-maintained Black towns.

I have not as yet been able to ascertain why certain indigenous communities seem to be progressing according to such indices as education and infrastructure, but one reason may be that government-sponsored initiatives and projects, such as INI, have opened doors to indigenous development. What is important here is that some Afro-Mexicans diverge, however tentatively, from the generalized negative view of *indígenas* by according contemporary indigenous peoples a degree of admiration that may serve as an interesting corollary to the dominant mestizo view of the "glorious" indigenous past.

Afro-Mexicans and the Greater Diaspora

All but the most educated people in the Costa Chica pueblos in which I have worked have had little consciousness of Africa and even less of their being part of any African diaspora. One of the few occasions in which the subject of Africa came up in normal conversation was during televised coverage of international soccer tournaments such as the World Cup. In these tournaments there are always Black players on the teams of several African countries as well as of other Latin American countries. While watching these games with young Afro-Mexican men I noticed that Black players were usually commented upon much like the other players except for the use of the term *moreno* to describe them: "¡Mira a ese moreno, como se cayó!" (Look at that *moreno*, how he fell down!); or when referring to the Nigerian national team: "Son puros morenos, ¿verdad?" (They're all Black, right?)

I never heard generalized statements about the Black players. The Black players were not lumped together in any way that I could discern, such as being said to be better, worse, slower, or faster than any other players. This was somewhat of a surprise to me, given that stereotypes abound in our own society about Black athletes. The young men with whom I would watch games also expressed no association between themselves and the Black players on the screen. They did not tend to root for the Black players or teams, even when the international competitions would pair a European team against an African team.[12]

With respect to their drawing connections between themselves and U.S. Blacks, they were rare. One of the first things that surprised me when speaking to Black Mexicans about race was how they reacted to me. One older Black woman who did not appear to be any lighter in skin complexion than myself told me that in Collantes I would find many people "de tu color" (of your color). She did not say these people were of *our* color, but that they were of *my* color. I would often hear this phrase *de tu color* as well as the phrase *gente como tú* (people like you) used to refer to Black people. It appears as though the distinction is clearly drawn between Afro-Mexicans and the Blacks of other countries. Although over the years I have developed a significant rapport with Afro-Mexicans with whom I have worked, my sense is that this rapport has more to do with the establishment of bonds of trust over time rather than any predilection they might have toward working with another *negro*. Notwithstanding our more or less similar physical characteristics, diaspora Blacks like me are *othered* in a way that limits Costeños from including themselves within a larger diasporic framework. This othering is not unexpected and is yet another example of the way race in general and blackness in particular are not matters of objective physical traits. Rather, those traits are embedded in a social (including national) framework that gives them meaning (Anthias and Yuval-Davis, 1992; Omi and Winant, 1986).

One way that Blacks in diverse national landscapes have given meaning to their Black identity is through embracing the languages, styles, and symbols of the diaspora (Gilroy, 1990:272). Many of these styles and symbols involve the consumption and production of popular music. In many countries where African diaspora people live, one finds the significant consumption of African-influenced music and/or drumming traditions such as reggae (Jamaica), salsa (Cuba, Puerto Rico, Colombia), calypso (Bahamas, Trinidad and Tobago), merengue (Dominican Republic), *bomba* and *plena* (Puerto Rico), *cumbia* and *vallenato* (Colombia), samba (Brazil), *punta* (Garifuna of Honduras), and jazz, blues, gospel, and hip-hop (United States), among others. In most places where small populations of African diaspora peoples exist, yet where unique commercially popular musical traditions may not have developed, Black people have nonetheless associated themselves with the international consumption of these musical products—Blacks and Garifuna in Honduras, Blacks in Nicaragua, and Blacks in Ecuador's Chota region, for example, consume reggae and hip-hop music.

In the Costa Chica there are essentially three types of music one is likely to hear in rural towns: *tropical, chilenas,* and *corridos.*[13] Space does not permit a discussion of these genres, other than a brief description of each. By far the most popular genre is *tropical.* The music's rhythmic foundation is the Colombian *cumbia* which *suffered* a transformation upon its arrival in Mexico in the 1960s. The music was simplified, and, principally in Acapulco with the formation of the group Acapulco Tropical, came to be known as *tropical* (Figueroa Hernández, 1996). *Tropical* is generally locally produced in Acapulco and is not available outside of the region. *Tropical* groups, typically consisting of a standard four- or five-piece rock ensemble, earn most of their income performing at weddings and such throughout the Costa Chica. The most popular groups include Los Costeños del Sur, Hawaii, Mar Azul, Metal, Los Negros Sabaneros, and Siglo XX.

The *chilena,* as its name suggests, was introduced to the coast by Chilean sailors in the mid-nineteenth century. These sailors were most likely on their way to the California coast during the gold rush and stopped for a time in Acapulco. There, they taught their music and dance, the *cueca,* to the Black dockhands, who spread their interpretation of it throughout the Costa Chica (Ochoa Campos, 1987). The *chilena* is now considered the single most characteristic art form of the Costa Chica and any association it may have with Chile or the *cueca* is not widely known among locals.

The coastal *corrido* (ballad) is perhaps the most recognizably Mexican of the musical genres of the Costa Chica, as it closely follows the form of the *corrido* found throughout the country. These *corridos* are generally ballads that tell of local feuds, murders, or other important events that seem to rise to the level of having a *corrido* composed in commemoration. For example, a *corrido* was composed recounting the events of Hurricane Pauline of 1997. What tends to separate the *corridos* of the Costa Chica from those of other regions are both their somber tone (further accentuated by their use of minor keys) and their violent content (Gutiérrez Avila, 1988; McDowell, 2000).[14]

Historians and folklorists might argue as to the African roots of the *cumbia* and what that may suggest with respect to its appropriation as *tropical* in the Costa Chica.

One can, in addition, make a case that the Chilean *cueca*'s possible African origin (Rojas, 2003) is an important element to consider when charting its eventual transformation into the *chilena*. Thus, while Blacks and others in the region consume music of African diasporic origin, Afro-Mexicans do not self-consciously consume it *because* it is diasporic. In this, as in many other respects, Costeños have not identified themselves with the diaspora—at least not until very recently. While their blackness has always been a very meaningful identity with concrete social implications in the local and national landscape, Afro-Mexicans are only now beginning to link their Black experience with that of the greater diaspora. This emerging consciousness is a result of increased exposure to the mass media (electricity became available in many towns as late as the 1970s), the increased migration of Afro-Mexicans to the United States where they are exposed for the first time to non-Mexican Blacks, and a growing interest in the Costa Chica among scholars and activists from the diaspora. Since the late 1990s, the occasional visits of Black scholars and activists, including myself, to the region have quite expectedly raised questions among Costeños as to what these strangers who look much like themselves might have in common. While the local discourse had previously been limited to questions about Blacks, whites, *indígenas*, and mestizos, now a new actor has emerged—one who belongs to the larger African diaspora. It is this larger identity that a local grassroots organization, México Negro, hopes to encourage as a possible avenue toward meeting the needs of everyday Costeños.

Black Politics in the Costa Chica: The México Negro Movement

Before the 1990s there had been no political organization of Afro-Mexicans. In the Costa Chica there has been little recent grassroots organizing even among Mixtec or Amuzgo. Unlike the rather successful indigenous organizing efforts among the Zapotec to the east of the Costa Chica,[15] little ethnic political activity has arisen in the Costa Chica.

There has never been a self-identified Black political leader on the national stage in Mexico, nor even on a statewide scale. It is significant that in 1999 an Afro-Mexican from Acapulco, René Juárez Cisneros, from the then ruling party PRI (Partido Revolucionario Institucional), was elected governor of the state of Guerrero. Judging from campaign posters and official Web sites, the governor has facial characteristics similar to those of any *moreno* from the Costa Chica. His surname, Cisneros, also bespeaks his Afro-Mexican heritage.[16] However, during his campaign, reference was never made to his color or ethnicity. He made no mention of blackness in his inaugural address, while though at various times referred to his concern for the political rights of indigenous people (Guerrero, 2000). In addition, Cisneros made no campaign appearance in the largest Afro-Mexican town in Guerrero, Cuajinicuilapa, probably because the town was firmly aligned with the opposition party, the PRD (Partido de la Revolución Democrática). One wonders how the Afro-Mexican candidate who apparently never had publicly associated himself with rural Afro-Mexicans would have addressed the largely Black community of Cuajinicuilapa.

The Cisneros campaign illustrates how one man's path to political power involved a conscious disassociation from an Afro-Mexican identity, as well as how in Mexican society today an overt assertion of one's blackness is largely a political and social liability.

It is within this uneasy political climate that Afro-Mexican activists have had to work. Rather than looking to politicians who might speak for them, efforts for social change have tended toward the grassroots. The following is a brief sketch of a new grassroots social and political movement among Blacks in the Costa Chica spearheaded by an organization called México Negro. I have been a friend of the organization since 1997 and have assisted in some of its organizing efforts.[17]

In the early 1990s Father Glyn Jemmott, a Trinidadian parish priest who arrived in the region in 1984, began to organize arts and crafts workshops for children of El Ciruelo, Oaxaca, eventually establishing a small library in the town of some 2,400 people. The broader movement began in 1997 with the first regionwide meeting of Afro-Mexicans. According to Father Glyn, "we began to plan the event a year in advance, and it was a dream a year before that." This Primer Encuentro de Pueblos Negros (First Encounter of Black Towns) took place in El Ciruelo as a three-day meeting with representatives from some twenty-five Costa Chica communities in attendance. The explicit thrust of the event—the first of its kind in Mexico—was to initiate a discussion among Afro-Mexicans of the Costa Chica as to their own racial identity and heritage. One of Father Glyn's driving motivations was his sense that perhaps "more social action could be taken by Blacks if they had a common cultural identity from which to draw strength." The first meeting, according to Jemmott, was an attempt to contemplate these issues, not from an academic perspective, but from a practical perspective that would engage everyday rural people.

Some comments from unnamed participants, compiled by Israel Reyes Larrea (1996), include:

> This encounter of Black people will allow us to speak openly. We can do things just like anyone else. We simply lack a push and we hope that in this encounter we can find it in order to move onward. (anonymous participant)

> [I hope] to find different people, get to know each other and dialogue. I hope to find people that really want to have solidarity with other communities. This encounter will help us to think about what we have to do as Black people. (delegate from El Ciruelo, Oaxaca)

According to the organizers of the event and some of the participants, the discussions were quite fruitful for several reasons. First, the meeting was the first time that these people had come together to discuss and valorize their own culture. The dances, songs, and poetry with which most everyone was familiar in their particular towns were now at center stage in a way that they had never previously been showcased. Also, this was the first attempt to convene and unite Afro-Mexicans from a number of towns in the Costa Chica. The event was thus regional in scope and gave participants a chance to visit with people from towns that they had surely heard of but had never visited. The organizers of the event maintain that this was a very important accomplishment. For the first time, Afro-Mexicans came together within the framework of their shared cultural and ethnic bonds. The distinctions among towns as well as between states of origin (i.e., Guerrero versus Oaxaca) were de-emphasized.

In my view one of the most important achievements of this first *encuentro*—and of subsequent *encuentros*—was to revindicate blackness. The event's name—displayed on posters, banners, and leaflets in various towns in the region—was El Encuentro de Pueblos Negros. Afro-Mexicans of the region did not (and do not) readily represent themselves to outsiders as *negros*, most often preferring *morenos*. Thus, the very use of the term *Pueblos Negros* signaled a certain contestation of dominant ways of denying blackness. Furthermore, the committee that organized the first encounter would soon evolve into a recognized nongovernmental organization called México Negro, thus continuing this discursively subversive move.

Tensions soon surfaced among some of the participants. One mestizo man who attended the first event approached Father Glyn and asked, ". . . and when are you going to have a meeting for us?" Father Glyn responded by trying to convince this man that the encounter was not exclusive, and anyone from the participating towns should feel welcome to participate. However, the priest admitted to me that the tension of potential exclusion is one with which the movement would have to continue to grapple. Perhaps this is the kind of ideological struggle that Jean Comaroff and John Comaroff (1993) point to—a struggle that is likely once the hegemonic racial discourse of nationalist *mestizaje* is rattled. The mestizo's comment illustrates the burden placed on these challenges to the status quo. Indeed, Afro-Mexican organizing critiques the exhausted "we are all mestizos" trope and inevitably faces the charge of being exclusionary, separatist, and even racist.

In terms of promoting the event, México Negro has struggled with several ideological conflicts that are emblematic of the difficulty in politicizing blackness in Mexico. Because the discourse of ethnic organizing in the context of blackness has been virtually absent in Mexico, it is almost impossible to articulate the purpose of México Negro to townspeople. This was a topic of discussion in one of the México Negro meetings I attended, and all of the members present expressed a similar discomfort. When speaking to people who are not familiar with México Negro, or with *encuentros*, one may be reluctant to state the official purpose of the *encuentro*, which is essentially "an event where people of African descent from the region will get together to examine and deliberate on organization, with the hopes of creating an inter-town network that would speak to the needs of Afro-Mexican communities."

Organizers expressed difficulty explaining the movement in these terms, primarily out of fear of appearing to be exclusionary or of appearing to characterize the primary problem of the Costa Chica as a race problem. Uneasiness at using racialized language that can be read as confrontational is a very delicate issue. Organizers, including me, therefore "confessed" to the group that they had been much more comfortable promoting the more innocuous aspects of the *encuentro*—the showcasing of regional dance and music of neighboring Afro-Mexican towns. The political goals of the *encuentro*—the discussions that would treat regional history, identity, social action, community economics—were thus glossed over in favor of the more spectacular performance of Black people's music and dance.[18]

Afro-Mexican activists, then, are faced with the challenge of fashioning a politics that might engage with larger cultural and political currents of the diaspora while continuing to reflect the priorities and lived experience of a community to whom the prospect of Black-based organizing is greeted with uneasiness at best and alarm at worst. It appears that the nature and measure of success of such future movements in the Costa Chica will depend not only on the efforts of the diaspora-influenced leaders in the region, but also on everyday Afro-Mexicans' encounter with the diaspora—an encounter that gathers steam as Afro-Mexicans join the persistent stream of Mexican migration to the United States.

"*Me Voy Pa'l Norte*" (Going North): Notes on Afro-Mexican Migration

Since the late 1980s increasing numbers of Blacks from the Costa Chica have left their hometowns in response to ever-worsening economic conditions. As rural Afro-Mexican people travel to urban settings one might expect exposure to a new way of life may later affect how they view themselves, their nationality, and their blackness.

The Costa Chica has not participated in the consistent streams of Mexican migration that began around the turn of the century. That migration was, and continues to be, drawn primarily from the western states of Jalisco, Guanajuato, and Michoacán. It was only in the late 1980s that evidence emerged of increased migratory flows from southern Mexico. There is little reliable data on the regional origins of Mexican migrants, and one wonders whether the increased migration of Costeños is part of a general shift in migration from the traditional western origins to the more peripheral regions.

Since the late 1980s Blacks and others from the Costa Chica have embraced the possibility of migration. As we have seen, the economic opportunities for most rural families in the Costa Chica are limited to poorly remunerated agriculture. In terms of basic needs, only a handful of families want for food, clothing, and basic shelter. Yet many families feel themselves trapped in a kind of economic stagnation. Many talk of lacking the ability to involve themselves in more profitable agricultural production. Most peasants find themselves locked into low-paying day labor on land owned by others and dedicated to more lucrative cash crops such as papayas, peanuts, or limes.

Until recently Acapulco and Mexico City were the most popular destinations for Costeños. Mexico City became the most common destination in the 1980s after small numbers of Costeños began their sojourns in the late 1970s. Migration to Mexico City comes as no surprise, as the metropolis has been aptly described as a city of migrants from all regions of Mexico. The dizzying growth of Mexico City was fed by these demographic shifts—movements of rural people seeking work in the urban economy. Costeños have participated in this migration, settling in lower-class popular barrios such as Ciudad Nezahualcóyotl and Xochimilco.

The frequency with which I saw California and North Carolina license plates on the few cars and pickup trucks in these Black towns was my first indication that Afro-Mexicans were not just migrating to Mexico City. By now the majority of Costeños are migrating to the United States, "El Norte." This migration apparently began in the mid-1980s, with people heading to Southern California at that time. As is the case with most Mexican migration to the United States (the most notable exception being that of farm workers), people tend to settle where others from their home cities or towns have settled previously, thus creating so-called enclave communities. In Southern California, Costeño enclave communities are to be found in several small neighborhoods of Pasadena and Santa Ana. A much larger number of Afro-Mexicans have settled in Winston-Salem, North Carolina. Winston-Salem became their destination of choice beginning around 1993. Afro-Mexicans seek out the labor-intensive packaging industry (much of it related to tobacco production) as well as Winston-Salem's relatively low-cost housing. Many Afro-Mexican immigrants believe that the Immigration and Naturalization Service is much less of a problem for undocumented workers in North Carolina than in California. Increasingly Costeños are also migrating to Phoenix, Arizona, and small numbers of Afro-Mexicans reside in Utah, New York City, and New Jersey.

I should emphasize that the sojourners to the United States undertake the journey at great risk. As is the case with most rural Mexicans, Costeños are generally not able to secure legal documents to enter the United States and therefore rely on clandestine networks to gain entry. They endure a two-day, physically taxing trek through the desert along the Mexico–California border, risking dehydration, exposure, as well as assaults by bandits. Actual crossing of the border is undertaken by night. For the successful, the frantic dash to evade border agents results in safe passage. For others, apprehension by mounted border agents results in bitter disappointment, further delay, and additional expense before a second attempt can be tried. Nearly all of my informants eventually succeeded even after two or three tries. I know of one young man who spent twelve days attempting to cross the border, before finally making it. In addition, the economic burden is great, for money must be borrowed or animals must be sold in order to finance the journey. The costs are such that in some cases the first several months of steady work must be dedicated solely to paying off these loans.

Immigration from Collantes to the United States parallels general trends of Mexican migration to the United States. The migrants from Collantes are generally young (aged fifteen to twenty-four) although I know of some men in their fifties and sixties who have migrated. Young men leave in greater numbers than their female counterparts, but my finding of an essentially 60:40 male–female ratio contrasts slightly with the general ratio of about 75:25 suggested by Jorge Durand, Douglas Massey, and René Zenteno (2001:121). Nearly all young men and most young women entertain the idea of going to El Norte soon after completing school.

The typical Costeño migrant tends to be a sojourner, returning home from the United States without forming strong ties, as opposed to a settler (see Cornelius [1992] for more on the sojourner and settler migration patterns). Rather than intending to settle indefinitely in the United States, the Costeño sojourner stays for about two years before returning home. Many visit home for a period of three to six months, usually during the winter. Durand and his colleagues (2001) suggest a correlation between the frequency of return migration and the migrant's legal status. Migrants who have a legal status are much more likely to make frequent trips back to Mexico, while undocumented Mexicans do not enjoy such a luxury, as the expense and risks of repeated clandestine border crossing is too great. As Chávez (1990:32) points out, "undocumented" is a political status that carries certain liabilities and constraints; in this way Costeños are constrained from making more frequent trips home.

An important area of inquiry is the extent to which Afro-Mexicans interact with African Americans with whom they often share neighborhoods. My preliminary observations in Santa Ana, Pasadena, and Winston-Salem suggest that Costeños tend to associate with Spanish-speaking people, primarily with their extended families, rather than with African Americans. None of my informants report any significant friendships with African Americans or other English-speaking Americans. Race—blackness in this case—is not a primary identity marker.

Social networks are circumscribed and rarely include non-Latinos. Most Costeños speak almost no English and therefore encounter great difficulty in establishing ties with English-speaking neighbors and coworkers. Self-segregation among recent Mexican immigrants is not unusual. It comes as no surprise, then, that Costeños do not interact with African Americans. Perhaps it is because of this lack of interaction that Costeños in the United States tend to subscribe at least in part to the prevailing stereotypes, seeing African Americans as violent, drug-addicted, and generally undesirable. There does not seem to be any sense of solidarity with African Americans. While casual interactions on the job are cordial and while some Costeño men play occasional "pick-up" games of basketball with African Americans at the neighborhood park, my informants had few substantive impressions of Blacks in these urban settings.

Where Costeños do come into contact with blackness in a substantive way is when they are often mistaken for African Americans. This marks a distinction between the Costeño immigrant experience and that of other Mexican counterparts. Afro-Mexicans are often approached by English speakers who assume that they are American Blacks. This confusion is seen as an advantage by most Afro-Mexicans in California, the conventional wisdom being that they are thus less likely to raise suspicions among immigration authorities; they can, in essence, "pass" for Black. Both men and women discovered that particular haircuts and clothing styles popular among African Americans allow them to blend in and attract little unwanted attention. Regardless of whether this "undercover blackness" actually helps Afro-Mexicans evade detection by INS agents, the prospect of such evasion gives some Costeños peace of mind and a feeling that their blackness has some practical benefit.

Costeños' blackness also masks their real identity when fellow Mexicans in the United States do not readily recognize them as Mexicans. There is a corollary of this mistaken identity that occurs frequently in Mexico, when Costeños travel outside of the Costa Chica. They are often asked where they come from and their response—"Guerrero" or "Oaxaca"—is usually met with skepticism. Most Mexicans in central and northern Mexico are not aware of the Afro-Mexican coast and therefore react with some surprise upon encountering Afro-Mexicans.[19] It is no surprise, then, that the Mexican immigrant community in the United States is equally unaware of Black Mexicans. Costeños, then, repeatedly find themselves addressing their blackness as they assert their nationality to the incredulous—be they African Americans, Anglo-Americans, or even their Mexican compatriots.

These encounters of blackness highlight for Black Mexicans the limits of nationalist conceptions of *mestizaje*. I have previously argued elsewhere that blackness is a very salient identity of social importance, despite hegemonic *mestizaje* discourses (Vaughn, 2001). In the United States, Costeños live their blackness juxtaposed not only with what it means to be *indio, blanco, negro,* or *moreno,* but also with what it means to be Mexican.

Notes

1. Importantly, in contradistinction to the later national period, in which almost no mention of Blacks is made, the colonial *casta* system was obsessed with blackness. If we consider fourteen of the most commonly cited categories (**negro, mulato, morisco, albino, negro torncatrás,** *español, castizo,* mestizo, *indio,* **coyote, tente en el aire, cambujo, chino,** and **lobo**), ten of them (in boldface) involve some degree of Black ancestry. In comparison, categories involving a degree of indigenous and Spanish ancestry are reflected in eight and seven *castas,* respectively. It thus appears that the specific quantity of "black blood," however small, was crucial to the imagination of the racial categories.
2. See Cope (1994) for an elaborate argument on the often ambiguous meanings of the *castas* status categories, at least with respect to their significance among urban plebeians.
3. Indeed, the Zapatista rebellion of 1994 was a clear demonstration of this disconnect between the continued celebration of the symbols of indigenous patrimony in the face of repression, marginalization, racism, and national indifference as to the concrete experience of indigenous people. The continuing political reverberations of that watershed event have brought about sharp critiques of previous homogenizing nationalist efforts, and as a result, calls for indigenous autonomy are gaining traction (Díaz-Polanco, 1997; Ramírez Cuevas, 2003; Stephen, 1997).
4. I use *Afro-Mexican* in line with common academic and popular usages of *Afro-Cuban,* *Afro-Peruvian, Afro-Colombian,* and *Afro-American.*
5. While this essay's focus is on Afro-Mexicans of the Costa Chica region, I address Afro-Veracruz in Vaughn (2001b). For more ethnography on Afro-Veracruzanos, see Cruz Carretero (1989), Cruz Carretero et al. (1990), and Cruz Carretero, Martínez, and Santiago (1990).
6. My work has centered almost entirely on Afro-Mexican and mestizo communities in the Costa Chica and has not as yet considered in ethnographic depth the attitudes of indigenous people with respect to Blacks.
7. See Alonso (1995:64) for a short historical discussion of the *gente de razón* status.
8. Although Blacks firmly assert their "*de razón*" status, mestizos may not necessarily agree that they both share this status. As Tibón (1981) reports, the mestizos in Pinotepa Nacional referred to the Blacks as "*gente de media razón*" (*media* means "half"). While I have not heard this turn of phrase in my own fieldwork, it rings consistent with the ways that blackness in the Costa Chica destabilizes supposedly fixed categories of *indígena* and non-*indígena*.
9. My analysis differs somewhat from that of Lewis (2000), who finds that many Afro-Mexicans assert an *indígena* heritage as a claim to Mexicanness. My findings suggest the opposite to be true and are more consistent with the asymmetric relations between Blacks and *indígenas* that extend back to the colonial era and continue to be evident in the 1970s (Flanet, 1977).
10. It is as yet unclear as to why this particular set of surnames emerges among Afro-Mexicans of the Costa Chica. Many are common surnames throughout Mexico, while others are almost

unheard of, i.e., Ayona, Bacho, Corcuera, Mariche, and Morga. In addition, the names do not correspond to the names of large slaveholding families mentioned in regional historical sources. These Afro-Mexican names include: Acevedo, Ayona, Bacho, Bernal, Calleja, Cisneros, Colón, Corcuera, Dominguez, Gonzalez, Hernández, Herrera, Liborio, Mariano, Mariche, Morga, Noyola, Petatán, Peñalosa, Saguilán, Salinas, Serrano, Silva, Toscano, and Vargas.

11. This conclusion is consistent with Carroll (1995) whose study of colonial Veracruz showed that in regions where Blacks, whites, and indigenous people lived in proximity, *indígenas* were far less likely to intermarry than were Blacks and whites. Indeed, he concludes that the intermarriage among black men and mestizas was the most consistent pattern of relations during the colonial era, thus producing a *raza cósmica* that is denied in Vasconcelos's *raza cósmica* (1979:432–433).

12. It has been my experience that barring strong team loyalties, Black Americans tend to favor Black teams and Black stars out of a sense of group solidarity.

13. Elsewhere (Vaughn, 2001a) I discuss some of the various folkloric dances native to particular towns, such as the *danza de los diablos* of Collantes, Oaxaca, Cuajinicuilapa, and Guerrero. Unlike the other musical genres discussed here, these dances are only performed on a particular holiday or, increasingly, only in regional dance festivals or contests.

14. McDowell (2000) is the first monograph-length study of the *corrido* of the Costa Chica. The folklorist has included with the book a CD that offers eleven field recordings of representative *corridos*.

15. See Campbell (1990) on Zapotec organizing in Tehuantepec.

16. See footnote 8.

17. I concentrated most of my efforts on working with others to help the organization raise relief funds in the aftermath of the devastating Hurricane Pauline which ravaged the region in October 1997.

18. I do not mean to underestimate the potential power of using regional dance and other performative culture as a vehicle toward, or entry point into, other more overtly political activities. The performance and celebration of Afro-Mexican dance and music are political acts and inherently involve the embracing of an Afro-Mexican discourse. The organizers, however, struggled with how to make such linkages explicit and move into a more manifestly political phase that transcended typical presentations of folklore. (I owe this observation to discussions with the Mexican anthropologist and percussionist Lilly Alcántara Henze.)

19. At times this general ignorance of the Afro-Mexican presence lends itself to abuse, as in cases where law enforcement officials have detained Costeños traveling to Mexico City. In one case of which I am aware, a group was detained under the pretense that they were suspected of being undocumented Central Americans, and when they could not sing the Mexican national anthem on demand, they ran into trouble. In this case, it appears as if the prevailing ignorance about Afro-Mexicans coupled itself unfortunately with the infamous corruption prevalent in Mexican law enforcement.

References

Aguirre Beltrán, Gonzalo. 1989. *Cuijla: Esbozo etnográfico de un pueblo negro*. Mexico City: Fondo de Cultura Económica.

Alonso, Ana María. 1995. *Thread of Blood: Colonialism, Revolution, and Gender on Mexico's Northern Frontier*. Tucson: University of Arizona Press.

Anderson, Benedict. 1991. *Imagined Communities: Reflections on the Origin and Spread of Nationalism*. New York: Verso.

Anthias, Floya, and Nira Yuval-Davis. 1992. *Racialised Boundaries: Race, Nation, Gender, Colour and Class and the Anti-Racist Struggle*. New York: Routledge.

Appiah, Kwame Anthony, and Henry Louis Gates Jr. 1999. Slavery in Latin America and the Caribbean. In *Encarta Africana*, ed. K. A. Appiah and H. L. J. Gates. Redmond, WA: Microsoft Corporation.

Basauri, Carlos. 1943a. *Breves notas etnográficas sobre la población negra del distrito de Jamiltepec, Oaxaca*. Mexico City: Primer Congreso Demográfico Interamericano.

———. 1943b. La población negroide mexicana. *Estadística* 1:96–107.

Brading, David. 1980. *Los orígenes del nacionalismo mexicano*. Mexico City: Ediciones Era.

Campbell, Howard. 1990. The COCEI: Culture, class, and politicized ethnicity in the isthmus of Tehuantepec. *Ethnic Groups* 8:29–56.

Carroll, Patrick J. 1991. *Blacks in Colonial Veracruz: Race, Ethnicity, and Regional Development*. Austin: University of Texas Press.

———. 1995. Los mexicanos negros, el mestizaje y los fundamentos olvidados de la "raza cósmica": Una perspectiva regional. *Historia Mexicana* 44 (3):403–438.

Chávez, Leo R. 1990. Coresidence and resistance: Strategies for survival among undocumented Mexicans and Central Americans in the United States. *Urban Anthropology* 19 (1–2):31–61.

Comaroff, Jean, and John L. Comaroff. 1993. *Of Revelation and Revolution*. Chicago: University of Chicago Press.

Consejo Nacional para la Cultura y las Artes. 2003. Programa Nuestra Tercera Raiz. http://www.cnca.gob.mx/cnca/popul/nuter.htm. macgrego@conaculta.gob.mx.

Cope, Douglas R. 1994. *The Limits of Racial Domination: Plebeian Society in Colonial Mexico City, 1660–1720*. Madison: University of Wisconsin Press.

Cornelius, Wayne. 1992. Sojourners to settlers: The changing profile of Mexican migration to the United States. In *U.S.-Mexico Relations: Labor Market Independence*, ed. Jorge A. Bustamante et al., 155–195. Stanford, CA: Stanford University Press.

Cruz Carretero, Sagrario. 1989. Identidad en una comunidad afromestiza del centro de Veracruz: La población de Mata Clara. Tésis de Licenciatura, Fundación Universidad de las Américas.

——— et al. 1990. *El carnaval en Yanga: notas y comentarios sobre una fiesta de la negritud*. Mexico City: Consejo Nacional para la Cultura y las Artes.

Cruz Carretero, Sagrario, Alfredo Martínez, and Angélica Santiago. 1990. Carnaval en El Coyolillo: Los negros disfrazados. *México Indígena* 10:41–45.

Díaz-Polanco, Héctor. 1997. *La rebelión Zapatista y la autonomía*. Mexico City: Siglo Veintiuno Editores.

Durand, Jorge, Douglas Massey, and René M. Zenteno. 2001. Mexican immigration to the United States. *Latin American Research Review* 36 (1):107–127.

Figueroa Hernández, Rafael. 1996. *Salsa mexicana: Transculturación e identidad*. Xalapa, Veracruz: ConClave.

Flanet, Veronique. 1977. *Viviré, si dios quiere: Un estudio de la violencia de la Mixteca de la costa*. Translated by T. Mercado. Mexico City: Instituto Nacional Indigenista.

Gilroy, Paul. 1990. One nation under a groove: The cultural politics of "race" and racism in Britain. In *Anatomy of Racism*, ed. D. T. Goldberg, 263–282. Minneapolis: University of Minnesota Press.

Guerrero, Gobierno de. 2000. Gobierno de Guerrero Official Web Site. http://www.guerrero.gob.mx/dominios/gobierno/Gobierno2.htm.

Gutiérrez Avila, Miguel Angel. 1988. *Corrido y violencia entre los afromestizos de la Costa Chica de Guerrero y Oaxaca*. Mexico City: Universidad Autónoma de Guerrero.

Gutiérrez, Natividad. 1999. *Nationalist Myths and Ethnic Identities: Indigenous Intellectuals and the Mexican State*. Lincoln, NE: University of Nebraska Press.

León, Nicolás. 1924. *Las castas del México colonial o Nueva España*. Mexico City: Talleres Gráficos del Museo Nacional de Arqueología, Historia y Etnografía.

Lewis, Laura. 2000. Blacks, black Indians, Afromexicans: The dynamics of race, nation, and identity in a Mexican *moreno* community (Guerrero). *American Ethnologist* 27 (4):898–926.

Martínez Montiel, Luz María. 1994. *Presencia africana en México*. Mexico City: Dirección General de Culturas Populares.

McDowell, John Holmes. 2000. *Poetry and Violence: The Ballad Tradition of Mexico's Costa Chica*. Urbana: University of Illinois Press.

Ochoa Campos, Moisés. 1987. *La chilena guerrerense*. Chilpancingo: Gobierno del Estado de Guerrero.

Omi, Michael, and Howard Winant. 1986. *Racial Formation in the United States: From the 1960s to the 1980s*. New York: Routledge & Kegan Paul.

Palmer, Colin A. 1976. *Slaves of the White God: Blacks in Mexico, 1570–1650*. Cambridge, MA: Harvard University Press.

Ramirez Cuevas, Jesus. 2003. La fiesta de los Caracoles: La autonomía indígena, basada en los incumplidos acuerdos de San Andrés. *La Jornada*.

Reyes Larrea, Israel. 1996. *Cimarrón*. Vol. 12. José María Morelos.

Rojas, Mario. 2003. *Cueca Chilena*. http://www.cuecachilena.cl.mrojasp@ctcinternet.cl.

Ronan, Charles E. 1977. *Francisco Javier Clavijero, S.J. (1731–1787), Figure of the Mexican Enlightenment: His Life and Works*. Chicago: Loyola University Press.

Stephen, Lynn. 1997. The Zapatista opening: The movement for indigenous autonomy and state discourses on indigenous rights in Mexico, 1970–1996. *Journal of Latin American Anthropology* 2 (2):2–41.

Tibón, Gutierre. 1981. *Pinotepa Nacional: Mixtecos, negros y triques*. Mexico City: Editorial Posada.

Valdés, Dennis Nodin. 1987. The decline of slavery in Mexico. *Americas* 44 (2):167–194.

Vasconcelos, José. 1979. *The Cosmic Race/La Raza Cósmica: A Bilingual Edition*. Los Angeles: California State University.

Vaughn, Bobby. 2001a. Mexico in the context of the slave trade. *Diálogo* 5:14–19.

———. 2001b. Race and nation: A study of blackness in Mexico. Ph.D. diss., Stanford University.

Vinson, Ben. 2000. The racial profile of a rural Mexican province in the "Costa Chica": Igualapa in 1791. *The Americas* 57(2):269–282.

Wagley, Charles. 1968. The concept of social race in the Americas. In *The Latin American Tradition*, ed. C. Wagley. New York: Columbia University Press.

CHAPTER 7

THE CHANGING WORLD OF BRAZILIAN RACE RELATIONS?

Anani Dzidzienyo

Introduction

Brazil has occupied a privileged position in discussions of comparative race relations and racializations since its earliest days. Though Brazil was the last country to abolish slavery—doing so in 1888, two years after Cuba—the quality of Brazilian race relations and the extent of racial mixture were topics of frequent commentary by travelers and nationals, in terms of the treatment of slaves, the possibilities for upward mobility for ex-slaves and their descendants, and, above all, its avoidance of the more vicious race relations order in the United States. Over the last three decades, a vigorous debate has emerged on the validity of the claims that Brazilian race relations are more benign than those in other parts of the hemisphere. At the same time, there is an increasing tendency to transcend the official and unofficial celebrations of what became popularly known as "racial democracy," which ostensibly provided "equality of opportunity" for all individuals to participate in the process of race mixture, irrespective of their racial backgrounds (Bacelar and Caroso, 1998; Crook and Johnson, 1999).

Any discussion of race relations in Brazil and Latin America as a whole must take into account the following two fundamental truths: (1) historically, disproportionate weight has been assigned to physical appearance (color/race), with whiteness and near whiteness being positively valued, while blackness and near-blackness have been valued negatively; and (2) whether willful or not, legally mandated or not, these race-based valorizations are incontrovertible aspects of race relations in Brazil and indeed in Latin America as a whole (Fontaine, 1980). Thus, race mixture, or *mestizaje*, like the notion of "racial democracy," has historically both included and excluded nonwhites, whether of African or indigenous descent, from the "commanding heights" of the sociopolitical, economic, and cultural orders of Latin American societies (Mallon, 1996; Wade, 1997; Martínez-Echazábal, 1996; Munanga, 1986, 1999).

While bearing these two points in mind, this chapter nevertheless suggests that, over the past twenty-five years, there have been clear and unambiguous transformations in Brazilian societal discourses, policy formulation, and the meanings and questioning of the conventional wisdom about Brazilian race relations. This is not to say that such shifts in thought, discourse, and action signify the total abandonment of the old ideas that continue to resonate throughout Brazilian society and its polity. Still, without denying Brazilian specificities, the following pages review the changes as reflected in recent scholarship as well as in Afro-Brazilians' political activities and the discussion of them in the Brazilian media, in order, ultimately, to situate Brazil within a broader international comparative framework. I conclude that the Brazilian "racial universe" and knowledge of its ongoing changes and debates can provide some useful insights for, and contribute to, the present discussion of changing majority-minority relations within the United States, especially, the prospect of a "Latin Americanization" of U.S. race relations given the magnitude of the Latin American and Latino population in that society today. Perhaps more than any other American country, Brazil has been the subject of an impressive array of studies and discussions directed at getting to the core of its race-relations conundrum: a self-proclaimed example of "nonracialness," simultaneously characterized by the conspicuous absence of Brazilians of African descent from critical areas of the polity and society (Hanchard, 1994, 1999; Reichmann, 1999; Chor Maio, 1996).

Moreover, the commitment to the general recognition of fluidity in individual racial, color identity has not meant the absence of acute and "finely tuned" racial, color distinctions. The meanings of and the challenges to these issues, both of which are undergoing intense discussions today, provide a mirror into history, race, nation, and identity. These in turn all intersect with the present and future discourses of inter- and intragroup relations within the United States.

The Historical Debates on Brazilian Race Relations

Today, unlike twenty-five years ago, very few people would assert with any confidence that Brazil has no racial problem (D'Adesky, 1996). Antonio Sérgio Guimarães (2003) summarizes the present state of the conflicting perspectives on the part of activists and militants, on the one hand, and academics, on the other. Briefly put, there has been a simultaneous increase in what Afro-Brazilian activists have characterized as the "demystification" of "racial democracy" and the consequent "dethroning" of Gilberto Freyre, the famous anthropologist and father of the study of modern Brazilian culture, with whom the thesis of Brazil as a "racial democracy" is usually associated. This process comes together with a growing and robust defense of Freyre by academics who now posit the notion of "the myth racial democracy" not as something negative, in need of demystification, or as a concept to be abandoned, but more as an ideal which, although based on an obvious falsehood, nevertheless can still serve as a guide for social conduct. According to these academics, "racial democracy" is to be assessed as symbolic of Brazilian race relations, an idea or concept that has long been acceptable to Brazilians, at least until the recent assaults on it by anti-Freyrean militants who do not reflect the generality of Afro-Brazilians, much less of Brazilians, who have yet to categorically reject the concept.

Afro-Brazilian activists and their anti-Freyrean academic allies, on the other hand, argue that "racial democracy" is not so benign—that it has indeed had a negative impact on Brazilian race relations by hiding the realities of discrimination against Afro-Brazilians and further silencing them when they protest such discrimination, and that it is contrary to "idealized" voices because of its total identification with "Brazilianness." The activists point out that whenever Afro-Brazilians criticize racial democracy, they are accused of assaulting Brazilian nationality and being. Similarly, their questioning of the legitimacy of "racial democracy" and their insistence on focusing specific attention on Afro-Brazilians, now identified "racially," are viewed by their critics as a throwback to pre-Freyrean Brazil, with its false notion of the existence of races with "essences." In short, while for the pro-Freyreans rejecting race inherently implies rejecting all racial associations, the Afro-Brazilian activists and their anti-Freyrean allies point out that there is no direct correlation between denying the existence of races and the attenuation or elimination of discrimination and its consequences. Instead, Afro-Brazilians argue that the maintenance or reproduction of social and political inequality in Brazilian society is not predicated upon the scientific legitimization of the existence of races.

In 1985 the Brazilian sociologist Oracy Nogueira (1985) argued that the difference between U.S. and Brazilian race relations lay in the fact that in the United States prejudice was based on origin, while in Brazil it was based on appearance. But the attempt to distinguish race and color, or physical appearance, from origin in defining Brazilian identity inherently assumes that it is possible to separate the two. Neither biological precision in designating an individual's race nor certainty in determining his/her color is self-evident. After all, if race is socially constructed, so is color. Mobility into or toward whiteness, like socioeconomic mobility, has been possible for "educated mulattos" and lighter Blacks. Their "cultural integration" and political and social cooptation came to be seen as proof of the existence of a racial democracy in Brazil, especially when it became the equivalent of an official state ideology.

As Guimarães (2001:164) notes, the powerful combination of disguised racist practices, hierarchical differentiations, a general acknowledgment of inequality (everyone knows his or her "place"), and the informality of social relations has allowed for different types of offensive verbal behavior and conduct that threaten individual rights. Although "race" has been abandoned as a concept, Guimarães goes on to argue that its underpinnings have remained. White/European culture is perceived as symbolizing civilization and is considered superior to Black/African culture, which is seen as "uncultured" and "uncivilized." The transformation of whites with dark hair and skin, or of darker individuals with "whiter" features, into another category (morenos/morenas) is common. This way, negative perceptions of Blacks have remained, as have the inequality of treatment before the law and the primacy of Black stereotypes and somatic traits in policing of public spaces. This reality notwithstanding, those who point to racialization and use it as the basis of antiracist actions are designated as "racist" or as engaging in "reverse racism" (2001:166).

With invisibility and denial as distinguishing characteristics of Brazilian racism, how, then, have Afro-Brazilian activists tackled the problem of making racism visible? Could a robust Black movement emerge—one dedicated to the rediscovery of Africa-connected values, to individual cultural uplift, to fighting exclusively for equal opportunity for Blacks within the polity and society? Undoubtedly, a certain "universalization" of demands for rights and freedoms for the poor and other disadvantaged sectors of the population, aimed at eventually reducing the socioeconomic gaps between "whites," "Blacks," and "nonwhites," stands a better chance of success than single movements devoted to the struggles of specific constituencies such as Afro-descendants. Still, the question remains: how to create a movement that makes visible the issue of racism in a society that denies the validity of racial difference?

The predominance of colorism in Brazilian society, even within families, and the privileging of lighter-skinned members has resulted in fragmenting racial solidarity among nonwhite individuals and seriously reducing the possibilities for political mobilization (Nobles, 2000). Nevertheless, there have been persistent criticisms of the existing Black Movement for being unduly distant and isolated from the majority of Black people and for not being very successful at mass mobilization and representation of their interests. In electoral terms, there is a perception that the Black vote—that is, Blacks voting for Blacks—has not been common practice. "O voto racial não pega"—that is, racial voting has no meaningful resonance, insofar as relatively powerless Blacks are not likely to "deliver" patronage. Hence, as Benedita da Silva noted in Austin in 1993, prior to her election as vice governor of the State of Rio de Janeiro, Blacks are more prone to seek "other" (white) patrons who are more able to "deliver" (Hanchard, 1999).

The way out of this difficulty lies in tying Black movement demands to the larger agenda for human rights groups and their activities. This broader strategy has the distinct advantage of impacting a larger number of people. Nonetheless, it is important to emphasize that this strategy itself is limited by the fact that Brazilian society has never shown any concern about police brutality or other forms of human rights violations in relation to those perceived as criminals, regardless of their race. As Abdias do Nascimento and Elisa Larkin Nascimento (2001:136–137) have noted, until recently, there has been a general resistance to issues of human rights, which are believed to criminals. Guimarães suggests that since Blacks and the poor are in fact interchangeable categories, the creation of coalitions uniting the two could be a viable option for escaping a reductionist trap likely to lead to a "minority politics" with very minimal benefits if any—a position similar to what William Julius Wilson advanced a few years ago in the United States. This kind of strategy could make elites move away from hiding behind "racial democracy" or economic underdevelopment as long-term but ill-defined sociopolitical ideals. Nevertheless, to the extent that, to date, elites have never shown any interest in improving the situation of either the poor or Blacks, it is not clear either how or why this strategy would elicit such a radical transformation in elite behavior.

Furthermore, there is strong resistance on the part of the pro-freyrean Brazilian academics and sectors of the dominant society to the current practice by Afro-Brazilian activists of dissolving the distinctions among nonwhites into a uniform "Black" category. Increasingly known as "Afrodescendentes" (i.e., of African descent), this category is considered by its opponents as unduly subverting the generally accepted Brazilian classification system and thus as not being representative of mainstream thought and behavior in Brazilian society. Eschewing individual identity and imposing a new Black one, which homogenized nonwhiteness, the pro-Freyrean academics charged, could only mean that Brazilian race relations were being "Americanized." Hence, Blacks were said to be de-characterizing conventional Brazilian racial practices through their movement, seeking instead to import and impose "foreign models," together with the latter's implicit connotations of violence.

As in other race relations contexts, such as the United States and the Republic of South Africa, the Black Movement in Brazil has had to rely on the support of white allies in the continuing battle with the white academic establishment, particularly in relation to the barriers against the admission of Blacks and the poor into the universities due to concerns about the undermining of intellectual standards (Marx, 1998). The legal (i.e., constitutional) terrain has become a conspicuous venue for movement forward in the ongoing struggle against racism in Brazil. The 1988 constitution introduced the idea of "collective rights," recognizing Blacks and indigenous peoples as subjects of the law. It also established a "Public Ministry," charged with monitoring the enforcement of legal rights and duties by public authorities such as prosecutors and public defenders. This development was significant in view of the popular perception in Brazil that a big gap exists between the letter of the law and its actual enforcement and that the law serves elites and nonelites differently.

As Guimarães (2001) has demonstrated, in practice, antidiscrimination laws have not entirely proven to be models of success in combating racial discrimination. This is due to the frequency with which allegations of racism are "downgraded" or transformed into cases of defamation of character, or injury to personal honor, because the latter stand a better chance of arriving at a judicial settlement. In this context, what long-term results can be contemplated for dealing with allegations of racial discrimination?

Furthermore, what had been considered to be a significant legal victory—the criminalization of racist behavior that was not subject to bail upon conviction and that carried a stiff penalty—has, in practice, turned out to be an ambiguous victory. Judges are reluctant to impose such harsh penalties for allegedly racist acts in a legal system in which judges and courts are overburdened with cases perceived to be graver than individual acts of racial discrimination.

In this context, in terms of its symbolic significance, whether internally or externally, perhaps no single action on the judicial front matches the appointment of an Afro-Brazilian, Joaquim Barbosa Gomes, to the Supreme Federal Tribunal in 2003. Still, as Guimarães (2001:174) notes, not even the powerful symbolism of this appointment obviates the continuing need for the struggle to influence public opinion about making the appearance of Black lawyers and prosecutors in the courts, and the recognition due them as professionals, both normal and routine in Brazilian society. Joaquim Gomes Barbosa (2001), as a law professor and public federal prosecutor, had argued that the Brazilian state had demonstrated a notable unwillingness to prosecute racial discrimination cases. He pointed to the need for a fund to train legal activists to handle such cases. Figures from Brazil in the area of employment are embarrassing from a North American perspective: of 800 federal judges in Brazil, perhaps 12 are Afro-Brazilians; while only 6 of the 550 federal prosecutors are Afro-Brazilians. Moreover, Gomes Barbosa characterized the diplomatic service as "the most racist of Brazilian institutions." Two years later the foreign ministry, popularly known as Itamarati, announced that it was setting up special scholarships for "African descendants," or Afrodescendentes, to prepare for the entrance examination to the Instituto Rio Branco, Brazil's foreign service training institute (*Jornal do Brasil*, 7/7/2002).

The small "victories" against discrimination represented, for example, by appointments such as Barbosa's do not extend to an opening up of the rest of Brazilian society to a more forthright discussion of the theories, "pacts," "practices" and "protocols" of race relations. Instead, they are limited generally to the creation of special police stations for racial crimes, similar to those aiming to protect women's rights. The election of activists coming mainly from center-left labor parties, the strengthening of identity affirmation through the formation of groups, and the promotion of cultural events are significant for the protection of the Black population. But what are the kinds of concrete struggles in which Blacks should engage? How should they approach their involvement in national struggles so that Blacks are only coresponsible for success or failure, rather than being made exclusively responsible? To what extent can Brazilian society be complicit in bringing about a new race relations order? Otherwise, Black challengers are left in an untenable position. They are allotted the responsibility of disrupting the race relations "pact" of the 1930s and 1940s, and then burdened again with a disproportionate share of the responsibility for crafting a new pact, ushering in a new racial order.

In thinking about the construction of a Black Movement through which a new socioracial pact might be collectively constructed by Brazilian society as a whole, it is also important to ask whether abandoning the "racialism" of racial descent (i.e., physical traits or biological lineage) in favor of a racialism of chosen identities could lead to the temptation to abandon majority politics for minority politics (Guimarães, 2001:177)? If, in fact, the Afro-descendente trope now functions as a broadly based designation, which transcends narrow colorism, is it not then majoritarian? By the same token, might possible affirmative action benefits dramatically expand the "Black" category, rendering it more "majoritarian"? Either way, there appears to be much less abandoning of majoritarian politics for the minoritarian. The post–Afrodescendente phase, after all, has the potential of embracing a much larger number of Brazilians than has previously been the case. What is less certain are the tests to be established for legitimizing claims to blackness for the purposes of distributing the "benefits" gained from policies related to affirmative action and "quotas."

The Present State of Afro-Braziliana: Initiatives and Responses

The significance of the recurrent charge that the "Black Movement" and its leadership are alienated from the majority of Blacks and hence cannot claim to represent a broad section of the Afro-Brazilian community should not be underestimated (Rufino dos Santos, 1988). In the first place, the vagueness of the term "Black Movement," variously employed to describe the original United Black Movement Against Racial Discrimination, which subsequently became the Unified Black Movement (MNU), and other organizations, leaves confusion in its analytical trail. It is not at all clear how or why the Movimento Negro is distinguishable from other Brazilian movements or organizations in terms of having automatic links, or not, to the bases or general population. How, realistically, could the MNU become the voice of all or most Afro-Brazilians in a state and society with a very inconsistent record of such organizations linking leadership and bases? This is not to plead for an alibi for the MNU; rather it is to suggest that perhaps from its very inception the MNU was faced with a difficult issue: Could a single movement or organization, no matter how innovative it may be, aspire to such unity after periods of intermittent activity on the part of both Brazil and Afro-Brazil, albeit for reasons primarily linked to the absence of democratic participation, irrespective of democratic volition on the part of Afro-Brazilians (dos Santos, 2001)?

It is impossible to assess any form of Afro-Brazilian political activity without fully situating it in the context of Brazilian society and polity. Do Nascimento and Larkin Nascimento (2001:138–139) have underscored the absence of well-organized political parties with the capacity (and interests) to transform demands into concrete executive and legislative actions in view of the society's overwhelming resistance to human rights and affirmative action initiatives. They also (2001:108, 126) note:

> Official Brazilian census data uses two color categories for African descendants: preto (literally, "Black") for the dark-skinned and pardo (roughly mulatto and mestizo) for others. This distinction has proved so arbitrary and subjective as to be essentially useless, yet it leads those unfamiliar with the Brazilian demographic content to mistake the smaller preto group for Black. It is now accepted convention to identify the Black population as the sum of the preto and pardo categories, referred to as negro, afro brasileiro, or afro-descendente.
>
> But, there has also existed a practice by which African-descended interviewees tended to classify themselves as (white or mulatto) lighter than they actually might appear because of the historical and continuing negativity of Blackness in Brazilian society and culture.
>
> A major consequence of de facto, as opposed to de jure, discrimination is that those excluded lose their voice. Indeed, if racism is deemed not to exist, with what legitimacy can its targets' voice be raised? While spokesmen have assumed and been granted the legitimacy to speak for Blacks, challenging this procedure has traditionally been considered "reverse racism."

A strong resistance to discussions of antidiscrimination measures is the direct outgrowth of the notion of the nonexistence of racism (Viotti da Costa, 1985). This resistance has strengthened the voices of nongovernmental organizations in their interaction with state agencies, particularly in the attention devoted to combating hunger, poverty, income inequality, and the inequality of living conditions, all of which invariably include addressing racial inequalities.

On a more positive note, the emergence of an Afro-Brazilian movement made up of nongovernmental organizations, community leaders actively engaged in labor unions, political parties, Christian churches, religious communities of African origin, and cultural organizations, among others, points to a new phase in Afro-Brazilian activities. Raising the "racial question" in each area, and often facing opposition and hostility, the Black Movement has won allies and raised consciences among Brazilians about Black issues such that in 1995, the Brazilian government agreed to recognize November twentieth as the National Day of Black Consciousness.[1]

Still, there is a need for caution about the extent to which even vigorous Afro-Brazilian actions have been able to influence official responses in the long run. In 1991, Leonel Brizola created the Extraordinary Secretariat for the Defense and Promotion of Black People (SEAFRO) in the state of Rio de Janeiro. Advances and gains have had to be taken into consideration, along with simultaneous setbacks even after initial gains. SEAFRO and its first secretary of state, Abdias do Nascimento, were charged with the articulation and implementation of public policies for the Afro-Brazilian community of Rio de Janeiro. Created by decree, there were subsequent legal challenges to it, such that by the time the next administration was sworn in, the secretariat had been abolished.

In contrast to SEAFRO, created by governor's decree, the establishment of the Municipal Secretariat for Black Community Affairs (SMACON) in Belo Horizonte, in the state of Minas Gerais, could not have been more different from the founding of SEAFRO—although both eventually met the same fate. In the case of SMACON, which was created by Mayor Célio de Castro, in December 1998, there was a long process of debate in the press and civil society, followed by a vote in the City Council ensuring that SMACON was recognized as a regular City Council agency. Nevertheless, like SEAFRO, SMACON was later abolished, this time in response to an alleged budget crunch. This was a much more serious blow for the Black community, considering the extensive groundwork that had preceded SMACON's creation, and that had included a broadly based national and international campaign of support. Thus, whether established by a gubernatorial decree, or engendered by full discussion in society and polity and subsequently established as part of the normal city administration, such secretariats, specifically targeted to support Blacks' struggle for equality, have not been allowed to thrive in Brazil.

These kinds of failed attempts to institutionalize government support for the advancement of Black rights, in the context of Brazilian racial democracy, can provide insights for Afro-Americans who are today having to confront the mainstream's assumptions concerning "the end of racism" in a post–Civil Rights U.S. society. From this perspective, the words of Elisa Larkin Nascimento (2003) provide a new twist on the "racial democracy" myth: "In societies where Civil Rights victories have changed institutional structures, the difficulties in denouncing and combating discrimination tend to become similar to those faced by the Afro-Brazilian movement to date [for example], denial of the racial nature of inequalities, appropriation by conservative forces of the discourse of equality, and allegations that anti-discrimination policy constitutes reverse discrimination."

John French (2000) argues that the post-1978 scholars of Brazilian race relations saw themselves as providing "evidence" to help the cause of activists battling the moribund "racial democracy" idea. They were implicitly adopting the Black Movement's binary division of Brazilian society into whites and Blacks—a division that goes against the conventional Brazilian practice of recognizing multiple racially based divisions in the population. The consequence of their work has not been a dramatic transformation of Brazilian race relations attitudes. Instead, what their work has done is to show the endurance of a range of perceptions concerning the relationship of race to various forms of social and economic inequalities in Brazil. French notes that, to date, this research has not been successfully mobilized to create a political response. Certainly, it is worth asking how feasible is the idea that scholars' research findings have any real chance of radically transforming overall societal designations within the Brazilian race relations order. At the same time, however, there is no doubt about the significance of the solidarity provided by these scholars, even if they were to appear to adopt the Black Movement's view of blackness and its binary understanding of Brazilian race relations.

French (2000:121) notes that, in recent decades, there has not been a single attempt by a Brazilian to build a scholarly case based on evidence, as opposed to ideal or myth, that Brazil is in fact a society without racism. "Simple affirmations of Brazilian racial democracy are encountered only in the folk wisdom of Brazilians who do not conduct scientific research on the topic." His characterization of a certain radical strand in Afro-Brazilian political activity as "a sense of alienation" (2000: 123n.5) is questionable. It is not at all clear that Caetano and Cunha (1992:86) provide any indication of alienation by noting the all-pervasiveness of racism in Brazilian national life, visibly corroborated by the fact that the majority of Brazilians have difficulty in identifying racism when it occurs because of its deep-rootedness in Brazilian life, resulting in the very victims' acceptance of racism as normal. That the majority does not protest is not in itself surprising. Tacit acceptance and collaboration are neither new nor unheard of in colonial or quasi-colonial hegemonic situations. The case can be made that, far from heading toward alienation, Caetano and Cunha might actually be articulating the results of long observation. What interests them is much more collective political action than individual heroics, significant as these may be. The centrality of agency does not subvert the unequal access to power and its manipulations. Therein, perhaps, lies a major reason for the collective weakness of Afro-Brazilian political activities.

Thomas Skidmore (2000:3) believes that the most important single factor in the transformation of Brazil's race relations over the past twenty-five years has been the collection of new census data, which has produced proof of discrimination against nonwhite Brazilians, thus transcending the old reliance on personal observation. Debates on the difference between prejudice and discrimination continue, and although one is sometimes posited to predominate over the other, no one has yet claimed that the two are completely absent from Brazilian society.

Skidmore also suggests that a major difference in the discussion has to do with the fact that today many more Americans study Brazilian race relations than do Brazilians themselves. Undoubtedly, the possibilities of increased Afro-Brazilian perspectives would add another dimension to such studies. But not only is there a lack of funds in Brazil, but Brazilian intellectuals reflect elite perspectives, which do not consider race as a central concern for contemplation or study. Initiatives since 1995 along with raging controversies about antidiscrimination moves are, perhaps, evidence of a changing climate for Brazilian race relations studies.

Are there other factors contributing to changes in Brazilian race relations?

Though, as Guimarães argues, "it would be mistaken to attribute the growth of 'Black consciousness' and the cultivation of racial identity in Brazil of the 1970s to foreign, especially U.S., influence" (2003:18), it would be equally difficult to totally exclude such influences. How Brazil could be receptive to all manner of extraneous influences in national life, culture, economy, and society, and yet remain fully protected against the influences of the United States, is puzzling. By the same token, how Brazil would be totally immune from developments in continental Africa and the rest of the Black world in relation to race relations discourses and practices is also intriguing. Moreover, that earlier phases of Black militancy might have been receptive to the idea of social integration by way of the racial democracy trope does not obviate radical changes in Black ideas or tactics in recent years. Exposure to these changes in ideology has enabled Afro-Brazilians to better situate Brazil and themselves as Brazilians within a broader universe of comparative race relations.

Carlos Alberto Medeiros (1998) has drawn attention to the need to move beyond the denunciation of individual acts of racial discrimination and to pay closer attention instead to mobilization and group activity. Thus, notwithstanding what D'Adesky (1996) characterized as the limitations of "brave efforts" by movement leaders, the overall political dividend is somewhat ambiguous. Granted that exhorting individuals to tackle the issue frontally and opt for blackness, in order to avoid playing the historical and contemporary ambiguity card—that is, "not allowing their color to be lost in the ambiguity shuffle"—was an important campaign. But how would it fundamentally shift individual and societal predisposition toward what Dárien Davis (1999) has characterized as the tendency to opt out of blackness when and where other options exist?

A hotly debated issue in Brazil today is the establishment of affirmative action policies, particularly in higher education. Helio Santos, rapporteur of the Interministerial Group created in 1995 by President Fernando Henrique Cardoso, has noted that in Brazil many social scientists have spoken favorably in support of "quotas" for the poor and that affirmative action has been described as "quotas." Santos emphasized that Black Movement members do not want radical quotas, which, he noted, already exist for all whites. In his view, affirmative action for Blacks is a matter of Brazilian society paying its debts to the Black population. Drawing attention to Brazil's obligations under international treaties such as the Inter-American Commission for Human Rights, Santos observed, would be a helpful reminder to the Brazilian government of its obligation to guarantee the full exercise of rights contained in the Inter-American Convention. Full rights and equality under the law was necessary. The government should include an international conceptualization of racism in the laws of Brazil. National and international conventions pertaining to human life and access to social goods and the protection of Blacks should become public policy.[2] Fernando Henrique Cardoso contributed to the discussion by noting that the problem with "quotas" and affirmative action was "racial hypocrisy" and the difficulties of fighting against what was not publicly acknowledged. He argued that it was necessary to consider both race and class. In some circles in Brazil, it was considered unpatriotic to bring up the racial question in public. He pointed out that the Foreign Ministry, or Itamaraty, was beginning to have Black diplomats and that there was a "*negro*"—not a mulatto—colonel in the office of the President.[3]

The complexity of the debate over affirmative action is illustrated by the fact that at one time the president of the Supreme Court fully endorsed affirmative action, noting that the Brazilian state had a responsibility to provide for the social well-being and equality of all Brazilians (2003). Similarly, Paulo Renato Souza, minister of education in the Cardoso government, who had publicly expressed his opposition while minister, observes that it was necessary to avoid offering "false solutions to Brazil's problems."[4] In 2002 the state government of Rio de Janeiro designated special "quotas" for Afrodescendentes in the state universities. Economist Roberto Borges Martins pointed to the increased attention being devoted to racial matters by the Brazilian government and the media both sectors were speaking forcefully in favor of affirmative action. In response to the argument about the difficulties in designating affirmative action initiatives, for example, Borges Martins noted that in the past there did not appear to be such difficulties on the part of both state and society in targeting or identifying the discriminated.

On the other side of the affirmative action divide, however, Solicitor General Geraldo Brindero appealed to the Supreme Federal Tribunal to declare the state of Rio de Janeiro's "affirmative action" initiatives to be unconstitutional. He argued that all students should have an equal right to compete for university places. The "formidable" extent of miscegenation, a Brazilian trademark, should be honored (*Estado de São Paulo*, 28/16/03).

Similarly, Minister of Education Cristovam Buarque (2003–2004) has noted, "Quotas will not resolve the problems of inequality." Hence he is against instituting quotas that impact on race or color but not class, which, he argues, is the biggest hurdle in Brazil (*Estado de São Paulo*, 19/3/2003). Indeed, all the ministers of education have pronounced themselves to be against any kind of affirmative action policies that focus exclusively on race, while claiming not to be against affirmative action per se. Again, complicating the problem is the fact that, in Brazil, the concepts of "affirmative action" and "quotas" are used interchangeably.

Afrodescendente intellectuals and scholars, such as Muniz Sodré (1999:259), have made another case for affirmative action, noting that there is a certain lack of candor in confronting racial inequalities in Brazil. Sodré argues that combating racism intellectually is not sufficient. While naming it publicly is desirable, such recognition does not control its advance. Various subtle forms of racism continue to multiply.

> Political democracy and economic mobility by themselves cannot overcome racial discrimination. Hence the euphoric media images of emerging Black middle-class consumers in both the USA and Brazil have to be considered with grains of salt; they merely hint at the end of racism, when in practice strategic discourses for reconstruction of the identities in economic and cultural terms have to be confronted. (Ibid., 263)

As Luiz Alberto, the federal deputy from Bahia has commented in relation to the Brazilian race relations conundrum, the transnational context is relevant for Brazil (*Jornal do Brasil*, 14/1/2001). Race relations are not just a Black problem, they are a national problem. The effects of neoliberalism have to be fought and the issues of affirmative action and indemnities have to be confronted by the society as a whole.

At the same time as the Foreign Ministry is touting its racially based scholarship program, a scholar of Brazilian international relations, Maria Regina Soares, has discussed the changes that Itamaraty had to undergo to keep up with globalization, without once mentioning the significance of racial demographics in this process and the consequent need for the ministry to adopt new recruitment modes that reflect this new international context.[5] Elisa Larkin Nascimento (2003, 383–387) has pointed out that Blacks as people have become incorporated into human rights and citizenship discourses without the racial continuity and "blind spot" disappearing. There is, in fact, a double blind spot on the part of the dominant Brazilian society within which domination is exercised (unconsciously) and at the same time any initiatives on the part of the "dominated" are characterized as manifestations of "reverse racism." By her assessment, a feature of the Brazilian race relations order is the "deafricanization" of Blacks; racial mixture will ultimately produce "o branco visual," the *visual white*.

Seth Racusen (2002) has shown the ways that personhood, race, the mobilization of the law, honor, and the matter of redressing acts of discrimination intersect and produce unintended results (see also Mallon, 1996; Martínez-Echazábal, 1996). Racusen's meticulous discussion raises complex problems as the very title of his dissertation, "A Mulatto Cannot Be Prejudiced," suggests. He observes that in the United States advocates for the introduction of a "multiracial" category have often claimed that Brazil's flexible color identity is a "more natural" model for organizing identity because it offers an opportunity for "choice," and he wonders about the reality of such choice in view of the general stigma attached to blackness (364). Brazilians looking north and North Americans looking south can learn much from the exchange, but there is little to be emulated in either direction, he argues. "Brazilian 'color blindness' cannot simply be declared as a destination reached" (2002:364).

The Elusive Meaning of Blackness in Brazil

Over the last several years Brazil has been increasingly characterized both in government and popular venues, as well as in academic studies (Andrews, 1993; do Nascimento and Larkin Nascimento, 1992 and 2001) and Black Movement discourses, as the country with the second largest population of Black people/people of African descent in the world, after Nigeria. However, this trend does not automatically clarify the persistent definitional or conceptual problem in Brazilian race relations discourses: who is Black in Brazil? If, according to both scholarly and popular discussions, uniform agreement on the answer to the question has never existed, it is worth asking whether the assignment of Brazil to the second position after Nigeria ultimately ends up conflating both definition and indefinition. After all, on the one hand, what makes Brazil "Brazil" is the possibility it offers its residents to define themselves in multiple ways; on the other hand, in a country in which blackness remains undefined and largely unacknowledged, how is it possible to affirm that it contains the second largest population of Blacks? Far from being a simple characterization of Brazilian society, the assertion in fact has a number of important political implications, both nationally and transnationally. If generalized claiming of African descent is, in fact, symptomatic of a major paradigm shift, then its transformation into political action, political participation, and the potential emergence of a constituency in Brazil's foreign relations, especially relations with Africa, would herald an unprecedented development. A shift of this magnitude could contribute significantly to providing fresh insights into the domestic and external permutations of Brazilian race relations. If, suddenly, claiming African descent has actually become fashionable, does this in turn also signal the abandonment of the ambiguities about Africa and blackness that have long characterized Brazil's multiple and often contradictory race relations discourses?

At the time of this writing, not even the most generous interpretation of the remarkable emergence of Afro-Brazilian political activism in recent years could assign a modicum of influence to any sectors of the Afro-Brazilian population in the matter of Brazil's relations with contemporary independent Africa. Neither impressive re-creations of historical Africana, nor religious-cultural manifestations, nor "Africanesque" modes of dressing directly address this issue. It is not a question of identifying arcane African linguistic patterns, liturgical practices, and dance steps—all of which lie along the slippery road to further hairsplitting about the "real" Africa in Brazil. Symbolic Africa as imagined or lived in religious and cultural settings has been recognized in both academic and popular discourses as significant, not just among Afro-Brazilians in Brazil but within the broader society, irrespective of racial governance.

A distinction, however, has to be made between the representation of symbolic Africa and the political significance of contemporary Africa in Brazilian life and society. The import of this distinction for international relations is the possibility of generating a new consciousness of Africa, which is not hostage to interesting but questionable debates about liturgical priorities, authenticity, and nationalization of Africana in Brazil (Dzidzienyo, 2002).

A brief look at the response of state agencies to Afro-Brazilian activism reveals the ways that official agencies, which once focused solely on Afro-Brazilians in the Brazilian polity, are now increasingly playing a role in the entry of Afro-Brazilians into the international arena. The Fundação Cultural Palmares, an official entity within the Ministry of Culture, has the mandate of articulating and supporting the historical and present contributions of people of African descent in Brazil. Part of its responsibility is to secure titles to lands now designated as historical spaces, which had once been inhabited by descendants of slaves who had established these places of refuge. Legalizing their tenancy would provide security from the threats of dispossession by the landowners. The ultimate objective is to empower African-descended Brazilians to exercise their citizenship rights within the political, economic, and social structures of Brazil, and also to overcome racial discrimination. Consciousness-raising for the whole nation implies becoming aware of commitments such as March 21, the international recognition and celebration of the International Day Against Racial Discrimination (Lindgren Alves, 2002).

The program of preparations for the Durban 2001 conference on race led to a period of intense activity on the part of the Palmares Foundation. Afro-Brazilians participated in both national and international gatherings charged with developing a common agenda for the Durban conference. The sheer number of Afro-Brazilians involved in such meetings, and of those who ultimately went to Durban, points to a dramatic increase in Afro-Brazilians/Afro-descendants conspicuously involved domestically and internationally in Brazilian public discussions about race relations and society at the present time (Dzidzienyo, 1991).

What accounts for this development? To answer this question adequately we must re-visit earlier international gatherings and the misadventures therein.

In 1966 Abdias do Nascimento and his Teatro Experimental do Negro were excluded from the Brazilian delegation to the First Festival of Black Arts and Culture, held in Dakar, Senegal. Transnationalizing the issue, Nascimento sent an open letter to the gathering, thereby ensuring that participants became informed of an alternative Afro-Brazilian reality. The point here was not that Afro-Brazilians were totally absent. It was much more the circumscribed nature of Afro-Brazilian representation.

Nothing in 1966 could have prepared either Brazilians or those gathered in Nigeria for the Second Festival of Black Arts and Culture in 1977 for the inseparability of the national and the broader international context within which the drama was played out. This time, the government delegation succeeded in keeping Abdias do Nascimento (at the time, a visiting professor in Nigeria) from presenting a paper on race and education in Brazil. Moreover, it went to the extent of casting Abdias as frustrated and unrepresentative of Afro-Brazilian views. But as irony would have it, a Nigerian newspaper serialized the entire paper that Abdias had prepared, thereby making the controversial discussion of Brazilian race relations accessible to a far wider audience. What might have been conceptualized as a preemptive measure to contain a particularly troublesome kind of Afro-Brazilian radicalism became the subject of a very public and unexpectedly critical discussion of Brazilian race relations.

The unexpected consequences of globalization have not always produced practical results for Brazil's Afro-descendants. Abdias do Nascimento's reflections on the need for institution building by the Black Movement are particularly apt: gains should never be centered on the achievements of one person, as that person's absence would ensure the disappearance of those gains.

Nevertheless, what characterizes Afro-Braziliana today is the impressive dynamism of discourses, publications, and debates, which have brought to prominence the issue of Afro-Brazilians within Brazilian society. The first of Bacelar and Caroso's two volumes on the fifth Afro-Brazilian Congress, held in 1998, offered a suggestive title: *Brasil, um pais de negros?* (1999). In the same year, Darien Davis's *Avoiding the Dark: Essays on Race and the Forging of National Culture in Modern Brazil* (1999) drew attention to the tensions surrounding Blacks and blackness in Brazilian national life. Kabenguele Munanga (1999) offered insightful comments on the ongoing tension between Brazilian national identity and black identity.

Publication of the anthology *Tirando a mascara* (Guimarães and Huntley, 2000) heralded a new stage in Brazilian race relations by removing the mask that hid the "realities" of racial discrimination and racist practices which Afro-Brazilian activists had been railing against for a long time. If in 1977 even the respected weekly magazine *Veja* had refused to publish an article on Blacks by one of its own respected journalists, by 2000 *Veja* was covering race-related matters with some frequency (Fontaine, 1980).[6]

Concluding Thoughts

Of what relevance is the discussion offered here to the question of Black-Latino relations in the United States? Technically Brazilians are not part of the Latino community; however, Brazil's prominence in the discourse on race relation worldwide, and its position within Latin America, guarantee it a special niche. Brazilian migration to the United States, and to the other countries of Latin America, has resulted inevitably in an interfacing of Brazilian and other Latin (Spanish) American race relations orders and practices. The Brazilian racial pluriverse and the complexities of Brazilian discourses about racial matters, which range from circumstances in the past to increasing public recognition and articulation of fault lines, and even more important, official efforts to come to terms with histories and practices of racialization and racial exclusion, provide an important guide for the way Black-Latino relations evolve in the United States. The benefits of Brazilian discussions on the intersections of race, color, gender, and language have the potential of contributing to new configurations of nation, society, racialization, and pan-Blackness (Monteiro, 2001). How Brazilians relate specifically to these issues and to the multinational Latino community remains to be seen. In the meantime, there is much to be gained from paying attention to transformations in the interfacing of the Brazilian and Afro-Brazilian societies.

For Brazilians in the United States, there are likely to be surprises of a different kind. In the first place, the sheer numbers of Black travelers they see at airports will be unusual for them, not because Blacks are not seen at airports in Brazil but Blacks in U.S. airports are not merely part of the workforce, usually at the lower levels. The interpretation of this visual imagery will depend on the "background" of Brazilians, that is, "Black Brazilians," or those who are visibly black, even if they are classified as something else, might discover a certain space for the expression of solidarity with African Americans and other Blacks. They might also find a direct connection to Latinos whose racial-color spectrum will be familiar. For that reason, then, identifying with "Latinos" is one option, depending on phenotype or a desire to connect to Latinidad or Latin American roots. For whiter Brazilians, the surprise might be the conditions under which they see Blacks in public spaces. Coming from a country with spaces traditionally considered to be the preserve of "whites," a certain readjustment of vision they may require (Boaventura Leite, 1996). Also, if their "whiteness" is not immediately perceptible to the eye, no amount of insistence on Brazilian color flexibilities and categorizations will be enough to absent them from U.S. race relations patterns. Consigning such individuals to a nonwhite (Latino?) category could be seen as either an affront to personal dignity or an opportunity to seek solidarity with non-Black Latinos.

Imposed categorization can result in the formation of new associations based on common nationality. Brazilians, particularly those who are aware of recent developments in race relations in their home country, may contribute important insights to the ongoing discussions of the boundaries and meanings of race relations and blackness; indeed, they may see more clearly the importance of differentiating between idealized national images and day-to-day realities of Black life (Sheriff, 2001). Far from imposing so-called foreign models or solutions on cherished national assets, comparative analysis, informed by direct experience of race relations in North America, might effectively deepen discussions of the nature and consequences of hemispheric encounters within the United States (Sansone, 2003). The prospect of a more robust politicization transnationally is at best uncertain, given the history and context of race and racialization in the United States. There can be no guarantee that the elasticities of either Brazilian or Latin American definitions of race will necessarily trump the corresponding rigidity common in North America; after all, the privileging of whiteness and the denigrating of blackness remain salient throughout the Americas (Pinheiro, 2000). What is new, perhaps, is the more visible challenge to this order that the U.S. encounter provides. Distinct possibilities can emerge for Brazilians and Afro-Brazilians to take a fresh look at Brazil (Mitchell, 2000; Medeiros, 1998).

It is not a matter of putting aside the ideals of mixture and indefinition or of becoming North Americans in order to combat racism, as some have said (Vianna, 1999:117). Nor is it a lack of acknowledgment of the visible changes in the composition of ministers of the Brazilian republic as Jorge da Silva (2001) and Roberto Freire (2003) have noted—that is, the reality of miscegenation is not reflected in the institutions of the republic. President Luiz Ignacio Lula da Silva's government has a record number of "Afro-descended" ministers and there is even a Secretariat for Racial Equality (Raça Brasil, 2003).

As Miriam Leitão (2004) recently observed, the argument that affirmative action is polemical because of its U.S. origins is not a convincing one. Affirmative action does not imply abandoning poor whites with regard to determining who stands to benefit from it: "Everybody knows, from police officers to doormen and employers." Hence, the sudden concern about the difficulties of "identifying individuals" is only part of the story. Interactions in the United States will quickly highlight an old Brazilian problem; that is, the very concept of what Turra and Venturi (1995) have called "cordial racism" might not travel well outside of Brazil. Herein lies a chance for rethinking Brazil, Afro-Brazil, and the U.S. Black–Latino relations and possible contributions of Brazilians to new ideas and discourses, to the benefit of all.

Notes

1. November 20, 1695, is the date that Zumbi, the Black national hero of Palmares, the largest Quilombo or refugee community of freed and runaway slaves, is believed to have died.

2. Helio Santos is a leading Afro-Brazilian university professor (São Paulo) who served as the coordinator of the Interministerial Group appointed by the government after public recognition of a racial "problem" by President Fernando Henrique Cardoso.

3. See Roberto Pompeu Toledo (1998:30–34). Quoted in the booklet *A construindo a democracia racial* (1998), which contains a record of initiatives, including the official recognition of November 20 as the National Day of Black Consciousness, the documents establishing interministerial working groups, the international seminar on Multiculturalism and Racism, and the role of affirmative action.

4. See *O Estado de São Paulo*, 28/6/03. See also *O Globo*, 20/6/03, p. 6. See also Roberto Borges Martins, "Affirmative Action and the Quest for Racial Justice in Brazil" (2003).

5. For a more direct criticism, see "Parlamentario negro acusa política externa de hipocrata," *A Tribuna Santos* (São Paulo), 28/5/83. See also Agremiro Procorpio, "O Itamaraty é racista," *Veja*, 15/6/1994, p. 142.

6. See two cover feature editions of: *Veja* "Do preconceito ao sucesso: A discriminação racial vista por quem venceu a barreira e chegou a la," 18/8/1999; and "A classe media Negra: advogados, professores, medicos, vendedores, empresários, Já são 8 milhões e movimentam 50 bilhoes de reais pon ano," 18/8/1999.

References

Andrews, George Reid. 1992. Racial inequality in Brazil and the United States: A statistical comparison. *Journal of Social History* 26 (1): 229–261.

Bacelar, Jefferson, and Carlos Caroso, eds. 1998. *Brasil, um país de negros?* Rio de Janeiro: Pallas Editora e Distribuidora.

Barbosa Gomes, Joaquim. 2001. *Ação Afirmativa e princípio constitucional da igualdade*. Rio de Janeiro and São Paulo: Renovar.

Boaventura Leite, Ilka, ed. 1996. *Negros no sul do Brasil: Invisibilidade e territorialidade*. Ilhae Santa Catarina/S.C.: Letras Contemporâneas.

Bourdieu, Pierre, and Loic J. D. Wacquant. 1999. On the cunning of imperialist reason. *Theory, Culture, and Society* 16 (1): 41–58.

Caetano, Miriam Expedita, and Henrique Cunha. 1992. Afro-Brazil: The Black Movement and community education. In *Community Education in the Third World*, ed. Cyril Poster and Jurgen Zimmer. London: Routledge, 84–90.

Chor Maio, Marcos. 1996. O projeto UNESCO e a agenda dasciencias sociais no Brasil dos anos 40 e 50. *Revista Brasileira de Ciencias Sociais* 140 (41):141–158.

Chor Maio, and Ricardo Santos, eds. 1996. *Raça, ciência e sociedade*. Rio de Janeiro: Editora Fiocruz, 107–124.

Crook, Larry, and Randal Johnson, eds. 1999. *Black Brazil, Culture, Identity, and Social Mobilization*. Los Angeles: UCLA Latin American Center Publication.

D'Adesky, Jacques. 1996. Pluralismo etnico e multiculturalismo: Racismo e anti-racismo no Brasil. Ph.D. diss., University of São Paulo.

da Silva, Jorge. 2001. Discrimination of Afro-Brazilians Naturalized. Paper presented at the workshop Race and Blackness in the Americas: Contemporary Perspectives. Providence, R.I.: Brown University.

———. 1994. *Direitos civis e relações raciais no Brasil*. Rio de Janeiro: Luam.

———. 1998. *Violência e racismo no Rio de Janeiro*. Rio de Janeiro: Eduff.

Davis, Darien. 1999. *Avoiding the Dark: Essays on Race and the Forging of National Culture in Modern Brazil*. Ashgate, Brookfield, USA, Singapore, and Sydney: Aldershot.

do Nascimento, Abdias. 2002. *O Brasil na mira do Pan Africanismo: O genocídio do negro brasileiro sitiado em Lagos*. 2nd ed. Salvador: EDUFBA/CEAP.

do Nascimento, Abdias, and Elisa Larkin Nascimento. 1992. *Africans in Brazil: A Pan-African Perspective.* Trenton, NJ: Africa World Press.

―――. 2001. Dance of deception: A reading of race relations in Brazil. In *Beyond Racism: Race and Inequality in Brazil, South Africa, and the United States,* ed. Charles Hamilton et al. Boulder and London: Lynne Reinner Publishers.

dos Santos, Ivanir. 2001. A exportação da mentira: O estado brasileiro investiu na propaganda do mito do país das relações étnicas. *Jornal do Brasil,* July 3.

Dzidzienyo, Anani. 1991. Afro-Brasileiros no contexto nacionale internacional. In *Desigualdade racial no Brasil contemporâneo,* ed. Peggy A. Lovell. Belo Horizonte: Editora 34 Ltda.

―――. 1993. Brazilian race relations studies: Old problems, new ideas? *Humboldt Journal of Social Relations* 19 (2):109–129.

―――. 1995. Conclusions. In *No Longer Invisible: Afro-Latin Americans Today.* London: Minority Rights Group.

―――. 2002. Triangular mirrors and moving colonialisms. *Etnografica* 6 (1):127–140.

Fontaine, Pierre Michel. 1980. Research in the political economy of Afro-Latin America. *Latin American Research Review* 15 (2):111–141.

French, John. 2000. The missteps of anti-imperialist reason: Bourdieu, Wacquants and Hanchard's "Orpheus and Power." *Theory, Culture, and Society* 17 (1): 107–129.

Fry, Peter. 2000. Politics, nationality, and the meanings of "race" in Brazil. In Brazil: The burden of the past, the promise of the future. Special issue, *Daedalus* 129, no. 2 (Spring):83–118.

Grin, Monica. 2001. Ação afirmativa e ajustas normativas. *Novos estudos CEBRAP* 59 (March):172–192.

Guimarães, Antonio Sérgio. 1999. *Racismo e anti-racismo no Brasil.* São Paulo: Editora 34 Ltd.

―――. 2003. Racial democracy.

―――. 2002. *Classes, raças e democracia.* São Paulo: Editora 34 Ltd.

―――. 2001. The misadventures of nonracialism in Brazil. In *Race and Inequality in Brazil, South Africa, and the United States,* ed. Charles Hamilton et al. Boulder, CO: Lynne Rienner Publishers.

Guimarães, Antonio Sérgio, and Lynn Huntley, eds. 2000. *Tirando a mascara: Ensaios sobre o racismo no Brasil.* São Paulo: Editora Paz e Terra.

Hanchard, Michael. 1994. *Orpheus and Power: The Movimento Negro of Rio de Janeiro and São Paulo Brazil, 1945–1988.* Princeton, NJ: Princeton University Press.

―――, ed. 1999. *Racial Politics in Contemporary Brazil.* Durham, NC: Duke University Press.

Larkin Nascimento, Elisa. 2003. *O sortilégio da côr: Identidade, raça e genero no Brasil.* São Paulo: Negro Edições.

Leitão, Miriam. 2004. Preto no branco do problema racial. *Diário de São Paulo,* February 8.

Lindgren Alves, J. A. 2002. A conferência de Durban contra o rascismo e a responsibilidade de todos. *Revista Brasileira de Política Internacional* 45 (22):198–223.

Mallon, Florencia A. 1996. Constructing mestizaje in Latin America: Authenticity, marginality and gender in the claiming of ethnic identities. *Journal of Latin American Anthropology* 2 (1):170–181.

Martínez-Echazábal, Lourdes. 1996. O culturalismo dos anos 30 no Brasil e na América Latina: Deslocamento retórico ou mudança de conceituação? In *Raça, ciência e sociedade,* ed. Marcos Chor Maio and Ricardo Ventura Santos. Rio de Janeiro: Editora Fiocruz.

Marx, Anthony. 1998. *Making Race and Nation: A Comparison of the United States, South Africa, and Brazil.* New York: Cambridge University Press.

Medeiros, Carlos Alberto. 2003. Legislação e relações raciais Brasil–Estados Unidos, 1950–2003: Uma visão comparativa. Master's thesis, Universidade Federal Fluminense, Rio de Janeiro.

―――. 1998. Lideranças do Movimento Negro no Rio de Janeiro. *Caderno de depoimentos.* Rio de Janeiro: CIEC.

Mitchell, Michael. 2000. *Building Democracy in Brazil?: Constitutional Foundations for Anti-Discrimination Law.* Washington, DC: NCOBPS.

Monteiro, Jorge Aparecida. 2001. *O empresario negro: Historias de vida e trajetória de sucesso em busca da afirmação racial.* Rio de Janeiro: Editorial Produto Independente.

Munanga, Kabenguele. 1999. *Rediscutindo a mestiçagem no Brasil: Identidade nacional versus identidade negra.* Petrópolis: Editora Vozes.

———. 1986. *Negritude: Usos e sentidos.* São Paulo: Atíca.

Murilo de Carvalho, José. 2000. Dreams come untrue. In Brazil: Burden of the past, promise of the future. Special issue, *Daedalus* 129, no. 2 (Spring):57–82.

Nobles, Melissa. 2000. *Shades of Citizenship: Race and the Census in Modern Politics.* Stanford, CA: Stanford University Press.

Nogueira, Oracy. 1985. *Tanto preto quando branco: Estudo de relações raciales.* São Paulo: T. A. Quieroz.

O Brasil racista. Pesquisa exclusiva mostra que o brasileiro admite o preconceito. 1996. *Isto é* 4 September 4.

Pinheiro, Paulo Sergio. 2000. Democratic governance, violence and the (un)rule of law. In Brazil: burden of the past, promise of the future. Special issue, *Daedalus* 129, no. 2 (Spring):119–141.

Pompeu Toledo, Roberto. 1998. *O presidente segundo o sociologo.* São Paulo: Companhia das Letras.

Racusen, Seth. 2002. A mulatto cannot be prejudiced: The legal construction of racial discrimination in contemporary Brazil. Ph.D. diss., Massachusetts Institute of Technology.

Reichmann, Rebecca, ed. 1999. *Race in Contemporary Brazil: From Indifference to Identity.* University Park, PA: Pennsylvania State University Press.

Rufino dos Santos, Joel. 1988. IPCN e cacique de Ramos: Dois, exemples de movimento negro na cidade do Rio de Janeiro. *Comunecações do ISER* 7 (2):5–20.

Sansone, Livio. 2003. *Blackness Without Ethnicity.* New York: Palgrave Macmillan.

———. 2000. From Africa to Afro: Use and abuse of Africa in Brazil. Paper presented at annual meeting of the Latin American Studies Association, Miami, FL.

Sim temos ministros. 2003. *Raça Brasil* 77 (November–December):50.

Sheriff, Robin D. 2001. *Dreaming Equality: Color, Race, and Racism in Urban Brazil.* Piscataway, NJ: Rutgers University Press.

Skidmore, Thomas E. 2000. Themes and methodologies in the current study of Brazilian race relations. Paper prepared for the 50th International Congress of Americanistas, Warsaw, Poland.

Sodré, Muniz. 1999. *Claros e escuros: Identidade, poro e midia no Brasil.* Petropolis: Editora Vozes.

Turra, Cleusa, and Gustavo Venturi, eds. 1995. *Racismo cordial: A mais completa analise sobre o preconceito de cor no Brasil.* São Paulo: Editora Atica.

Vianna, Hermano. 1999. *The Mystery of Samba: Popular Music and National Identity in Brazil.* Edited and translated by Charles Chasteen. Chapel Hill and London: University of North Carolina Press.

Vidal Porto, Alexandre. 2001. Racismo brasileiro, sim. *Jornal do Brasil,* July 3.

Viotti da Costa, Emilia. 2000. *The Brazilian Empire: Myths and Histories.* Revised edition. Chapel Hill and London: University of North Carolina Press.

Wade, Peter. 1997. *Race and Ethnicity in Latin America.* London: Pluto Press.

Winndance Twine, France. 2001. *Racism in a Racial Democracy: The Maintenance of White Supremacy in Brazil.* Piscataway, NJ: Rutgers University Press.

PART 3
THE POLITICS OF RACIALIZATION IN THE UNITED STATES

CHAPTER 8

FRAMING THE DISCUSSION OF AFRICAN AMERICAN–LATINO RELATIONS: A REVIEW AND ANALYSIS

John J. Betancur

This chapter studies African American–Latino relations in the United States. Drawing on existing literature, it examines their nature, dimensions, and methodological questions while, at the same time, advancing some proposals. Still in its infancy, the study of African American–Latino relations has profited from its white–African American counterpart. At the same time, it has reflected the shortcomings of that debate and construct. Forecasts estimate that minorities will constitute around 50 percent of the U.S. population in the year 2050 (McLeod, 1996). A large recent inflow of migrants from the Third World is already altering U.S. racial dynamics deeply. Under these circumstances, the discussion assumes an increasing role and urgency in the construction of more desirable relations. The following is an attempt in that direction.

Methodological Questions Associated with the Analysis of Latino–African American Relations

Like majority-minority relations, African American–Latino relations may have gone through different stages and assumed different forms. Research needs to determine them and to establish possible variations related to the circumstances in which African Americans and Latinos came together, the nature of the specific groups involved, and the role of whites in each particular case. In what follows, we point to some of the methodological questions for research emerging from the literature.

First, analysis has to pay attention to the fact that racism and race relations operate in specific environments and sociopolitical contexts and thus are subject to multiple variations. Factors such as location, mix, and makeup of groups, histories, group size, time and conditions of entry, intensity of interactions and community building can produce different outcomes as can experiences that Latinos bring from their home countries, the timing of their immigration, the nationalities and classes involved in the mix, and their level and forms of incorporation into the U.S. economy.[1] Dynamics differ, for instance, according to who is the numerical majority, who is the most organized and in what terms, and the role of each group in the local economy.

A different but equally important second issue is the reductionism often involved in characterizations of racial groups as monolithic formations. In contrast, intragroup differences can include multiple "races,"[2] cultures, religions, and languages among others. Thus, generalizations referring to Latino–African American relations as including all Latinos and all African Americans are terribly misleading. For instance, relations between African American and Latino elites can vary significantly from relations between their grassroots (Sales and Bush, 1997; Bonilla and Stafford, 2000). Hence, there is a need to identify the specific segments involved and all other differentiating factors.

A third issue has to do with the ways in which racial formations "are tied to particular labor, political, and class relations" (Chang and Diaz-Veizades, 1999: 138; Jaynes, 2000). Different industries have recruited different national or racial groups, at various times, for particular locations/economies or have segregated them by occupation, often generating crowded labor enclaves of exclusion. Charlie LeDuff (2000) illustrates this around the Smithfield Packing Co. near Chapel Hill. There, racial groups break by occupation/pay and residence into a highly differentiated social order converging at the workplace, yet kept socially and economically separate. In this case, employers and the housing market primarily dictate their relationships. Thus, conflict or collaboration may have more to do with the roles that each group has been made to play in the socioeconomic system and in particular localities than with the groups' choices. Employer preference for one group over the other (e.g., Latinos over African Americans in Chicago; see Tienda and Stier, 1996), or local white–African American or white-Latino coalitions that exclude the other minority, may have serious long-term impacts on African American–Latino relations.

Fourth is the role of whites and white–African American relations in the construction of Latino–African American relations. European Americans have had the upper hand even in the determination of interminority relations. Thomas Nakayama (2002:96), for instance, argues that the construction of Asians as the model minority is used to defend the allegedly unbiased character of our institutions and "tends to deflect attention away from the social and structural constraints that lead to inequality in the U.S." Similarly, referring to the role of New York's media in the Korean–African American conflict in that city, Edward Chang and Jeannette Diaz-Veizades (1999:73) argue, "By focusing on the Korean–American conflict, the white establishment is disguising the real issue of institutional racism and racial inequality in America." This is not to say that whites act as a monolithic group either. However, systemic factors give them collective advantage regardless of their individual perceptions or actions.

Fifth is the question of race and class. In spite of a tremendous overlapping between low class and minority condition, Latinos and African Americans break also by class and engage in intracommunity class relations. Whether relationships are controlled by middle or lower classes in each of the groups can bear different dynamics related to the dominant class element in the relationship at stake.

Approaches to the Study of African American–Latino Relations

For much of the twentieth century, the classical immigration-assimilation paradigm of the Chicago School dominated the discussion of race relations in the United States. The School looks at group relations as reflective of their degrees of assimilation. Allegedly, as immigrants progress from the traits of the home country toward Americanization, they achieve structural assimilation. Hence, like Europeans, in due time minorities will become like the white majority (Park, 1950; Gordon, 1964; Glazer, 1971). African American–Latino relations thus would follow the same dynamics and trends of any group in the mobility queue. However, the experiences of African Americans and other minority immigrants (immigrants from former colonies) have differed radically from those of Europeans (Blauner, 1969; Barrera, 1979; Acuña, 1988). Hence, addressing African American–Latino relations in terms of queues or processes of competition, accommodation, and assimilation is an unwarranted reductionism.

A second approach, derived from the study of African American–Korean relations, and perhaps applicable to successful Latino businesses—for example, Cubans in Miami—is the middleman theory (Chang, 1990; Light and Bonacich, 1988). As Korean merchants enter African American areas, a relationship emerges between them and their local customers. Marginalized by racism and lacking the resources to get into businesses even in their own communities, African Americans see Korean merchants as a symbol of what they have been denied and direct their hostility at them. Korean merchants are viewed as "middlemen," " 'outsiders' who are ripping . . . or exploiting the African American community" (Chang and Diaz-Veizades, 1999:52). Claire Kim (2000:76) claims that this approach "spares elites . . . from direct challenge," and criticizes it for its "crude determinism and neglect of strategic and purposive agency." Certainly, it is restricted to interminority relations involving a merchant customer relationship, a situation not typical of African American–Latino encounters.

Third is the rational action approach (Kim, 2000:77). This perspective assumes that, as rational actors, participants in race relations engage in "preference-maximization and cost benefit analysis." The approach explains collective action by the benefits of participation. Kim argues that, while including purposive agency, the approach is reductionist and "too abstract and decontextualized to apply to real life collective action." Meanwhile, it fails to consider not-so-rational factors such as feelings, contagion, solidarity, racism, following of leaders, or simple habit.

Kim (2000:77) proposes the concept of strategic agency of social movement scholars. In her approach, action is socially embedded "or shaped by the actors' specific social location, community context, and collective identity and belief." This approach places action in its historical and structural context and allows for consideration of factors such as class, identity, momentum, experience, perception, and history. Along with this, we suggest considering the dialectics between individuals and groups and between rationality and irrationality, external provocation, and mediating circumstances.

These approaches have not been tested systematically. Most of them assume self-determination and the same agency on the part of minorities and whites. Studies should give serious consideration to the insights tying class and race of authors like

Mario Barrera (1979), Rodolfo Acuña (1988), and Robert Blauner (1969). It is important to examine African American–Latino relations in their historical moment, context, and specific dynamics while taking into consideration systemic factors, individual and collective experiences, class, and local variations.

Main Issues and Findings from the Literature

The academic literature includes very limited research directly or explicitly dedicated to the discussion of African American–Latino relations. The earliest work we identified dates back to the late 1970s. The media has addressed the topic most frequently within a sensationalist tone of conflict. General African American or Latino literatures provide relevant elements. Overall, the topic is largely unexplored, ranging from vague generalities to limited local cases. This section addresses major issues emerging from the literature.

African American–Latino relations take place in a highly constrained context and are determined by structural conditions over which the actors have little control. In this sense, the primary question has to do with their ability to relate as two independent subjects. This question is not addressed thoroughly in the literature.

Studies of Miami (Grenier and Pérez, 1996; Perez-Stable and Uriarte, 1993), Los Angeles (Bozorgmehr, Sabagh, and Light, 1996; Chang and Diaz-Veizades, 1999), Chicago (Betancur and Gills, 2000; Betancur, Córdova, and Torres, 1993), Washington (Manning, 1996), Philadelphia (Whalen, 2000), and New York (Binder and Reimers, 1996; Bonilla and Stafford, 2000) suggest variations related to factors such as context, circumstances of encounters, nationality, group size, past experiences, level of diversity, time, condition, class, economic incorporation, organization, and the actions of the white majority.

In Miami the immigration of the middle and upper classes of Cuba took place at exactly the time when civil rights gains promised African Americans economic and political gains. Aided by U.S. policies never available to African Americans in the same scope and largesse, Cuban refugees pulled ahead in a relatively short time, frustrating the aspirations of African Americans. As a result, the general context became one of bitterness, separation, and contestation—courtesy of national geopolitics.

In Los Angeles relations have changed over time. Following the civil rights movement, African Americans were able to carve out important positions in local politics and institutions before Latinos. The recent, dramatic growth of Latinos led to intense conflicts around political representation, multiculturalism in schools, use of English in public matters, distribution of affirmative action goods (Horton, 1989). Originally, Mexicans had been the only Latinos. Most recently, a flood of very low-income Central Americans and a growing South American migration have made the community much more diverse and complex. Introductions of new players and issues, and changes in proportions, have had a tremendous impact on African American–Latino relations. Now, the same "minority" pie has to feed more mouths and has to be distributed in new ways. Edward T. Chang and Jeannette Diaz-Veizades

(1999:110) point to the difficulty of reconciling "Latinos' demand for equal representation and the African American's feeling of displacement" in Los Angeles.

For the city of Washington (Manning, 1996), two new factors, the move from a biracial city in which African Americans were the only minority to a multicultural metropolis including Latinos and Asians and the correspondence between the recent dramatic growth of Latinos and the decline of African Americans, have brought out latent tensions in new ways. As most Latino newcomers are low-income refugees, the struggle for scarce unskilled jobs, affordable housing, and social services has intensified conflicts with African Americans. In turn, the tenuous immigrant status of Central Americans has made their situation desperate, adding to the potential for conflict with their most direct and visible "competition," African Americans.

In New York relations between African Americans and Latinos (predominantly Puerto Ricans and Dominicans but increasingly Colombians and Mexicans) have not been smooth. Limited to the worst areas and in constrained competition for the scarce opportunities available to them, African Americans and Latinos have clashed particularly around electoral politics and control of strategic institutions. Similarly, the outcome of a civil rights era focused on assistance to the African American community left Puerto Ricans angry and doubly marginalized (Barbaro, 1977). Skirmishes between Latino and African American leaders—especially over political and affirmative action—have become a common feature.

The impact of contention between Latino and African American elites is significant. Research in New York (Sales and Bush, 1997; Bonilla and Stafford, 2000) and in Chicago (Betancur and Gills, 2000) identified different experiences in Latino–African American relations at the grassroots and those among elites. According to these studies; relations between leaders and elites set the tone for the rest. However, at the grassroots, Latinos and African Americans work together and achieve better results in the solution of common problems than do their elite counterparts. Elites clash more frequently and bitterly around the distribution of institutional power and divisible gains and often lead their communities against each other as a means to enhance their own interests—even at the expense of their majority poor.

Finally, in Chicago, African Americans consolidated first into the dominant minority securing significant advances (political and institutional mainly). With a recent dramatic increase, Latinos entered the struggle for public jobs and representation. As the minority pie remained the same, African Americans felt that anything Latinos obtained came at their expense. A progressive citywide coalition and movement between them and white liberals led to the election of African American administrations (1983–1989) that opened up more opportunities (Clavel and Wiewel, 1991). Unfortunately, factors such as nationalism, internal bickering for position, and the death of Mayor Harold Washington disbanded the coalition (Betancur and Gills, 2000). Each community turned inward and played into the hands of a white-dominated Democratic machine that took back many of the gains. However, the long-term options of collaboration between progressive forces on both sides are still open. Meanwhile, the sharing of neighborhoods, particularly schools and institutions, has been an ongoing source of collaboration and contention.

Other analyses have illustrated cooperation at the grassroots (Morales and Pastor, 2000; Betancur and Gills, 2000; Bonilla and Stafford, 2000; Córdova et al., 2000; Barbaro, 1977; Garcia, 2000; Uhlander, 1991) and also among the elites (Portes, 1990; Betancur and Gills, 2000). Generally, competition seems to emerge when African Americans and Latinos have to wrestle for limited opportunities, services, and resources (the poverty budget). In this case, they are operating within a constrained environment and have little control. In contrast, cooperation seems to be associated with initiatives coming from the communities. As such, it seems to be more self-directed. It occurs mostly when they join forces to fight against a condition imposed on both, when together they seek the expansion of the minority pie, or when they pursue indivisible goods. Bickering also seems to be related to individual or class claims as opposed to collective, general gains.

Overall, tensions between Latinos and African Americans come from different and sometimes conflicting agendas associated with each group's unique conditions.[3] Immigration is one of them. Many African Americans feel that Latino immigrants shrink the pie, making their life more miserable. Thomas Espenshade (2000) concluded that this was not generally the case but might be so under particular conditions—for example, level of substitutability and employer markets. A second point relates to public-sector job opportunities. For Gerald Jaynes (2000:28), "in public sector employment . . . African Americans have found a haven from the high levels of discrimination in the private sector." To some extent mobility for them is a function of access to these jobs. Hence, they feel threatened when Latinos pursue this path.

A third sensitive topic is bilingual education. Many African Americans join whites to oppose it because they view it as an extra expenditure and "privilege." Affirmative action programs are a fourth particularly contentious issue with their extension to groups who apparently don't need or deserve them. This has caused much grief and has opened wedges between and within the two groups as African Americans see immigrants taking away from them opportunities that they fought and longed for. Most recently, districting has become an additional bone of contention in areas with growing Latino populations. As their proportions decline, African Americans see or fear the dwindling of political representation earned in long and hard struggles. Latinos, meanwhile, use the same arguments of African Americans to claim representation.

In spite of such factors, both groups have engaged in negotiation and a better understanding of each other and have cooperated around the same sources of difference.

African American–Latino Cooperation and Coalition

Commonalities associated with their minority condition (vis-à-vis opportunity and access) provide the grounds and potential for cooperation. A common question in the literature and in public conversation is why African Americans and Latinos do not coalesce more around their common condition and needs. Explanations and opinions vary according to the analytical perspective used. I highlight three main factors: (1) distribution of the gains resulting from the civil rights and similar movements, (2) the increasing diversity of the two communities, and perhaps most important, (3) the nature of white mediation.

The Civil Rights Movement

Fred Barbaro (1977) argues that the Kennedy–Johnson poverty domestic programs responding to the civil rights movement caused minority groups to break up and "move inward" rather than work together in a common struggle. By directing most resources to African Americans (a political strategy of the Democratic Party at the time), programs conveyed a message of exclusion to other groups who then had to part waters and stage their own movements and separate community building. The result was interminority rivalry, the breakup of civil rights collective efforts, and separate agendas and strategies related to paternalism and factionalism. For Barbaro the transformation of the civil rights movement into an "African American power" movement shifted the struggle from a collective cause of all dominated groups to a separate African American fight for resources and power. Meanwhile, the resources allocated were so meager that they could not possibly meet even the needs of a single group—hence the bickering for the crumbs. Barbaro concludes with an obvious statement (1977:92): "African Americans have little interest in forming coalitions if the price they must pay is to share limited program resources for an unspecified goal of intergroup harmony." Meanwhile, the search for identity and separate agency on the part of each racial group reflects real differences and unique needs. We should see this as a positive event to the extent that the incorporation of difference provides a more solid foundation to their joint efforts. We cannot build justice on the basis of suppression of the other; rather, we must accept all groups as legitimate and equal subjects and partners.

Increasing Diversity

Authors point to the increasing immigration of minorities and their concentration in central cities as a major cause of conflict ("competition") among them. We need to go beyond this and understand the reasons for concentration of poverty, powerlessness, and need in cities. We should pay attention to white monopoly of resources and opportunities and the decision of whites to leave cities and minorities behind. Minorities did not cause their concentration, their condition, or their lack of opportunity. They certainly do not control distribution in this society. We should look at the conflicts associated with their concentration and growth within this context. Absent a critical analysis, the problem tends to be defined as a race problem rather than as a problem of distribution—or a combined class/race question and a matter of self-serving white control.

White Mediation

The white majority has controlled construction of the United States. Along the way, they produced separate and contending conditions for different workforces by race and nationality. Slavery, indentured or coerced, and other forms of cheap or unpaid minority labor and ensuing race-based wages produced much of the wealth that allowed the United States to pull ahead. The white power establishment made sure to monopolize the benefits while putting in place a structure of ongoing white privilege. Historically, it has deprived nonwhites of the American dream through a mix of de jure and de facto interventions generating chronically underdeveloped and subjected labor pools and politically weak minorities. Civil rights legislation tried to correct this. However, legislation alone cannot bring down the accumulated and reified conditions of centuries of exclusion—especially when structural factors continue reproducing them. Even affirmative action has been a managed system of promotion producing a highly dependent minority middle class (tied, in some cases, to affirmative action jobs in the public sector), which often acts as gatekeepers or is at any rate unable to bring fellow minorities along. Affirmative action, in fact, may have benefited females more than racial minorities.

Meanwhile, denial that race is a factor has become a convenient excuse. Enjoying the privilege of its accumulated advantage, European Americans have no practical reason to level the playing field. Today's dominant discourse blaming minorities and welfare for their condition has become a formidable obstacle to their advancement. Equating formal equality in the eyes of the law with actual equality causes the majority to profess that equal opportunity has been achieved. Only when statistics show a random distribution of poverty and wealth can we be sure that effective equal opportunity has occurred.

The white dominant establishment produced a context of race relations that generates contention among minorities. Most recently, it has engaged heavily in management of interminority relations. Chang and Diaz-Vaizades (1999:139) document efforts of the Los Angeles Human Relations Commission to mediate between them. Copied and repeated throughout U.S. cities, such initiatives are important for mutual awareness and a sense of common plight. Unfortunately, they are often merely symbolic and manipulative. In the authors' words, "dialogue alone cannot reconcile structural differences." By using paternalistic and abstract methods of conflict resolution with no bearing on structural factors and the forces pitting them against one another, such initiatives may not go beyond "feel good" acquaintances. The authors contrast the ways in which the media, reflecting local dynamics, took sides with Koreans against African Americans in New York while doing the opposite in Los Angeles.[4] A great illustration of this manipulation is Jack Miles's (1992) portrayal of African American–Latino issues. The author blames Latinos for taking the jobs of African Americans—pitting one group against the other, while exonerating the white establishment.

Discursive constructs have become increasingly important in shaping interminority relations. To the extent that arguments stirring conflict continue circulating, African Americans and Latinos will be pressed to focus on this aspect of their relations—at the expense of a search for deeper structural solutions. Perhaps the most damaging discourses are those claiming groups' entitlement to affirmative action, blaming minority conditions on minority competition and deficits, establishing hierarchies of the "model" minority type, or disengaging middle- and upper-class minorities from their communities.

What Have We Learned?

Students of African American–Latino coalitions have developed general conclusions. Howard Winant (1994) identified factors of convergence of race and class in the minority inner city. Analyzing the 1992 Los Angeles riots, which included Latinos and African Americans, he suggested that the factor bringing them together was "the unity—partial but real—that links the urban poor regardless of race." Similarly, discussing rioting in Mount Pleasant, Adams Morgan, and Columbia Heights in Washington, D.C., Robert Manning (1996) refers to the convergence of Latinos, African Americans, and some whites around police brutality. Chang and Diaz-Veizades (1999:138) argue that if we look at interminority conflict from an economic and political perspective, we need to understand and address the way in which these groups are linked to the ongoing "creation and maintenance of an economic system." In other words, we need to address issues of capital and labor relations, disinvestment, marginalization, democratic participation, employment, and educational, health, and other services, that is, structural differences. Similarly, Barbaro (1977) argues that no single minority group has the numbers to influence the legislative agenda required to address them meaningfully. Experience, he concludes, demonstrates that together minorities can achieve this within a broad perspective recognizing differences and the equal rights of all.

Along these lines, Alejandro Portes (1990) claims that Latinos and African Americans have similar reactions to discrimination. Hence, they may be closer to each other politically than given credit for and, in fact, have coalesced on many fronts and continue to do so. Gerald Jaynes (2000:15) describes interminority relations as a "love-hate" affair including both competition and collaboration. Programs like affirmative action stir the former; common perceptions of discrimination and white privilege facilitate the latter. John Garcia (2000) argues that the decisive factor between coalition and competition is how much discrimination and poverty African Americans and Latinos experience in the United States. In turn, Carole Jean Uhlander (2000) ties coalition and competition to the actions of leaders—their ability and interest in collaboration; She (1991) points to the convergence of common interest and perceived discrimination as a strong basis for coalitions. Yolanda Flores Nieman (1999) calls for awareness about the actual conditions of the other. In this way, they can learn about their affinities and the array of elements limiting opportunity, access, and resources for both.

Lloyd Warner (1936) characterizes intracommunity relations as class relations—in contrast with majority-minority relations, which he defines as caste relations. Class is definitely an internal source of contending interests. This, however, is not the only internal source. Analysts need to look into this. Meanwhile, there is a need to develop models and document successful experiences incorporating and actually celebrating difference. In short, *rather than asking why African Americans and Latinos do not collaborate more with each other, we should ask how and why they have collaborated so much.*

Finally, summarizing the work of twenty researchers who examined African American–Latino relations throughout the United States, Douglas Gills and I

(Betancur and Gills, 2000) conclude that these can assume multiple forms and combinations and usually take place within a creative tension. Grassroots, place- and issue-based coalitions, and coalitions among segments of classes or groups sharing the same interests emerge as the most successful and long lasting. In turn, electoral coalitions have great potential only when representing grassroots movements. Otherwise, they can be highly contentious and elitist. Whereas competition is an ongoing source of conflict, collaboration in the pursuit of indivisible good tends to bring the communities together more successfully. In their daily interaction in neighborhoods and workplaces, African Americans and Latinos have learned how far they can go when they change the context of exclusionary competition for one of collaborative emulation. More research documenting these experiences can help expand successful experiences. While some issues can be addressed at the small-group level (e.g., between African American and Latino parents whose children attend the same school), others require comprehensive interventions. Informal collaborations build the foundations for complex ones. Finally, we call attention to the need for intracommunity building to facilitate intercommunity collaboration.

The Challenges Ahead

A growing literature on interminority relations testifies to the efforts of minorities—and their associates—to gain subjectivity and speak their own words.[5] African Americans and Latinos have been interacting for centuries around their places and conditions of convergence. The literature has focused mostly on their conflicts and deficiencies. As they start taking possession of their relations, they have an uphill battle entailing both the deconstruction of their representation and manipulation and the construction of their willful collaboration. They need to confront the antithetical definition of their identity—the stereotypes and constructs socializing them about and against each other,[6] structural mechanisms of race-based exclusion, and their internalization of alienation. While building on past experiences, construction of their collaboration needs to work out a new philosophy and practice. The seeds in our judgment come from progressive efforts to build togetherness within difference. They include concentration on actions

> against structural factors maintaining oppression; around the provision of collective, indivisible goods; inclusive of other forces fighting for effective equal opportunity; excluding of race antagonism and race-based opportunism; celebrating of difference and diversity; to the extent possible controlled by grassroots forces and focusing on those who have been most affected by racism, especially the poor. (Betancur and Gills, 2000)

So far, studies of African American–Latino relations focus mostly on political coalitions within a framework of conflict resolution and management of relations. Research needs to rescue grassroots experiences, especially those integrating difference and leading to long-term, positive relationships. Such histories may teach important lessons to leaders and elites who often engage in paternalistic or self-serving interventions. Experience shows that the collective struggle of Latinos and African

Americans has gained most from social protest, resistance, and organizing (Morris and Herring, 1996; Vigil, 1996). Differently, negotiations among elites often compromise past gains and collective interests.

A major ongoing challenge comes from globalization and restructuring (Betancur and Gills, 2000). The imbalance between large migrations of Third World unskilled workers and the export of low-skilled jobs to underdeveloped countries is increasing the pool of low-income minorities with poor education at a time when the economy is polarizing, unskilled livable wage jobs are disappearing, and the opportunities of mobility for such immigrants are disappearing. The result is a growing pool of reserve workers with an ever-larger representation of minorities. Unless the mechanisms of distribution are dramatically improved, the struggle for the minority pie may become fiercer. This makes collaboration around structural improvements most difficult. Hope comes from daily interaction at the grassroots around collective needs. Meanwhile, as gains become more complex and require deeper changes, Latinos and African Americans need to rely more heavily on each other.[7] Any gains of one group at the expense of the other are losses for both, as they weaken their collective cause. At the same time, numbers alone would be a strong argument whenever these two communities come together. The challenge is for their leaders to develop the vision and commitment to turn these interactions into a large movement for social change benefiting everybody.

Notes

1. Authors like Eva Morawska (1990) and Sucheng Chan (1990) suggest that specific labor-market conditions at the time of a group's immigration and the points at which they enter explain their success or failure or their ability to develop their own resources. To this, we can also add political climate and white perceptions/decisions.

2. The term *race* gets stretched to the point that it does not even resemble its epistemological roots. At the end of the day, it stands for region and country of origin. The case of Latinos is particularly interesting: many African Americans from Latin America prefer to identify themselves as Latinos; similarly, many whites from the region prefer their Hispanic (from Spain) over their Latin American heritage (as in Latino).

3. Chang and Diaz-Veizades (1999:56) put it this way: "Their competition for jobs and scarce resources is exacerbated by their cultural disparities, ranging from differences in language to music to the way in which people use and decorate their houses."

4. Interestingly enough, the same media praising Koreans in Los Angeles referred to Latinos in derogatory terms (e.g., "thugs" and "illegal immigrants").

5. This is not to exclude others from the struggle—and research. Charles Willie (1977:12) establishes relationships between who writes and who listens between and who writes and what the focus is. According to him, whites trust studies done by whites, and African Americans doubt the accuracy of studies conducted by whites. Similarly, whites pay most attention to minority weaknesses and deficiencies; in contrast, minorities pay more attention to white racism and their own strengths. At the same time, many people in the majority have joined the cause of minorities both practically and academically. Similarly, many Latinos and African Americans have joined forces to study each other and their collaborations. This dialogue and joining of forces are crucial.

6. Minorities are often consumers of media stereotypes describing African Americans as murderers, rapists, drug addicts, and lazy (Romo, 1996); Latinos as greasers, spics, superstitious, and hot-blooded (Castro, 2002); and whites as victims, carriers of civilization, and defenders of the faith (Miller, Like, and Levin, 2002).

7. Looking back at the history of their struggle, we see steady advances up to the emergence of affirmative action. Here, white resistance and institutional arrangements prove more resilient. This may have to do with the required reparations. Working- and middle-class whites fear that minority advancement may lead to more white poverty. They don't like what they see in the minority community and fear that it can happen to them. Furthermore, the condition of minorities makes whites feel good about themselves.

References

Acuña, Rodolfo. 1988. *Occupied America: A History of Chicanos*. 3rd ed. New York: Harper-Collins.

Barbaro, Fred. 1977. Ethnic resentment. In *African American/Brown/White Relations: Race Relations in the 1970s*, ed. Charles V. Willie, 77–94. New Brunswick, NJ: Transaction Books.

Barrera, Mario. 1979. *Race and Class in the Southwest: A Theory of Racial Inequality*. South Bend, IN: Notre Dame University Press.

Betancur, John J., Teresa Córdova, and Maria de Los Ángeles Torres. 1993. Economic restructuring and the process of incorporation of Latinos into the Chicago economy. In *Latinos in a Changing U.S. Economy*, ed. Rebecca Morales and Frank Bonilla, 109–132. Newbury Park, CA: Sage Publications.

Betancur, John J., and Douglas C. Gills, eds. 2000. *The Collaborative City: Opportunities and Struggles for African Americans and Latinos in U.S. Cities*. New York and London: Garland.

Binder, Frederick M., and David M. Reimers. 1996. New York as an immigrant city. In *Origins and Destinies: Immigration, Race, and Ethnicity in America*, ed. S. Pedraza and R. G. Rumbaut, 334–345. Belmont, CA: Wadsworth Publishing.

Blauner, Robert. 1969. Internal colonialism and ghetto revolt. *Social Problems* 16:393–408.

Bonilla, Frank, and Walter Stafford. 2000. African Americans and Puerto Ricans in New York: Cycles and circles of discrimination. In *The Collaborative City*, ed. J. J. Betancur and D. C. Gills, 41–58. New York and London: Garland Publishing.

Bozorgmehr, Mehdi, Georges Sabagh, and Ivan Light. 1996. Los Angeles: Explosive diversity. In *Origins and Destinies: Immigration, Race, and Ethnicity in America*, ed. S. Pedraza and R. G. Rumbaut, 346–359. Belmont, CA: Wadsworth Publishing Company.

Castro, Diego O. 2002. "Hot blood" and "easy virtue": Mass media and the making of racist Latino/a stereotypes. In *Images of Color, Images of Crime: Readings*, ed. C. R. Mann and M. S. Zatz, 82–91. 2nd ed. Los Angeles: Roxbury Publishing Company.

Chan, Sucheng. 1990. European and asian immigration into the United States in comparative perspective, 1820s to 1920s. In *Immigration Reconsidered: History, Sociology, and Politics*, ed. Virginia Yams-McLaughlin, 37–75. New York and Oxford: Oxford University Press.

Chang, Edward T. 1990. New urban crisis: Korean-African American conflict in Los Angeles. Ph.D. diss., University of California at Berkeley.

Chang, Edward T., and Jeannette Diaz-Veizades. 1999. *Ethnic Peace in the American City: Building Community in Los Angeles and Beyond*. New York and London: New York University Press.

Clavel, Pierre, and Wim Wiewel. 1991. *Harold Washington and the Neighborhoods: Progressive City Government in Chicago, 1983–1987*. New Brunswick, NJ: Rutgers University Press.

Córdova, Teresa, Jose T. Bravo, Jeanne Gauna, Richard Moore, and Ruben Solis. 2000. Building networks to tackle global restructuring: The environmental and economic justice movement. In *The Collaborative City*, ed. J. J. Betancur and D. C. Gills, 177–196. New York and London: Garland Publishing.

Espenshade, Thomas J. 2000. Immigrants, Puerto Ricans, and the earnings of native African American males. In *Race and Immigration: New Challenges for American Democracy*, ed. Gerald D. Jaynes, 125–142. New Haven and London: Yale University Press.

Flores Nieman, Yolanda. 1999. Social ecological contexts of prejudice between Hispanics and African Americans. In *Race, Ethnicity, and Nationality in the United States: Toward the Twenty-first Century*, ed. Paul Wong, 170–190. Boulder, CO: Westview Press.

Garcia, John A. 2000. Coalition formation: The Mexican-origin community and Latinos and African Americans. In *Race and Immigration*, ed. Gerald D. Jaynes, 255–275. New Haven and London: Yale University Press.

Glazer, Nathan. 1971. African Americans and ethnic groups: The difference and the political difference it makes. *Social Problems* 18:444–461.

Gordon, M. M. 1964. *Assimilation in American Life*. New York: McGraw-Hill.

Grenier, Guillermo J., and Lisandro Pérez. 1996. Miami spice: The ethnic cauldron simmers. In
Origins and Destinies: Immigration, Race, and Ethnicity in America, ed. S. Pedraza and
R. G. Rumbaut, 360–372. Belmont, CA: Wadsworth Publishing Company.

Horton, John. 1989. The politics of ethnic change: Grassroots responses to economic and demographic restructuring in Monterey Park. *Urban Geography* 10:578–592.

Jaynes, Gerald D., ed. 2000. *Race and Immigration: New Challenges for American Democracy*. New
Haven and London: Yale University Press.

Kim, Claire Jean. 2000. The politics of African American–Korean Conflict: African American
power protest and the mobilization of racial communities in New York City. In *Immigration
and Race: New Challenges for American Democracy*, ed. Gerald D. Jaynes, 74–97. New Haven
and London: Yale University Press.

LeDuff, Charlie. 2000. At a slaughterhouse, some things never die: Who kills, who cuts, who bosses
can depend on race. *New York Times*, June 16. http://query.nytimes.com/search/article-printa-
page.html?res=9E07E.

Light, Ivan, and Edna Bonacich. 1988. *Immigrant Entrepreneurs: Koreans in Los Angeles*. Berkeley
and Los Angeles: University of California Press.

Manning, Robert D. 1996. Washington, D.C.: The changing social landscape of the international
capital city. In *Origins and Destinies: Immigration, Race, and Ethnicity in America*, ed. S. Pedraza
and R. G. Rumbaut, 373–389. Belmont, CA: Wadsworth Publishing Company.

McLeod, Ramon G. 1996. U.S. population expected to be half minorities by 2050. *San Francisco
Chronicle*, March 14, A3.

Miles, Jack. 1992. Immigration and the new American dilemma. *Atlantic*, October.

Miller, Jody, Toya Z. Like, and Peter Levin. 2002. In *Images of Color, Images of Crime: Readings*, ed.
C. R. Mann and M. S. Zatz, 100–114. 2nd ed. Los Angeles: Roxbury Publishing Company.

Morales, Rebecca, and Manuel Pastor. 2000. Can we all just get along? Interethnic organization for
economic development. In *The Collaborative City: Opportunities and Struggles for Blacks and
Latinos in U.S. Cities*, ed. John Betancur and Douglas C. Gills, 157–176. New York and
London: Garland Publishing.

Morawska, Ewa. 1990. The sociology and historiography of immigration. In *Immigration
Reconsidered: History, Sociology, and Politics*, ed. Virginia Yans-McLaughlin, 187–238. New York
and Oxford: Oxford University Press. .

Morris, Aldon, and Cedric Herring. 1996. The civil rights movement: A social and political watershed. In *Origins and Destinies: Immigration, Race, and Ethnicity in America*, ed.
S. Pedraza and R. G. Rumbaut, 206–223. Belmont, CA: Wadsworth Publishing Company.

Nakayama, Thomas K. 2002. Framing Asian Americans. In *Images of Color, Images of Crime:
Readings*, ed. C. R. Mann and M. S. Zatz, 92–99. 2nd ed. Los Angeles: Roxbury Publishing
Company.

Park, Robert E. 1926/1950. *Race and Culture*. Glencoe, IL: Free Press.

Perez Stable, Marifeli, and Miren Uriarte. 1993. Cubans and the changing economy of Miami. In
Latinos in a Changing U.S. Economy, ed. R. Morales and F. Bonilla, 133–159. Newbury Park,
CA: Sage Publications.

Portes, Alejandro. 1990. From south of the Border: Hispanic minorities in the United States. In
Immigration Reconsidered: History, Sociology, and Politics, ed. Virginia Yans-McLaughlin,
160–184. New York and Oxford: Oxford University Press.

Romo, Ricardo. 1996. Mexican Americans: Their civic and political incorporation. In *Origins and
Destinies: Immigration, Race, and Ethnicity in America*, ed. S. Pedraza and
R. G. Rumbaut, 84–97. Belmont, CA: Wadsworth Publishing Company.

Sales, William W. Jr. and Roderick Bush. 1997. African American and Latino coalitions: Prospects
for new social movements in New York City. In *Race and Politics*, ed. James Jennings, 135–148.
London and New York: Verso.

Tienda, Marta and Haya Stier. 1996. The wages of race: Color and employment opportunity in
Chicago's inner city. In *Origins and Destinies: Immigration, Race, and Ethnicity in America*,
ed. S. Pedraza and R. G. Rumbaut, 417–431. Belmont, CA: Wadsworth Publishing Company.

Uhlander, Carole Jean. 2000. Political activity and preferences of African Americans, Latinos, and Asian Americans. In *Race and Immigration: New Challenges for American Democracy*, ed. Gerald D. Jaynes, 217–254. New Haven and London: Yale University Press.

———. 1991. Perceived discrimination and prejudice and the coalition prospects of African Americans, Latinos, and Asian Americans. In *Racial and Ethnic Politics in California*, ed. Brian O. Jackson and Michael Preston. Berkeley: IGS.

Warner, Lloyd. 1936. American class and caste. *American Journal of Sociology* 42:234–237.

Whalen, Carmen T. 2000. Displaced labor migrants or the "underclass": African Americans and Puerto Ricans in Philadelphia's economy. In *The Collaborative City*, ed. J. J. Betancur and D. C. Gills, 115–136. New York and London: Garland Publishing.

Willie, Charles V. 1977. Introduction: race, power and social change. In *African American/ Brown/White Relation: Race Relations in the 1970s*, ed. C. V. Willie, 11–18. New Brunswick, NJ: Transaction Books.

Winant, Howard. 1994. *Racial Conditions*. Minneapolis and London: University of Minneapolis Press.

Vigil, James Diego. 1996. Que viva la raza: The many faces of the Chicano movement, 1963–1971. In *Origins and Destinies: Immigration, Race, and Ethnicity in America*, ed. S. Pedraza and R. G. Rumbaut, 224–237. Belmont, CA: Wadsworth Publishing Company.

Chapter 9

Neither White nor Black: The Representation of Racial Identity Among Puerto Ricans on the Island and in the U.S. Mainland[1]

Jorge Duany

How is racial identity represented in an Afro-Hispanic Caribbean nation like Puerto Rico? And how do racial and ethnic categories shift in the diaspora? In 1990 I directed an ethnographic study of the sociocultural causes of the census undercount in Barrio Gandul, a poor urban community in Santurce (Duany et al., 1995). At the beginning of our fieldwork, my colleagues and I asked our informants: "What race do you consider yourself to belong to?" Responses to this seemingly innocuous question ranged from embarrassment and amazement to ambivalence and silence: many informants simply shrugged their shoulders and pointed to their arms, as if their skin color were so obvious that it did not need to be verbalized. When people referred to others' race, they often used ambiguous euphemisms (such as "he's a little darker than me"), without making a definite commitment to a specific racial label. Sometimes they would employ diminutive folk terms like *morenito* or *trigueñita* (referring to dark-skinned persons), which are difficult to translate into U.S. categories. For the purposes of this research, it seemed culturally appropriate to collect our impressions of people's phenotypes as coded in Hispanic Caribbean societies such as Puerto Rico and the Dominican Republic. However, this procedure left open the question of the extent to which the researchers' racial categories coincided with the subjects' own perceptions.

My field notes for that project are full of references to the intermediate physical types of many residents of Barrio Gandul, including *moreno* and *trigueño*. For statistical purposes, these terms are usually grouped under the generic label "mulatto," but Puerto Ricans make finer social distinctions in their daily lives. For instance, our informants used the terms *grifo*, *jabao*, and *colorao* to refer to various combinations of hair types and skin tones. At least nineteen different racial categories are commonly used in Puerto Rico. Contrary to the collapsing of racially mixed persons in the United States into the nonwhite category, residents of Barrio Gandul recognized intermediate groups. In U.S. racial terminology, most of our subjects would probably classify themselves as "other," that is, as neither white nor Black.

Popular racial taxonomies in Puerto Rico cannot be easily reduced to the white/Black antithesis prevalent in the United States. Puerto Ricans usually group people into three main racial groups—Black, white, and brown—based primarily on skin pigmentation and other physical traits, such as facial features and hair texture, regardless of their ancestry. In the United States the dominant system of racial classification emphasizes a two-tiered division between whites and nonwhites deriving from the principle of hypo-descent—the assignment of the offspring of mixed races to the subordinate group (Davis, 1998; Harris, 1964). According to the "one-drop rule," anyone with a known African ancestor is defined as Black, regardless of his or her physical appearance. In Puerto Rico that same person would be classified according to her skin color, facial features, and other visible characteristics of her body. This clear-cut opposition between Puerto Rican and U.S. conceptions of racial identity has numerous repercussions for social analysis and public policy, among them the appropriate way to categorize, count, and report the number of people by race and ethnicity.

The problem of representing the racial identity of Puerto Ricans, both on the island and in the U.S. mainland, has troubled U.S. scholars, census enumerators, and policymakers at least since the end of the nineteenth century. Two key issues have pervaded academic and public debates on race in Puerto Rico. On the one hand, the proliferation and fluidity of racial terms to describe the island's population have attracted much attention. According to a recent analysis, such "slippery semantics" may be a strategy to recognize the high incidence of racial mixture on the island, while avoiding the binary oppositions between white and black (Godreau, 2000). On the other hand, census tallies report a growing proportion of whites in Puerto Rico between 1899 and 1950, and then again in the year 2000. Even though the census's racial categories changed several times during this period, the white category remained intact, and the number of persons counted as white increased from one census to another. As I discuss later in this chapter, the evasion of blackness and its perceived negative connotations is a recurring theme in the history of Puerto Rican race relations, dominated by slavery for nearly four centuries. Moreover, the downplaying of the African heritage is a constant practice in the dominant discourse that tends to idealize the Hispanic and indigenous "roots" of national culture, often at the expense of Blacks.[2]

In the United States, Puerto Rican migrants do not fit well in the conventional white/Black dichotomy and therefore challenge the hegemonic discourse on race and ethnicity (Rodríguez, 1994, 2000). Recent research by the U.S. Bureau of the Census has focused on determining why so many mainland Puerto Ricans, as well as other Hispanics, choose the "other" category when asked about their racial identity. In the 2000 census, 42.2 percent of all Hispanics in the United States declared that they belonged to "some other race" besides white, Black or African American, American Indian and Alaska Native, Asian, or Native Hawaiian and other Pacific Islander (U.S Bureau of the Census, 2001). The existence of a large and growing segment of the U.S. population that perceives itself ethnically as Hispanic or Latino, while avoiding the major accepted racial designations, is a politically explosive phenomenon. It is no wonder that the federal government has so far resisted public pressures to include a separate multiracial category (as opposed to "more than one race") in the census and other official documents. So have many African American, Latino, and Asian American lobbying groups, which perceive a threat to their numbers, as a multiracial category would create further divisions within racial minorities. For these groups, checking more than one race in the census questionnaire means reducing their influence on public policy making (Schemo, 2000).

In this chapter I examine how Americans have represented the racial identity of Puerto Ricans, as well as how Puerto Ricans have represented themselves racially, both at home and in the diaspora. First I review census data on the racial composition of the island's population between 1899 and 1950 and then again in 2000. Next I analyze estimates of the racial composition of Puerto Rican migrants between 1940 and 2000. I show that U.S. racial categories have historically been at odds, and continue to be so, with prevailing self-concepts among Puerto Ricans. My premise is that the changing racial categories used by the census in Puerto Rico and in the diaspora articulate the hegemonic discourse on race in the United States. However, Puerto Ricans continue to represent themselves differently from official views on race and ethnicity, both on the island and in the mainland. Whereas Americans tend to draw a rigid line between white and Black people, Puerto Ricans prefer to use a fluid continuum of physical types. In essence, different and competing racial discourses have produced incompatible portraits of racial identity on the island and in the U.S. mainland. On the island the vast majority of Puerto Ricans regard themselves as white. In the mainland most consider themselves to be neither white nor Black but members of some other race. To many Americans, Puerto Ricans occupy an ambiguous position between whites and people of color.

"The Whitest of the Antilles": Representing Race in Puerto Rico

One of the first official acts of the U.S. government in Puerto Rico after acquiring the island in 1898 was to conduct a census of its population. The War Department assumed that task in 1899. Since 1910 the Department of Commerce has been in charge of the census in Puerto Rico as well as in the mainland. Until 1950 the U.S. Bureau of the Census attempted to quantify the racial composition of the island's population, while experimenting with various racial taxonomies. In 1960 the census dropped the racial identification question for Puerto Rico but included it again in the year 2000. The only category that remained constant over time was white, even as other racial labels shifted greatly—from "colored" to "Black," "mulatto," and "other"; back to "colored" and "other races"; then to "nonwhite"; again to "Negro" and "other races"; and finally to "Black or African American" and "other races." Regardless of the precise terminology, the census reported that the bulk of the Puerto Rican population was white from 1899 to 2000.

From the beginning of the twentieth century American observers remarked on the "surprising preponderance of the white race" on the island (*National Geographic*, 1900:328). One travel writer called Puerto Rico "the whitest of the Antilles" (White, 1898).

Table 9.1 Racial composition of the Puerto Rican population, as reported by the census, 1802–2000 (in percentages)

Year	White	Nonwhite[a]
1802	48.0	52.0
1812	46.8	53.2
1820	44.4	55.6
1827	49.7	50.3
1830	50.1	49.9
1836	52.9	47.1
1860	51.1	48.5
1877	56.3	43.7
1887	59.5	40.5
1897	64.3	35.7
1899	61.8	38.2
1910	65.5	34.5
1920	73.0	27.0
1930	74.3	25.7
1935	76.2	23.8
1940	76.5	23.5
1950	79.7	20.3
2000	80.5	19.5

Sources: Administración de Reconstrucción de Puerto Rico (1938); Departamento de la Guerra (1900); U.S. Bureau of the Census (1913, 1921, 1932, 1943, 1953a, 2001).
[a]Includes Black, colored, mulatto, mixed blood, and other races.

In a widely distributed piece, a geologist (Hill, 1899:93) wrote that the island was "notable among the West Indian group for the reason that its preponderant population is of the white race." In a more academic book he reiterated that "Porto Rico, at least, has not become Africanized, as have all the other West Indies excepting Cuba" (Hill, 1903:165). Such authoritative reports helped to allay the common racist fear that the U.S. government had annexed a predominantly Black population after the war of 1898. Such a view still surfaces in contemporary debates about the island's political status, albeit indirectly.

Table 9.1 compiles the available census statistics on the proportion of whites and nonwhites in Puerto Rico between 1802 and 2000. The Spanish censuses show that Puerto Ricans were about evenly divided between whites and nonwhites until the mid-nineteenth century. Since 1860 the proportion of the island's population classified as white has increased steadily, except for the year 1899, when the first U.S. census registered a small decrease. Correspondingly, the proportion of people reported as nonwhites (including Blacks and mulattos) has diminished, again except for 1899. In the 2000 census 80.5 percent of the island's residents classified themselves as white, with only 8 percent Black and 11.5 other races. According to these statistics, the Puerto Rican population has become increasingly whiter, especially during the first half of the twentieth century.

What social factors account for this dramatic transformation in the official representation of Puerto Rico's racial composition? To some extent, the gradual lightening of the
island's population was due to European immigration, especially during the second half
of the nineteenth century (Hoetink, 1967). But the number of white immigrants was
not large enough to produce such a significant shift in racial groups during the first half
of the twentieth century. Nor was there a massive outflow of Black people to the United
States or other countries at this time. Barring major population movements into and out
of the island until the 1940s, scholars have proposed several additional hypotheses.

Charles Rogler (1940:16) put forth one of the most popular explanations: "The
census includes as colored both full-blooded and mixed. The census estimate is probably low because many who are known to have colored blood are counted as
white. . . . Because of the absence of marked race prejudice, and also because of the
tendency to deal with color as a class rather than a race phenomenon, the attitude of
the community as a whole operates to reduce materially the percentage classified as
colored and to classify many quadroons and octoroons as white." While Rogler points
out that light mulattos are often accepted as whites in Puerto Rico, he fails to acknowledge that "passing" also takes place in the United States, although it operates differently there and without official approval. Moreover, the whitening of the Puerto Rican
population is hardly due to the absence of racial prejudice but rather to its very
presence: many people prefer to identify as white to avoid racial stigmatization. Nor is
it a question of conflating color and class, although the two factors are closely linked.
Finally, racial categories such as quadroons and octoroons are meaningless in contemporary Puerto Rico, precisely because it is practically impossible to determine the
degree of racial mixture in much of the population (Fitzpatrick, 1987).

Rogler (1972a:62) provides a second explanation: "This apparent decline [in the
nonwhite population] is probably the consequence of changing race conceptions or,
more specifically, the social definition as to who is a person of color. In other words,
these percentages would suggest that many persons of color are moving into the white
race." I would accept the first premise of this proposition—that census categories
reflect changing discourses on race—but would reject its second implication—
that Puerto Ricans jumble together white and black people. On the contrary, the
Puerto Rican scheme of racial classification is primarily concerned, perhaps even
obsessed, with distinguishing various shades of skin color. However, such definitions
of race clash with the categories imposed by the U.S. Bureau of the Census. Hence,
the problem is not, as Morris Siegel (1948:189) believed, that "the reliability of
Puerto Rican racial classifications is open to serious criticisms." *All* such classifications are historically contingent, culturally relative, politically contestable, ultimately
arbitrary, and of dubious scientific value (see Omi and Winant, 1994).[3]

The Bureau of the Census itself has offered a third explanation for the apparent
increase in Puerto Rico's white population: "The percentage of the population which
was colored, according to the census returns, declined from 38.2 percent in 1899 to
23.8 percent in 1935. A part of this nominal decline, however, was without doubt
the result of the gradual change in the concept of the race classification as applied by
the census enumerators" (Administración de Reconstrucción de Puerto Rico, 1938:17).

I doubt that Puerto Rican census takers substantially changed their racial concepts during this period and therefore counted more people as white. Since 1899 enumerators have been recruited from the island's population and have presumably applied local standards of racial classification. According to *National Geographic* (1901:80), "The facts presented in the reports were gathered in all cases by the [Puerto Rican] people themselves, as the most intelligent of the better classes were induced to compete for positions as census-takers by the relatively handsome salaries offered by the U.S. government." Until the 1960 census enumerators in Puerto Rico as well as in the U.S. mainland usually judged their informants' physical appearance as a visual cue of racial identity (Ruggles et al., 1997; Lillian Torres Aguirre, letter to the author, January 21, 2000). Only in the 2000 census was the racial question based on self-classification in Puerto Rico.

My own interpretation of the island's changing racial statistics focuses on the transactions between state-supported and popular representations of race. From the beginning, the U.S. government attempted to divide the Puerto Rican population neatly into "two main classes, pure whites and those who are not" (Departamento de la Guerra, 1900:57). In turn, Puerto Ricans insisted on distinguishing Blacks from mulattos and blurring the boundaries between "pure whites" and "mixed blood." In 1930 the Bureau of the Census dropped mulattos from its count of the Puerto Rican population and lumped them together with Blacks under "colored." This change anticipated the collapsing of Blacks and mulattos into a single category in the U.S. mainland (Davis, 1998; Domínguez, 1998). Between 1900 and 1930 the U.S. census counted persons of mixed Black and white ancestry as a separate group. But in 1940 such persons were considered Black or Negro. On the island census enumerators tended to avoid the "colored" and "Black" labels altogether and to identify their informants as whites. Thus, the official disappearance of racially intermediate types accelerated the movement from nonwhite to white categories on the island.

In short, the U.S. government sought to apply a binary race model to the fluid multiracial situation in Puerto Rico. As an official report to the local House of Representatives noted, "The population is extremely mixed and there are not just two colors but rather an infinite number of hues" (*El Mundo*, 1945). Although the census recognized that most "colored" people were mulattos rather than "pure Blacks" (the term used by the census), the dominant discourse on race silenced that trend after 1930. From an American standpoint, only two distinct races existed in Puerto Rico—white and Black (variously called Negro, colored, or nonwhite). Well into the 1940s the Bureau of the Census claimed that racial terms "probably need no definition" (U.S. Bureau of the Census, 1946:2). However, it instructed local enumerators to classify persons of mixed ancestry as colored rather than white (U.S. Bureau of the Census, 1953a:100). As a U.S. Bureau of the Census (1963:ix) report understated, "It is likely that the commonly held conceptions of race among Puerto Ricans in Puerto Rico, among Puerto Ricans in the United States, and among other persons in the United States are somewhat different, and there was a considerable variation in the classification." For instance, the 1950 census categorized persons of mixed ancestry according to the race of the nonwhite parent, following the rule of hypo-descent

(U.S. Bureau of the Census, 1953a:53-V). In contrast, Puerto Ricans classified them primarily according to their physical appearance. Whereas the census insisted on distinguishing only two groups, white and nonwhite, Puerto Ricans continued to use three or more categories, including *trigueño, moreno, indio*, and other folk terms. Many people in Puerto Rico contested the racial practices articulated by the Bureau of the Census.

The racial politics of census enumeration in Puerto Rico reveal a sharp discrepancy between self-representations and representations by others. In 1899 nearly two-thirds of all Puerto Ricans were considered to be white. By 2000 more than four-fifths classified themselves as white. However, many Americans—including visiting scholars and public officials—mistrusted such statistics, believing instead that the island's "colored" population was much larger than suggested by the census. Some Puerto Rican authors granted that the majority of the local population was composed of mulattos (Blanco, 1985 [1942]; Rodríguez Cruz, 1965). In 1960 the federal government eliminated any references to race or color from the census of Puerto Rico, apparently because it considered such references to be unreliable and practically useless. A brief note in the 1950 census reads: "There is considerable evidence which indicates that color is misreported [in Puerto Rico]. The comparison of the 'white' and 'nonwhite' total from census to census reveals the tendency of the enumerator to report persons with varying amounts of Negro blood as 'white' " (U.S. Bureau of the Census, 1952:viii). Racial statistics on the island did not generate a portrait compatible with the dominant discourse on race in the United States.

For its own reasons, the Puerto Rican government attempted to erase race from most official documents on the island. According to the director of the Office of the Census of the Puerto Rican Planning Board, Lillian Torres Aguirre (letter to the author, January 21, 2000), the race question was dropped because the Commonwealth's constitution prohibits discrimination by race or color, and because the local government is not required by law to collect racial statistics in order to provide public services. In 1978 an attorney working for the Office of Legal Affairs of the Puerto Rican Planning Board recommended that "the most adequate and convenient solution for our economic, social, and cultural reality is not to include the question about racial determination in the 1980 census questionnaire" (Mercado Vega, 1978:3). Between 1960 and 1990 the census questionnaire in Puerto Rico did not ask about race or color. Racial categories therefore disappeared from the dominant discourse on the Puerto Rican nation.

However, the 2000 census included a racial self-identification question in Puerto Rico and, for the first time ever, allowed respondents to choose more than one racial category to indicate mixed ancestry. (Only 4.2 percent chose two or more races.) With few variations, the census of Puerto Rico used the same questionnaire as in the U.S. mainland. This decision was a response to intense lobbying by former governor Pedro Rosselló's administration to include Puerto Rico in federal census statistics, along with the fifty states (Mulero, 1999). According to census reports, most islanders responded to the new federally mandated categories on race and ethnicity by insisting on their "whiteness"; few declared themselves to be Black or some other race (U.S. Bureau of the Census, 2001). Clearly, many of the census's racial categories—such as American Indian, Alaska Native, Asian, Hawaiian, or Pacific Islander—are irrelevant to most of the Puerto Rican population.

White, Black, or Other? The Racial Representation of Puerto Rican Migrants

If classifying the race of Puerto Ricans on the island was complicated, the task became even more daunting to government authorities in the U.S. mainland. Since the beginning of the twentieth century the Bureau of the Census has frequently altered its racial designation of Puerto Rican and other Hispanic immigrants. For instance, the census counted Mexicans as a separate (nonwhite) race in 1900 and 1930, as white between 1940 and 1970, and as being of any race they reported between 1980 and 2000. Until 1970 most Puerto Ricans living in the United States were considered to be white, "unless they were definitely Negro, Indian, or some other race" (Domínguez, 1998). In 1980 the census introduced two separate self-identification questions, one on Hispanic origin and one on race, based on the premise that Hispanics could be of any race. Consequently, the federal government encouraged Puerto Ricans to classify themselves primarily as Hispanics rather than as white or Black.

Table 9.2 presents census data on the racial composition of Puerto Ricans in the United States from 1940 to 2000.[4] First, the proportion of mainland Puerto Ricans who were reported to be white decreased drastically after 1980, largely as a result of the inclusion of the new Hispanic category. In the year 2000 the proportion of Puerto Ricans who classified themselves as white (about 46 percent) was slightly more

Table 9.2 Racial composition of Puerto Ricans[a] in the United States, as reported by the census,[b] 1940–2000 (in percentages)

Year	White	Nonwhite[c]	Other
1940	86.8	13.2	–
1950	92.0	8.0	–
1960	96.1	3.9	–
1970	92.9	5.3	1.8
1980	48.3	4.3	47.5
1990	45.8	7.1	47.2
2000	46.4	7.9	45.8

Sources: Almaguer and Jung (1998); Inter-University Program for Latino Research (2002); U.S. Bureau of the Census (1953b, 1963, 1973).
[a] For 1940, refers only to persons of Puerto Rican birth; for other years, includes persons of Puerto Rican birth or parentage.
[b] Until 1970, "race" was based on the census enumerators' judgment; since then, it has been based on the respondents' self-reports.
[c] Includes Negro or Black, Native American or American Indian, and Asian and Pacific Islander.

than half the 1940 figure (87 percent). Second, the proportion of Black Puerto Ricans has remained extremely low since 1950 (between 4 and 8 percent). Third, those reporting other races jumped from less than 2 percent in 1970 to almost 46 percent in 2000. Thus, over the past three decades, Puerto Ricans in the United States have changed their racial self-perception from a predominantly white population to a hybrid one.[5] Contrary to the dominant trend among Puerto Ricans on the island, fewer of those residing in the mainland reported that they were white between the 1970 and 2000 censuses.

Let me review some possible reasons for this change and then offer my own explanation. Several authors have argued that Puerto Ricans in the United States tend to reject their labeling as Black, because that would mean accepting an inferior position within American society. From this perspective, the migrants assert a separate cultural identity to evade rampant prejudice and discrimination against African Americans (Fitzpatrick, 1987; Montero Seplowin, 1971; Rodríguez-Morazzani, 1996; Seda Bonilla, 1968; Wolfson, 1972). Although this argument may help to explain why many dark-skinned Puerto Rican migrants do not identify themselves with African Americans, it misses two basic points. First, about the same proportion of Puerto Ricans on the island and in the mainland (8 percent, according to the census) classify themselves as Black rather than white or of other races. Second, proportionally fewer Puerto Ricans in the mainland than on the island classify themselves as white when offered an opportunity to declare other races. The key question then becomes why so many U.S. Puerto Ricans chose the "other" category—neither white nor Black—in the last two censuses.

Clara Rodríguez believes that Puerto Ricans in New York City continue to define their racial identity according to a color continuum from white to Black. As in Puerto Rico, this continuum is based on phenotypic categories ranging in pigmentation, hair form, and facial features. Surprisingly, few of her Puerto Rican interviewees reported that they were "other" because of racial mixture as such. The majority stated that they had chosen the "other race" option because of their culture, family, birthplace, socialization, or political perspective. However, most respondents placed themselves in racially intermediate positions between Black and white. They rarely used conventional U.S. terms to describe their racial identity and preferred to say that they were Spanish, Puerto Rican, Boricua, or *trigueño* (Rodríguez, 1990, 1992, 2000; Rodríguez and Cordero-Guzmán, 1992). From this perspective, the growing use of the term "other" among Puerto Rican and other Hispanic immigrants reflects their disapproval of the American racial classification system.[6]

Despite its eloquence, this thesis raises some unresolved issues. As Rodríguez (1997) recognizes, the meaning of census racial categories has shifted greatly for Puerto Ricans and other Latinos in the United States. Thus, it is difficult to simply juxtapose American and Latin American discourses of race and to suggest that the latter are more attuned to large-scale racial mixture and conceptual fuzziness. Both types of discourses may be converging: American Black/white relations have been complicated by the growth of "brown" groups such as Asian Americans or Latinos, while Latin American race relations, at least in Brazil, are increasingly polarized between whites and nonwhites (Winant, 1994).

Furthermore, the rise of new ethnic/racial labels, such as "Hispanics" and "Latinos," has affected the self-definition of Puerto Ricans and other Latin American immigrants in the United States (see *Latin American Perspectives*, 1992; Oboler, 1995). Among other repercussions, the official adoption of the Hispanic label by the Bureau of the Census and other federal government bureaucracies often treats Puerto Ricans as racially distinct from both non-Hispanic whites and Blacks. The quasi-racial use of the term "Hispanic" has led many Puerto Ricans to move away from the Black/white dichotomy in the United States.

Finally, many Puerto Ricans choose the catchall "other" as a proxy for brown or tan—that is, as neither white nor black, but an in-between color (Fitzpatrick, 1987). As several researchers have found, migration to the mainland tends to produce a "browning effect" (Ginorio, 1979; Martínez, 1988; Rodríguez, 1996), as opposed to the whitening of the island's population. The contemporary self-representation of Puerto Ricans in the United States may therefore constitute a rupture, rather than a continuity, with the dominant racial discourse on the island. However, most migrants have not adopted the U.S. racial model wholesale but have adapted it to their particular situation of racial mixture and heterogeneity.

Recent studies by the Bureau of the Census provide empirical support for this alternative conception of the othering trend among Puerto Rican migrants (Tucker et al., 1996). The 1995 Current Population Survey supplement included four versions of the race and Hispanic origin questions, with and without a multiracial category. More than 70 percent of Puerto Ricans in the United States identified as Hispanic in a combined race and ethnicity question. Only 7 percent chose the multiracial category in the separate race and Hispanic origin panel, while less than 3 percent did so in the combined panel. However, more than 32 percent of the respondents classified themselves as "all other" when they were asked separate race and ethnicity questions as currently formulated in the decennial census. In short, "other" seems to be increasingly used as a racialized synonym for Hispanic. These data confirm that many Puerto Ricans prefer to label themselves as neither white nor black when they have another option presumably indicating mixed descent.

In sum, census figures suggest two main trends in the racial self-identification of Puerto Ricans in the United States. On the one hand, mainland Puerto Ricans classify their "racial" identity primarily as Hispanic, regardless of federal government policy stating that Hispanics can be of any race. Most Puerto Ricans prefer to place themselves in an intermediate position between white and black, even when offered a multiracial option. This preference seems most popular among those who call themselves *trigueño* on the island (Landale and Oropesa, 2002). On the other hand, if forced to separate their Hispanic origin from their racial identity, many Puerto Ricans choose to call themselves "other." This option seems to provide a third alternative, conceptually equivalent to brown, which eludes the white/Black dichotomy altogether. Either as Hispanics or as others, Puerto Ricans in the United States are increasingly racialized. Rather than repudiating the dominant American scheme of group classification, mainland Puerto Ricans may be assigning new meanings to existing racial and ethnic categories.[7] In other words, migrants may be using the terms "Hispanic," "Latino," or "other race" as analogues for *trigueño* or *moreno*, rather than identifying themselves as either white or Black.

Conclusion

During the twentieth century the problem of defining, classifying, and representing the racial identity of Puerto Ricans was officially addressed in two main ways. On the island the Bureau of the Census did not collect any racial statistics between 1950 and 2000, largely because they were incompatible with the dominant U.S. scheme of racial classification. Furthermore, Commonwealth officials were interested not in dividing the Puerto Rican population by race but in uniting it under a common nationality. In the mainland the 1980 census asked people to identify themselves as either Hispanic or not Hispanic, and then as white, Black, American Indian, Asian, or other. Whereas most islanders describe themselves as white, most mainland Puerto Ricans now consider themselves to be neither white nor black but other. Many use Hispanic, Latino, or Spanish origin as racial self-designators. The increasing racialization of such pan-ethnic terms has numerous implications for American society, such as the possible broadening of a binary racial order into a tripartite color scheme including white, Black, and brown (Winant, 1994).

Between 1899 and 1950 the U.S. Bureau of the Census computed the number of white and nonwhite people in Puerto Rico. In spite of changing racial categories, as well as their popular contestation, the census reported that Puerto Ricans were becoming whiter over time. This trend continued with the 2000 count. The "bleaching" of the island's population is partly due to the propensity to incorporate light mulattos (*trigueños*) into the white category, as well as the common belief in "improving one's race" through intermarriage with lighter-skinned persons. But the main reason for the transformation of Puerto Rico's racial statistics was the growing polarization between whites and others (variously called Black, Negro, colored, or nonwhite) in the census. The American scheme of racial classification diverged from local discourses and practices, which paid more careful attention to gradations in skin color and recognized multiple physical types in between white and Black, such as *trigueño*, *indio*, and *jabao*, as well as the more exotic *café con leche*, *piel canela*, and *blanco con raja*.

Since 1940 the Bureau of the Census has faced the challenge of counting a growing number of Puerto Ricans in the continental United States. At first the U.S. government considered most Puerto Ricans to be whites, whose mother tongue happened to be Spanish. By 1980 the census had adopted "Hispanic" as a quasi-racial term and encouraged Puerto Ricans and other Latin American immigrants to identify with that category, rather than with non-Hispanic whites or Blacks. In 1990 and 2000 an even larger proportion of Puerto Ricans, Mexicans, Dominicans, and other Hispanics reported that they belonged to other races (*Latin American Perspectives*, 1992; Rodríguez, 1992, 2000). For U.S. Puerto Ricans, "other" has multiple semantic connotations, including *trigueño*, tan, brown, Spanish, Hispanic, Latino, Boricua, or simply Puerto Rican. Contrary to the whitening of the island's population during the first half of the twentieth century, mainland Puerto Ricans underwent a browning tendency during the second half of the century.

Throughout this chapter I have argued that the popular racial categories used by Puerto Ricans on the island and in the diaspora depart from dominant U.S. racial codes. Although the official racial terminology in the United States has changed over time, the two main categories—white and Black—have remained relatively stable, distinct, and opposed to each other (Domínguez, 1998). The presumed purity and homogeneity of the white and Black races, however, clashed against the prevalence of racial mixture among Puerto Ricans. The multiplicity of physical types, produced by seemingly endless combinations of skin color, facial features, and hair texture, could not easily be accommodated within the U.S. hegemonic racial taxonomy. From the standpoint of the federal government, Puerto Ricans on the island had to be labeled according to discrete racial groupings—or not at all. But most islanders insisted that they were white, even if they knew they had some African ancestry. Here again, the denial of blackness is rooted in a long history of racial discrimination against people of African origin in Puerto Rico. In contrast, migrants to the mainland responded to a binary racial order by choosing a third alternative, other, which increasingly mirrored their Hispanic identity. That choice was conditioned, in part, by the resistance of many Puerto Ricans to identifing themselves as Black or African American.

The contested representation of the racial identity of Puerto Ricans has wider theoretical and practical implications. This case study confirms that all racial classification systems are scientifically invalid as representations of human biological diversity. They are even less appropriate as explanations for social and cultural differences. Although some group variations related to skin, hair, and eye pigmentation, stature, and body form are hereditary, such variations are difficult if not impossible to categorize in a reliable way. Phenotypically, Puerto Ricans display the full range of characteristics traditionally associated with both whites and Blacks. According to U.S. standards, they should be counted as people of color because of their mixed ancestry. According to Puerto Rican standards, they should be considered white if they have light skin color, thin lips, elongated noses, and straight hair. It is sterile to argue that one scheme is right and the other wrong, or that one is morally superior to the other. Instead, both systems are historically and culturally grounded in racist projects originating in colonialism and slavery (see Omi and Winant, 1994). The persistence of the myth of racial democracy in Puerto Rico suggests that it plays an important role in the nationalist discourse that glorifies the island's Hispanic culture vis-à-vis the ubiquitous influence of the United States.

The practical implications of this analysis are ominous, especially for racial counting efforts such as the census. Allowing respondents to choose more than one racial category did not change substantially the proportion of Puerto Ricans on the island or in the mainland who classified themselves as whites or Blacks. Instead, the racial self-identification question has opened a Pandora's box in Puerto Rico. Most islanders—more than 80 percent—checked the "white" box on the 2000 census questionnaire because local standards of race allow them to consider themselves white even though some of them might not be accepted as such according to American standards. Like Hispanics in the mainland, islanders could have chosen "other," or they might have opted for both "Black" and "white." Then again, Puerto Ricans could have defined themselves according to multiple racial categories, but most did not. In the 1998 status plebiscite island residents had to choose among four alternatives: the current Commonwealth, free association, independence, and statehood. The largest proportion of voters supported "none of the above." Perhaps, to recycle that formula, the best response to the racial question in the 2000 census would also have been "none of the above."[8]

Notes

1. This chapter is a revised and abridged version of a paper presented at "The Meanings of Race and Blackness in the Americas: Contemporary Perspectives," a conference held at Brown University, Providence, Rhode Island, February 10–12, 2000. I thank Suzanne Oboler and Anani Dzidzienyo for their kind invitation to present this paper, and for their fine suggestions to revise it for publication. Lillian Torres Aguirre and Roberto R. Ramírez provided access to census data on race among Puerto Ricans on the island and in the United States. Isar Godreau, Juan José Baldrich, Arlene Torres, Louis Herns Marcelin, Marvin Lewis, and María Zielina offered useful comments to strengthen my argument. Amílcar Tirado invited me to present the paper at the Documents and Maps Collection of the library at the Río Piedras campus of the University of Puerto Rico on May 1, 2001. A longer version of this essay was published as chapter 10 of my last book (Duany, 2002).
2. Elsewhere I have argued that some nationalist intellectuals have tended to "make Indians out of Blacks," by symbolically displacing the African heritage with the Taíno in many scholarly analyses and public representations of Puerto Rican identity on the island and in the U.S. mainland (Duany, 2002: chapter 11). In a different historical context, the dominant discourse about race in the Dominican Republic has canceled out Blacks and turned them into *indios*, while reserving the pejorative term *negro* for Haitians.
3. Virginia Domínguez (1998) has reviewed changing racial taxonomies in the United States, especially as reflected in Hawaiian censuses during the twentieth century. She found much categorical flip-flopping in U.S. concepts of race since the first census of 1790. Since 1900 the census has used twenty-six different terms to identify the racial composition of the U.S. population.
4. Before 1940 it is practically impossible to obtain separate cross-tabulations for Puerto Ricans and race in the United States.
5. This change is similar to the early-twentieth-century shift among Brazilian elites from an ideology of whitening to the celebration of race mixture (Skidmore, 1974). As the editors of this collection have suggested, Puerto Ricans in the U.S. mainland who claim to be white are often subjected to ridicule by non–Puerto Ricans.
6. Similarly, Benjamin Bailey (1999) found that young Dominican Americans in Providence, Rhode Island, variously describe their race as Spanish, Hispanic, Dominican, or Latino, but never as black or white.
7. As Angela Ginorio (1979:107) argues, the recognition of a third racial group such as brown or other to designate Native Americans, Chicanos, Puerto Ricans, and other Latinos does not constitute a fundamental challenge to the American system of racial classification. Rather, it merely adds another discrete category based on ethnic background.
8. The racial implications of the various status options for Puerto Rico lie beyond the scope of this chapter. However, many Black Puerto Ricans have historically supported the island's total annexation to the United States, while the pro-independence movement has been predominantly white. The impact of racial distinctions on local elections remains unknown as a result of lack of research.

References

Administración de Reconstrucción de Puerto Rico. 1938. *Censo de Puerto Rico: 1935. Población y agricultura.* Washington, D.C.: Government Printing Office.

Almaguer, Tomás, and Moon-Kie Jung. 1998. The enduring ambiguities of race in the United States. Working paper 573, Center for Research on Social Organization, University of Michigan.

Bailey, Benjamin. 1999. Language and ethnic/racial identity of Dominican American high school students in Providence, Rhode Island. Ph.D. diss., University of California, Los Angeles.

Blanco, Tomás. 1985 [1942]. *El prejuicio racial en Puerto Rico.* 3rd ed. Río Piedras, P.R.: Huracán.

Davis, F. James. 1998. *Who Is Black? One Nation's Definition.* University Park: Pennsylvania State University.

Departamento de la Guerra, Dirección del Censo. 1900. *Informe sobre el censo de Puerto Rico, 1899.* Washington, DC: Government Printing Office.

Domínguez, Virginia. 1998. Exporting U.S. concepts of race: Are there limits to the U.S. model? *Social Research* 65 (2):369–400.

Duany, Jorge. 2002. *The Puerto Rican Nation on the Move: Identities on the Island and in the United States.* Chapel Hill: University of North Carolina Press.

Duany, Jorge, Luisa Hernández Angueira, and César A. Rey. 1995. *El Barrio Gandul: Economía subterránea y migración indocumentada en Puerto Rico.* Caracas: Nueva Sociedad.

Fitzpatrick, Joseph P. 1987. *Puerto Rican Americans: The Meaning of Migration to the Mainland.* 2nd ed. Englewood Cliffs, NJ: Prentice-Hall.

Ginorio, Angela Beatriz. 1979. A comparison of Puerto Ricans in New York with native Puerto Ricans and Native Americans on two measures of acculturation: Gender role and racial identification. Ph.D. diss., Fordham University.

Godreau, Isar P. 2000. La semántica fugitiva: "Raza," color y vida cotidiana en Puerto Rico. *Revista de Ciencias Sociales* (new series) 9:52–71.

Harris, Marvin. 1964. *Patterns of Race in the Americas.* New York: Norton.

Hill, Robert T. 1899. Porto Rico. *National Geographic* 11 (3):93–112.

———. 1903. *Cuba and Porto Rico, with the Other Islands of the West Indies.* 2nd ed. New York: The Century.

Hoetink, Harmannus. 1967. *Caribbean Race Relations: A Study of Two Variants.* London: Oxford University Press.

Inter-University Program for Latino Research. 2002. Race for Puerto Ricans by state. http://www.nd.edu/~iuplr/cic/his_org_9-02/4.htm.

Landale, Nancy S., and R. S. Oropesa. 2002. White, Black, or Puerto Rican? Racial self-identification among mainland and island Puerto Ricans. *Social Forces* 81 (1):231–254.

Latin American Perspectives. 1992. The politics of ethnic construction: Hispanic, Chicano, Latino . . .? Special issue, vol. 19, no. 4.

Martínez, Angel R. 1988. The effects of acculturation and racial identity on self-esteem and psychological well-being among young Puerto Ricans. Ph.D. diss., City University of New York.

Mercado Vega, César A. 1978. Memorandum to Rosendo Miranda Torres, November 13. Photocopy. Junta de Planificación de Puerto Rico, San Juan.

Montero Seplowin, Virginia. 1971. Análisis de la identificación racial de los puertorriqueños en Filadelfia. *Revista de Ciencias Sociales* 15 (1):143–148.

Mulero, Leonor. 1999. Ingresa la Isla a las estadísticas del censo federal. *El Nuevo Día* January 9, 10.

El Mundo. 1945. Comité Bell preocupado con gobierno insular. May 2, 5.

National Geographic. 1900. The first American census of Porto Rico 11 (8):328.

———. 1901. Cuba and Porto Rico 12 (2):80.

Oboler, Suzanne. 1995. *Ethnic Labels, Latino Lives: Identity and the Politics of (Re)Presentation in the United States.* Minneapolis: University of Minnesota Press.

Omi, Michael, and Howard Winant. 1994. *Racial Formation in the United States: From the 1960 to the 1990s.* 2nd ed. London: Routledge.

Rodríguez, Clara E. 1990. Racial identification among Puerto Rican men and women in New York. *Hispanic Journal of Behavioral Sciences* 12 (4):366–379.

———. 1992. Race, culture, and Latino "otherness" in the 1980 census. *Social Science Quarterly* 73 (4):930–937.

———. 1994. Challenging racial hegemony: Puerto Ricans in the United States. In *Race*, ed. Steven Gregory and Roger Sanjek, 131–145. New Brunswick, NJ: Rutgers University Press.

———. 1996. Puerto Ricans: Between Black and white. In *Historical Perspectives on Puerto Rican Survival in the United States*, ed. Clara E. Rodríguez and Virginia Sánchez Korrol, 23–36. Princeton, NJ: Markus Wiener.

———. 1997. Rejoinder to Roberto Rodríguez-Morazzani's "Beyond the Rainbow: Mapping the Discourse on Puerto Ricans and 'Race.'" *Centro* 9 (1):115–117.

———. 2000. *Changing Race: Latinos, the Census, and the History of Ethnicity in the United States*. New York: New York University Press.

Rodríguez, Clara E., and Héctor Cordero-Guzmán. 1992. Placing race in context. *Ethnic and Racial Studies* 25(4):523–542.

Rodríguez Cruz, Juan. 1965. Las relaciones raciales en Puerto Rico. *Revista de Ciencias Sociales* 9 (4):373–386.

Rodríguez-Morazzani, Roberto P. 1996. Beyond the rainbow: Mapping the discourse of Puerto Ricans and "race." *Centro* 8 (1–2):150–169.

Rogler, Charles C. 1940. *Comerio: A Study of a Puerto Rican Town*. University of Kansas.

———. 1972a [1946]. The morality of race mixing in Puerto Rico. In *Portrait of a Society: Readings on Puerto Rican Sociology*, ed. Eugenio Fernández Méndez, 57–64. Río Piedras, P.R.: University of Puerto Rico Press.

———. 1972b [1944]. The role of semantics in the study of race distance in Puerto Rico. In *Portrait of a Society: Readings on Puerto Rican Sociology*, ed. Eugenio Fernández Méndez, 49–56. Río Piedras, P.R.: University of Puerto Rico Press.

Ruggles, Steven, et al. 1997. Integrated public use microdata series: version 2.0: Enumerator instructions. http://www.ipums.umn.edu.

Schemo, Diana Jean. 2000. Despite options on census, many to check "Black" only. *New York Times*, February 12. http://archives.nytimes.com.

Seda Bonilla, Eduardo. 1968. Dos modelos de relaciones raciales: Estados Unidos y América Latina. *Revista de Ciencias Sociales* 12 (4):569–597.

Siegel, Morris. 1948. A Puerto Rican town. Center for Social Science Research, University of Puerto Rico, Río Piedras.

Skidmore, Thomas E. 1974. *Black into White: Race and Nationality in Brazilian Thought*. New York: Oxford University Press.

Tucker, Clyde, Ruth McKay, Brian Kojetin, Roderick Harrison, Manuel de la Puente, Linda Stinson, and Ed Robison. 1996. Testing methods of collecting racial and ethnic information: Results of the Current Population Survey Supplement on Race and Ethnicity. *Bureau of Labor Statistical Notes*, no. 40.

U.S. Bureau of the Census. 1913. *Thirteenth Census of the United States Taken in the Year 1910: Population*. Washington, DC: Government Printing Office.

———. 1921. *Fourteenth Census of the United States: 1920. Bulletin. Population: Porto Rico. Composition and Characteristics of the Population*. Washington, DC: Government Printing Office.

———. 1932. *Fifteenth Census of the United States: 1930. Agriculture and Population: Porto Rico*. Washington, DC: Government Printing Office.

———. 1943. *Sixteenth Census of the United States: 1940. Puerto Rico: Population. Bulletin No. 2: Characteristics of the Population*. Washington, DC: Government Printing Office.

———. 1946. *Sixteenth Census of the United States: 1940. Puerto Rico: Population Bulletin No. 4: Migration Between Municipalities*. Washington, DC: Government Printing Office.

———. 1952. *United States Census of Population: 1950. General Characteristics: Puerto Rico*. Washington, DC: Government Printing Office.

———. 1953a. *Census of Population: 1950. Volume II. Characteristics of the Population. Parts 51–54: Territories and Possessions*. Washington, DC: Government Printing Office.

U.S. Bureau of the Census. 1953b. *U.S. Census of Population: 1950. Special Reports: Puerto Ricans in Continental United States.* Washington, DC: Government Printing Office.

———. 1963. *U.S. Census of Population: 1960. Subject Reports: Puerto Ricans in the United States.* Washington, DC: Government Printing Office.

———. 1973. *1970 Census of Population. Subject Reports: Puerto Ricans in the United States.* Washington, DC: Government Printing Office.

———. 2001. American factfinder: Census 2000 data. http:www.census.gov/main/www/cen2000.html.

White, Trumbull. 1898. *Our New Possessions.* Boston: Adams.

Winant, Howard. 1994. *Racial Conditions: Politics, Theory, Comparisons.* Minneapolis: University of Minnesota Press.

Wolfson, Alan R. 1972. Raza, conocimiento del inglés y aprovechamiento social entre los inmigrantes puertorriqueños de Nueva York: Una aplicación de la teoría de grupos de referencia. Thesis project, School of Social Work, University of Puerto Rico.

CHAPTER 10

SCRIPTING RACE, FINDING PLACE: AFRICAN AMERICANS, AFRO-CUBANS, AND THE DIASPORIC IMAGINARY IN THE UNITED STATES

Nancy Raquel Mirabal

Scripting Race: Historical Articulations

Invisible things are not necessarily not there.
— Toni Morrison

Diaspora, like death, interrupts all conversation.
— Jorge Luis Arcos

The historical question of race, of its multiple articulations and meanings, figured greatly in the shared trans-American visions of Cuban diasporic movement, geography, and self. An important element in the re-historicizing of experience was the theoretical reworkings of what constitutes "historical diasporic blackness" from multiple vantage points. Critical to this analysis was the creation of a dialogue—loosely defined as speeches, newspapers, journals, pamphlets, and recorded club activity—that influenced how the Cuban nation was historically reimagined outside of Cuba by Cuban migrants and exiles. Key to this reimagining was the redefinition of "blackness" in relation to the Cuban national project, while at the same time calling for the erasure of "blackness" in the development of a shared Cuban nationalist identity. This historical dilemma of racial discourse and Cuban nation building inspired the Cuban poet Nicolas Guillén to note that the "problem of the Cuban Black is simply cultural" (1929).

Unlike African Americans who were historically positioned outside of the United States nation-building project, despite historical evidence to the contrary, Afro-Cubans both in and outside of the island, figured greatly in the Cuban revolutionary war efforts, exile nationalist movements, and the transnational reconfiguring of *Cubanidad*. Created during the late 1880s, *Cubanidad* was intended to assert an oppositional Cuban identity that challenged Spanish colonial rule. In addition, it also fostered and supported a nationalist language predicated and based on not only multiraciality but also the belief that there was no such thing as race.[1]

This rhetoric of racelessness, of a "raceless nationality," held much currency among not only Afro-Cubans in Cuba and Afro-Cuban migrants in the United States, but also among African Americans who by the late nineteenth and early twentieth centuries were more involved in pan-African, global, and other transgeographical definitions of race. By this time, Cuba, as fiction, as racial paradise, loomed large in the imagination of African Americans. As David Hellwig (1998) has observed, "Except for Haiti, no New World society received as much attention from black North Americans in the nineteenth century as did Cuba."[2] The beginning of the twentieth century signaled a rethinking of "blackness," a creation of a new dialogue on Africa, and a willingness to look past the United States for alternative definitions to race and race making. The end of slavery, Reconstruction, the incorporation of state-sanctioned racial segregation, and the use of Black troops to fight imperialist wars inspired African Americans to challenge U.S. racial supremacy and privilege. As James Grossman (2000) has written, African Americans faced innumerable economic, social, and political barriers as they worked toward undoing past injustices and "argued among themselves as to what those barriers were made of; exactly where they were situated; how permanent they were; and whether they should be destroyed, circumvented or hurdled."

An important part of this negotiation was the development and use of a shared dialogue, one carried out forcefully in Black newspapers and among figures like W. E. B. DuBois, Ida B. Wells, and Langston Hughes that not only rethought "blackness" but also reached past U.S. geographical imaginings to include a global framing of Afro-diasporic culture and politics. One of the countries that African Americans looked toward during this period was Cuba, one of the ideas they responded to was the concept of a "raceless" nation and nationality, a concept articulated and promoted by José Martí and the Partido Revolucionario Cubano (Cuban Revolutionary Party) during the late nineteenth century when he lived and worked in the United States.

During the last decade scholars working in the fields of Latin American and Latina/o studies, including Agnes Lugo-Ortiz (1999), Julio Ramos (2001), Kristen Silva Gruesz (2002), and José David Saldívar (1991), have resituated Martí as a trans-American writer and thinker who transcended nationally drawn borders and, in doing so, questioned the politics of location. According to Julio Ramos (2001), Martí is first and foremost a writer who travels to New York, not because of any specific exilic, romantic, or political reasons, but because at this time New York was the publishing capital of the United States. This is not to say, as Ramos reminds us, that Martí is not deeply affected by the growing imperialism of the United States and the shifting of borders, in particular, between the United States and Mexico and between the United States and the Caribbean. That Ramos refuss to see Martí as mainly a political figure, offering instead a vision of an intellectual who conceives of revolutionary and nationalistic politics, is part of a larger project on literary imaginings that in many respects forces a rethinking of the production of knowledge and the process involved in historical writing, especially when it comes to Martí's articulations of race.

For the late French historical philosopher Michel de Certeau (1988) such revisionism was both "natural" and indicative of the process involved in historical reproductions and the incessant re-creation of knowledge—processes that reveal the precarious and changeable natures of historiographies. In many respects, Martí and the symbolism/symbol of Martí, reveals the changeable nature of historiographies— a dangerous meditation if we are to believe in fixed and static historical "truths." Martí seemingly belongs to everyone and no one. He is both political and apolitical, direct and mysterious, genuine and strategic—his truth residing in large part in the imagination of those who think and write about him. It is within this context, rife with possibility and inconsistencies but always directed toward a specific goal, that Martí's analysis of race and gender must be understood.

By the time Martí arrived in New York, the city already had a reputation among Cuban immigrants and exiles as a site for political organization and activism. In 1823 the separatist newspaper *El Habanero* was first published in New York City, and by the 1830s the work of Father Felix Varela[3] in Philadelphia and later in New York was well known to the members of the Cuban independence movement. During the 1880s and the late 1890s the Cuban nationalist movement was at its peak. The founding of the Partido Revolucionario Cubano and the popularity of its newspaper *Patria* solidified New York City as a site for activism and political organization. Furthermore, the high numbers of Afro-Cubans involved in the separatist uprisings of 1868 and 1880 in Cuba directly impacted the political organization of the Cuban community in the United States. Exile separatists and nationalists were now seriously considering the end of slavery and the future incorporation of Afro-Cubans into the Cuban social structure. Before the wars the language used to promote nation building was invested in calling for the "gradual" abolition of slavery and either the annexation of Cuba to the United States or an "independent" Cuba with strong economic and political ties to Spain.

An example of the earlier Cuban exile politics can be found in the pro-annexationist newspaper *La Verdad*, established in 1849 in New York City. The editors represented the interests of the annexationists who, on the one hand, advocated for the independence of Cuba from Spain but, on the other, believed in the annexation of Cuba to the United States At the root of this argument was nothing less than the fear of a potentially powerful Black majority in Cuba. Looking to Haiti, Jamaica, and the Dominican Republic, the editors of *La Verdad* questioned whether Cubans could in fact govern themselves or their affairs, given the racial character of the population.

> In Hayti [*sic*] the negroes have had unlimited power, as in Jamaica they have had unlimited equality and what advances have they made in happiness or civilization? In the plenetude [*sic*] of their undisputed sway, they have murdered, insulted it; and driven out the whites in St. Domingo, and no authority prevented; they have governed themselves and no man has said them nay.[4]

The failure of the Ten Years' War in 1878 and La Guerra Chiquita in 1880 to gain independence from Spain, as well as the high level of Afro-Cuban involvement and participation in the wars, dramatically changed the racial politics among Cubans in New York City. No longer could Cuban exiles and migrants subscribe to or even tolerate the racial politics and tactics espoused by newspapers like *La Verdad*. For the separatists, any past discussions that associated blackness with being uncivilized or unable to govern were seen as running counter to any and all efforts to gain independence from Spain. By the 1880s Cuban separatists promoted a dialogue that emphasized blackness within the insurgent ranks and connected it to both the nationalist and independence movements. In short, blackness was code for Cuban liberation.

The change in politics and perspective was evident in the literature published during this period. *El Mulato*, an antislavery newspaper published in New York, argued that it was necessary "to attack slavery in whatever way it was disguised." Other New York newspapers, including *El Habanero*, *La Independencia*, and *La Revolucion*, called for racial unity and total independence at all costs. Yet, despite the determination to move forward, the nationalist movement was fragmented and its members were distrustful of one another. To unify the struggle, organizers centered race as part of a larger dialogue on freedom and independence. In the late 1880s José Martí (1972:276) gave a speech in Tampa that redirected the uses and meanings of race within the nationalist movement.

> Shall we fear the black, the noble black, and the black brother who has forgiven the Cubans who still mistreats him? The revolution, which has brought together all Cubans regardless of their color, whether they come from the continent where the skin burns, or from people of a gentler light, will be for all Cubans.

Although Martí attempts to speak for the Afro-Cuban population, who he is really responding to are the white Cubans listening in the audience. Martí understood that if the movement was finally to succeed he needed to convince white Cubans to change their ideas about race and war as well as to revise the nationalist movement's revolutionary platform so that it took seriously racial equality and civil rights. One of the strategies that Martí used to accomplish this tenuous balance was to both name and "erase" the meanings and impact of race. On the one hand, he asks white Cubans to not be afraid of the "black brother," while, on the other, he emphasizes that "regardless of color" the revolution will be for all Cubans. Highlighting a process of "being" Cuban allowed Martí and the Partido Revolucionario Cubano to create unity in a time of disunion and, moreover, to bypass and avoid having to truly confront the racial problems and divisions facing the Cuban immigrant community.

An understudied and rarely discussed element of *Cubanidad* has been the different articulations of not only blackness but also whiteness to neutralize racial tensions. For blackness to work as a tool of Cuban liberation that challenged historical notions of Spanish colonial rule and slavery, it could not lessen the uses of whiteness or the power of white Cuban insurgents and *independistas* in the movement. As such, whiteness was normalized and erased from the discussion, making it possible for Martí to use blackness to articulate *Cubanidad* as a tool for engineering political unity among a community still deeply affected and divided by a long history of slavery and colonial racial hierarchies.

Refusing to Erase: War and the Geographical Reimaginings
of Blackness in the Diaspora

We may blow all we want but the victory at San Juan Hill belongs to the colored boys. I was there, and for my part, I would not be so mean as to rob them of it.
— Reverend Astwood, A.M.E. Missionary (Lynk, 1899:54)

. . . one "silences" a fact or an individual as a silencer silences a gun.
— Michel Rolph Trouillot (1995)

The United States' intervention in the Cuban War for Independence in 1898, or the Spanish-American War, as it is commonly known in U.S. historiography, is one of the most revised and silenced wars in our collective U.S. historical memory. Few know exactly how and why it began, and even fewer know how it ended. It is not uncommon in the United States' historical memory to bypass the Cuban revolutionary wars (i.e., the Ten Years' War, La Guerra Chiquita, and El Grito de Baire) as well as long-standing Cuban exile and immigrant nationalist activity in the United States. In addition, the passages of the Foraker Act in 1900 and the Platt Amendment in Cuba in 1901 are rarely part of the historical discourse.[5] And yet they were critical to U.S. empire building in the Caribbean and to Puerto Rican and Cuban postwar nationalist movements, migrations, and diasporic experiences. These silences, as the Haitian anthropologist Michel Rolph Trouillot (1995) has observed, are part of a larger project of historical silencing sanctioned by a Western historiography that is incapable of "expressing the unthinkable," as well as one that promotes a politics of erasure (1995:101). For Puerto Ricans, Filipinos, Cubans, and African Americans, however, the war and its colonial aftermath would not be easily forgotten nor erased. In fact, unlike U.S. historical productions, it would remain a large part of what would constitute historical memory, experience, and the process of nation building.

The period during and after the war also marked a turning point in the diasporic articulations of race. Along with being the first war that the United States fought "abroad," it was also the first war to draft "free" African American men to fight. The drafting of African American male bodies was an ironic and insidious twist in a post-slavery politics that viewed this policy as proof that African Americans were now full "citizens" of the United States. This irony was not lost on African Americans as they debated and questioned the nation's intentions in using its racialized bodies to fight other "foreign" racialized bodies in an attempt to carry out and win what was for many an imperialist war. African American participation in a war designed to create and implement empire initiated a dialogue focused on colonialism, race, empire, civil rights, and citizenship. It also signaled the creation of a language that spoke to larger discussions of "blackness," one that attempted to give meaning to diasporic connection and displaced geographies. While mainstream U.S. newspapers scripted empire by glorifying war and supporting colonialism, the majority of Black newspapers remained deeply ambivalent and torn. A number of African American editors and reporters were not completely convinced of President McKinley's reasons for intervening in Cuba and, as such, considered it a deeply racist war. As an editor for the

Kansas City American Citizen put it, "the fear of Negro dominancy in Cuba was the root of the United States' desire to annex the island" (Gatewood, 1975).

The *Indianapolis Freeman* published an article depicting most African Americans as "indifferent patriots," while another article printed in the same edition of the *Freeman* called for African Americans to make specific demands on the U.S. government before engaging in any form of military battle.

> If the government wants our support and services, let us demand and get a guarantee for our safety and protection at home. We want to put a stop to lynch laws, the butchering of our people like hogs, burning our houses, shooting our wives and children and raping our daughters and mothers. (March 19, 1898)

At the same time, the highly racialized nature of the war caused one reporter for the *Kansas City American Citizen* to question the mainstream press's support for Cuban independence.

> When it is remembered that the majority of the Cuban insurgents and soldiers are colored people this unanimity of demand [for Cuban independence] on the part of the press of the country can hardly be understood. . . . Cuba is extremely near our Southern border and everybody knows that the South is wedded to the doctrine of "white supremacy." (October 4, 1895)

The opinions and strategies among African Americans as reflected by the Black press informed the workings and direction of a public dialogue that took seriously the possibility of an ideological alliance between African Americans and Afro-Cuban revolutionaries, an alliance that had at its core a shared and mutual understanding of "freedom" and protection. Such understanding could not be ignored considering that at the same time that African American soldiers were fighting an imperialist war on behalf of the United States, African Americans were experiencing racial terror, disenfranchisement, and segregation.

In March 1898, the eve of the United States' entrance into the war, the editors of the *Richmond Planet* wondered, "Who will be expected to do the fighting? The Negro-haters have declared this to be a white man's country, and the Negroes themselves have inquired, why should not the white man fight for it." A few months later the *Iowa Bystander* published the comments of an African American male on the impending war: "I will not go to war. I have no country to fight for. I have not been given my rights here" (May 20, 1898).

The relationship between civil rights at home and war abroad was a continual and insistent theme in the Black newspapers published during this period. While many— as the quotes above illustrate—questioned the war, a number argued that African American involvement in the war would prove their worth as a community to a white population that mistreated them. Many believed that if they fought hard and devoted themselves to ending Spanish tyranny in Cuba, they could change the minds of white Americans who viewed them as inferior. In "The War Will Help the Negro" a reporter for the *Iowa Bystander* outlined the various reasons why African American men should fight in the war: "We think that the present war will help the colored man in America, that is, his real worth will be more respected; his help is needed; his loyalty will establish a friendlier feeling in the South between the two races, his bravery and patriotism in the hour of need will hereafter grant equal justice and freedom" (April 28, 1898). Along with viewing the war as a catalyst for change, some African Americans used the Black press to argue that the involvement of the Black troops was an "obligation of citizenship."

This argument, however, would prove futile in the face of the decision in *Plessy v. Ferguson* (1896), which legalized racial segregation in the United States. The passage of this court decision two years before the war only reinforced the position of leaders such as Booker T. Washington who doubted that the war would "blot out racial prejudice" (Gatewood, 1970). For George W. Prioleau, a chaplain of the Ninth Cavalry, African American participation in the Spanish-American War was an increasingly ironic comment on the United States' refusal to respond to its own problems. "Talk about fighting and freeing poor Cuba from Spain's brutality . . . is America better than Spain?" (Gatewood, 1975). Another African American chaplain, T. G. Steward, of the 25th Infantry, further echoed Prioleau's ironic sentiments when he observed that Afro-Cubans faced the "glorious dilemma" of being relieved of Spanish tyranny only to be "pushed into the condition of the American Negro" (Gatewood, 1970).

Steward's prophetic observations were for many African Americans and Afro-Cubans a testament to the potential danger of U.S. imperialism. Not only would the United States' highly racialized perception and execution of the war push Cubans into the "condition of the American Negro," but it would also strengthen racial segregation and discrimination at home. The period between 1898 and 1933 was one of transition and change. During this period both African Americans and Afro-Cubans attempted to reimagine a postslavery, postreconstruction, and postwar "blackness" that would at its very root be empowering and self-defined. The constant violence, lynching, and widespread segregation and discrimination convinced many African Americans to look outside of the United States. For some, Cuba was the ideal place for resituating blackness. Booker T. Washington, for instance, believed that Cubans had "surpassed the United States in solving the race problem in that they have no race problem." The African American writer John Cromwell echoed Washington's sentiments when he observed that Cubans both black and white lived "on terms of perfect equality." Before Washington and Cromwell's public statements on Cuba, the Reverend John L. Waller had already formed the Afro-American Cuban Emigration Society in 1899, an organization devoted to moving African Americans to Cuba. Waller went so far as to ask the U.S. Congress for $20 million to move close to 2,000 African Americans to Cuba. Although a number of congressmen supported the idea, the project was never funded.

For many African Americans, Cuba remained a necessary site for examining the possibility, the potential, and even the failures of race relations. According to David Hellwig (1998), African Americans viewed the island not as an accessible holiday retreat for the wealthy or an outlet for investments but rather as a "setting for an experiment in race relations offering hope that former slaves and slave masters could live together harmoniously." Envisioning this potential was necessary for, at the very least, any attempt to re-create such coexistence, not to mention the belief that coexistence was even possible. In 1912, however, the "Race War" in Cuba would change the parameters of potential, causing African Americans to seriously reconsider the image of Cuba as racial paradise.

In 1908 Evaristo Estenoz founded the Partido Independiente de Color (PIC) as a forum for advocating change and equality for Afro-Cubans during the post-1898 period in Cuba.[6] The PIC called for an end to racial discrimination, the integration of Afro-Cubans into the Cuban social, economic, and political structure, and an end to the ban on "nonwhite" immigration to Cuba.[7] While the PIC did focus on issues related to Afro-Cuban equality, it also made demands for improving the conditions of the popular classes regardless of race. These included, among many things, the expansion of compulsory free education, abolition of the death penalty, and distribution of national lands to Cubans. By 1911 the PIC had grown into a powerful political party that boasted a membership of close to several thousand members. The publication of the influential and radical newspaper *Previsión* made the PIC a target for the Cuban government who were threatened by the organization's growing power among Afro-Cubans.

On May 20, 1912, the members of the PIC organized an armed protest to pressure the Cuban government into allowing them to participate in the November elections and repealing the Morúa amendment, which banned any club or political party organized on the basis of race. The government responded to the protest by labeling it a "race war" and sending military troops to deal with the protestors. Within days hundreds of PIC members and supporters had been killed and others had been jailed. On June 27 Estenoz was shot and killed. A month later another key figure of the PIC, Pedro Ivonnet, was also killed.

Before 1912 editors of Black newspapers rarely covered Cuban politics in detail. One of the few exceptions was when an American-owned hotel refused to serve two Afro-Cuban congressmen in 1910. In 1912, however, Black newspapers began to take notice. The African American publication *The Crisis* published an article written by the Puerto Rican activist Arturo Schomburg, a well-known archivist of African American culture and history,[8] in which he detailed the events leading up to the revolt in Cuba. After chronicling the rise and fall of Estenoz and the PIC, Schomburg went on to criticize the racist politics of the Cuban government, declaring that "many Negroes curse the dawn of the Republic." The republic, as Schomburg argued, did little to honor all that Afro-Cubans had done in "the time of hardship during the days of revolution." Schomburg concluded the article by noting that although "the Negro had done much for Cuba, Cuba had done nothing for the Negro" (Schomburg 1912). This was a particularly troubling comment considering that Schomburg along with being a close ally of José Martí, had a long history of activism in the Cuban and Puerto Rican nationalist movements of the 1890s. Furthermore Schomburg was committed to the idea of a global Afro-diasporic identity that could transcend racial barriers and encompass a larger, more expansive view of "blackness."

He cultivated long-term friendships with Afro-Cuban writers, thinkers, and activists and traveled to Cuba frequently, creating and cementing collaborations and alliances.

Schomburg's analysis of Cuban racial politics thus marked a departure from his earlier writings, which tended to cast Cuba as a racial paradise. Also, its appearance in *The Crisis* was a clear indication that African American perceptions of Cuban racial politics were also changing. Instead of praising the Cuban government, Black newspapers were now questioning the Cuban government's policies and openly challenging the U.S. government's role in the uprising, especially with the U.S. intervention and subsequent occupation in 1906 and 1912. While the theme of racial equality in Cuba as opposed to that in the United States would continue to be debated, Schomburg's comment on the state of Cuban racial affairs was a wake-up call to Afro-diasporic populations looking to Cuba for alternative definitions of global blackness.

Pivotal Politics and Revolutionary Migrations. Diasporic Race Making in New York, 1930s–1990s

... the problem of the American Negroes and Cuban Negroes are essentially different although both have in common, the racial problem.

—Marcus Garvey[9]

La question de la raza, digamos, los problemas entre los negros y los blanco cubanos no se hablaba mucho, y menos en Nueva York

—Lydia "Tata" Caraballosa[10]

When asked how race operated in New York during the late 1940s and early 1950s, Lydia "Tata" Caraballosa answered that, for the most part, it was not "talked about" among Cubans arriving in New York. Although initially reluctant to discuss the differences among Cubans, especially when it came to race, Caraballosa was like many Cuban migrants of that period who employed a diasporic language that privileged the workings of culture and ethnicity, all the while knowing it did not reveal the full story. Not revealing the full story was for many racialized Cuban migrants a necessary strategy for negotiating the migrant experience in New York during this period. Although Caraballosa passed for *not* "being Black," she was also *not* "white." As a mixed-race Cuban woman, she occupied a racialized, "foreign" in-betweenness that allowed for mobility and access but never enough to truly pass or be considered white by U.S. racial definitions. Once in the United States, Cubans redefined their own notions of "blackness," "whiteness," and "in-betweenness" by attaching meanings and delineations to the very process of exile and migrant race making.

For Melba Alvarado who migrated to New York City in the 1930s, the process of race making meant repositioning and expanding "blackness" to include the building of political movements and activism that, although focused on Cuba and Cuban issues, such as the founding of El Club Cubano InterAmericano, welcomed African Americans, Puerto Ricans, and Dominicans as members. Blackness was the unspoken variable in the creation of political clubs that had as their organizing principle culture and ethnicity.[10] By defining a club as *Cuban*, migrants could render exclusivity and reset the parameters of race making by using *Cuban* or *Cubanidad* both to decenter the importance of race and to signal "blackness" among Cubans and other Afro-diasporic communities in New York. And yet the very process of naming an organization or club *Cuban* was designed to limit the workings of "blackness" among its members.

This seemingly opposing process, that is, the multiple uses and articulations of race, was common among Afro-Cuban migrants who chose to operate within, and continually cultivate, the spaces "in-between." It was in these "in-between spaces" in these particular sites of contestation and convergence that definitions of race were rescripted to suit a shared diasporic imaginary. An important element in this reconfiguration was, and continues to be, the uses of silences to discuss and understand how Cuban migrants and exiles defined race. The uses of multiple silences in the production of knowledge and historical thinking help to explain Caraballosa's contention that race was "not talked about"; and, too, they operate as a tool for interrogating a process that also involves a reassertion of self and community, factors necessary to the processes and workings of Afro-Latinidad. In addition, an important but rarely discussed element of Afro-Latinidad is the production of "whiteness" as defined by privilege and access.

In 1922 an Afro-Cuban lawyer by the name of Bernardo Ruíz Suarez (1922) published a pamphlet with the title *The Color Question in the Two Americas*. In it he attempted to explain the *differences* between Afro-Cuban and African American men. Although never fully defined, "culture," he argued, was what caused migrants from "Spanish-American" countries to declare that they were "not an American negro" (16). For Ruíz Suarez, this contention was predicated on the belief that since Afro-Cubans played a large role in the independence movements in Cuba, they could rightfully declare themselves not only Black but also "Cuban." Designating oneself as part of the nation-state or, more important, the nation-building project, allowed Afro-Cubans to distinguish themselves from African Americans and to complicate definitions of blackness, culture, nationality, and self. At the same time, Ruíz Suarez's contention was dependent on a shared assumption that African Americans were *not* seen by the white population as critical to the nation-building project: "the black American, generally and practically speaking is not even a citizen of his country" (47). Ruíz Suarez's discussion of citizenship, or the lack thereof, is best understood as it relates to cultural citizenship, that is, a politics of citizenship which defines belonging as cultural acceptance; for Afro-Cuban men this would mean reinscribing them into the process of cultural production (Rosaldo, 1997). At the same time, in situating African American citizenship on the margins of the nation, Ruíz Suarez interprets their disenfranchisement and disempowerment as being both without culture and without the rights of citizenship.

In addition to reifying citizenship and culture to discuss difference, Ruíz Suarez also problematizes "whiteness." While Ruíz Suarez makes a case for *Cubanidad* in shaping Afro-Cuban migrant identity, he also questions how "white" Cubans refuse to be accountable for their own brand of racism. His frustration is particularly palpable when he compares how white Cubans treat Afro-Cubans with how white Americans treat African Americans.

> In the one case, the white man pretends to give him the hand of fellowship, as to a brother reared in the same cradle. The [white] American, on the other hand, regards him with haughty disdain and considers him not at all as a man, a black man, and a citizen, but simply as a negro, an indefinite and indefinable thing, at best. (Ruíz Suarez, 1922:24)

Ruíz Suarez's argument concerning the workings of "whiteness" was, in a very different sense, partly shared by the Afro-Cuban poet Nicolás Guillén. In 1929 Guillén authored an article entitled "El blanco: es ahí el problema" (The white: There is the problem) which directly addressed Cuban racism and the uses of whiteness. For Guillén what made Cuban racism so intolerable was that it was couched in a language of tolerance, unity, and cultural pride, which served to diffuse the quotidian racism that Afro-Cubans endured. Guillén noted that "as long as the whites are not disposed to recognize that under equal conditions we ought to enjoy identical rights, there will not be a single firm step taken toward bringing together the two great nuclei that make up the Cuban population."[12]

What makes this text invaluable as a source is that it historically contextualizes a public discourse on the perceived and "real" differences between Afro-Cuban and African American men in New York on the basis of citizenship and culture. An important part of that production, however, was the creation of a deeply masculinist language that underpinned the fundamental workings of privilege, authority, power, and place under the rubric of masculinity. Women rarely enter the dialogue of racialized productions of Afro-Cuban or African American identity, community, and self. When they do, it is solely to point out and exult the "feminine charms" of Cuban and American women. Consisting of three pages, the main argument of the very brief chapter "Women in the Two Americas" is a comparison between the "Anglo-American" and "her Spanish-American sister." Remarkably, Afro-Cuban and African American women were not even mentioned by Ruíz Suarez, making it clear that it is men who decide the answers to the "color question."

The masculinist undertaking of rewriting cultural racial politics is a problematic in the historical reconstitution and rethinking of race by Afro-Cubans and African Americans. The famous collaboration between Nicolas Guillén and Langston Hughes, while fruitful and important, reveals little about the role of women and everything about how men viewed their place within the politics of race making. The connection between both writers, that is, their willingness to see connections and create a language that spoke to universal and global racial problems, was instrumental in the movement toward a larger understanding of Afro-diasporic thinking. For both men, their creative work also translated into activism. Both were active in fighting against U.S. imperialism, neocolonialism, and racism. In 1937 both men traveled to Spain to help defend the Spanish Republic. Greeted by Spaniards and the African American men who were part of the Abraham Lincoln Brigade, both men were outspoken opponents of fascism. As the Spanish newspaper *Estampa* reported in September 1937 concerning Guillén and Hughes's visit, "Ellos llevarán a la América negra y la America blanca el dolor de nuestra España" (They will take back to Black America and white America the pain of our Spain).[13]

While Guillén and Hughes's creative collaborations and mutual political work were welcomed by both communities, Marcus Garvey and the Universal Negro Improvement Association (UNIA) were never fully embraced by Afro-Cuban migrants in New York. In 1914 Marcus Garvey founded the UNIA in his native Jamaica. Soon thereafter, the UNIA spread to the United States, Central America, and rest of the Caribbean. Garvey's vision of a pan-Africanist movement aimed at joining African peoples across the globe received a decidedly mixed response from Afro-Cubans in Cuba and in the United States. His idea was put to the test seven years later, in 1921, when Garvey visited Cuba. Although Afro-Cubans did not fully welcome him or his message, his visit made sound political sense, as close to 50,000 Jamaican immigrants and a significant number of Haitians were then living and working in Cuba.

While the West Indian population in Cuba supported Garvey, the Afro-Cuban newspapers, including *La Antorcha* and *La Prensa*, were quick to challenge his politics. The newspapers dismissed the idea of going back to Africa, of creating an altogether new homeland, since most Afro-Cubans had no interest or intention of leaving Cuba for Africa. Despite this, Spanish editions of the UNIA newspaper, the *Negro World*, were circulated and small chapters of the UNIA were organized. In the late 1920s, however, the UNIA and the *Negro World*, and by 1930 Marcus Garvey himself, were banned from Cuba. Citing the Morúa Law, which prohibited the formation of race-based organizations, President Gerardo Machado justified his actions by claiming that there was "no racial problem in Cuba" (Robaina, 1998:121–122). Afro-Cuban resistance to Garvey in Cuba influenced how Afro-Cuban migrants would respond to the rise of Garveyism in New York. While many left Cuba in protest, few Afro-Cuban migrant organizations and mutual-aid societies would make the connection between Machado's refusal to address racial inequities in Cuba and the goal of the UNIA. For Melba Alvarado's father who was politically active in both Cuba and New York, the UNIA was a movement that demanded a certain renunciation of the nation-state. According to Alvarado, her father believed that Garveyism "was Jamaican politics, not Cuban."[14] Despite the broken promises and the refusal of the nation-state to allow Afro-Cuban participation in nation building, it appeared that Afro-Cubans were still not willing to relinquish the nation for a larger global rethinking.

During the early part of the twentieth century the migration of Cubans to the United States increased significantly. By 1930 close to 19,000 Cubans lived and worked in the United States, an increase of 5,000 from 1920.[15] Much of this migration was a result of President Gerardo Machado's policies in Cuba as well as the subsequent overthrow of his government in 1933. Elected on a reform platform in 1924, Machado promised to end political corruption and initiate policies and programs designed to modernize Cuba. As part of his agenda, he also called for an end to U.S. influence, specifically questioning the role of the Platt Amendment, a visible and recognizable vestige of U.S. policies in Cuba. By 1929, however, it was clear that Machado was more interested in protecting the assets of Cuba's upper classes, foreign capital, and business interests. A few years earlier Machado had targeted the newly formed Communist Party and labor unions such as the Confederación Nacional Obrera de Cuba. Workers, students, labor organizers, and Socialist Party members were periodically beaten and imprisoned. The repression led to more demonstrations, chaos, and calls for the end of Machado's presidency. In addition, Cuba, like most of Latin America, was hit hard by the economic depression, adding fuel to the already unstable political situation. Strikes and work stoppages in lucrative and key industries, such as sugar, cigars, railroads, construction, and manufacturing, made the political and economic situation in Cuba unbearable. Within a few years and after the United States had been called in to mediate, President Machado was overthrown.

It was during this period, in 1931, that Melba Alvarado's father migrated to New York. Frustrated by the economic and political chaos, Alvarado's father did what many Afro-Cubans had already done, which was to move to New York. An early supporter of Machado, Alvarado's father soon changed his mind as he witnessed the violence and repression in Cuba. Five years later Alvarado would migrate with her family, settling in an upstairs apartment located on 113th street and Fifth Avenue in New York City. Alvarado shared in her father's later politics, openly supporting student activist and founder of the Cuban Communist Party, Julio Antonio Mella. Alvarado's support for Mella would continue long after his assassination in Mexico and influence her politics for the next thirty years.

This period also witnessed an increase in the migration of women to the United States. Although difficult to assess fully because of the frequent returns and transnationalist movements of Cuban migrants, close to a third of the Cubans who migrated to the United States were women. Of that number, it is estimated that a third were Afro-Cuban women. Records of Afro-Cuban social clubs in New York, along with oral histories, show a steady increase in the migration of Afro-Cuban women during the late 1930s and early 1950s. In 1949 Lydia Caraballosa left Santiago de Cuba to be with her husband who had left months earlier for the United States. Once there, she found work in the garment industry. As Caraballosa put it, "Me fui para Nueva York, pa' hacer un poquito de agua y carbon."[16] Similar to many Cuban women who migrated during this period, Caraballosa traveled to the United States on a B-29 tourist visa and simply stayed. Intended to allow immigrants to stay in the country a maximum of twenty-nine days, the B-29 visas quickly became a well-known strategy for entering the United States to find work.[17] For the next forty years Caraballosa would continue to work in one capacity or another in the garment industry. Alvarado would also find work in the garment industry and stay there until her retirement. Afro-Cuban labor participation in the garment industry was so pervasive that local Cuban clubs and organizations offered classes where migrant women could learn to sew well enough to gain employment in the factories.[18]

The migrations of the 1930s and 1940s were smaller in number than the pre-1898 and post-1959 migrations. Yet they were significant in redefining the Cuban migrant community because they attracted not only Afro-Cuban political migrants but also economic migrants who tended to settle in large urban areas like New York City. Afro-Cuban male migrants were soon impacting and affecting sports, in particular boxing and baseball, as well as music and literature. Afro-Cuban male musicians, including Mario Bauza, Luciano "Chano" Pozo, Perez Prado, and Frank "Machito" Grillo, were influencing jazz, bebop, and what Dizzy Gillespie would later categorize as Cu-Bop, by fusing jazz with Cuban music. According to Geoffrey Jacques (1998), what connected these musicians was Africa and African music. Citing Dizzy Gillespie's characterization of Pozo as not Cuban, but "really African, you know," he goes on to explain how a shared and imagined sense of being from Africa informed the relationship among musicians:

> Of course, the Cubans themselves more openly proclaimed the African roots of their music, and this made it easier for American jazz musicians to appropriate the identifications with Africa for their own purposes. The references to Pozo's Africanness, while taking full account of the drummer's relationship to religious survival in Cuba, also helped black American musicians to use Cuban culture to expand the African-American cultural palette and identity.

The cultivation of shared musical spaces among African American and Afro-Cuban musicians was also influencing the creation of shared political spaces.

The 1940s and 1950s was a period of much collaboration and political realignment among communities. The end of World War II, the Civil Rights Movement, the Cuban Revolution, and the Black Power Movement, inspired many, especially second-generation Afro-Cubans, to organize across "culture" and create a fused political agenda that emphasized shared African roots, slavery, colonialism, and disenfranchisement at the hands of European populations. These alliances ranged from Afro-Cubans becoming active and part of the Civil Rights Movement to African-Americans supporting the Cuban Revolution. The spaces for organizing, however, were at times contested. As past president of El Club Cubano InterAmericano Alvarado was instrumental in drafting bylaws that prohibited any discussion of politics, let alone activism. The club was designed to be a social space that welcomed not only Afro-Cubans but also Puerto Ricans, Dominicans, African Americans, and West Indian migrants. Cuban migrants, as Alavarado recounted, were divided when it came to the revolution and the politics of Batista. "It was to respect the club to not take sides," she said. "And very funny, the white ones thought that we were pro-Batista and many of the pro-Batistas thought we were communist, but in the club we don't take sides."[19] It is interesting to note how in this instance Alvarado links "whiteness" and the political beliefs of white Cubans with perceptions of what constitutes Afro-Cuban revolutionary politics.

It was as a result of such potential confusion that Alvarado was adamant that the club should not be used as a site for political debate. Yet, as she herself noted, she was nonetheless politically active outside of the club supporting the Cuban Revolution even though she never publicly supported Fidel Castro. Alvarado, however, was an exception. As she herself conceded, "Yo no creo que habia apoyo entre los cubano de color [por Fidel Castro]; el 90 percent era más Batistero que otra cosa" (I don't believe that there was support among Cubans of color [for Fidel Castro]; 90 percent were more pro-Batista than anything else). It is not clear from the records why Afro-Cubans would support Batista when the revolutionary rhetoric responded to and openly addressed Cuban racism. Because of the differences in opinions, especially when it came to Cuban revolutionary politics, Alvarado believed that the club needed to be free of dissension and division, and the only way to guarantee this was to prohibit politics and emphasize culture. Despite the changes taking place in the Afro-Cuban migrant community, "culture" would continue to be used as a strategy to remake and sustain community even as it was being crossed in larger political arenas.

Club members also used culture as a means of prolonging the group's tenure by accepting non-Cuban Afro-diasporic members, specifically other Black immigrants and African Americans. During the 1950s and 1960s the influx of new non-Cuban members effectively changed the club's orientation; it would now cater to a diverse Afro-diasporic community. The connections between the different communities inspired Afro-Cubans to become more involved in the civil rights and later the third world liberation movements, including the Young Lords; and African Americans, for their part, would organize in support of the Cuban Revolution.

The success of the Cuban Revolution in 1959 and the subsequent exile further complicated how earlier Afro-Cuban migrants produced and articulated blackness. The large numbers of Cuban exiles who arrived in the United States were white and from the middle and upper classes. Exiles would refashion a Cuban migrant identity that could not be separated from the revolution or the politics of exile. At the same time, because the revolution promised to end racism on the island, a number of Afro-Cubans chose to stay on the island and support a revolution they believed would at last respond to the racial inequities of past generations. As a result, a disproportionate number of Afro-Cubans remained in Cuba during most of the 1960s and 1970s. It would not be until 1980 with the Mariel boatlift that Afro-Cubans would leave the island and live in exile in the United States. The combination of factors as well as the formation of an exile community that rarely discussed or posited "blackness" as a necessary and important part of community making, would in the end challenge the power and sustainability of "culture."

The late twentieth century would continue to complicate and change racial discourses among Cuban migrants, as well as those among Afro-Cubans and African Americans. The liberation movements of the 1960s and 1970s, along with the Mariel boatlift of the 1980s, emphasized "blackness" and at the same time erased it, especially in the realm of Cuban identity making in the late twentieth century. While Cuba was not cast as the racial paradise of past generations, it was seen as the potential and radical future of African peoples around the world. In contrast to past migrations, the Mariel boatlift of 1980 and the Balseros of 1994 included a large number of Afro-Cubans. The recent migrations of Afro-Cubans again reconfigured a language of race, sexuality, culture, and gender that was not always understood or employed in community making among Cuban exiles.

Notes

1. In his most famous and, subsequently, most quoted essay, "Mi Raza," José Martí wrote that being Cuban was "Más que negro, más que blanco, más que mulatto" (More than Black, more than white, more than mulatto). He also went on to argue against the very existence of racial differences when he wrote that "there can be no race hatred, because there are no races." Yet as historians Ada Ferrer (1999), Aline Helg (1995), and Alejandro de la Fuente (2001) have argued, this rhetoric of race lessness was designed not necessarily to "erase" race but to somehow neutralize and subsume it under the rubric of a shared Cuban nationality. This, as historians have argued, led to a later contestation of race and its role in the building of the Cuban republic.

2. See also Lisa Brock (1998); St. Clair Drake (1982); Paul Gilroy (1993); Robin D. G. Kelley (1994); Robin D. G. Kelley and Earl Lewis (2000); and Michael Coniff and Thomas J. Davis (1994).

3. Father Felix Varela was exiled from Cuba by Spanish authorities for openly advocating independence and criticizing Spanish colonial rule. Varela lived in the United States until his death in St. Augustine, Florida, in 1853. See Felix Varela (1977).

4. *La Verdad*, 1849. Special Collections, New-York Historical Society.

5. In 1900 the U.S. Congress passed the Foraker Act. Named after Senator Joseph B. Foraker of Ohio, the act made Puerto Rico a "non-incorporated" territory belonging to the United States but not really a part of the United States. The Foraker Act gave the United States control over a wide range of political, social and economic institutions and relations. It terminated the military government that had been put into place by the U.S. government when it arrived in Puerto Rico and replaced it with a civil structure. The U.S. president appointed the governor, cabinet members, and even the justices of the Supreme Court. Although Puerto Ricans were given the right to vote for members of the lower house, this appointive structure gave the United States control of the three branches of government and the central decision-making process. In addition to the governmental restructuring, English was made the official language and flying the Puerto Rican flag was considered unlawful. The following year, in 1901, the Platt Amendment was incorporated into the Cuban constitution. This amendment, named after Orville Platt, was designed to give the United States political, economic, and social control of the island. The amendment allowed the United States to intervene in Cuba anytime it deemed necessary. The amendment also provided for the Guantanamo Naval Base. The Platt Amendment was repealed in 1931, while the Foraker Act remained in place until 1917, when it was replaced with the Jones Organic Act, which rendered U.S. "citizenship" to all Puerto Ricans.

6. During the building of the Cuban Republic the politics and meanings of blackness went from being highly identified with the building of nation and independence to being part of a postwar rhetoric on equality that had little to do with incorporation. According to Aline Helg (1995), the shift corresponded to the "Western ideal of white supremacy at the turn of the century." As a response, Afro-Cuban male leaders advocated two fundamental strategies: a moderate, integrationist model that emphasized participation in the Cuban electorate and a more radical front that demanded equality and an end to racial discrimination. The integrationist model encouraged by Martin Morúa Delegado and to a lesser extent Juan Gualberto Gómez held education as the most important tool in integrating Afro-Cubans. The latter model was favored by Evaristo Estenoz and was a significant part of the PIC's platform. Please see Alejandro de la Fuente (2001) and Rafael Fermoselle (1974).

7. From 1902 to 1919 immigration to Cuba increased significantly. Many of those who immigrated were from Spain. According to Louis A. Pérez Jr. (1988:202–203), the Cuban government encouraged this migration as a way to "whiten" the island as well as appease U.S. business interests in Cuba that preferred higher "whites" to work for them. Afro-Cuban leaders viewed this strategy as one more obstacle to gaining economic and political equality.

8. For a literary-historical analysis of Schomburg, see Lisa Sánchez-González's insightful and brilliant chapter in Sánchez-González (2001).

9. Quoted in Robaina (1998).

10. Translated this reads: "The question of race, that is the problem between Black and white Cubans was not talked about much, and less in New York." Interview with Lydia "Tata"

Caraballosa conducted by Nancy Raquel Mirabal, November 26, 2001, Los Angeles, California.

11. Interview with Melba Alvarado, conducted by Nancy Raquel Mirabal, July 28, 2002. Also see records of El Club Cubano InterAmericano, Special Collections, Schomburg Public Library, New York City.

12. From *Diario de la Marina*, June 9, 1929, quoted in Ellis, 1998.

13. "Dos poetas negros sobre España," *Estampa* (Madrid), September 25, 1937.

14. Interview with Melba Alvarado, conducted by Nancy Raquel Mirabal, July 28, 2002.

15. The exact number in 1920 was 14,872. In 1930 the exact number totaled 18,493. The passage of the Johnson-Reed Act of 1924, designed to curb immigration from Europe, had an effect on the number of Caribbean migrants entering the United States. Census records show that in 1924, 17,559 Caribbean migrants arrived in the United States. A year later only 2,106 Caribbean migrants made the trip. Cuban migration would remain stagnant until 1933, when President Gerardo Machado of Cuba was ousted from office. See U.S. Bureau of the Census, *Historical Statistics of the U.S.: International Migrations and Naturalization*, Series C228–295 (1870–1930).

16. "I left for New York *to make a little water and coal*"—that is, to make money. An old Cuban *dicho*, the expression refers to the water and coal used to power steam trains.

17. While no formal study has yet been made of the impact of the B-29 on Cuban female migrations during the 1940s and early 1950s, it was frequently mentioned in the oral history of Cuban women migrants to the United States. For instance, according to Nieves Garcia the use of tourist visas, specifically the B-29, was a common migration strategy among women. Among Cubans already residing in New York and looking for work and housing, it was a common practice to identify themselves as Puerto Rican and therefore citizens of the United States. Interview with Nieves Garcia, conducted by Nancy Raquel Mirabal, December 18, 2001, Los Angeles, California.

18. The factories were one of the sites where African American, West Indian, and Afro-Cuban women met, and created informal social and economic networks. The factories, as Caraballosa remembered, were racially and "culturally" segregated, with African American women often working as pressers, a low-paying and disagreeable job, while the majority of Cuban, Puerto Rican, Dominican, and West Indian women were hired as seamstresses. None of these women, however, were hired or promoted to positions of management until the 1960s.

19. Interview with Melba Alvarado, conducted by Nancy Raquel Mirabal, July 28, 2002.

References

Arcos, Jorge Luis. 1995. Epistle to José Luis Ferrer (from Havana to Miami). In *Bridges to Cuba, Puentes a Cuba: Cuban and Cuban-American Artists, Writers, and Scholars Explore Identity, Nationality, and Homeland*, ed. Ruth Behar. Ann Arbor: University of Michigan Press.

Brock, Lisa. 1998. Introduction. In *Between Race and Empire: African-Americans and Cubans before the Cuban Revolution*, ed. Lisa Brock and Digna Castañeda Fuertes. Philadelphia: Temple University Press.

———. 1996. Questioning the diaspora: Hegemony, Black intellectuals and doing international history from below. *Issue: A Journal of Opinion*, 24 (2).

Brock, Lisa, and Digna Castañeda Fuertes, eds. 1998. *Between Race and Empire: African-Americans and Cubans Before the Cuban Revolution*. Philadelphia: Temple University Press.

Coniff, Michael, and Thomas J. Davis. 1982. *Africans in the Americas: A History of the Black Diaspora*. New York: St. Martin's Press.

de Certeau, Michel. 1988. *The Writing of History*. New York: Columbia University Press.

de la Fuente, Alejandro. 2001. *A Nation for All: Race, Inequality, and Politics in Twentieth-Century Cuba*. Chapel Hill: University of North Carolina Press.

———. 1998. Recreating racism: Race and discrimination in Cuba's "special period." Georgetown University Cuba Briefing Paper 18 (July).

Drake, St. Clair. 1982. Diaspora studies and pan-Africanism. In *Global Dimensions of the African Diaspora*, ed. Joseph E. Harris. Washington, DC: Howard University Press.

Ellis, Keith. 1998. Nicolás Guillén and Langston Hughes: Convergences and divergences. In *Between Race and Empire: African-Americans and Cubans before the Cuban Revolution*, ed. Lisa Brock and Digna Castañeda Fuertes. Philadelphia: Temple University Press.

Fermoselle, Rafael. 1974. *Politica y color en Cuba: La guerrita de 1912*. Montevideo, Uruguay: Ediciones Geminis.

Ferrer, Ada. 1999. *Insurgent Cuba: Race, Nation and Revolution, 1868–1898*. Chapel Hill: University of North Carolina Press.

Fields, Barbara Jeanne. 1985. *Slavery and Freedom on the Middle Ground: Maryland during the Nineteenth Century*. New Haven: Yale University Press.

Foner, Eric. 1998. *Reconstruction: America's Unfinished Revolution, 1863–1877*. New York: Harper-Collins.

Gatewood, Willard B., Jr. 1975. *Black Americans and the White Man's Burden, 1898–1903*. Urbana: University of Illinois Press.

———. 1971. *"Smoked Yankees" and the Struggle for Empire: Letters from Negro Soldiers, 1898–1902*. Urbana: University of Illinois Press.

———. 1970. Negro troops in Florida, 1898. *Florida Historical Quarterly* 49 (July).

Gilroy, Paul. 1993. *The Black Atlantic: Modernity and Double Consciousness*. Cambridge, MA: Harvard University Press.

Graham, Richard, ed. 1988. *The Idea of Race in Latin America, 1870–1940*. Austin: University of Texas Press.

Gray, Brenda Clegg. 1993. *Black Female Domestics during the Depression in New York City 1930–1940*. New York: Garland.

Grossman, James R. 2000. A chance to make good, 1900–1920. In *To Make Our World Anew: A History of African Americans*, ed. Robin D. G. Kelley and Earl Lewis. New York: Oxford University Press.

Guillén, Nicolás. 1929. El camino de Harlem. *Diario de la Marina* (Havana), April 21.

Helg, Aline. 1995. *Our Rightful Share: The Afro-Cuban Struggle for Equality, 1886–1912*. Chapel Hill: University of North Carolina Press.

Hellwig, David. 1998. The African-American press and the United States' involvement in Cuba 1902–1912. In *Between Race and Empire: African-Americans and Cubans before the Cuban Revolution*, ed. Lisa Brock and Digna Castañeda Fuertes, 71. Philadelphia: Temple University Press.

Higginbotham, Evelyn. 1993. *Righteous Discontent: The Woman's Movement in the Black Baptist Church, 1880–1920*. Cambridge, MA: Harvard University Press.

Hine, Darlene Clark, and Jacqueline McLeod, eds. 1999. *Crossing Boundaries: Comparative History of Black People in the Diaspora*. Bloomington: Indiana University Press.

Holt, Thomas. 1977. *Black over White: Negro Political Leadership in South Carolina during Reconstruction*. Urbana: University of Illinois Press.

Iglesias, Cesar A., ed. 1984. *Memoirs of Bernardo Vega: A Contribution to the History of the Puerto Rican Community in New York*. New York: Monthly Review Press.

Jacques, Geoffrey. 1998. "CuBop!": Afro-Cuban music and mid-twentieth century American culture. In *Between Race and Empire: African-Americans and Cubans before the Cuban Revolution* ed. Lisa Brock and Digna Castañeda Fuertes. Philadelphia: Temple University Press.

James, Winston. 1998. *Holding Aloft the Banner of Ethiopia: Caribbean Radicalism in Early Twentieth-Century America*. New York: Verso Press.

Kelley, Robin D. G. 1999. But a local phase of a world problem: Black history's global vision *Journal of American History* 86, no. 3 (December).

———. 1994. *Race Rebels: Culture, Politics, and the Working Class*. New York: Free Press.

Kelley, Robin D. G., and Earl Lewis, eds. 2000. *To Make Our World Anew: A History of African Americans*. New York: Oxford University Press.

Lemelle, Sidney, and Robin D. G. Kelley, eds. 1994. *Imagining Home: Class, Culture, and Nationalism in the African Diaspora*. New York: Verso Press.

Lopez-Mesa, Enrique. 2002. *La comunidad cubana de New York: Siglo xix*. Havana: Centro de Estudios Martianos.

Lugo-Ortiz, Agnes. 1999. *Identidades imaginadas: Biografia nacionalidad en el horizonte de la guerra (Cuba 1860–1898)*. Rio Piedras, P.R.: Editorial de la Universidad de Puerto Rico.

Lynk, Miles V. 1899. *Black Troopers or the Daring Heroism or the Negro Soldiers in the Spanish American War*. New York: AMS Press.

Martí, José. 1972. *Obras Completas*. Vol. 4. Havana: Editorial Nacional de Cuba.

Mirabal, Nancy Raquel. 2001. No country but the one we must fight for: The emergence of an Antillean nation and community in New York City, 1860–1901. In *Mambo Montage: The Latinization of New York*, ed. Agustin Lao-Montes and Arlene Davila. New York: Columbia University Press.

Morrison, Toni. 1989. Unspeakable things unspoken: The Afro-American presence in American literature. *Michigan Quarterly Review* 28 (1):1–34.

Patterson, Tiffany, and Robin D. G. Kelley. 2000. Unfinished migrations: Reflections on the African diaspora and the making of the modern world. *African Studies Review* 43 (1).

Pérez Louis A., Jr. 1988. *Cuba: Between Reform and Revolution*. New York: Oxford University Press.

Poyo, Gerald. 1989. *With All and for the Good of All: The Emergence of Popular Nationalism in the Cuban Communities of the United States, 1848–1898*. Durham, NC: Duke University Press.

Radhakrishnan, Rajagopalan. 1996. *Diasporic Meditations: Between Home and Location*. Minneapolis: University of Minnesota Press.

Ramos, Julio. 2001. *Divergent Modernities*. Durham, NC: Duke University Press.

Reid, Ira De A. 1939. *The Negro Immigrant: His Background, Characteristics and Social Adjustments, 1899–1937*. New York: Arno Press.

Robaina, Tómas Fernández. 1998. Marcus Garvey in Cuba: Urrutia, Cubans, and Black national ism. In *Between Race and Empire: African-Americans and Cubans before the Cuban Revolution*, ed. Lisa Brock and Digna Castañeda Fuertes. Philadelphia: Temple University Press.

———. 1990. *El negro en Cuba, 1902–1958: Apuntes para la historia de la lucha contra discrimini-ación racial*. Havana: Editorial de Ciencias Sociales.

Roediger, David. 1991. *The Wages of Whiteness: Race and the Making of the American Working Class*. London: Verso Press.

Rosaldo, Renato. 1997. Cultural citizenship, inequality, and multiculturalism. In *Latino Cultural Citizenship: Claiming Identity, Space, and Rights*, ed. William V. Flores and Rina Benmayor. Boston: Beacon Press.

Ruíz Suarez, Bernardo. 1922. *The Color Question in the Two Americas*. New York: Hunt Publishing Co.

Sánchez-González, Lisa. 2001. Boricua modernism: Arturo Schomburg and William Carlos Williams. In *Boricua Literature: A Literary History of the Puerto Rican Diaspora*, 42–71. New York: New York University Press.

Saldívar, José David. 1991. *The Dialectics of Our America: Genealogy, Cultural Critique, and Literary History*. Durham, NC: Duke University Press.

Schomburg, Arthur A. 1912. General Evaristo Estenoz. *The Crisis* 4 (July):143–144.

Scott, Rebecca. 1985. *Slave Emancipation in Cuba: The Transition to Free Labor, 1860–1899*. Princeton, NJ: Princeton University Press.

Silva Gruesz, Kristen. 2002. *Ambassadors of Culture: The Transamerican Origins of Latino Writing*. Princeton, NJ: Princeton University Press.

Trouillot, Michel-Rolph. 1995. *Silencing the Past: Power and the Production of History*. Boston: Beacon Press.

Varela, Felix. 1977. *Escritos politicos*. Havana: Editorial de Ciencias Sociales.

Watkins-Owens, Irma. 1996. *Blood Relations: Caribbean Immigrants and the Harlem Community, 1900–1930*. Bloomington: Indiana University Press.

White, Deborah Gray. 1999. *Too Heavy a Load: Black Women in Defense of Themselves, 1894–1994*. New York: Norton.

———. 1985. *Ar'N't I a Woman?: Female Slaves in the Plantation South*. New York: Norton.

Whitten, Norman E., Jr., and Arlene Torres. 1992. Blackness in the Americas. *NACLA Report on the Americas* 25, no. 4 (February).

Wiencek, Henry. 2003. *An Imperfect God: George Washington, His Slaves, and the Creation of America*. New York: Farrar, Straus & Giroux.

CHAPTER 11

IDENTITY, POWER, AND SOCIORACIAL HIERARCHIES AMONG HAITIAN IMMIGRANTS IN FLORIDA

Louis Herns Marcelin

This chapter provides a preliminary exploration of the ideologies of race and color among Haitians in Miami-Dade County.[1] It examines the ways in which these ideologies are configured and reappropriated within the new transnational contexts created between Haiti and South Florida. Particular focus is placed on the cultural variation of racial and derivative color-line stereotypes that underlie inter- and intra group relationships and that impact both the sociocultural marginalization and subordination of working-class Haitians in Miami-Dade County and the reconfiguration of social boundaries and political processes within Haitian communities.[2] The argument starts with a discussion of the contingency of race and racial configuration in Miami-Dade. As we will see, the case of Miami-Dade well illustrates that racial practices and politics have no automatic effects and "can therefore be made to serve different ends" (Gilroy, 2003). It is therefore important in the study of socioracial practices among immigrants in Miami-Dade to take into account their previous national experiences and histories as well as the local racial grammar in defining this context. Next, the text provides a brief overview of the historical and sociocultural baggage that Haitians brought along with them to the United States. Then, it describes how Haitians became a "racialized" group in Miami-Dade County and how, as a minority group, they process the constant tension between rejection and internalization of racial objectification. What role does this tension play in the subjectivity formation of this minority group? How does the experience of denigration mediate the interaction between history and everyday life, ontology and politics? And how do these intersections complicate issues of race in Miami-Dade as framed within the binary Black versus white? Finally, the article explores how different segments of the Haitian population use identity as a site of sociopolitical struggle to strategically forge their "imagined communities" (Anderson, 1991) in relation to other groups in Miami-Dade.

Miami-Dade's Socioracial Configurations

Recent research has examined how the influx of new immigrants to the United States has helped to destabilize a dominant conception of race, framed through the binary identity of Black versus white, and to challenge prevailing modes of identity positioning and political organization (Glick-Schiller et al., 1992; Goode, 1998; Lowe, 1996; Oboler, 1995; Omi and Winant, 1994; Urciuoli, 1996; Vickerman, 1999; Waters, 1999; Zéphir, 1996, 2001). Findings from this body of scholarship suggest that new immigrants constantly participate in generating situations of heterogeneity in which practices of differences are redefined on the basis of their previous sociocultural experiences (for example, Lowe, 1996). In a context such as Miami-Dade County, where immigrants from the Caribbean and Latin America constitute the majority of its population (Census, 2000), this destabilization seems to operate simultaneously in multiple directions and involves contradictory strategies of contestation and incorporation of different groups' cultural expectations regarding objectification of differences. While Miami Dade's Caribbean and Latin American immigrants appear to reject, by virtue of culture and history, the validity of the United States' mainstream established codes that define racial differences and locate groups or individuals in society, they create a framework that relocate "Blacks" or people of African descent to the confines of racial subjects. For most Haitians, especially in the context of Miami-Dade, "cultural considerations" that should theoretically work to destabilize the Black versus white paradigm—as it does for other groups—have been systematically portrayed in such a negative light that even Haitians themselves contribute to fostering the imposed racial conditions. In this way, immigrants' experiences of race and color in Miami-Dade County are lived within a sociocultural framework that only appears to subvert the Black versus white paradigm that defines racial subjects and privileges in the United States. Indeed, Miami-Dade's context is interesting for understanding how racial politics selectively incorporates this paradigm within its institutional and everyday practices.

Lee Drummond (1980) argues that in the Caribbean, as in Latin America (see Nelson, 2003; Skidmore, 1990; Wade, 1993, 2002), hierarchical premises[3] based on colonial values that privilege light skin color, configured within the plantation societies, pervade representations of social status and national identity. Although profound structural crisis has undermined the sociopolitical fabric of Haitian society and generated massive emigration of its population, this ethos continues to regulate the daily life of Haitians throughout the Haitian Diaspora. The Haitian experience in Miami-Dade County, its own specificity notwithstanding, draws upon this larger sociocultural, historical, and political background.

Racial issues historically emerge in articulation with mutually determining categories such as place, class, gender, and ethnicity (Hall, 1996). They are a manifestation of people's "practical sense" (Bourdieu, 1990), governed by incorporated history, culture, and power. Thus, neither race nor color can be isolated as a single causal category in the analytical process. In this vein, the neologism "socioracial" refers in this chapter to sociocultural processes in which race or color lines and class are inextricably embedded.

Socioracial phenomena take on unique configurations in Miami-Dade County and set Miami apart from other American cities. Miami-Dade County is one of the rare places in the United States where a national ethnic minority, white Cubans and their descendants, shares substantial control of socioeconomic, symbolic, and political power with the native-born white Americans. This situation has been fostered by U.S. government programs that provided economic and social supports to the Cuban exile community for geopolitical purposes.[4] South Florida's history of racial segregation and discrimination, together with the intense immigration of populations from more than thirty Caribbean and Latin American countries, has also contributed to shaping Miami-Dade County into a complex site of sociocultural production and of economic and political struggle among ethnic/racial groups.

Accordingly, the configuration of social/racial groups in Miami does not follow the typical and well-documented pattern by which white Americans maintain undisputed control over the political and economic life of the city (Massey and Denton, 1993). Instead, U.S. white hegemonic domination has given way to what Alejandro Portes and Alex Stepick (1993:8) describe as "parallel social structures, each complete with its own status hierarchy, civic institutions, and culture." Because the groups that make up the city have no shared experiences, except for the larger history of colonization, slavery, and migration, they can only generate competing discourses and embodied practices of class hierarchies and socioracial differences. This results in a variety of local racisms, which refer back to a multiplicity of national racisms. However, the competing social structures in Miami-Dade County are not equally weighted. They are framed within a dominant racial paradigm that nurtures the ideology and materiality of whiteness as the ultimate definition of power and privilege, thus reinforcing the traditional hierarchy in which groups with African ancestry are always located at the bottom.

Background

The racialization of Haitians in Miami-Dade County, or for that matter elsewhere in the United States, is reflective of sociohistorical processes that define the relations between Haiti and the United States, if not the Western world, since Haiti's emergence as a nation state (Dash, 1997; Hurbon, 1987; Trouillot, 1995). Western narratives about and silences toward Haiti (Buck-Morss, 2000; Tavares, 1992; Trouillot, 1995) are largely shaped by this process (Dash, 1997).

Haitian society emerged from a radical revolution against slavery and colonization. What came to be referred to as the first Black republic in the modern world faced a singular dilemma: Should Haiti reconstruct and reappropriate its past for itself, reconfiguring it within the confines of the nation-state, or should it erase its African heritage and embrace Western values in order to show the world that it is a "civilized" country? Two cultural worlds had developed from this fundamental question: the French-oriented cultural practices embraced by the upper classes and the African-oriented culture of the rural areas (Barthélemy, 1989; Lundahl, 1979). These constituted a system of two autonomous cultural worlds within which discourses on and of identities as well as sociopolitical practices would develop. As in other Caribbean and Latin American countries (Drummond, 1980; Nelson, 2003; Skidmore, 1990; Stepan, 1991; Wade, 1993), the ideology that sustains Haitian elites' representation of the nation equates civilization with whiteness and permeates Haiti's class relations and sociopolitical processes (Labelle, 1986; Nicholls, 1986). Thus, the really difficult tasks of Haitian elites included, but are not limited to, erasing from the "national type Haitian" every possible mark of blackness (Hurbon, 1987): the satanic African religion called vodun, a stigmatized language called Creole (that is nevertheless spoken by 100 percent of the population), and barbaric cultural practices from the rural area (where more than three-quarters of the population resides). Although a segment of these elites have formulated counterarguments that insist on Haiti's African heritage (for example, Price-Mars, 1918, 1928) in the making of its national project, when entering the political terrain, the advocates of these arguments have also ignored the rural and urban masses that constitute the majority in that country (Trouillot, 1990).

The ethos that has historically governed relationships between classes in Haiti has never assumed a truly universalistic nature. Instead, a double-bind mechanism has always allowed upper-class Haitians to invoke universalism when it comes to negotiating their location in the Western world, but display their exclusiveness when it comes to their own Haitian subjects (Nicholls, 1986; Trouillot, 1990). It is within this complex framework of hierarchy of class, location, and color that Haiti's sociocultural-political and economic system has been built.

Haitian Immigrants in Miami-Dade's Public Imagination

The ways in which the settlement of the new Haitian immigrants in South Florida has been implemented, combined with the degraded status of Haiti within the international arena, not only shape immigrants' individual and collective identities but also define the immigrant group's position within mainstream imaginaries and social life. This section highlights the ways in which (a) sociocultural conditions in Haiti, (b) conditions of immigration, and (c) other groups' reactions to the arrival of Haitians in South Florida inform both Miamian social imaginaries and Haitians' self-identity processes and positioning in relation to blackness and Haitianness.

Literature on recent Haitian immigration to the United States, particularly to South Florida, has largely documented the conditions under which migration and settlement of this population have taken place (Laguerre, 1984, 1998; Portes and Stepick, 1993; Stepick, 1992). Although it has become commonplace to describe the persistent prejudice, poverty, and multiple marginality faced by most Haitian immigrants, it is more difficult to fully appreciate the power of these processes in generating popular stereotypes as well as individual and collective responses in Haitian communities.

Haitians have been migrating to the United States in significant numbers for almost a century; cities such as New York, New Jersey, Chicago, Boston, and Miami have had relatively large populations of Haitians (Laguerre, 1984, 1998). However, between 1977 and 1985, Haitian migration underwent a significant redefinition in its process, pattern, and destination. Due to Haiti's political repression and socioeconomic crisis, more than 80,000 people fled the country during that time frame. Borrowing a term applied to earlier transnational migrants from Southeast Asia, these Haitians have been called "boat people." Alejandro Portes and Alex Stepick (1993:51) described the phenomenon:

> More than numbers, it was the manner of their arrival that garnered attention, both locally and nationwide. Photographs of shirtless Black refugees huddled aboard barely seaworthy craft evoked images buried deep in the American collective mind. Like the slave ships of yore, these boats also brought a cargo of Black laborers, except that this time they came on their own initiative, and this time nobody wanted them. Still more pathetic were those black bodies washing ashore on Florida's pristine beaches when their craft did not make it.

The sociopolitical context of the arrival of the Haitian boat people could not have been more hostile. Metropolitan Miami was just beginning to recover from its post-1960s socioeconomic, racial, and moral crisis, when the Cuban immigrant population swelled far beyond what was expected by the local establishment (Dunn, 1997; Portes and Stepick, 1993). Economic competition and the redefinition of the social makeup of the local middle-class population led to widespread discontent and an explosion of riots in 1980 among Miami's Black population (Dunn, 1997; Harris, 1999; Portes and Stepick, 1993). During the same year an immigration crisis exacerbated tensions between Cuba and the United States when more than 100,000 Cuban refugees left the Cuban port of Mariel in a flotilla heading for Miami (Masud-Piloto, 1985; Portes and Stepick, 1993).

The new Cuban immigrants, called *"los Marielitos,"* were mostly Blacks and of mixed race. For the local Anglo community as well as for the predominantly white, middle-class Cuban Americans in Miami, the *entrée en scène* of *los Marielitos* was shocking and distressing. According to a Cuban-American city official quoted in Portes and Stepick (1993, 21):

> "Mariel destroyed the image of Cubans in the United States and, in passing, destroyed the image of Miami itself for tourism. The *marielitos* are mostly Blacks and mulattoes of a color that I never saw or believed existed in Cuba."

During the same time period, as the sociopolitical situation in Haiti worsened, other Caribbean countries such as the Dominican Republic, Jamaica, Puerto Rico, and the Bahamas initiated self-protective measures against Haitian illegal immigrants (Helton, 1999; Mitchell, 1999).

Both in the United States and the Caribbean, characterizations of Haitians as disease-ridden, dirty, barbaric "voodoo" practitioners were circulated by the media (Farmer, 1992; Lawless, 1992; Nachman, 1993; Stepick, 1992). In Miami an outbreak of tuberculosis attributed to Haitians prompted the Immigration and Naturalization Service to take special measures regarding the illegal Haitian immigrants detained at Krome Detention Center (Nachman, 1993). In 1981 the Centers for Disease Control and Prevention characterized Haitians as one of the four risk groups that carry AIDS (at that time called 4Hs, the other Hs being heroin addicts, homosexuals, and hemophiliacs)[5], giving rise to a social panic in the United States.

In Miami-Dade reports that Haitians had been quarantined at hospitals, at Krome Detention Center, in schools, and in other public facilities filled the local press. Scientific publications and educational materials for schools and college students also helped to shape popular beliefs about and perceptions of Haitians (Farmer, 1992). These perceptions led the local health department and hospitals to adopt special prevention campaigns that disseminated information on Haitians as a "risk group" for contracting AIDS (Lawless, 1992), thus contributing to the stigma suffered by all Haitian immigrants.

The Newcomers: Boat People and Illegal Aliens

These new Haitian immigrants have been located geographically and sociologically within the socioracial order that characterizes Miami. Although the "Little Haiti" neighborhood of Miami contains the greatest concentration of Haitian immigrants, there are fast-growing populations of Haitians throughout South Florida, including rural Immokalee, Belle Glade, Palm Beach, Homestead, and Florida City. Most of the immigrants are unskilled seasonal farm workers; others are part-time workers, working single mothers, and others employed in service industry jobs at minimum wage. Most adults among this segment of Haitian immigrants can speak only Creole and most of their children speak English; vodun and Catholicism are part of their daily life, even though evangelical institutions are gathering them under new denominations. Many are undocumented and, as such, have very little access to public services. Over the years, they have come to constitute new ghettos within South Florida, principally in Miami-Dade County where other social problems compound the effects of increasing marginalization and exclusion (Marcelin, 2000). These new Haitian ghettos are both geographically part of, and culturally distinct from, traditional Black ghettos of Dade County.

There is no exact count of how many Haitians are living in Florida. Estimates from S. Michel Laguerre's study (1998) suggest a range of 500,000 to 1,000,000. Conservative estimates from local agencies and community-based organizations suggest that the number of Haitians in South Florida alone is 300,000, of which over 150,000 are in Miami-Dade County. In fact, not even the U.S. Bureau of the Census has accurate information. The massive census data collected from this population in 2000, from both the long and the short forms, revealed that more than 80 percent of Haitians classified themselves as "Haitians" for the question related to "race" (Marcelin and Marcelin, 2001). The U.S. Bureau of the Census, however, dismissed the Haitian claim and tabulated them as "Black," therefore omitting them as a relevant group that should have an active participation in the public debate. By doing so, the U.S. Bureau of the Census both negated Haitian identity and reinforced a demographic tradition that constructs the Black population in the United States as an undifferentiated whole, ignoring its sociocultural diversity (Marcelin and Marcelin, 2001).

Middle and Upper Class: Separate Ways

Although Haitian boat people grabbed the public imagination, a more discreet immigration of Haitians to South Florida (Miami, Fort Lauderdale, and West Palm Beach) had already been taking place for years. As was the case for other cities such as New York, Boston, and Chicago, most of the Haitians who migrated to Miami-Dade through the mid-1970s were professionals and entrepreneurs from the middle class and the elite. These segments of the Haitian immigrant population are spatially distributed throughout virtually every county in South Florida. Professionals of Haitian descent are consolidating and extending their networks in affluent neighborhoods and invest significantly in small enterprises, services, university systems, and the entertainment industries. It is also important, however, to mention salient differences within these segments: they do not constitute an undifferentiated whole. A subsegment of this population is made up of members of the traditional light-skinned Haitian elite. They congregate in wealthy, upper-middle-class Hispanic, and, sometimes, middle-class white gated communities; they speak both French and English and are frequently entrepreneurs who own factories, large enterprises, and industries in Haiti. They are also merchants, traders, landowners, and investors in sectors in Haiti, such as communications and energy. Most of them hold U.S. and French passports in addition to their Haitian passports. They are politically connected within the United States. They channel and mediate international aid and cooperation with Haiti. However, they tend not to identify themselves with "Haitians."

Close to, but not assimilated into, this subgroup are other professionals and intellectuals from the Haitian middle class. Most of them are physicians, lawyers, college professors, or former Haitian politicians/statesmen, many of whom live in predominantly Hispanic middle-class neighborhoods. Most of them invest in "business activities" in Port-au-Prince, Haiti's capital, even though they do not have strong economic interests in Haiti. Because the phenotypically Black subgroup cannot "pass" for white, they tend to reappropriate traditional Haitian markers of distinction including use of the French language for intragroup communication and promulgation of their European heritage. Respondents in this subgroup tend to reinvent a family history focused on their nonslave origin. Within this segment of the population, the work of reinventing identity is pervasive. Reinventing the past, as a strategy, has the magical virtue of erasing the traditional view of race (Trouillot, 1994:149).

Although, in Miami-Dade the elite and middle-class Haitian subgroups do not interact socially, except within specific contexts, such as the workplace, they hold the same vision of "the polluting danger" of rural and lower-class Haitians. They also share similar prejudices of native white Americans regarding Blacks and blackness, and Haitians and Haitianness. Most Haitian immigrants in Miami-Dade create layers of distance, first, between themselves and middle-class persons of rural or more humble origins and, second, between themselves and what they call "real" Haitians. For them, "real" Haitians are exotic, Black, poor, barely literate, monolingual, and mostly stereotyped as peasants living in the urban areas (whether in Haiti or in South Florida).

The "real" Haitians mostly live in Black neighborhoods in Miami-Dade, Broward, Palm Beach, or Immokalee, that is, in more demographically concentrated Haitian immigrant communities. According to this view, sociopolitical and economic crisis in rural and urban Haiti has led them to "invade" not only urban shantytowns in Haiti and the Dominican Republic but also the ghettos of Southeast Florida.

As the constant negativity and panic about diseases, contamination, and danger permeated media reports, reinforcing the Miamian social imaginary about radical otherness, many middle-class and elite Haitians responded with strategic conceal-ment of their identity and avoidance of "real" Haitians living in the inner cities of Miami-Dade.

The Location of Blackness: Black Populations and Hispanics in Miami-Dade

In Miami-Dade County physical places not only embed socioracial locations but also moral attributes (Allman, 1987; Dunn, 1997; Peacock et al., 1997; Portes and Stepick, 1993). No matter their social history, the dominant narrative assumes that all Blacks are the same and located as such. Thus, location creates a territory of black-ness; a community of essence, positioned at the bottom in the hierarchy of power, perpetuates the hierarchy of territories of race, color, and privileges in the city (Allman, 1987; Peacock et al., 1997; Portes and Stepick, 1993). This imagined linkage, reinforced with a strong tradition of segregation, was the backdrop that informed Haitian settlement in the city.

According to the 2000 census, the Black[6] populations represent 20 percent of the population in Miami-Dade, most of them live in the north section of the county (in Overtown, Liberty City, Brownsville, Little Haiti, with clusters in North Miami), with significant numbers living in the south of Dade (South Miami, Coconut Grove, Richmond Heights, Goulds, Homestead, and Florida City). Here, Miami displays a configuration of lower-class neighborhoods in which ethnicity and class collide. They are comprised of different national, cultural, religious, and linguistic backgrounds. They include native African Americans, descendants of Bahamians—who still perceive themselves as distinct from native African Americans and other Blacks from the Caribbean—Jamaicans, Haitians, and Afro-Cubans. Except for the Afro-Cubans who are diluted within the socioracial hierarchies of Cuban enclaves in Miami, each of these populations constitutes a distinct sociocultural group within distinct geographical "enclaves." Neighborhoods such as Little Haiti (predominantly Haitians), Liberty City (African Americans), Overtown (African Americans), Black Coconut Grove (Bahamian Americans), and Richmond Heights (predominantly Jamaicans) are all characterized by their ethnic homogeneity where interpersonal and family relations are deeply shaped by common experiences, language, and immigra-tion background. As Marvin Dunn suggests, besides the commonality of skin color Black communities in Miami are as distant from one another as they are from other racial or non-Black ethnic groups (Dunn, 1997; but see also Croucher, 1997, 1999, and Peacock et al., 1997).

The spatial division and social isolation (Wilson, 1987) that characterize these locations have, among other consequences, contributed, to the weakening of the potential for a "pan-Black" political movement in Miami-Dade (Dunn, 1997). In these neighborhoods interethnic interactions are minimal; casual contacts in stores and on sidewalks, or relationships at work and through social services, do not extend to other domains of everyday life. Even for the younger generation, for which school-based friendship plays a critical role in their sociability, cross-ethnic relationships are still difficult to achieve. Yet, despite differences and fragmented identities among Black enclaves in Miami-Dade, the younger generation of all ethnic backgrounds finds a common expressive language, notably in hip-hop music, street codes, and alternative lifestyles such as drug use or dress codes. Nonetheless, commonalities among Black youths do not always prevail: rivalries between groups, cliques, or youth street gangs, as well as competition for dominating public space, lead to creation of territories within and between neighborhoods and stimulate antinomies between young Blacks belonging to different cultural backgrounds.

The sociocultural diversity of Black populations in Miami provides a complex frame for each of these groups to define and experience blackness. However, in a city which has been established on clear principles of racial hierarchy (Allman, 1987; Massey and Denton, 1993), Miamian Blacks' experiences of discrimination and racism has constituted a continuous basis for Black solidarity and ad hoc political alliance. Along this line, Haitians have benefited from the support of African American leadership in efforts to combat perceived discriminatory measures taken by the INS against Haitian immigrants. This solidarity, however, is being eroded by larger sociopolitical forces in the city, such as neighborhood politics, the divide-and-conquer strategy of the dominant groups, historical neglect by the dominant white supremacists, structural marginalization, and social isolation (Massey and Denton, 1993).

Likewise, enclaves such as Little Havana (predominantly working-class Cubans), Little Managua (Nicaraguans), and Hialeah (Cubans) constitute separate worlds in themselves, where common languages and sociocultural experiences as well as residential and work patterns combine with the imaginary of Latin America to generate a specific affirmation of identities. Spatial distance between Black and Hispanic neighborhoods and the lack of public transportation from one to another contribute to structural socioethnic isolation. This state of affairs is no accident. Systematic urban-planning policies and the politics of incorporated cities have had an undermining effect on political solidarity among groups. Within each of these neighborhoods ethnically owned small businesses, churches, and community-based organizations structure everyday activities and reinforce each group's cultural practices and Miami's ethnic clustering, thereby minimizing situations of interactions between non-Hispanic Black populations belonging to different ethnic networks and Cubans or Nicaraguans or Mexicans, except in work situations. Even in the workplace relations between lower-class English-speaking Blacks, Haitians, and Hispanics of different ethnicities are contained within ethnic lines. Portes and Stepick (1993), and later Stepick and his colleagues (2003), have provided ethnographic accounts of interethnic relations at the workplace (but see also Grenier and Stepick, 1993). Conversely, despite the ethnic clustering and because of the commonalities of language and spatial proximity, everyday interactions among Mexicans, Nicaraguans, and Cubans are relatively intense (compared with Black/Hispanic interactions). In these socioethnic contexts, blackness, for example among Black Cubans, is defined within a different sociocultural frame in which intraethnic socioracial hierarchies play a fundamental role. Nonetheless, Black Cubans' interactions with non-Hispanic Blacks follow the same pattern laid out at the beginning of this section.

While Miami displays a configuration of neighborhoods that conflates ethnicity and class for lower-class populations, most of the middle- and upper-middle-class neighborhoods, such as Kendall, Pinecrest, or Coral Gables, manifest civility among individuals of different ethnic backgrounds. In such neighborhoods one can find small numbers of Blacks from all backgrounds who interact individually with Hispanics or whites in multiple contexts. Individual interactions with friends, neighbors, schoolmates, and workmates help create a civil atmosphere in the neighborhoods. Here "whiteness" becomes the articulating principle that requires a manipulation of one's identity to the point that it "erases" any *visible* trace of "difference." It is against this background that the sections below discuss the uses of identity among Haitian immigrants.

From Haitianness to Blackness: Performances and Objectifications

The difficulty of sustaining a positive relationship to blackness informs the ambivalence of Haitians of all social classes in relation to what they call "Black Americans" and to Haitianness itself. While for middle- and upper-class Haitians living in Miami-Dade the fundamental activity of their identity-building consists of distinguishing themselves from Haiti, Haitians, and blackness by overemphasizing mixture—cultural or biological—with Western Europe (the French), inner-city Haitians build up their social identity by distinguishing themselves from African Americans. Although, as Blacks and as immigrants, these newcomers/boat people/undocumented are at the very bottom of Miami-Dade society and experience economic and social marginalization similar to that of the majority of their fellow "Black Americans" (which is how Haitians in these segments identify African Americans), they share a vision of themselves as different from African Americans because of their history. As many interviewees remarked, "We are Haitians no matter what."

From this perspective, the claim of "Haitianness" resonates as an ideology that manifests its persistence through cultural forms and symbols that are meaningful to Haitian immigrant youth in their marginal context. These cultural forms and symbols are mediated among the children of the newcomers through practices such as music (the *new rap*), forms of sociability (gangs, cliques, and groups), language (Zo), alternative lifestyles, and other expressive forms, such as the Haitian flag, that are incorporated within their narratives on identity. This claim is also an expression of resistance to and contestation of the power structure and relations that govern their daily life in South Florida's ghettos. Its complements are severe marginalization and institutional racism. As one of the study participants mentioned, "It's a new Haitian generation here. Ain't afraid anymore to show who I am. We stand for ourselves. . . . We fight for our respect. Haitians will stand up in this country!" For some of these youths, "Haitianness" in this context can be nothing else but a vanishing expression of faith, a marginal fiction with neither substance nor potential for political effect. It remains, however, an ideological base, deeply entrenched in the sociocultural terrain that defines the conditions for its expression.

While middle- and upper-class Haitians locate the inner-city Haitians outside the confines of "civilization," the latter build the notion of otherness by considering African Americans living in the same environment to be barbarians. African Americans living in the inner cities hold a reciprocal view of Haitians. Moreover, while middle- and upper-class Haitians reject any association with their Haitianness or their blackness, Haitians in the inner cities celebrate their Haitianness and selectively reject blackness *as they experience it* in the United States. This positioning contrasts with the time when Haitianness was rejected even by newcomer Haitians, because of hostility experienced in the host country (Laguerre, 1984; Nachman, 1993; Stepick, 1998).

The physical deterioration of the neighborhoods of Little Haiti, which symbolically represents the Haitian presence in Miami, led to great health and security concerns on the part of county officials. As a result, properties are losing value and Haitians themselves are fleeing the neighborhood. Simultaneously, there is a progressive gentrification of adjacent communities. Real estate enterprises are investing in the reconfiguration of nearby neighborhoods. The city has developed a Miami Design District in the heart of Overtown, a predominantly African American neighborhood about twenty blocks from Little Haiti, leading to a skyrocketing of housing prices, which are then no longer affordable for low-income Haitians or African Americans. This in turn creates a new environment in which higher-income residents move to new residential homes in the neighborhoods because of their proximity to the new Design District, the downtown area, South Beach, and Miami Beach. Cultural artifacts and places that used to be associated with the Haitian presence during the 1980s and the 1990s are now at risk of disappearance.

Some new community-based organizations created by new generations of Haitians, mostly educated in the United States, are trying to slow down the process of gentrification by helping Haitians who reside in these neighborhoods to evaluate their options and explore the possibility for public funding for home ownership in what is still a low-income area. Still, most Haitians are at odds with the process. First, for most Haitians, moving out of Little Haiti is a must, a goal that symbolizes a graduation from poverty, from a stigmatized environment, and from a certain definition and practice of blackness (proximity to historically African American neighborhoods, crime, prostitution, poor schools, and delinquency). Second, Haitians with economic and social capital would prefer to move to new, "de-ethnicized" neighborhoods where blackness per se is not the primary principle that articulates outsiders' and insiders' perceptions of the social landscape.

Where I live, my kids' friends are whites or Hispanics. I think that the Haitian or Black identity thing is for losers. America is no longer Black and white. The big thing now is those who
know how to win. And then there are those who are *born* to be losers. I am teaching my kids
how to play . . . to stay a winner. (Forty-year-old Haitian health professional)

Yet, further discussion with this male informant revealed that the "losers" all have
one face: Blacks (African Americans), Haitians, and Africans. Another male informant referred to Little Haiti as a "no-man's-land," where prostitution, chronic
violence, magical rituals including voodoo and sorcery, and other social and cultural
ills predominate. These, according to the informant, are the defining features of the
people living in that environment. "That's the way *they* are." Another participant, a
26-year-old female, also did not believe that redemption is possible for other Black
individuals living in the ghettos of the United States: "People living in the ghetto can
get out of the ghetto but the ghetto would never get out of them." The irony is that
this participant lived in Little Haiti for more than fifteen years, before moving to
North Miami, a more upscale section of town. The participant has family members,
including a brother, still living there. For this informant, leaving Little Haiti was
"graduating" from a particular location that sanctions a particular subjectivity associated with a specific ethnic condition in Miami-Dade. Graduating from Little
Haiti is "graduating" from *being* Haitian and thereby de-ethnicizing or, ultimately,
de-racializing the self to becoming a "born again" persona, with new social networks,
new environments, and a new sociopolitical project.

Visible racial segregation and sociocultural estrangement of the African American
population in Miami-Dade County have helped to structure a shared representation
of Blacks as both powerless and radical others. It is no surprise, therefore, that Black
immigrants such as Haitians ambivalently position themselves as "different" from
African Americans, while sharing the same socioeconomic and cultural estrangement
from the local mainstream society and living their own unique condition as "Black
disease-ridden illegal alien" (Stepick, 1992). The whole system seems to be built
upon a terrible irony: middle- and upper-class Haitians are invested in overtly
disclaiming their Haitianness on racial grounds in order to blend into the non-Black
whole, whereas the Black lower-class Haitian immigrants must work the most to
distinguish themselves locally on cultural or ethnic (not racial) grounds. It is because
they are the most visibly stigmatized group in Miami-Dade that they provide the
favored reference for the viewpoints of higher-situated Haitians who see Haitianness
in racial terms, that is, as Black.

Contact Zones and Strategic Concealment

Haitians in Miami-Dade find themselves situated within a complex, but not rigid, socioracial and ethnic hierarchy. In turn, the Haitian community is subdivided by a combination of shifting boundaries and contradictions. However, some contact zones exist
between these groups. In this context, "contact zone" refers to arbitrary or opportunistic
spaces for "claiming" or "disclaiming" Haitianness. Most of these contact zones are
provided by private or state institutions that work with marginalized Haitians and by

international organizations that channel international aid to Haiti. The city and its public and private institutions also provide rare alternative spaces—through national celebrations, public festivals, and art exhibits—where Haitians can display their cultural practices. When this happens, these spaces are opportunities for Haitians of different social classes to represent (in the sense of Goffman, 1967) and renegotiate their status in public—the former boat people who "made it big" in the United States, the petit bourgeois who have experienced a reversal of status in the new country, and, rarely, the "cultivated elite" who insist on carrying the French heritage through language, manners, and appearances that distinguish them from the rest. In such contexts these spaces become mirroring theaters where different groups of Haitians "read each other."

Unlike the Cuban elites in Miami-Dade County, the Haitian elites have not assumed any leadership role in socially and economically structuring a Haitian enclave. The Haitian community has not been able to generate even a viable enclave economy, despite the availability of a cheap workforce and potential for an ethnic market. As in Haiti, this potential has been left mostly to racketeers and *rentiers*. The prominent businesses at the core of the Miami Haitian communities are mostly owned by Cubans or newly middle-class Haitians who have associated themselves with more "reliable" Latino groups or white Americans. The capital has never come from prominent, economically solvent Haitians, although most of them do invest in the larger speculative market or own interests in Cuban businesses in Miami. One respondent suggests that these investors follow a *habit* of *not* associating their investment with the human development of Haitians in Haiti—where the rules of the socioeconomic game are relaxed and more permissible. To invest in Haiti would require first a shared belief in the possibility of a stable market in an ordered, stable, and viable society. In the Haitian community in Miami, this investment would require a type of leadership that is essentially *stained* by its own ethnic audience of Haitians, an identity that no one wants to be associated with. The shared myths predominant in public and private discourses from Haiti to South Florida have constantly been structured around the impossibility for Haitians to generate a rational organization of society or to be rational and modern themselves. Thus, the belief expressed in the proverb *"Ayiti se te glise"* (Haiti is a slippery land) has become *"Ayisyen pap janm anyen"* (Haitians will never make it). This is a view that is shared by the majority of Haitians of all classes in Miami.

For upper- and middle-class Haitian respondents, Haiti is a "war zone," where no one is safe, especially "people who attract envy" from the mass of the dispossessed. They relocate themselves in Miami to find a "safe zone" to invest in the future. The idea of the "safe zone" is recurrent in conversations among Haitians. It can be understood here as a symbolic space, appropriated for a new process of establishing oneself; a place where they can reinvent new forms of sociability and create new political, economic, or matrimonial alliances. Their investment in Miami as the place where their future lies is, in fact, an investment in a new articulation of power within and beyond the borders of Haiti. As one informant from the upper middle class confirms, "It is an intelligent investment as far as I am concerned; it is protected from social turmoil, unpredictable riots, and political uprising."

Between Ontology and Politics: Building Up the Haitian Community

However, there are instances in which it is advantageous to be Haitian. The Miami-Dade setting configures complex sociopolitical relations among ethnic groups. In such a context, ethnic politics become a powerful tool to reach individual goals. When local or federal institutions are in need of qualified intermediaries capable of formulating or implementing specific programs for Haitian immigrants in need, being "Haitian" may indeed be an asset. Claiming Haitian ancestry and knowledge of the Haitian language and "culture" become strategic for competition in status-driven positions.

On the other hand, in Miami-Dade County, political struggles based on identity are performed for multiple audiences and for multiple reasons. Haitian activists and a handful of professionals, including some of those who used to dissociate themselves from their identity as Haitians, are increasingly investing in "the Haiti community as a potential for sociopolitical advancement." The Haitian community is also projected in the local public imagination as a potential market. Activists' engagement through neighborhood politics, community and civic organizations, radio communication, and other organizational venues, including the youth associated with the new street cultural practices, are challenging the arbitrariness of local hierarchies and the ethnic socioracial order in Miami-Dade County. There is a growing perception that Haitians in South Florida's inner cities deserve better conditions through the creation of work opportunities, access to and utilization of social and heath services, and better education.

In terms of Miami-Dade County ethnic politics, however, Haitians are not a powerful enough community to mobilize the finances and other public resources for community building and empowerment of a population that in the public imagination still represents a group of refugees that "nobody wants," to paraphrase Stepick (1992). Yet, investment in these projects by prominent Haitian capital holders is perhaps the least likely possibility.

Conclusion: New Questions, Old Problems

In Miami-Dade, if not in the United States, the category "Haitian" conflate simultaneously "race," "ethnicity," and "class." In other words, "Haitian/Black/poor" seems to be the defining feature of the "other" not only for popular media representations and public imagery cultivated for some type of consumption, but also as a trope that indexes Haitians in scholarly publications. The heterogeneous character of this population is more often than not only recognized in footnotes, hence doing less than justice to its historical complexity. This may be due to the fact that most experts on Haitian issues (or those of other racialized minorities in the United States) are not sufficiently reflective about the extent to which their own analytical paradigm of difference, applied to the study of this racialized group, is embedded within a specific cultural conception of race, which Michael Omi and Howard Winant designated as a "fundamental axis of social organization in the United States" (1994:13)

This conflation frames the population both in biological and reified cultural terms to the point that it stigmatizes its position and posits its members as a reverse of the desirable image of the American nation. On the one hand, it typifies Haitianness as unable to fit into the projects of the city or to become fully American. On the other hand, this conflation is safe, because it grounds itself within the notion of "cultural difference," which justifies social exclusion and cultural marginalization.

This conflation is a manifestation of the racializing process not only of Haitians but also of "Blacks" as "radical other." It permeates sociocultural relations and hierarchies between and within groups in Miami-Dade. As we have seen, although the context of Miami-Dade seems to generate a cultural framework that destabilizes the mainstream Black versus white paradigm, which articulates differences in American society, providing Caribbean and Latin American immigrants with a multiplicity of standards of locations, Haitian immigrants have only two standards. First, the Black versus white paradigm is used by middle- and upper-class Haitians. Most individuals who belong to different ethnic groups, including light-skinned Haitians, may position themselves according to a multiplicity of standards made available to them by the very paradigm they contest. Indeed, the dominant paradigm shapes the Haitian communities in Miami-Dade in such a way that discrimination becomes a strategic tool manipulated by Haitians themselves. However, the majority of Haitians do not have this option. Thus, Haitians of lower status make use of cultural "tradition" in an attempt to distinguish themselves from Black Americans, understood as a uniform whole, although this strategy encompasses the Black versus white paradigm. This use of cultural difference, instead of destabilizing the dominant paradigm, reinforces it.

Miami-Dade's setting offers a singular opportunity for studying how transnational processes shape this urban context in such a way that hierarchies between and within groups recycle national and local patterns of characterizing and locating people in society to generate new socioracial configurations and political dynamics. Miami-Dade's economic and political centrality in the international region, due to its geographical proximity to the Caribbean and Latin America (Nijman, 1996:20) and the socioethnic variation of its demography, makes it a success story for most of the nationals from these regions. At the same time, it also generates a peculiar context in which interactions between and within groups are regulated by primordial differences (Croucher, 1997). This context creates a specific repertory of multiplicity of local racisms and marginalization of Blacks, which refer back to a multiplicity of national racisms and socioracial exclusion. In this sense, socioracial dynamics in Miami-Dade are largely shaped by broader sociopolitical and transnational processes which, instead of fostering cross-ethnic integration—even in the name of the market or global capitalism—reinstate socioracial differences as a baseline of social identity and political practices. The case of the Haitians in Miami-Dade clearly illustrates the paradox of a city that presents itself and defines its policies within the framework of multiculturalism—or even within what Guillermo Grenier and Max Castro (1999) would call a "triadic" frame, including Latinos, Blacks, and white Americans—while the larger sociopolitical and economic institutions reinforce socioracial differentiation to justify the marginalization of racialized groups.

Given the complexity at play here, one may wonder if there is any room in this analysis for transcending race and its political derivative in Miami-Dade. When will it be possible to claim, after Roger Sanjek (1998), "the future of us all"? What are the prospects for Black and Latina/o relations in Miami-Dade? The forces that regulate the formation of social imaginaries about differences are inscribed in the complex configuration of history, power, and practice. They permeate the institutional dynamics and the "fundamental axis of social organization" not only of the United States (Omi and Winant, 1994) but also of the post-plantation Americas and the Caribbean. They generate resources to forge new identities, modes of positioning, hierarchies, inequalities, and naturalness of local, national, and regional orders. The emergence of Miami-Dade as a privilege site for new socioracial configurations that appropriate in immigrant situations national patterns of hierarchies suggest that race and racialization in its many forms combine and coexist with new transnational or global processes.

Notes

1. Miami-Dade refers to an agglomeration of incorporated cities, including the city of Miami which is located in Miami-County of Dade in South Florida. In this text I use Miami-Dade and Miami-Dade County interchangeably.

2. This paper is based on more than five years of systematic and *longue durée* observations as well as on individual biographies and interviews of Haitians, both in Haiti and in South Florida. An earlier version of this paper was presented at "The Meanings of Race and Blackness in the Americas," a conference held at Brown University in February 2000 and March 2001. I thank all participants for their comments and suggestions. I am grateful to Anani Dzidzienyo and Suzanne Oboler for inviting me to this event and for their helpful editorial comments. This current version has benefited from the editorial prowess of Aurolyn Luykx and Christine Miles. Aurolyn Luykx, Michael Houseman, Louise Marcelin, Erica James, Edward Lipuma, Bryan Page, and Rose-Marie Chierici have provided me with useful comments. I thank them for their generosity.

3. For extensive discussions on "hierarchy," see Louis Dumont (1967); for a discussion on the sociocultural meanings of hierarchy in Caribbean societies, see R. T. Smith (1988) and Lisa Douglass (1992).

4. The Marielitos did not receive such settlement benefits as were present in the case of the white Cubans; see Emily Skop (2001). Ramón Grosfoguel (1995:161) wrote: "A conservative estimate of the total amount of social capital transferred by the US state to the Cuban [exile] community would be approximately 1.3 billion dollars (one billion from the refugee programme, more than 50 million from the SBA [Small Business Administration] in Miami, and around 250 million dollars from the CIA payroll and subsidies to Cuban businesses). The Cubans (around 700,000 people by 1975) received in a matter of fifteen years close to half of the total amount of the US foreign aid that Brazil (a country of more than 100 million people) received between 1945 and 1983." On the sociopolitical genesis of the Cuban enclave in Miami, see A. Portes and A. Stepick (1993).

5. Centers for Disease Control, Surveillance Data on Acquired Immunodeficiency (AIDS 1981).

6. For a history of the Black population in Miami-Dade, see Thomas Boswell (1991), Marvin Dunn (1997), Paul George (1978), and Raymond Mohl (1990).

References

Allman, T. D. 1987. *Miami, City of the Future*. New York: Atlantic Monthly Press.

Anderson, Benedict. 1991. *Imagined Communities: Reflections on the Origin and Spread of Nationalism*. New York: Verso.

Barthélemy, Gérard. 1989. *Le Pays en Dehors*. Port-Au-Prince: Le Natal.

Boswell, Thomas D. 1991. The settlement of Blacks in South Florida. In *South Florida: The Winds of Change*, ed. Thomas D. Boswell. Prepared for the annual conference of the Association of American Geographers, Miami.

Bourdieu, Pierre. 1990. *The Logic of Practice*. Stanford, CA: Stanford University Press.

Buck-Morss, Susan. 2000. Hegel and Haiti. *Critical Inquiry* 26 (Summer): 921–965.

Croucher, Sheila L. 1999. Ethnic inventions: Constructing and deconstructing Miami's culture clash. *Pacific Historical Review* 68 (2):233–251.

———. 1997. *Imagining Miami: Ethnic Politics in a Post-Modern World*. Charlottesville: University of Virginia Press.

Dash, J. Michael. 1997. *Haiti and the United States: National Stereotypes and the Literary Imagination*. 2nd ed. London: Macmillan.

Douglass, Lisa. 1992. *The Power of Sentiment: Love, Hierarchy, and the Jamaican Family Elite*. Boulder, CA: Westview Press.

Dumont, Louis. 1967. *Homo hierarchicus: Essai sur le sysème des castes*. Paris: Gallimard.

Dunn, Marvin. 1997. *Black Miamians in the Twentieth Century*. Tampa: University of Florida Press.

Drummond, Lee. 1980. The cultural continuum: A theory of intersystems. *Man* 15 (2):352–374.

Farmer, Paul. 1992. *AIDS and Accusation: Haiti and the Geography of Blame*. Berkeley: University of California Press.

———. 1994. *The Uses of Haiti*. Monroe, ME: Common Courage Press.

George, Paul S. 1978. Colored town: Miami's Black community, 1869–1930. *Florida Historical Quarterly* 57:434–450.

Gilroy, Paul. 2003. After the great white error . . . the great Black mirage. In *Race, Nature, and the Politics of Difference*, ed. Donald S. Moore, Jake Kosek, and Anand Pandia. Durham, NC: Duke University Press.

Glick Schiller, Nina, Linda Basch, and Christina Blanc-Szanton, eds. 1992. *Towards a Transnational Perspective on Migration: Race, Class, Ethnicity, and Nationalism Reconsidered*. New York: New York Academy of Sciences.

Goffman, Erving. 1967. *Interaction Ritual: Essays on Face-to-Face Behavior*. Garden City, NY: Anchor Books.

Goode, Judith. 1998. The contingent construction of local identities: Koreans and Puerto Ricans in Philadelphia. *Identity* 5(1):33–64.

Grenier, Guillermo, and Max J. Castro. 1999. Triadic politics: Ethnicity, race, and politics in Miami, 1959–1998. *Pacific Historical Review* 68 (2):273–292.

Grenier, Guillermo J., and Alex, Stepick. 1992. *Miami Now!: Immigration, Ethnicity, and Social Change*. Gainesville: University of Florida Press.

Grosfoguel, Ramón. 1995. Global logics in the Caribbean city system: The case of Miami. In *World Cities in a World System*, ed. Paul L. Knox and Peter J. Taylor. Cambridge: Cambridge University Press.

Hall, Stuart. 1996. Gramsci's relevance for the study of race and ethnicity. In *Stuart Hall: Critical Dialogues in Cultural Studies*, ed. David Morley and Kuan-Hsing Chen. New York: Routledge.

Harris, Daryl B. 1999. *Logic of Black Urban Rebellions: Challenging the Dynamics of White Domination in Miami*. Westport, CT: Praeger.

Helton, Arthur C. 1999. Establishing a comprehensive scheme for refugee and migration emergencies in the Caribbean region: Lessons from recent Haitian and Cuban emergencies. In *Free Markets, Open Societies, Closed Borders? Trends in International Migration and Immigration Policy in the Americas*, ed. M. J. Castro. Coral Gables, FL: North-South Center Press.

Hurbon, Laennec. 1987. *Le barbare imaginaire*. Port-au-Prince, Haiti: Deschamps.

Labelle, Micheline. 1986. *Idéologies de couleurs et classes sociales en Haïti*. Montréal: CIDHICA.

Laguerre, S. Michel. 1984. *American Odyssey: Haitians in New York City*. Ithaca, NY: Cornell University Press.

———. 1998. *Diasporic Citizenship*. New York: St. Martin's Press.

Lawless, Robert. 1992. *Haiti's Bad Press: Origins, Development, and Consequences*. Rochester, VT: Schenkman Books.

Lowe, Lisa. 1996. *Immigrant Acts: On Asian-American Cultural Politics*. Durham, NC: Duke University Press.

Lundahl, Matts. 1979. *Peasants and Politics: A Study of Haiti*. London: Croom Helm.

Marcelin, L. Herns. 2000. Changing contexts and perceptions of HIV/AIDS risks among minority populations in South Florida, United States. In *Proceedings of the XIII International AIDS Conference, 9–14 July 2000, Durban, South Africa*. Rome: Monduzzi Editore.

Marcelin, L. Herns, and Louise M. Marcelin. 2001. *Ethnographic Social Network Tracing among Haitian Migrant Workers in South Florida*. Decennial Management Division, U.S. Bureau of the Census, Washington, DC.

Massey, Douglas, and Nancy Denton. 1993. *American Apartheid: Segregation and the Making of the Underclass*. Cambridge, MA: Harvard University Press.

Masud-Piloto, Felix R. 1985. *The Political Dynamics of the Cuban Migration to the United States*. Ann Arbor, MI: University Microfilms International.

Mitchell, Christopher. 1999. Migration and geopolitics in the Caribbean: The cases of Puerto Rico, Cuba, the Dominican Republic, Haiti, and Jamaica. In *Free Markets, Open Societies, Closed Borders?: Trends in International Migration and Immigration Policy in the Americas*, ed. Max J. Castro. Coral Gables, FL: North-South Center Press, distributed by Lynne Rienner Publishers.

Mohl, Raymond. 1990. On the edge: Blacks and Hispanics in metropolitan Miami since 1959. *Florida Historical Quarterly* 69:37–56.

Nachman, Steven. 1993. Wasted lives: Tuberculosis and other health risks of being Haitian. *Medical Anthropology Quarterly* 7 (3):227–259.

Nelson, Diane. 2003. "The more you kill, the more you will live": The Maya, "race," and biopolitical hopes for peace in Guatemala. In *Race, Nature, and the Politics of Difference*, ed. Donald S. Moore, Jake Kosek, and Anand Pandia. Durham, NC: Duke University Press.

Nicholls, David. 1986. *From Dessalines to Duvalier: Race, Colour, and National Independence in Haiti*. New Brunswick, NJ: Rutgers University Press.

Nijman, Jan. 1996. Breaking the rules: Miami in the urban hierarchy. *Urban Geography* 17 (1):5.

Oboler, Suzanne. 1995. *Ethnic Labels, Latino Lives: Identity and the Politics of (Re)Presentation in the United States*. Minneapolis: University of Minnesota Press.

Omi, Michael, and Howard Winant. 1994. *Racial Formation in the United States: From the 1960s to the 1990s*. New York: Routledge.

Peacock, W. G., B. H. Morrow, and H. Gladwin. 1997. *Hurricane Andrew: Ethnicity, Gender, and the Sociology of Disasters*. New York: Routledge.

Portes, Alejandro, and Alex Stepick. 1993. *City on the Edge: The Transformation of Miami*. Berkeley: University of California Press.

Price, Hannibal. 1900. *De la réhabilitation de la race noire*. Paris: Vérollet.

Price-Mars, Jean. 1928. *Ainsi parla l'oncle*. Port-au-Prince, Haiti: Imprimerie de Compiègne.

———. 1918. *La vocation de l'élite*. Port-au-Prince, Haiti: Imprimerie de Compiègne.

Sanjek, Roger. 1998. *The Future of Us All: Race and Neighborhood Politics in New York City*. Ithaca, NY: Cornell University Press.

Skidmore, Thomas. 1990. *The Idea of Race in Latin America, 1870–1940*. Rev. ed. Austin: University of Texas Press.

Skop, Emily H. 2001. Race and place in the adaptation of Mariel exiles. *International Migration Review* 35(2):449–471.

Smith, Raymond T. 1988. *Kinship and Class in the West Indies: A Genealogical Study of Jamaica and Guyana*. New York: Cambridge University Press.

Stepan, Nancy Leys. 1991. *The Hour of Eugenics: Race, Gender, and Nation in Latin America*. Ithaca, NY: Cornell University Press.

Stepick, Alex. 1992. The refugees nobody wants: Haitians in Miami. In *Miami Now! Immigration, Ethnicity and Social Change*, ed. Guillermo Grenier and Alex Stepick. Gainesville: University of Florida Press.

———. 1998. *Pride against Prejudice: Haitians in the United States*. Boston: Allyn and Bacon.

Stepick, Alex, G. Grenier, M. Castro, and M. Dunn. 2003. *This Land Is Our Land: Immigrants and Power in Miami*. Berkeley: University of California Press.

Tavares, Pierre-Franklin. 1992. Hegel et Haiti, ou le silence de Hegel sur Saint-Domingue. *Chemins Critiques* 2:113–131.

Taylor, Charles. 2002. Modern social imaginaries. *Public Culture* 14 (1):91–124.

Trouillot, Michel-Rolph. 1990. *Haiti, State Against Nation: The Origins and Legacy of Duvalierism.* New York: Monthly Review Press.

———. 1995. *Silencing the Past: Power and the Production of History.* Boston: Beacon Press.

———. 1994. Culture, color, and politics in Haiti. In *Race,* ed. Steven Gregory and Roger Sanjek. New Brunswick, NJ: Rutgers University Press.

Urciuoli, Bonnie. 1996. *Exposing Prejudice: Puerto Rican Experiences of Language, Race, and Class.* Boulder, CO: Westview Press.

Vickerman, Milton. 1999. *Crosscurrents: West Indian Immigrants and Race.* New York: Oxford University Press.

Wade, Peter. 1993. *Blackness and Race Mixture: The Dynamics of Racial Identity in Colombia.* Baltimore, MD: Johns Hopkins University Press.

———. 2002. *Race, Nature, and Culture: An Anthropological Perspective.* London: Sterling.

Waters, Mary C. 1999. *Black Identities: West Indian Immigrant Dreams and American Realities.* New York: Russell Sage Foundation.

Wilson, William Julius. 1987. *The Truly Disadvantaged: The Inner City, the Underclass, and Public Policy.* Chicago: University of Chicago Press.

Zéphir, Flore. 1996. *Haitian Immigrants in Black America: A Sociological and Sociolinguistic Portrait.* Westport, CT: Bergin & Garvey.

———. 2001. *Trends in Ethnic Identification among Second-Generation Haitian Immigrants in New York City.* Westport, CT: Bergin & Garvey.

CHAPTER 12

INTERMINORITY RELATIONS IN LEGISLATIVE SETTINGS: THE CASE OF AFRICAN AMERICANS AND LATINOS

José E. Cruz

Historically, the most important aspect of race relations in the United States has been the reluctance of Anglo-whites to accept other ethnic groups as their equals. Codified in 1789 as the "three-fifths" clause of Article I of the Constitution, this attitude guided political practice for one hundred years after the abolition of slavery by the Thirteenth Amendment and for nearly a century after the Fifteenth Amendment established the right of citizens to vote regardless of race.

After the Civil War gave the North its victory, westward expansion became synonymous with Indian removal and extermination. During this period of almost forty years, racial conflict pitted Anglo-whites against Blacks and Native Americans. With the Indian problem "solved" by the turn of the century and relations between Anglo-whites and white ethnics subsumed under the rubrics of Progressivism and machine politics, the prominence of Blacks in the hierarchy of race relations became so significant that, despite the existence of an important "Mexican problem," race became synonymous with black skin, and race relations came to be understood predominantly as relations between Blacks and whites.

While in *Race, The History of an Idea in America*, Thomas F. Gossett (1997:xiii) wrote that race relations in the United States were multiethnic and multiracial, in Gunnar Myrdal's (1962:1) view interracial relations were strictly between "Negroes" and whites. This is how he conceived the project that would later become *An American Dilemma*: "The study . . . should aim at determining the social, political, educational, and economic status of the Negro in the United States as well as defining opinions held by different groups of Negroes and whites as to his 'right' status." With the publication of Myrdal's study (originally released in 1944) and the emergence of the Civil Rights Movement, the binary view of race relations in the United States became hegemonic, prevailing within both civil society and political society for most of the second half of the twentieth century.

During the 1990s this focus on a dual racial hierarchy shifted. Just as before, throughout the twentieth century the question of race encompassed issues related to the presence within American society of a variety of ethnic groups, not just African Americans. But it was not until the 1990s that most analysts came to understand that the problem of race in the United States could no longer be fully appreciated in terms of a Black–white dichotomy (Wallace and Chavez, 1992). Thus, during this decade the 1992 Los Angeles riots, sparked by the acquittal of the policemen accused of beating Rodney King, became, for both scholars and lay commentators, the prime example and key reference point of the multiracial nature of political conflict in the United States, even though multiracial political conflict was evident earlier. According to James Jennings (1992:3), ethnic conflict among nonwhite groups represented a "major new challenge" for white and nonwhite elites as well. For their part, Charles Kamasaki and Raul Yzaguirre (1994–1995:17) argued that "growing tension between [them], threatens the ability of Blacks and Hispanics to develop strong, sustainable coalitions." Wilbur Rich (1996:1–2), on the other hand, noted a different type of problem among minorities: "Lacking any common racial experience in America, minority groups remain separate. Each subgroup has sought a separate accommodation with the white majority (a vertical linkage), and in most cases groups have eschewed relationships with other minority groups (a horizontal linkage)".

It is in the context of this shift that I analyze the relationship between the Congressional Black (CBC) and Hispanic (CHC) caucuses. Doing so carries not just the vantage point of an interminority perspective but also the recognition that legislative settings are critical arenas of interaction between minority groups. This is the case in terms of how institutions mirror trends within the civil society and in terms of the impact that policy-making processes have as well. If coalition building is crucial to effective policy making—an assumption that is warranted by the decentralized and fragmented nature of interest representation in Congress—it follows that alliances among minority legislators are an important element of successful minority legislative behavior.

Just as it is no longer possible to ignore the multifarious nature of the racial hierarchy in the United States, it is difficult to accept the notion that commonalities of suffering override conflicting interests among minorities. Therefore, the factors that shape coalition building among minority political elites cannot be taken for granted. Accordingly, my purpose is to identify those factors. To do so, I address three basic questions: What is the nature of the working relationship between the minority caucuses in Congress? How effective is this relationship and why? What factors explain cooperation and conflict among minority political elites in this specific setting? Race is the implicit variable in these questions in the sense that all political relations in the United States are—to some extent—racial relations. In Congress racial discourse may not be explicit or prominent but, as far as minority legislators are concerned, all aspects of their institutional performance—from election to interest representation—are either determined or shaped by racial concerns. In other words, whether legislators choose to address issues related to economic or social policy, chances are they will have to take into account disparities in treatment performance, and achievement that run along racial lines.

To answer these questions, I conducted interviews with members of the Congressional Black and Hispanic caucuses, beginning in the fall of 2000. Between September and December 2000 a total of eleven interviews were conducted with three members of the CHC and eight members of the CBC. This represents 15 percent of the CHC's membership, 21 percent of CBC affiliates, and 19 percent of the caucuses' combined membership of fifty-nine representatives. All interviews were conducted over the phone, following repeated efforts to make contact with each member and coordinate appropriate dates and times. Interviews lasted between thirty and forty-five minutes each. Time and financial constraints did not allow for face-to-face interviews. Research suggests that telephone interviews affect the quantity of information obtained, but the validity of information is just as good as that of information obtained through face-to-face interviews (Weisberg, Krosnick, and Bowen, 1989:100–101).

A significant group of members were unwilling to grant an interview. Some declined as a matter of policy and others were just not interested in participating in the project—according to the staff of the latter group, participation was not a priority item. One explanation was that a request for an interview from an academic who was not a constituent did not help. A total of sixteen representatives refused to be interviewed, ten from the CBC and six from the CHC. The rest were simply impossible to pin down despite repeated requests. The interview materials were used as guideposts and supplemented by secondary sources, roll-call data, and news accounts.

Legislative Minorities in the Literature

Studies of minority groups in Congress concentrate on describing them, documenting their growth, and specifying their function (Cranford, 1992; Richardson, 1990; Hammond et al., 1983; Fiellin, 1962; Bositis, 1994). Scholars have also analyzed how these groups expand existing opportunities and open new avenues of action for minority legislators (Stevens et al., 1981; Barnett, 1975). Minority caucuses can be more unified than political parties (Gile and Jones, 1995), but they are not necessarily better at providing substantive representation for their constituencies (Kerr and Miller, 1997; Hero and Tolbert, 1995; Levy and Stoudinger, 1978).

Between 1969 and 2003 the growth in the number of special-interest caucuses in Congress was dramatic, rising to one hundred eighty-one, from three. This growth is attributed to the diversity of American society and the lack of consensus on issues within Congress (Hammond, 1989:369).[1] More specifically, ascriptive traits, such as race, have been found to provide a stronger stimulus for group formation than region, ideology, or gender (Jones, 1987). Some see these groups as a reflection of weak partisanship, both causing and deepening the Balkanization of American politics (Brady and Bullock, 1981:201). Others argue that even though minority caucuses do increase the fragmentation of Congress, they also provide and expand representation (Loomis, 1981). Additional benefits include facilitating access to information, providing a vehicle for the emergence of leaders, and giving members a structure for agenda setting (Hammond, 1989:363–366).

On the question of relations *between* minority groups, the literature is basically silent. The focus of attention concerns relations between minorities and whites, a fact that illustrates how race relations are approached predominantly in binary terms. A critical issue within this literature is the small number of minority legislators and their need to win the support of their white counterparts to accomplish their goals (Singh, 1998:138; Jones, 1987).

A second issue of importance relates to the means minorities use to channel their activities. According to Cheryl Miller (1990), at the state level, coalition-building efforts are more effective when pursued through formal, as opposed to informal, structures. In that sense, a caucus is a better vehicle than an informal association or network.

The advantage of a formal organization is that its cohesion compensates for small numbers. And cohesion is measured in terms of the ability to engage members in bloc voting. In Congress bloc voting is considered essential in several ways: as a legislative tool (Jones, 1985:192) and as a source of both bargaining power and respect (Ehrenhalt, 1977). The formula is simple: with a formal organization in place instead of striking x number of deals in exchange for support, x number of votes can be delivered in one deal.

On the issue of formal versus informal organization, the ancillary issues of cohesiveness and the conditions that lead to unified collective action are also important. While bloc voting does not require a commonality of interests between minority legislators and their majority counterparts, cohesion within the minority group is essential to its ability to trade votes (Hammond, 1989; Jones, 1987; Levy and Stoudinger, 1978). The ability to vote en bloc is indicative of cohesiveness, but that still begs the question concerning the factors that make cohesive behavior possible. Among these variables, ideology, constituency preferences, and a homogeneous identity play a critical role.

Still, most analyses focus on the role that a cohesive organization plays in the political behavior of Black and white legislators, whether as a caucus-party dyad or in terms of the relationship between minority caucuses and their partisan adversaries (Hammond, 1989:361–362, 366); regarding interminority behavior, these analyses have nothing to say.

Numerical Strength

In Congress, African Americans are 9 percent of the total number of representatives; Latinos constitute 6 percent of the total. At the time of writing, no African Americans or Latinos sit in the Senate. During the 104th Congress (1995–1996), Blacks were 19 percent of the Democratic Caucus—whose members were 47 percent of all representatives—and Latinos were 10 percent. While the relative strength of Blacks and Latinos is higher within the Democratic Caucus than within Congress as a whole, their numbers are still not sufficient to make each an independent force. During the 108th Congress (2003–2004), the relative strength of African Americans within the Democratic Caucus decreased slightly, down to 18 percent, while the relative strength of Latinos increased by one percentage point. In November 2002,

Robert Menendez, a CHC member, was elected chair of the Democratic Caucus, becoming the first Hispanic elected to a leadership position in the House.

Formal Organization

African Americans have been organized formally through the Congressional Black Caucus since 1971. The caucus was established during the 92nd Congress with 13 members. Current membership totals 39, including two nonvoting representatives—the delegates from the U.S. Virgin Islands and the District of Columbia. (See Tables 12.1 and 12.2.) Representative J. C. Watts from Oklahoma, the sole black Republican in Congress up until its 107th session, was never affiliated with the caucus.

Table 12.1 Congressional Black Caucus founding members

Member of Congress	State
Rep. Shirley Chisholm	New York
Rep. William Clay	Missouri
Rep. George Collins	Illinois
Rep. John Conyers	Michigan
Rep. Ronald Dellums (Chair 1989–1990)	California
Rep. Charles Diggs (Chair 1971–1972)	Michigan
Rep. Walter Fauntroy (Chair 1981–1982)	Washington DC
Rep. Gus Hawkins	California
Rep. Ralph Metcalf	Illinois
Rep. Parren Mitchell (Chair 1977–1978)	Maryland
Rep. Robert Nix	Pennsylvania
Rep. Charles Rangel (Chair 1975)	New York
Rep. Louis Stokes (Chair 1973–1974)	Ohio

Table 12.2 Congressional Black Caucus members 108th Congress (2003–2004)

Member of Congress	State
Rep. Frank Ballard	North Carolina
Rep. Sanford D. Bishop Jr.	Georgia
Rep. Corrine Brown	Florida
Rep. Julia M. Carson	Indiana
Rep. Donna M. Christian-Christensen	Virgin Islands
Rep. William L. Clay	Missouri
Rep. James E. Clyburn	South Carolina
Rep. John Conyers Jr.	Michigan
Rep. Elijah E. Cummings	Maryland
Rep. Arthur Davis	Alabama
Rep. Danny K. Davis	Illinois
Rep. Chaka Fattah	Pennsylvania
Rep. Harold E. Ford Jr.	Tennessee
Rep. Alcee L. Hastings	Florida

Table 12.2 (Continued)

Member of Congress	State
Rep. Eleanor Holmes-Norton	Washington, DC
Rep. Jesse Jackson Jr.	Illinois
Rep. Sheila Jackson-Lee	Texas
Rep. William J. Jefferson	Louisiana
Rep. Eddie Bernice Johnson	Texas
Rep. Stephanie Tubbs Jones	Ohio
Rep. Carolyn Cheeks Kilpatrick	Michigan
Rep. Barbara Lee	California
Rep. John Lewis	Georgia
Rep. Denise Majette	Georgia
Rep. Kendrik Meek	Florida
Rep. Gregory W. Meeks	New York
Rep. Juanita Millender-McDonald	California
Rep. Major R. Owens	New York
Rep. Donald M. Payne	New Jersey
Rep. Charles R. Rangel	New York
Rep. Bobby L. Rush	Illinois
Rep. David Scott	Georgia
Rep. Robert Scott	Virginia
Rep. Bennie G. Thompson	Mississippi
Rep. Edolphus Towns	New York
Rep. Maxine Waters	California
Rep. Diane E. Watson	California
Rep. Melvin L. Watt	North Carolina
Rep. Albert R. Wynn	Maryland

Latinos formed their own group, the Congressional Hispanic Caucus, in December 1976 during the 94th Congress. Originally comprising five representatives, currently the caucus has 20 members out of the 24 Latinos that serve in Congress. (See Tables 12.3 and 12.4). One CHC member—Puerto Rico's resident commissioner—is a nonvoting member. Between the 95th and 100th Congress, encompassing the period from 1977 to 1988, Manuel Luján, a Republican from Texas was a CHC member. In September 1989, during the 101st Congress, the newly elected Republican representative from Florida, Ileana Ros-Lehtinen also joined. She dropped out during the 102nd Congress (1991–1992) and rejoined during the 103rd (1993–1994), along with Republicans Henry Bonilla and Lincoln Diaz-Balart from Texas and Florida, respectively. The 104th Congress (1995–1996) was the last to see Republican Latinos as members of the CHC. In 2003 there were four Latino Republicans in the House: Henry Bonilla (TX), Lincoln Diaz-Balart (FL), Mario Diaz-Balart (FL), and Ileana Ros-Lehtinen (FL). None were CHC members. In March 2003, with the participation of Devin Nunes, a Republican of Portuguese ancestry from California, they formed the Congressional Hispanic Conference to support President Bush's policies and to oppose the CHC (Gamboa, 2003).

Table 12.3   Congressional Hispanic Caucus founding members

Member of Congress	State
Rep. Herman Badillo	New York
Rep. Baltasar Corrada del Río	Puerto Rico (resident commissioner)
Rep. E. "Kika" de la Garza	Texas
Rep. Henry B. González	Texas
Rep. Edward Roybal	California

Table 12.4   Congressional Hispanic Caucus members 108th Congress (2003–2004)

Member of Congress	State
Rep. Aníbal Acevedo-Vilá	Puerto Rico (resident commissioner)
Rep. Joe Baca	California
Rep. Xavier Becerra	California
Rep. Dennis Cardoza	California
Rep. Charles A. González	Texas
Rep. Raúl Grijalva	Arizona
Rep. Luis V. Gutiérrez	Illinois
Rep. Rubén Hinojosa	Texas
Rep. Robert Menéndez	New Jersey
Rep. Grace Napolitano	California
Rep. Solomon P. Ortíz	Texas
Rep. Edward Pastor	Arizona
Rep. Silvestre Reyes	Texas
Rep. Ciro Rodríguez	Texas
Rep. Lucille Roybal-Allard	California
Rep. Linda Sánchez	California
Rep. Loretta Sánchez	California
Rep. José E. Serrano	New York
Rep. Hilda Solís	California
Rep. Nydia M. Velázquez	New York

Cohesion

According to Robert Singh (1998:141), the CBC qualifies as a cohesive organization on the basis of its predominantly liberal ideology.

> [CBC members] consistently maintain a homogeneous ideological stance on roll-call votes: They strongly oppose Republican presidential positions, support the Democratic party on "party votes" . . . and oppose the preferences of the Conservative Coalition. CBC members unfailingly earn high ratings from liberal groups and low ones from conservatives.

In contrast, in terms of voting behavior the CHC has been found to be less cohesive than the Black Caucus, northern Democrats, southern Democrats, and House Republicans (Vega, 1993:84). On occasion, this lower level of voting cohesion has diminished the attractiveness of the CHC as a coalition partner. Furthermore, as was the case in 1986, when the members of the caucus split their vote on the Simpson-Mazzoli immigration reform bill, lack of cohesion has led to legislative failure.

Looking at foreign and economic policy roll calls, Charles Menifield found "consistent levels of voting unity" within the CHC. The caucus was also found capable of affecting the voting behavior of its members across different types of votes. Nevertheless, Menifield confirmed the fact that the cohesion level of the CHC "tends to be lower than that of the other caucuses and the parties as well. This is especially true when the comparison is made with the Congressional Black Caucus" (1998:41).

Building on an extensive literature (Weisberg, 1978; Matthews and Stimson, 1975; Clausen, 1973; Kingdon, 1973), Arturo Vega (1993) found that district electoral preferences influence the cohesiveness of minority voting behavior. Districts with strong Democratic preferences in congressional and presidential elections tend to provide clear voting cues along liberal lines. African American districts fit this pattern. In contrast, districts with marginal Democratic preferences tend to do the opposite, and Hispanic districts typically fall within this group. Incentives for consistency in voting are greater for districts favoring the Democratic Party than they are for those that do not, and for this reason CBC members display more cohesive behavior in voting than their Hispanic counterparts.

Even though the Black population in the United States is more ethnically diverse today than during the 1960s, historically similarities of ancestry, heritage, and life experience among Blacks have been greater than the differences. These similarities have resulted in the formation of a Black consciousness and a race-based belief system (Allen et al., 1989:421), which has encouraged unity and collaboration among Blacks in Congress. The fact that African Americans constitute a racial minority bound by a set of values and beliefs helps explain why Black leaders in Congress can claim to represent not just their individual districts but also the interests of all African Americans in the United States (United States, 1982:29).

Historically, the leadership of the CHC has made similar claims. In the words of Robert García, who chaired the CHC in 1982: "Representatives in Congress who are black, Hispanic, or women, have, in addition to their own constituency, a national constituency which looks to them for leadership and help at the federal level of government" (U.S. Congress, 1982:90). Yet this assertion lacks the foundation that underlies African American assumptions. Latinos share a common Spanish heritage but this translates into commonalities of religion and language that are not substantial enough to transform national identities into a singular pan-ethnic identity.

The problem is not so much that Latino elites lack a strong ethnic or racial consciousness, as Vega (1993:81) suggests, but that the historical experiences of Latino groups are quite diverse. The political incorporation of Mexicans, Puerto Ricans, and Cubans—to mention just the principal groups—into the U.S. political system took place not only at different times for each group but also in different regional settings and through different mechanisms. These differences tend to outweigh group similarities. In fact, even those who argue that the combination of language, heritage, class, and experience with discrimination favors the development of a Latino identity recognize the absence of that identity despite long-standing efforts to make it a reality (DeSipio, 1996).

Thus, the lower level of cohesion of the CHC relative to the CBC should not be surprising. This is a historical difficulty that, as Maurilio Vigil puts it, "will probably continue to be an obstacle to unity along with natural differences that will emerge over specific issues" (1997:259). Of course, none of this is meant to suggest that cleavages among African Americans along lines of class (Wilson, 1987), ethnicity (Torres, 1995), nativity (Waldinger, 1996), occupational status (Anderson, 1999), culture (Dawson, 1999), public policy (Swain, 1995), and even color (Gates, 1994; Zack, 1993) do not exist. The point is that group identity is objectively weaker among Latinos than among African Americans.

Coalition-Building Factors

On the question of Blacks and coalition politics, Jerry Gafio Watts (1996) argues that, more often than not, when political scientists talk about coalitions they are actually talking about illusory alliances whose coordinates are reified identities and symbolic appropriation of those identities by nonparticipants. He uses as an example the case of Andrew Goodman, the CORE activist murdered in Mississippi in 1964, whose objectified and expropriated identity became emblematic of a black–Jewish coalition that was more symbolic than real. According to Watts, this is a problem—a "paradigmatic failure"—that promotes a false view of actual relations.

Watts's solution to this problem is a more conceptually precise idea of political coalitions. He rejects nonpurposive, spontaneous, or circumstantial configurations of diverse populations as too broad to qualify as coalitions. Instead, he suggests two ideal types: "disjointed" and "shared core" coalitions.

Disjointed coalitions are those in which "groups band together because they do not believe that they have sufficient resources to articulate successfully their goals by themselves" (1996:41). Shared core coalitions develop "when various disparate groups come together because they support a common issue agenda" (1996:43). Watts endorses Barbara Hinckley's definition of coalitions, even though his conceptualization is at odds with hers. People do not join coalitions for purely instrumental or communitarian reasons, as Watts would have it, but, as Hinckley (1981:32) notes, on the basis of mixed motives and concerns.

On the nature of coalitions Wilbur Rich echoes Theodore Caplow's (1956) thesis that coalitional relationships reflect the relative resources controlled by political actors. Regarding motives, he declares that groups collaborate simply to maximize political preferences (1996:6). While incontrovertible, these claims fail to include other relevant factors. In addition to the level of resources controlled by participants, coalitions tend to reflect the ideology, reputational ambition, type of goal pursued and its importance, and the scope of member interests. Further, coalition partners not only participate for different reasons but also, depending on their specific motivation, play different roles (Deleon, 1991:184–185; Hula, 1999:93–94, 111).

My analytical framework does not rule out instrumental or communitarian motives as coalition-building factors. In highlighting these motives, Watts is on the mark. Rich is also correct in pointing out the importance of resources and preferences.

Yet Watts's approach suggests that participants are driven by either one of two mutually exclusive motives. On the other hand, if Rich were right, coalitions would always be dominated by the group with the greatest amount of resources, and coalition members would never make compromises. For these reasons, a nondichotomous approach to the question of coalition building seems appropriate.

In terms of Black-Latino coalitions, Paula McClain (1996:55–57) suggests that the disposition of each group is shaped by a combination of objective, subjective, and relational factors. Common concerns with poverty and discrimination, among others, are a source of coalitional behavior between Latinos and African Americans. But once either group begins to feel that the alliance does not produce the expected rewards, its disposition changes from a cooperative to a conflictive stance. If Black perceive Latinos as less likely to be prejudiced, their willingness to develop alliances is greater. Also, differences in the size of African American and Latino groups affect their disposition to establishing alliances. If one group feels that it has sufficient demographic strength to act on its own, it will be less willing to work with a lesser group. If the larger group begins to receive increasing shares of socioeconomic and political rewards, or if it starts to act as an oppressive majority, the smaller group will be unwilling to work as its partner.

My own research (Cruz, 2000) identifies a set of contextual and relational factors that can run purposive coalitions among political elites into the ground. If the historical premises of interelite attitudes are incongruent and the level of dissonance between actions and perceptions is high, it is hard for purposive coalition building to either get started or succeed once initiated. How minorities negotiate dilemmas of representation, especially in the context of relative degrees of empowerment status among groups, is also an important factor. Once the initially difficult process of coalition building is set in motion, it tends to succeed or fail depending on the strength or weakness of collective memory. In addition, the distribution of responsibilities, particularly the opportunity to exercise power, is as critical to coalitional stability as the distribution of social and economic rewards.

Nature of Interminority Relations in Congress

All CBC informants had a high regard for the relationship between their caucus and the CHC. Responses to the question concerning the nature of the working relationship between the caucuses ranged from "excellent" to "cordial." Half of CBC informants considered the relationship at least "good," and half of this group characterized it as "excellent." The other half considered it "cordial." For their part, the majority of CHC informants described the relationship as "minimal" and "uneven." This group did not consider the relationship to be close, and in their view, it took place mostly at the individual level. Almost all informants agreed that the caucuses do not work together often enough. Only three informants believed that the caucuses worked together about the right amount of time.

While the relationship between the caucuses seems to lack sufficient purposive contact, coincidental collaboration appears to be strong. During the first session of the 107th Congress, the members of the CBC and CHC voted exactly alike in seventeen out of nineteen selected roll calls involving the passage of difficult as well as easy resolutions and legislation.[2]

Collaboration

The most frequent reason to collaborate is the existence of common interests between the caucuses. Of a total of fourteen selections of reasons for collaboration, "common interests" was chosen ten times, for 71 percent of the choices. "Effectiveness" was chosen only three times, for 21 percent of the choices, whereas "full agreement on the issues" was chosen only once. When either group had a marginal interest in the issue at hand, the most frequently chosen reason to collaborate was "solidarity," with four choices out of nine, or 44 percent. The second most important reason, chosen three out of nine times, was "reciprocity," that is, the expectation that the favor of assistance would be returned.

When asked how frequently the caucuses were concerned about their relative size when deciding to work together, a majority declared that this was rarely or never a concern. Interestingly, CHC informants were less concerned about relative size than CBC members. A solid majority of those interviewed felt that in most cases their constituents would approve collaboration between the caucuses. In this regard, the response of CBC informants was virtually unanimous.

Race as an Issue

In order to avoid loading the question on race, I formulated it in general terms. I asked each informant the following: Has the issue of race ever come into play in the relationship between your caucus and the CBC/CHC? Each was given a choice of yes or no for an answer and an opportunity to elaborate. Because of the controversial nature of race, there was a risk that in the absence of specific cues most informants would simply adopt a safe stance and choose the "no" option. On the other hand, I estimated that if they were not prompted, informants would be more likely to offer candid responses. More than half agreed that the issue of race had never come into play in the relationship between the caucuses. The assessment of CHC informants who believed race to be an issue was positive, that is, race was seen either as a unifying factor or as a marker of differences in terms of status or issues of importance to each group. In contrast, the informants from the CBC who believed race to be an issue were concerned that the distribution of rewards based on race may not be commensurate with effort. Also, they did not approve the practice of lumping together African Americans and Latinos on account of race.

Importance and Usefulness of Collaboration

All CHC informants agreed that working in collaboration with the CBC was "important." Only one CBC informant disagreed. One CBC informant declared that collaboration was "somewhat important" and six others stated that it was "very important." Overall, a solid majority of informants agreed that working together was "very important." On the other hand, while all informants agreed that collaboration was "useful," two CHC informants agreed that it was "very useful" and five CBC informants concurred. A little over one-third of the informants believed that collaboration was merely "somewhat useful."

Failure to Collaborate

Informants selected numerous reasons to explain the failure of their caucuses to collaborate in situations where they should have done so. The most frequently chosen reason was "lack of communication"; also selected were "lack of coordination," "personality conflicts," "division over issues," "time constraints," and "competition over resources and benefits." Overall, these reasons were chosen with the same frequency, but CBC informants selected "division over issues" and "time constraints" twice as many times as CHC informants. Other reasons offered once each exclusively by CBC informants included "lack of foresight" about the importance of collaboration, the decentralized nature of Congress, and the inability of caucus members to formulate adequate strategies.

Race or Party?

During the 1980s the position taken by national Black leaders on the question of immigration often stood in sharp contrast with the attitudes of Black leaders in cities such as Los Angeles, New Orleans, and Miami. National Black leaders were concerned about economic displacement of Blacks by Latino immigrants, but they were also careful to avoid open conflict with Latino leaders. "As a consequence," wrote Lawrence Fuchs, "national black leaders began to move toward supporting Mexican American leaders on the illegal immigration issue. That was partly because of their strong common interest in other political issues, but also a result of the fact that nearly all of them were Democrats." During the 1984 debate and action on the Simpson-Mazzoli immigration bill, the CBC was so eager to cooperate with Hispanic congressional leaders that they ignored the preferences not only of the House Democratic leadership but also of Black constituents who supported English-language requirements in the amnesty provisions of the bill (Fuchs, 1990:301, 304).

In April 2001 a similar situation developed in Congress, this time involving a decision made by Latino leaders: CHC members agreed to withhold their support of Latino challengers in primaries against incumbent Democrats. According to the chair of the CHC, Silvestre Reyes (D-TX), to do otherwise would cost more in terms of lost support from Democratic colleagues than it would pay in terms of added descriptive representation in Congress. One could argue that in 1984 CBC members put race ahead of party, even if it is true that their decision was also influenced by their shared Democratic affiliation with CHC members, as Fuchs suggests. Accordingly, it is interesting that in the 2001 CHC decision, party clearly trumped race. In this case reciprocity based on partisanship was considered more important than descriptive representation. As Robert Menendez (D-NJ), CHC member and Democratic Caucus vice chair, put it: "Clearly, if we want members to vote with us on the issues of importance to our community, we need to support them" (Wallison and Mercurio, 2001). Thus, the CHC agreed that recruiting and supporting Latino challengers in Republican-controlled districts with growing Latino populations was more important than displacing Democratic incumbents with Latino representatives.

Discussion

Watts's reconceptualization of political coalitions may be more precise than previous formulations, but his model is not echoed by the perceived reality of coalitional behavior among African Americans and Latinos in Congress. Ironically, it is precisely the analytical sharpness of his distinction between disjointed and shared core coalitions that makes these concepts inapplicable to a situation in which coalition building appears to share elements of both. Indeed, the interviews for this study suggest that purposive alliances based on common issue agendas are never free of the instrumental elements that define disjointed collaboration. In that sense, the more fluid version of coalition building espoused by Hinckley, Hula, and Deleon, in which mixed motives and concerns shape the timing and content of alliances, appears more relevant even if less sharply delineated.

Similarly, Rich's idea that coalition prominence is inevitably tied to resources is not confirmed by the interviews of CBC and CHC members. Size, for example, barely registered as a concern in the decision to collaborate. The factors that according to McClain triggered collaboration or conflict between Latinos and Blacks in Los Angeles, such as prejudice and expected rewards, do not seem to have the same effect in the congressional setting, although personality conflicts and lack of communication in this study had the same effect as prejudice in McClain's, and one could argue that in racial relations those types of conflicts are potentially informed by prejudicial attitudes. The concern with the size of distributive shares as a coalition-building or coalition-maintenance factor was in evidence in the urban setting analyzed by McClain and in the legislative setting of this study as well.

Nevertheless, the legislative setting appears to have a dynamic of its own. Factors that in my research on urban settings I identified as having a disruptive impact on coalition building do not appear to have a similar effect in Congress. These factors include the historical premises of elite attitudes, the strength or weakness of collective memory, and the distribution of responsibilities among coalition partners. Another element suggesting that the legislative setting has a distinctive but not unique dynamic is that, as Marie Hojnacki (1997) found the case to be with interest groups, both caucuses put a premium on collaboration because it is considered, in theory if not always in practice, pivotal to success. How minorities negotiate the choice of virtual or direct representation, a factor of some importance at the city level, seems also to be important at the legislative level. This is clearly illustrated by the CHC's decision to favor Democratic incumbents over Latino challengers.

That CBC and CHC informants downplayed race as an issue is not altogether surprising. Yet the high response to "common interests" as a reason for collaboration, in contrast to the virtual exclusion of "full agreement on the issues," suggests that race is more critical to collaboration than caucus members are willing to admit. In other words, in the absence of a known agreement on the issues as a reason to work together, race must be an important proxy for common interests.

Of course, the absence of a known agreement could also mean that partisanship rather than race is the proxy for "common interests." Yet, when informants referred to the distinctiveness of the relationship between the two caucuses, they did so using such terms as "natural affinities," "broad concerns such as fairness and justice," and "minority status." Clearly, there is partisan affinity between them, but that is hardly a "natural" quality. Interest in "fairness and justice" is not an exclusive attribute of racial groups, but it points to a defining concern. Minority status is not a partisan trait at all. Thus, it is highly likely that as a proxy for "common interests," race is at least equally critical as party.

The interviews support what is by now a demonstrated assumption concerning interminority relations: that racial affinity does not automatically lead to collaboration (Uhlaner, 1991:370). For informants, race was an implicit reference point for decision making; the racialization of identity in particular—especially the lumping together of Blacks and Latinos on account of race—was a source of intergroup tension. This did not seem to be, prima facie, an obstacle for either purposive or coincidental collaboration. It is not clear what "lack of communication" means in racial terms, but in regard to collaboration it seemed to be a problem related more to the fragmentation and compartmentalization of Congress than to racially determined social distance.

Eyes on the Prize?

The position taken by Blacks in 1984 was part of a shifting debate over the responsibility of immigrants for the racialization of economic opportunity in the United States. The decision of the CHC in 2001 was influenced not just by partisan considerations but also and perhaps more importantly, by the coincidence of Black racial identity and Democratic incumbency. By going against the House Democratic leadership in 1984 Black leaders gave race more weight than they did partisanship. Remarkably, they put solidarity with an out-group ahead of in-group interest representation. Latinos acted similarly in 2001, except that their decision was less clearly delineated by race and it did not preclude pushing for in-group interest representation vis-à-vis Republican incumbents.

What is interesting in the Latino case is that even though partisanship may appear to be more important in determining action, race is inevitably implicated as well. In other words, by being overtly concerned with substantive as opposed to descriptive representation, decisions made on the basis of partisanship may appear to be racially neutral. But to the extent that substantive representation aims at producing benefits to Latinos or Blacks, it is shaped by racial concerns. Similarly, if privileging partisanship over identity helps one group avoid conflict with another, the end result is racial even if the strategy is not.

This is most clearly the case in the decision made by the CHC. By emphasizing partisanship, CHC members increased their chances of accomplishing at least three racial goals: (1) avoiding conflict with Black Democrats such as Maxine Waters, Juanita Millender-McDonald, and Diane Watson, all CBC members who may face Latino challengers in the future; (2) earning brownie points with the CBC, which means that in the next round of the congressional game of give-and-take, Latinos will be poised to "take" rather than "give"; and, (3) concentrating their energy and resources on increasing descriptive representation in districts with Republican incumbents.

Whether this strategy will work or not remains to be seen. For now, several key insights emerge from the analysis above. First, models of coalition building that are analytically precise may not be descriptively accurate and therefore not entirely useful in practice. Also, different settings seem to require attention to different sets of coalition-building strategies. This introduces an element of contingency to the question of interminority relations that increases their challenge. Second, symmetry of interests and needs is important if minorities are to fashion collaborative arrangements, but this does not automatically induce collaboration, especially in a context in which fragmentation and compartmentalization prevail. In this regard, the role that fragmentation and compartmentalization play is interesting because their effect has been the opposite within the pressure system. Outside of Congress, atomization has pushed interest groups *toward*, rather than away from, coalition strategies (Loomis, 1986); this reinforces the point about legislative settings having a coalitional dynamic of their own. Third, it seems that in order to fashion collaborative relations, minority elites in legislative settings must keep their eyes on the prize while pretending to look away. In other words, even if race is an issue, a positive relation between out-groups may require that race be downplayed as a factor. Sometimes racial objectives will be best accomplished by favoring party affiliation instead of race. There will be instances when race will be the critical parameter even if it registers only as subtext. At times out-group solidarity will take precedence over in-group interest representation. But in the same way that altruism often serves selfish ends, it may be that in such cases the best way to serve in-group racial interests is to put them aside for the sake of tactical collaboration and the promise of future gain.

Notes

1. In September 2003 there were 162 member organizations in the House and 19 in the Senate.
2. The selected roll calls took place between January 3 and May 26, 2001. Roll calls that did not consider the question of passage were excluded from the pool examined. The majority of roll calls, 106 out of 150, were of this kind.

References

Allen, Richard L., Michael C. Dawson, and Ronald E. Brown. 1989. A schema-based approach to modeling an African-American racial belief system. *American Political Science Review* 83 (June):421–441.

Anderson, Elijah. 1999. The social situation of the Black executive: Black and white identities in the corporate world. In *The Cultural Territories of Race*, ed. Michèle Lamont, 3–29. Chicago: University of Chicago Press.

Barnett, Marguerite Ross. 1975. The CBC. *Proceedings of the Academy of Political Science* 32:34–50.

Bositis, David A. 1994. *The Congressional Black Caucus in the 103rd Congress*. Washington, DC: Joint Center for Political and Economic Studies.

Brady, David W., and Charles S. Bullock III. 1981. Coalition politics in the House of Representatives. In *Congress Reconsidered*, 2nd ed., ed. Lawrence Dodd and Bruce Oppenheimer. Washington, DC: Congressional Quarterly Press.

Caplow, Theodore. 1956. A theory of coalitions in the triad. *American Sociological Review* 19:23–29.

Clausen, Aage. 1973. *How Congressmen Decide*. New York: St. Martin's Press.

Cranford, Janet R. 1992. The new class: More diverse, less lawyerly, younger. *Congressional Quarterly Weekly Report*, 7–10.

Cruz, José E. 2000. Interminority relations in urban settings: Lessons from the Black-Puerto Rican experience. In *Black and Multiracial Politics in America*, ed. Yvette M. Alex-Assensoh and Lawrence J. Hanks, 84–112. New York: New York University Press.

Dawson, Michael C. 1999. "Dis beat disrupts": Rap ideology, and Black political attitudes. In *The Cultural Territories of Race*, ed. Michèle Lamont, 318–342. Chicago: University of Chicago Press.

Deleon, Richard. 1991. The progressive urban regime: Ethnic coalitions in San Francisco. In *Racial and Ethnic Politics in California*, ed. Bryan O. Jackson and Michael B. Preston, 157–192. Berkeley: IGS Press.

DeSipio, Louis. 1996. More than the sum of its parts: The building blocks of a pan-ethnic Latino identity. In *The Politics of Minority Coalitions*, ed. Wilbur C. Rich, 177–189. Westport, CT: Praeger.

Ehrenhalt, Alan. 1977. Black Caucus: A wary Carter ally. *Congressional Quarterly Weekly Report* 35 (May 21):967–972.

Fiellin, Allan. 1962. The functions of informal groups in legislative institutions. *Journal of Politics* 24 (February):72–91.

Fuchs, Lawrence H. 1990. The reaction of Black Americans to immigration. In *Immigration Reconsidered: History, Sociology, and Politics*, ed. Virginia Yans-McLaughlin, 293–314. New York: Oxford University Press.

Gamboa, Suzanne. 2003. Republican Hispanics form own congressional group. *San Diego Union-Tribune*, September 12, 2003. http://www. signonsandiego.com/news/politics/20030318–1600-republicanhispanics.html.

Gates, Henry Louis, Jr. 1994. *Colored People*. New York: Vintage Books.

Gile, Roxanne L., and Charles E. Jones. 1995. Congressional racial solidarity: Exploring Congressional Black Caucus voting cohesion, 1971–1990. *Journal of Black Studies* 25:622–641.

Gossett, Thomas F. 1997. *Race, The History of an Idea in America*. Oxford: Oxford University Press.

Hammond, Susan W., 1989. Congressional caucuses and the policy process. In *Congress Reconsidered*, ed. Lawrence Dodd and Bruce Oppenheimer. Washington, DC: Congressional Quarterly Press.

Hammond, Susan W., Arthur G. Stevens Jr., and Daniel P. Mulholland. 1983. Congressional caucuses: Legislators as lobbyists. In *Interest Group Politics*, ed. Allan J. Cigler and Burdett A Loomis, 275–295. Washington, DC: Congressional Quarterly Press.

Hero, Rodney, and Caroline Tolbert. 1995. Latinos and substantive representation in the U.S. House of Representatives: Direct, indirect, or nonexistent? *American Journal of Political Science* 39 (August):640–652.

Hinckley, Barbara. 1981. *Coalitions and Politics*. New York: Harcourt Brace Jovanovich.

Hojnacki, Marie. 1997. Interest groups' decisions to join alliances or work alone. *American Journal of Political Science* 41 (January):61–87.

Hula, Kevin W. 1999. *Lobbying Together: Interest Group Coalitions in Legislative Politics*. Washington, DC: Georgetown University Press.

Jennings, James. 1992. New urban racial and ethnic conflicts in United States politics. *SAGE Race Relations Abstracts* 17, no. 3 (August):3–36.

Jones, Charles E. 1987. United we stand, divided we fall: An analysis of the Congressional Black Caucus's voting behavior, 1975–1980. *Phylon* 48:26–37.

————. 1985. Three conditions for effective Black participation in the legislative process: An inquiry of the CBC, 1971–1982. Ph.D. diss., Washington State University.

Kamasaki, Charles, and Raul Yzaguirre. 1994–95. Black-Hispanic tensions: One perspective. *Journal of Intergroup Relations* 21, no. 4 (Winter):17–40.

Kerr, Brinck, and Will Miller. 1997. Latino representation, it's direct and indirect. *American Journal of Political Science* 41:1066–1071.

Kingdon, John. 1973. *Congressmen's Voting Decisions*, 2nd ed. New York: Harper and Row.

Levy, Arthur B., and Susan Stoudinger. 1978. The Black Caucus in the 92nd Congress: Gauging its success. *Phylon* 39:322–332.

Loomis, Burdett A. 1986. Coalitions of interests: Building bridges in the Balkanized state. In *Interest Group Politics*, 2nd ed., ed. Allan J. Cigler and Burdett A. Loomis, 258–274. Washington, DC: CQ Press.

————. 1981. Congressional caucuses and the politics of representation. In *Congress Reconsidered*, 2nd ed., ed. Lawrence Dodd and Bruce Oppenheimer, 204–220. Washington, DC: Congressional Quarterly Press.

McClain, Paula D. 1996. Coalition and competition: Patterns of Black–Latino relations in urban politics. In *The Politics of Minority Coalitions*, ed. Wilbur C. Rich, 53–63. Westport, CT: Praeger.

Matthews, Donald, and James Stimson. 1975. *Yeas and Nays: Normal Decision Making in the U.S. House of Representatives*. New York: John Wiley.

Menifield, Charles F. 1998. A loose coalition or a united front: Voting behavior within the Congressional Hispanic Caucus. *Latino Studies Journal* 9, no. 2 (Spring):26–44.

Miller, Cheryl. 1990. Agenda-setting by state legislative Black caucuses: Policy priorities and factors of success. *Policy Studies Review* 9:339–354.

Myrdal, Gunnar. 1962. *An American Dilemma*. New York: Pantheon Books.

Richardson, Sula P. 1993. *Caucuses and LSOs of the 103rd Congress*. Washington, DC: Congressional Research Service.

————. 1993a. *LSOs: An Informational Directory*. Washington, DC: Congressional Research Service.

————. 1990. *Caucuses and Legislative Service Organizations of the 101st Congress: An Information Directory*. Washington, DC: Congressional Research Service.

Rich, Wilbur C. 1996. Introduction. In *The Politics of Minority Coalitions*, ed. Wilbur C. Rich, 1–9. Westport, CT: Praeger.

Singh, Robert. 1998. *The Congressional Black Caucus: Racial Politics in the U.S. Congress*. Thousand Oaks, CA: Sage Publications.

Stevens, Arthur G., Daniel P. Mulholland, and Paul S. Rundquist. 1981. U.S. congressional structure and representation: The role of informal groups. *Legislative Studies Quarterly* 6:415–437.

Swain, Carol M. 1995. *Black Faces, Black Interests: The Representation of African Americans in Congress*. Cambridge, MA: Harvard University Press.

Torres, Andrés. 1995. *Between Melting Pot and Mosaic: African Americans and Puerto Ricans in the New York Political Economy*. Philadelphia: Temple University Press.

Uhlaner, Carole J. 1991. Perceived discrimination and prejudice and the coalition prospects of Blacks, Latinos, and Asian Americans. In *Racial and Ethnic Politics in California*, ed. Bryan O. Jackson and Michael B. Preston, 339–371. Berkeley, CA: IGS Press.

U.S. Congress, Committee on House Administration, Ad Hoc Subcommittee on Legislative Service Organizations. 1982. *Report of the Ad Hoc Subcommittee on Legislative Service Organizations of the Committee on House Administration, House of Representatives*. Washington, DC: Government Printing Office.

Vega, Arturo. 1993. Variations and sources of group cohesiveness in the Black and Hispanic congressional caucuses. *Latino Studies Journal* 4, no. 1 (January):79–92.

Vigil, Maurilio E. 1997. Hispanics in the 103rd Congress: The 1990 census, reapportionment, redistricting, and the 1992 elections. In *Pursuing Power: Latinos and the Political System*, ed. F. Chris García, 234–264. Notre Dame, IN: University of Notre Dame Press.

Waldinger, Roger. 1996. *Still the Promised City? African-Americans and New Immigrants in Postindustrial New York*. Cambridge, MA: Harvard University Press.

Wallace, Amy, and Stephanie Chavez. 1992. Understanding the riots six months later. *Los Angeles Times*, November 16.

Wallison, Ethan, and John Mercurio. 2001. Caucus' move could limit Hispanic gains, challengers unhappy with decision. *Roll Call*, April 23.

Watts, Jerry Gafio. 1996. Blacks and coalition politics: A theoretical reconceptualization. In *The Politics of Minority Coalitions*, ed. Wilbur C. Rich, 35–51. Westport, CT: Praeger.

Weisberg, Herbert F. 1978. Evaluating theories of congressional roll-call voting. *American Journal of Political Science* 22:554–577.

Weisberg, Herbert F., Jon A. Krosnick, and Bruce D. Bowen. 1989. *An Introduction to Survey Research and Data Analysis*. 2nd ed. Glenview, IL: Scott, Foresman.

Wilson, William J. 1987. *The Truly Disadvantaged*. Chicago: University of Chicago Press.

Zack, Naomi. 1993. *Race and Mixed Race*. Philadelphia: Temple University Press.

CHAPTER 13
AFRICAN AMERICAN AND LATINA/O COOPERATION IN CHALLENGING RACIAL PROFILING

Kevin R. Johnson

By the dawn of the new millennium the formal and informal targeting of African Americans, Latinas/os, and other racial minorities for police stops on account of race, popularly known as racial profiling, had grabbed national attention. The federal government promised to use the weapons at its disposal to end racial profiling in the United States. About the same time, the flaws of race-based enforcement of U.S. immigration laws, which expanded as the government escalated efforts to deport undocumented immigrants in the 1990s, also had gained increasing public awareness.

African Americans and Latinas/os, as well as other racial minorities, have common concerns about governmental reliance on race in the enforcement of criminal and immigration laws.[1] Civil rights deprivations result from law enforcement officers' relying on group probabilities as an indicator of unlawful conduct. Common interests among minority groups create the potential for political alliances designed to fight for the removal of the taint of race from law enforcement. Moreover, such coalitions are necessary to achieve social change in light of the fact that a majority of the voters are white. With respect to racial profiling, it is highly unlikely that the consideration of race can be eliminated from enforcement of the laws against Latinas/os while maintaining it against African Americans, or vice versa. Once race enters the realm of legitimate law enforcement, the logic of racial stereotypes makes *all* minority groups subject to profiling.

More generally, the criminal justice system in the United States, which skews enforcement, prosecution, and imprisonment toward young African American and Latino males, represents a legitimate target for concerted action. African Americans and Latinas/os are overwhelmingly overrepresented in the prison population compared with their respective proportions of the general population. According to some studies, rates of criminal conduct for these groups are equal to, or lower than, those for whites.

Eliminating racial bias from law enforcement through multiracial coalitions will no doubt prove to be a difficult project, marked by setbacks as well as breakthroughs. Barriers exist to the building of political coalitions between and among African Americans and Latinas/os; this is true for other minority communities as well. Trust will need to be built among groups who often view themselves as locked in competition. Racism by minorities against other minorities will need to be addressed and remedied, not ignored and avoided. Various groups often see themselves as having competing interests—that is, they may lose if others gain and vice versa. Similarly, one minority group may attempt to side with whites, while sacrificing the interests of other groups, a strategy employed by minorities at various times in U.S. history.

In the long run, political realities dictate that alliances are essential to the quest for racial justice in the United States. Although the much-publicized growth in the minority population in the United States over the last few decades bodes well for political activism, several factors make political change unlikely absent multiracial coalitions. Low voter turnout rates among African Americans, Asian Americans, Latinas/os, and Native Americans, the disenfranchisement of persons convicted of felonies, economic disparities between whites and minority groups that limit the political influence of racial minorities, and the citizenship requirement for voting (which greatly affects Latina/o and Asian American voting power) are a few factors limiting the political power of minorities despite their growing numbers.

The events of September 11, 2001, dramatically affected the nation's collective view of racial profiling in ways that make multiracial cooperation all the more necessary. Before September 11 a national consensus had emerged on the need to end racial profiling. However, after that fateful day the federal government began to engage in racial, religious, and nationality profiling on a grand, nationwide scale. With the assistance of state and local authorities, the U.S. Department of Justice questioned, interrogated, detained, and deported hundreds, if not thousands, of Arab and Muslim noncitizens, even though there was no evidence that they had any involvement with terrorism.

Importantly, a general public reconsideration of racial profiling followed September 11. Racial profiling made a comeback. The very propriety of efforts to eradicate racial profiling now are being questioned. Some observers claim that racial profiling makes sense in the "war on terror." National security has taken priority over concerns with the civil rights of Arabs, Muslims, African Americans, Latinas/os, Asian Americans, Native Americans, and other minority groups.

The first part of this essay sketches the legal problems with racial profiling in criminal and border enforcement, showing how both forms adversely impact Latinas/os, African Americans, and other minority groups, as exemplified by the post–September 11 "war on terror." The second part studies the common interests of Latinas/os and African Americans in eliminating race-based law enforcement. The third part analyzes the efficacy of coalitions to remedy the racism at the core of law enforcement in the United States. Difficult as it may be, collective action is essential to bring about much-needed racial reform in law enforcement.

Race Profiling in Law Enforcement

Racial profiling in both criminal and immigration law enforcement adversely affects African Americans, Latinas/os, and other racial groups. Misconceptions and stereotypes result in law enforcement's excessive reliance on physical appearance as a proxy for legal wrongdoing. Stereotyping by law enforcement authorities causes concrete injuries. First, if stopped, racial minorities are more likely to be arrested and convicted of a crime. Reliance on race in law enforcement thus has become a self-fulfilling prophesy. Second, the dignity of innocent racial minorities is assaulted by being stopped for nothing other than fitting a racial stereotype.

Based on similar logic and having comparable impacts, racial profiling in criminal law differs little in kind and substance from that employed in immigration enforcement. Before September 11 undue reliance on race had proven difficult to eliminate from law enforcement. Importantly, race cannot be removed from one form of law enforcement and not another. History suggests that once race taints one aspect of law enforcement (criminal law, for example), it almost inevitably infects other areas (such as immigration). Consequently, the most durable solution to remedying racial discrimination is to seek to remove the illegitimate use of race entirely from all forms of law enforcement.

The state employs race in both domestic and international law enforcement. Race-based law enforcement helps control the minority population in U.S. society and also limits migration of people of color into the United States. Although the immigration laws enacted since 1965 have not explicitly discriminated on the basis of race, they, through a variety of means, operate to exclude large numbers of racial minorities from the United States.

The relationship between domestic and international race-based law enforcement becomes especially clear in evaluating the war on terror. After the events of September 11, 2001, the U.S. government focused on Arab and Muslim noncitizens in the United States. Relying on the extensive powers afforded the political branches over immigrants and immigration, the federal government utilized a dragnet to arrest and detain Arab and Muslim noncitizens and to deport large numbers who had nothing to do with terrorism.

Criminal Law Enforcement

Few dispute that African American men for years have been routinely stopped by police for "driving while Black." This practice is one of many forms of discrimination against the African American community in this nation's criminal justice system. Similarly, police officers stop Latinas/os for "driving while brown." As African Americans have been targets of law enforcement, police departments in urban metropolises like Chicago, Los Angeles, and New York City, for years have focused the criminal justice machinery on Latinas/os. Studies have consistently shown that police are stopping Blacks and Latinos at much higher rates than they are stopping whites.

Few deny the concrete harms of racial profiling. When criminal investigation focuses on African Americans and Latinas/os, more members of these groups will be arrested and convicted of crimes, thereby contributing to disparate incarceration rates. Importantly, racial profiles punish, embarrass, and humiliate innocent people whose skin color is used as a proxy for criminal conduct. Moreover, as U.S. society becomes increasing multiracial, the possibility for error when using race in law enforcement increases because group identification is more difficult.

Racial profiling, as part of a long history of discriminatory law enforcement, fosters a deep cynicism among racial minorities about the criminal justice system. Fearing the police, many African Americans and Latinas/os are unwilling to cooperate in the reporting and investigation of criminal activity. Ultimately, the targeting of African Americans and Latinas/os for police stops increases the likelihood that they will suffer police brutality. The more interaction with police, the more likely that racial minorities will experience a violent outcome.

In addition, Asian Americans at times have suffered from racial profiling, sometimes of a different form from that experienced by African Americans and Latinas/os. The Wen Ho Lee case, in which an Asian American scientist was jailed on trumped-up espionage charges, is a well-known recent example. Although a naturalized U.S. citizen, Lee as an Asian American was stereotyped as a "foreigner," which helped make the bogus claims of espionage go unquestioned in the media despite the lack of any corroborating evidence. At least since the first significant migration from China in the nineteenth century, Asians have been classified as "foreigners" who are potential enemies of the state. Although proclaimed by some to be a "model minority" whom African Americans and Latinas/os should emulate to achieve the American Dream, Asian Americans at the same time are suspected traitors. Such stereotyping contributed to the infamous internment during World War II of more than 100,000 persons of Japanese ancestry, U.S. citizens and aliens alike.

Police in some localities also employ gang profiles to target Asian American youth in ways that mirror the treatment of young African Americans and Latinas/os. Local police often consider young Chinese men in New York and Vietnamese youth in California, for example, to be potential gang members. This problem has grown as the socioeconomic diversity of the Asian American community, with a significant population of poor and working immigrants, has become better known.

To comply with the Constitution, police officers ordinarily must have individualized reasonable suspicion of criminal conduct before conducting an investigatory police stop. Racial profiles based on alleged group propensities generally violate the law. Unfortunately, the courts have not been particularly effective in removing race and racism from criminal law enforcement. The Supreme Court has repeatedly rejected efforts to remedy racial discrimination in the criminal justice system. It has rejected challenges to the discriminatory impacts of the "war on drugs" and the imposition of the death penalty on the grounds that the persons affected are disproportionately African American. Moreover, police departments across the country also have proven to be resistant to legislative and other reform efforts. Consequently, reports of racial profiling continue.

Many reasons exist for the law's failure to remove racial discrimination from criminal law enforcement. Racism is a central organizing principle in U.S. social life and is incapable of eradication through law alone. Political activism is necessary to make the dramatic changes in race relations that cannot be accomplished through the incremental, and inherently conservative, rule of law.

Since the 1970s a conservative U.S. Supreme Court has whittled away at the rights of criminal defendants. For example, the Court in *Whren v. United States*[2] refused to invalidate a stop as an unreasonable search and seizure under the Fourth Amendment, even assuming that the legal infraction that police claimed to justify the traffic stop was in fact a pretext for race. This ruling effectively eliminated the Fourth Amendment as a tool to fight racial profiling; so long as a police officer could articulate some legitimate justification for a stop, he or she could in fact rely on race without violating the Fourth Amendment.

The Court in *Whren* emphasized that a victim of discrimination could pursue a claim of denial of equal protection of law under the equal protection clause.[3] However, such claims are notoriously difficult to prove, with the plaintiff bearing the heavy burden of showing that the police acted with a racially discriminatory intent.[4] Except in the most extreme cases, plaintiffs cannot satisfy this heavy burden.

More important, there is an exception to the prohibition of considering race in criminal law enforcement. Efforts to eradicate racial profiling are hampered by the legal rule that if a victim of a crime identifies the race of the alleged perpetrator of the crime, then law enforcement officers can legitimately consider race in the criminal investigation, including decisions to question suspects. This exception to the rule may seem reasonable at first glance. However, as a practical matter, it results in over-reliance on race in the investigation of crime. When the perpetrator of a crime is identified as being of a certain race, race becomes the predominant factor relied on by police in a criminal investigation.

The case of *Brown v. City of Oneonta*[5] is a rather extreme example of the lawful reliance on race in criminal investigation. In that case, a victim of a burglary and assault alleged that the perpetrator was an African American man who had suffered a cut on his hand in committing the crime. Police decided to question all African American men in the small rural college town where the crime occurred, starting with the university: "This endeavor produced no suspects. Then, over the next several days, the police conducted a 'sweep' of Oneonta, stopping and questioning nonwhite persons on the streets and inspecting their hands for cuts. More than two hundred persons were questioned during that period, but no suspect was apprehended." As the court observed, the police stopped an African American woman during the sweep, which "may indicate that [the police] considered race more strongly than other parts of the victim's description." *race considered over gender* {handwritten annotation}

Despite the egregiousness of the police officers' conduct, the court of appeals found that the police had not violated the equal protection rights of African Americans caught in the dragnet. Under the reasoning of *Brown v. City of Oneonta*, once a crime perpetrator is identified as a racial minority, then all members of that group instantly become suspects subject to questioning. Overreliance on race in the investigation is nearly impossible to challenge legally.

As *Oneonta* demonstrates, it has proven difficult to prevail in lawsuits brought to challenge racial profiling. It, however, remains a political issue that minority communities have pressed to remedy across the United States. These political pressures bore fruit. Several states have passed a variety of laws in this regard, ranging from the collection of statistical data to determine the magnitude of the problem, to requiring local police agencies to adopt policies on racial profiling. Although success is difficult, civil rights lawsuits, including some by the federal government, have kept the pressure on state and local police to attempt to do what is possible to eliminate racial profiling in criminal law enforcement.

Racial profiling is just one of many discriminatory aspects of the criminal justice system adversely affecting African Americans and Latinas/os. Both groups are demonized as criminals, drug dealers, and gang members, are the most likely victims of police brutality, and are disproportionately represented in the prison population. This reflects disparities in class and access to education, as well as the segregation endemic in the job and housing markets and overt discrimination.

Immigration Enforcement

Judicially sanctioned racial profiling is central to the U.S. government's enforcement of the immigration laws.[6] Race-based immigration enforcement is inconsistent with the color blindness in governmental programs demanded by the current Supreme Court.[7] In limited situations when racial classifications can be considered, such as affirmative action programs, the Court has required that race be part of a narrowly tailored program designed to satisfy a compelling state interest.[8]

At the border the law permits racial profiling, just as it does in immigration law enforcement generally. Indeed, the Supreme Court has held that the U.S. government has free rein to conduct warrantless searches without probable cause at ports of entry. As the Court explained, "[s]ince the founding of our Republic, Congress has granted the Executive *plenary authority* to conduct routine searches and seizures at the border, without probable cause or a warrant, in order to regulate the collection of duties and to prevent the introduction of contraband into this country."[9] As one court emphasized in rejecting the challenge of a lawful U.S. immigrant from Nigeria to a search, the claim that a border search is unconstitutional if based on race "*is groundless.*"[10]

In *United States v. Brignoni-Ponce*[11] the Supreme Court in 1975 stated that "[t]he likelihood that any given person of Mexican ancestry is an alien is high enough to make Mexican appearance a relevant factor" to the Border Patrol in making an immigration stop within the United States. Given this encouragement, Border Patrol officers for years have routinely admitted that a person's Hispanic appearance contributed to the decision to question that person. Plaintiffs in lawsuits regularly allege that the Border Patrol relies almost exclusively on race in immigration enforcement.[12] One noted court of appeals judge observed that "of all of the cases involving people who were stopped or searched because of their 'foreign-looking' appearance or 'foreign-sounding' names, we are not aware of any in which the targeted individuals were Caucasian."[13]

The Border Patrol's undocumented immigrant profile contains socioeconomic class as well as racial elements. For example, in one case, an Immigration and

Naturalization Service (INS) officer testified that along with Hispanic appearance, an officer might properly rely on a "hungry look" and the fact that a person is "dirty, unkempt," or "wears work clothing," in deciding to question a person about his or her immigration status.[14] Poorer Latinas/os thus are more likely to be stopped and questioned. That, however, does not mean that economically better-off Latinas/os are not subject to the indignities of an immigration stop.

As is the case for racial profiling in criminal law enforcement, race-based immigration enforcement constitutes an assault on the dignity of Latinas/os. Harms to Latinas/os lawfully in the United States, including embarrassment, humiliation, and other attacks on their very membership in U.S. society, result from the unjustified interrogation of their citizenship status based on skin color. The vast majority (roughly 90 percent) of the Latinas/os in the United States are lawful immigrants or citizens, thereby making Latina/o ancestry a poor indicator of undocumented immigrant status. That the Border Patrol targets persons of "Hispanic appearance" almost invariably contributes to the fact that *close to 90 percent* of all deportations are of Mexican and Latin American immigrants, even though they constitute somewhat slightly more than one-half of the total undocumented population in the United States.

Race-based immigration enforcement may well contribute to well-documented Border Patrol abuse of persons of Mexican ancestry. The more that members of particular groups are stopped and questioned, the more likely that members of that group will suffer hostility and violence. This is true even if the person stopped has been wrongly accused. Amnesty International and Americas Watch have published numerous reports documenting human rights abuses of persons of Mexican ancestry, including U.S. citizens, by the Border Patrol. A few years ago, a young goatherder, a U.S. citizen of Mexican ancestry without a criminal record, was killed by a military patrol operating near the border.

Importantly, race-based border enforcement adversely impacts racial minorities other than Latinas/os. Incidents of discrimination in customs searches at ports of entry are regularly reported. A 2000 U.S. General Accounting Office study of searches by U.S. Customs Service officers showed that Black women citizens entering the country were nine times more likely to be subject to intrusive searches than white women who were U.S. citizens.[15] In one lawsuit it was claimed that an African American woman, a U.S. citizen returning from Nigeria who complained about customs inspectors' treatment of a Nigerian citizen, was herself subjected to a full pat down and strip search, and many other intrusive procedures, including examination of her rectal and vaginal cavities, in an unsuccessful hunt for drugs.[16] In another case an African American woman, the only African American on her flight, was subjected to the embarrassment and humiliation of a strip search by customs officers upon entering the country.

Persons of African ancestry who arrive at airports often are presumed to be entering the country unlawfully. In one case the INS accused a Black college student, returning from a visit to Jamaica with lawful immigration status, of entering the United States with false documents, then strip-searched, shackled, and detained him. At San Francisco International Airport immigration officials shackled an African American citizen returning from Africa, accusing her of unlawfully entering the United States.

In *Orhorhaghe v. INS*[17] the court of appeals found that the INS was wrong to investigate a person's immigration status based on his possession of a "Nigerian-sounding name," which the court reasoned might serve as a proxy for race. Such abuses fit into a larger pattern of exclusion of immigrants of African ancestry from the United States, with Africa historically sending few immigrants to this country. The pattern of race policing at the border reflects reliance on stereotypes about persons of African ancestry as lawbreakers, the same preconceptions that contribute to race profiling in domestic criminal law enforcement.

Similarly, as for Latinas/os, persons of Asian ancestry have suffered from race-based immigration enforcement. In one case a court ruled that the "appearance of being oriental" combined with other factors justified continued observation by an INS officer.[18] Similarly, the Board of Immigration Appeals stated that "Oriental appearance, combined with the past history of illegal alien employment at that particular restaurant, and [an] anonymous tip" justified INS questioning of restaurant workers about their immigration status.[19] Not that long ago, Portland was dubbed "Deportland" because of the INS's rigorous scrutiny of the immigration status of Asian tourists, which caused a major airline carrier to end direct flights from Japan to the city.

In the name of fighting terrorism, the U.S. government has harshly treated persons of Arab ancestry and Muslim faith, classified as suspected terrorists. Based in part on stereotypes of Arabs and Muslims as terrorists, Congress in 1996 passed two harsh immigration laws designed, among other things, to fight terrorism. All of this occurred before September 11, 2001. After that date the profiling of Arabs and Muslims became an official part of federal policy.

Racial profiling makes little sense in criminal law enforcement, immigration enforcement, or the "war on terror" that followed September 11, 2001. In our democracy the law demands that individuals be judged as individuals and not on the basis of alleged statistical probabilities tied to group membership. Racial profiling assaults the dignity of minority groups and, moreover, can thwart legitimate law enforcement efforts. Minorities who feel threatened by governmental authorities are less likely to cooperate with criminal, immigration, or antiterrorism investigations.

September 11, 2001, and Racial Profiling

September 11 had a dramatic impact on the nation's collective view of racial profiling. After that fateful day the nation reconsidered the reliance on race, racial stereotypes, and statistics in law enforcement activity. The focus on terrorism and national security deflected attention from efforts to eliminate racial profiling from domestic law enforcement. Energies instead were directed at national security and avoiding another terrorist plot.

The U.S. government reacted quickly and decisively to the massive loss on September 11. Hundreds of Arab and Muslim noncitizens were arrested, questioned, detained, and deported. The dragnet was directed at large groups of people and based loosely on race, nationality, national origin, and religion different from the Anglo norm in the United States. Arab and Muslim noncitizens were subjected to special registration procedures, with some arrested and deported when they reported to the immigration authorities in an effort to comply with the law. Arabs and Muslims were subjected to special scrutiny at airports across the country, and the phrase "flying while Arab" entered the national vocabulary.

The federal government utilized the immigration laws to protect national security. Hundreds, if not thousands, of Arab and Muslim noncitizens were arrested, detained, and deported. As a matter of law, this is a convenient tool because of the great deference afforded the federal government in immigration matters. The U.S. Supreme Court has emphasized repeatedly that "[i]n the exercise of its broad power over naturalization and immigration, Congress regularly makes rules that would be unacceptable if applied to citizens."[20] The federal government's plenary power over immigration, as it is called, has resulted in a long history of exclusion of racial minorities, political dissidents, the poor, gays and lesbians, and other groups. In times of crisis it has exercised its power to target certain immigrant groups for special reporting requirements and deportation.[21]

It is difficult to deny that the treatment of Arabs and Muslims after September 11 does not amount to racial profiling, based on any commonsense definition of the practice. The focus of the nationwide dragnet was on one group of people without any specific belief of their involvement in terrorist activities of any kind. Statistical probabilities were used to justify the federal government's policies in the "war on terror." Racial, religious, and nationality classifications were employed as indicators of possible sources of information about, and potential for, terrorist activity.

Despite previous consensus on the need to eliminate racial profiling, the public voiced little objection to the racial profiling of Arabs and Muslims. The nation seemed willing to minimize the chances of another September 11 whatever the cost. Soon after that day, Congress passed the USA PATRIOT Act,[22] which restricted civil rights of immigrants and citizens in new ways by expanding the surveillance powers of the federal government. Because Arabs and Muslims were the primary victims of many civil rights deprivations in the "war on terror," the government's conduct received popular support. The Bill of Rights exists in the U.S. Constitution, however, to protect unpopular minorities from the majority, especially in times of social stress. Because tensions ran high in the days after September 11, the civil rights of a discrete and insular minority were undervalued.

The excesses of the U.S. government's conduct are only now coming to light. In April 2003 the Office of the Inspector General released a report detailing the abuse of noncitizens held on immigration charges after September 11, which included failure to notify detainees of the immigration charges against them in a timely manner, making it difficult for them to obtain bond and meet with attorneys, detaining them in harsh conditions (e.g., leaving lights on in their cells for 24 hours), and subjecting them to verbal and sometimes physical abuse.[23] In the future the United States as a nation will likely come to regret the treatment of Arabs and Muslims after September 11; this period may well be one of those historical episodes that bring shame, not pride, to the nation.

The Relationship Between Different Forms of Race-Based
Law Enforcement

Similar harms to African Americans and Latinas/os flow from the influence of race in the enforcement of the criminal and immigration laws. Importantly, race-based law enforcement is part of a system of institutions and cultural practices that relegate racial minorities to a castelike second-class citizenship in the United States. Both African Americans and Latinas/os have suffered serious limitations on their citizenship rights, often finding those rights manipulated through law. Both groups can move toward securing full membership if overreliance on race in law enforcement is eliminated.

The operation of the criminal justice system deeply shapes the lives of African Americans and Latinas/os in the United States. These groups, both overrepresented in our jails and prisons, must work together politically to eradicate the endemic racism in the criminal justice system. Past successful multiracial coalitions, such as the civil rights movements of the 1960s, suggest the possibility of future ones.

Specifically, African Americans and Latinas/os disproportionately suffer harms from racial profiling in criminal law enforcement. Discrimination against Blacks and discrimination against browns in the criminal justice system are deeply interrelated. Not coincidentally, many lawsuits challenging race profiling by police departments claim that police discriminate against both African Americans and Latinas/os. Similarly, race-based border enforcement not only adversely affects Latinas/os but injures persons of African and Asian ancestry. Given the similar injuries caused by the influence of race on law enforcement, minorities have common interests in removing race from the enforcement calculus.

The Los Angeles Police Department (LAPD), which has a long history of violating the civil rights of Latinas/os and African Americans, offers a case study in the relationship between race-based criminal and immigration enforcement. During the Depression, the LAPD helped facilitate the forced "repatriation" to Mexico—in the name of reducing the welfare rolls—of U.S. citizens, as well as immigrants, of Mexican ancestry. The police participated in raids of Mexican American communities and assisted in placing them on buses and trains destined for Mexico.

Later, during the infamous Zoot Suit riots in which mobs of white servicemen attacked Mexican and African American "gang" members at the time of World War II, the LAPD declined to protect the minority crime victims. The police instead arrested the "zoot suiters" who were beaten, and left their assailants alone.

In 1992 the violence sparked by the legal vindication of police officers who brutalized Rodney King was followed by police abuse of African Americans and Latinas/os, many of whom were rounded up by the LAPD and turned over to the INS for removal as part of the massive effort to quell the violence. Over the last few years media attention has focused on the infamous LAPD Ramparts Division for, among other transgressions, its systematic violations of the civil rights of African American and Latina/o youth. Police officers also conducted street sweeps, arrested Latinas/os, and turned over to the INS noncitizens who could not be subject to criminal prosecution owing to a lack of evidence, all of which violated official departmental policy.

As this brief history of the LAPD suggests, local police often have assisted federal authorities in immigration enforcement, which has increased in recent years. Congress has moved toward giving local police greater authority in the enforcement of the immigration laws. After September 11 the Justice Department solicited local assistance in questioning Arab and Muslim noncitizens. The federal government also considered entering into agreements with state and local police agencies to afford their officers training in the enforcement of the immigration laws.

Besides the LAPD case, there are many other examples of local police violations of immigrants' civil rights. Consider a few examples of civil rights abuses at the hands of local authorities. In 1996 local police in Riverside County, California, were videotaped beating two unarmed undocumented Mexican immigrants who fled the Border Patrol. In a much-publicized 1997 effort to rid the community of undocumented immigrants, police in a Phoenix, Arizona, suburb violated the constitutional rights of U.S. citizens and lawful immigrants of Mexican ancestry by stopping persons because of their skin color or their use of the Spanish language. One can expect civil rights violations when local law enforcement authorities, who generally are not well versed in the federal immigration laws, are enlisted to enforce those laws.

Two notorious recent incidents of police brutality involved immigrants of African ancestry, showing how the use of race by police can affect minorities and immigrants. Amadou Diallo, an immigrant from Guinea, and Abner Louima, a Haitian immigrant, were the subjects of notorious examples of brutality at the hands of New York police. Diallo was shot and killed while Louima was beaten and tortured. Neither had committed any crime. Both were Black.

The racial focus of the "war on drugs" both in our cities and at our borders also shows how criminal and border (customs and immigration) enforcement are deeply intertwined. Blacks and Latinas/os are the prime targets of the "war on drugs." Many commentators have observed that drug enforcement has distinctly racial impacts and facilitates the incarceration of African Americans in numbers greatly disproportionate to their drug use. Drug enforcement remains popular despite its devastating impacts on African Americans and Latinas/os. Police often use race profiles in traffic stops as a tool to uncover drugs, just as immigration and customs officers employ drug courier profiles at the border stops.

Race-based law enforcement suggests a potential for coalition building among racial groups that seek to end the use of race in criminal and immigration enforcement. There is no evidence suggesting that race can be removed from one mode of law enforcement without its elimination from the other. To the contrary, the use of race by governmental officials appears to be part of a whole. Once allowed to seep into the calculus, race comes to dominate law enforcement.

Put differently, reliance on race is difficult to cabin or limit. Use of racial profiles builds and reinforces popular stereotypes about the propensity for criminality among racial minorities. One can easily picture the stereotypes, for example, used in targeting African Americans, Latinas/os, and Arabs and Muslims for law enforcement activity. Unfortunately, once race is considered in one area of law enforcement, it often directly or indirectly taints other areas as well. At a most fundamental level, relying on the race of one group for targeted enforcement makes it easier to rationalize the same practice directed toward other racial minority groups.

Multiracial Coalitions and Challenging Racial Profiling in Law Enforcement

Because African Americans and Latinas/os suffer common harms from racial profiling in law enforcement, they would seem natural allies in seeking to eliminate the practice. However, cooperation between the African American and Latina/o communities in the United States faces formidable barriers. Competition for scarce resources, with civil rights viewed as a scarce resource, is one. Possible coalitions with whites also may seem attractive to certain racial minorities at particular historical moments.

In seeking to remedy the racism in the criminal justice system, we must acknowledge and address the formidable impediments to interracial cooperation. Not infrequently the relations between African Americans and Latinas/os have been marred by stress, strain, and conflict. Perceived economic and political competition, due in no small part to the changing demographics caused by immigration, help fuel such tension.

Barriers to Cooperation

As a purely historical matter, durable coalitions between African Americans and Latinas/os have not proven to be easy. Even intellectual exchanges among minority scholars about the scope of civil rights scholarship have at times been hostile. Conflict can be seen in dialogues between influential African American and Latina/o intellectuals. Jorge Klor de Alva and Cornel West jabbed at each other about the tensions between African Americans and Latinas/os, with Klor de Alva contending that African Americans were "Anglos" and West countering that Latinas/os were effectively "white."[24]

In the pages of the *New York Times* the prominent African American sociologist Orlando Patterson criticized the publicity surrounding the suggestion, based on the 2000 census, that whites would soon be a minority, because, in his words, many Latinas/os are "white in every social sense of this term." Patterson proceeded to blame the media for the loss of support for efforts to remedy past discrimination, naming their reports of the decline of the white population and inclusion of Latinas/os in affirmative action programs. He also questioned whether coalitions between African Americans and Latinos could benefit Blacks.[25] The claim that Latinas/os are functionally "white" ignores a rich history of well-documented discrimination suffered by persons of Mexican ancestry in the Southwest, as well as the colonization of the Puerto Rican people. At times, however, Latinas/os have emphasized their Spanish ancestry and have been classified as white by law, even though subject to discrimination.

Nor are the barriers to coalitions simply intellectual ones. At the grassroots level racism toward African Americans unquestionably exists in the Latina/o and Asian American communities. Non-Black minorities often have distinguished themselves from, and at times expressly denigrated, Blacks. In turn, African Americans are not immune from nativist anti-Latina/o and anti-Asian sentiments. Such animosity militates against broad-based coalitions between African Americans and Latinas/os, even when the leadership reaches agreement.

Moreover, fault lines between minority groups exist on certain substantive issues. Importantly, African Americans often have been concerned about the negative impacts of immigration on their community and less concerned than Latinas/os with immigration enforcement as a civil rights issue. Many poor and working-class African Americans compete with Latina/o immigrants for low-wage jobs and have seen some industries move from having predominantly Black to mostly Latina/o workforces. Some observers claim that employers prefer hiring undocumented Latinas/os over domestic African Americans. The rivalry between Blacks and Latinas/os is fueled by competition over jobs and access to education and housing. Blacks often see Latinas/os as able to be treated as white. Such sentiments tend to foster African American support for immigration restrictions and heightened immigration enforcement.

However, this may be changing. The treatment of Haitian refugees in the 1990s raised African American consciousness about the centrality of race to immigration law and policymaking in the United States. African Americans protested the treatment of the Haitians and claimed that racism infected the U.S. government's interdiction of Haitian boats on the high seas so that the asylum seekers could be returned to Haiti. In addition, the security measures directed at Arabs and Muslims after September 11 have provoked criticism from African American, as well as Asian American and Latina/o, activist groups.

Common Cause

Despite race and class differences, African Americans and Latinas/os must recognize their common interests in removing race from law enforcement, immigration as well as criminal. Perhaps more clearly with respect to law enforcement than other civil rights issues, African Americans and Latinas/os share common interests in extracting race from the justice system. By working together, they might best be able to improve and reform the system for the benefit of their respective communities.

Political realities show the need for coalitions. The Bureau of the Census projects that by 2050 Hispanics will constitute nearly 25 percent of the U.S. population African Americans need Latinas/os' growing political numbers; the Latina/o community, which includes immigrants who cannot vote and a citizen population that at least until recently has a low voter turnout record, will require the assistance of the mobilized African American community. Both groups need the moral and political force of the other to challenge the devastating impact that law enforcement has on their communities. If either balks, neither stands to secure meaningful change of the status quo.

The classic Prisoner's Dilemma describes a case in which prisoners are placed in a position in which one gains substantially if he or she betrays the other first, and loses substantially if betrayed first; if both prisoners cooperate, both can gain, although not as much as if they were the first to betray the other. Incentives exist to act in a way that maximizes personal benefit and being the first to act. Cooperation is the only way that both groups may gain. It is more difficult to achieve, however, because it requires trust and collaboration.

The Prisoner's Dilemma offers useful insights about the potential for African American–Latina/o coalition. For example, Latinas/os may see themselves as the beneficiaries of the profiling of Blacks by police, while African Americans may believe that they benefit by race profiling of Latinas/os (especially in immigration enforcement). Many groups may consider the profiling of Arabs and Muslims in the "war on terror" to be acceptable. Such positions are shortsighted. Once race is let out of the proverbial genie's bottle, it is difficult to limit where and when it will be considered by law enforcement authorities. If African Americans and Latinas/os do not cooperate to seek to change the police's discriminatory practices, both will suffer in the long run.

The Probable Nature of African American–Latina/o Coalitions

Political coalitions between diverse communities are complex and often fragile. The problems of building coalitions and developing political agendas bring us face-to-face with the reality that different racial and ethnic groups have distinct histories and interests. Groups centering on discrete identities struggle to find a rallying point from which to advocate social justice and coalition building. Alliances within and among communities of color require an appreciation of the position of noncitizens of color within the racial hierarchy. Therefore, the hierarchies of race and oppression must be overcome to form effective intragroup and intergroup coalitions.

Building such alliances requires significant care and attention as well as time and effort. Groups will need to work through the tensions and animosities in an effort to find common ground and work together for the common good. This part of the project often is where it ends, with the tensions overcoming the commonalities.

By necessity, such coalitions will be most feasible on narrow issues. Divisiveness is less likely to arise with narrow goals and objectives. It also will be easier to organize around one or several critical issues rather than starting with an entire array of them.

Rather than engaging in the difficult task of coalition building, minority groups could choose to pursue independent agendas without regard to other minority groups. As Richard Delgado posed the question, will African Americans and Latinas/os "be able to work together toward mutual goals—or [will] the current factionalism and distrust continue into the future, with the various minority groups competing for crumbs while majoritarian rule continues unabated"?[26]

There is room, however, for more narrowly focused groups that may be unwilling to compromise core principles in the interest of building coalitions. Those identity groups must exist, and will continue to do so. They offer their members many benefits, including building solidarity and self-esteem and focusing interests on minority group concerns. The existence of nationalistic groups is not necessarily inconsistent with these groups' building strategic coalitions on certain issues.

In contemplating alliances, Latina/o and African American leaders must consider the means of seeking to bring about meaningful social change. Both legal and political mechanisms may be used to challenge the use of race in law enforcement. Litigation may offer certain benefits, although it has its limits (as seen in the efforts to eliminate racial profiling from criminal law enforcement). Political action has the potential to bring about more drastic reforms and to create a means of enforcing the law. The use of race in law enforcement may prove to be a powerful organizing issue among minority communities, and among sympathetic whites as well, especially in a time when the color-blindness principle dominates the political landscape.

Conclusion

African Americans, Latinas/os, and other racial minorities have common interests in eliminating race profiling from criminal and immigration law enforcement. Race-based law enforcement damages all communities of color, immigrants and citizens alike, at our borders and in our cities. Similar practices injure different groups in similar ways and require similar remedies.

The common interests of racial minorities for ending race-based law enforcement are all the more apparent after the events of September 11 2001. Before September 11 the nation collectively condemned racial profiling in traffic stops. After September 11, however, the nation reevaluated and the U.S. Justice Department engaged in a campaign of measures—from questioning and arrest to detention of Arab and Muslim noncitizens—based on principles that were the equivalent of racial profiling. The attention paid to racial profiling of African Americans and Latinas/os in criminal law enforcement waned as racial profiling drew new credibility from the efforts of the federal government. The nation saw a resurgence of racial profiling, which was a central part of the entire "war on terror."

Political coalitions of racial minorities will be necessary to change the current status quo. Even with a rapidly growing minority population, whites will comprise a majority voting bloc for the near future. With proper efforts, minorities as a collective can move to attack racial profiling. The beginnings of such multiracial coalitions can be seen in the protests of many different groups to the post–September 11 security measures targeting Arab and Muslim noncitizens.

It is easy to see that Asian American–Latina/o coalitions are complex and difficult to construct. Despite the formidable challenges posed by multiracial coalitions, such alliances must be pursued and fostered in the fight for social justice by those truly committed to that goal. There is no viable alternative.

Notes

1. Parts of this article are adapted from Kevin R. Johnson, "The Case for African American and Latina/o Cooperation in Challenging Race Profiling in Law Enforcement," *Florida Law Review* 55 (2003):341.
2. 517 U.S. 806 (1996).

3. See *Whren*, 517 U.S. at 813: "We of course agree . . . that the Constitution prohibits selective enforcement of the law based on consideration such as race. But the constitutional basis for objecting to *intentionally discriminatory* application of laws is the Equal Protection Clause, not the Fourth Amendment" (emphasis added).

4. See *Washington v. Davis*, 426 U.S. 229 (1976).

5. 221 F. 3d 329 (2d Cir. 2000), *cert. denied*, 534 U.S. 816 (2001).

6. Arguments for ending the practice are elaborated on in detail in Kevin R. Johnson, "The case against race profiling in immigration enforcement," *Washington University Law Quarterly* 78 (2001):675.

7. See, e.g., *Adarand Constructors, Inc. v. Peña*, 515 U.S. 200 (1995); *City of Richmond v. J. A. Croson Co.*, 488 U.S. 469 (1989).

8. Compare *Grutter v. Bollinger*, 123 S. Ct. 2325, 2341–42 (2003), holding that a law school's consideration of race in an affirmative action program was narrowly tailored to further a compelling state interest, with *Gratz v. Bollinger*, 123 S. Ct. 2411, 2427–31 (2002), holding that an undergraduate admission system's reliance on race was not narrowly tailored to further a compelling state interest.

9. *United States v. Montoya de Hernandez*, 473 U.S. 531, 537 (1985) (citations omitted; emphasis added).

10. *United States v. Ojebode*, 957 F.2d 1218, 1223 (5th Cir. 1992) (emphasis added), *cert. denied*, 507 U.S. 923 (1993).

11. 422 U.S. 873, 886–887 (1975). But see *United States v. Montero-Camargo*, 208 F.3d 1122 (9th Cir. 2000) (en banc), disregarding language in *Brignoni-Ponce* and holding that Border Patrol cannot lawfully consider Hispanic appearance in deciding to make an immigration stop.

12. See, e.g., *Hodgers-Durgin v. de la Vina*, 199 F.3d 1037 (9th cir. 1999) (en banc); *Nicacio v. INS*, 797 F.2d 700 (9th cir. 1985); *LaDuke v. Nelson*, 762 F.2d 1318 (9th cir. 1985), modified, 796 F.2d 309 (9th cir. 1986); *Ramirez v. Webb*, 787 F.2d 592 (6th cir. 1986) (per curiam); *Illinois Migrant Council v. Pilliod*, 540 F.2d 1062 (7th cir. 1976), modified, 548 F.2d 715 (7th cir. 1977) (en banc); *Murillo v. Musegades*, 809 F. Supp. 487 (W. D. Tex. 1992).

13. *Orhorhaghe v. INS*, 38 F.3d 488, 498 n.16 (9th cir. 1994) (Reinhardt, J.).

14. *Nicacio v. INS*, 797 F.2d 700, 704 (9th cir. 1985).

15. See U.S. General Accounting Office, *U.S. Customs Service: Better Targeting of Airline Passengers for Personal Searches Could Produce Better Results*, report to Senator Richard J. Durbin, March 2000.

16. See *Brent v. United States*, 66 F. Supp. 2d 1287 (S.D. Fla. 1999), aff'd sub nom., *Brent v. Ashley*, 247 F.3d 1294 (11th cir. 2001).

17. 38 F.3d 488, 498 (9th cir. 1994).

18. See *Cheung Tin Wong v. INS*, 468 F.2d 1123, 1127 (D.C. cir. 1972).

19. Matter of King and Yang, 16 I. & N. Dec. 502, 504–05 (BIA 1978).

20. *Matthews v. Diaz*, 426 U.S. 67, 79–80 (1976), upholding denial of public benefits to lawful immigrants in federal program, which were available to U.S. citizens; see *Demore v. Kim*, 123 S. Ct. 1708, 1716 (2003), quoting *Mathews v. Diaz* and upholding mandatory detention of immigrants convicted of certain crimes pending a deportation hearing.

21. See, e.g., *Narenji v. Civiletti*, 617 F.2d 745 (1979), *cert. denied*, 446 U.S. 957 (1980), requiring registration of Iranian noncitizen students during times of difficult foreign relations with Iran; *Ghaelian v. INS*, 717 F.2d 950 (6th cir. 1983), holding that the court lacked jurisdiction to review an equal protection challenge to regulation in an action to deport an Iranian noncitizen; *Dasltmalchi v. INS*, 660 F.3d 880 (3d cir. 1981) (same); *Nademi v. INS*, 679 F.2d 811 (10th cir. 1982), upholding regulation allowing Iranian citizens only 15 days before voluntarily departing the country; *Malek-Marzban v. INS*, 653 F.2d 113 (4th cir. 1981) (same).

22. Uniting and Strengthening America by Providing Appropriate Tools Required to Intercept and Obstruct Terrorism (USA PATRIOT Act) Act of 2001, Pub. L. No. 107–56, 115 Stat. 272.

23. See U.S. Office of the Inspector General, *The September 11 Detainees: A Review of the Treatment of Aliens Held on Immigration Charges in Connection with the Investigation of the September 11 Attacks*, September 2004; see also U.S. Office of the Inspector General, *Report to Congress on Implementation of Section 1001 of the USA PATRIOT Act*, June 2003, which

concludes that more than 1,000 claims of civil rights violations had been reported as a result of the implementation of the USA PATRIOT Act.

24. See "Our Next Race Question: The Uneasiness Between Blacks and Latinos," Harper's, April 1996, 55.
25. Orlando Patterson, "Race by the Numbers," *New York Times*, May 8, 2001, A27.
26. Richard Delgado, "Rodrigo's Fifteenth Chronicle: Racial Mixture, Latino-Critical Scholarship, and the Black-White Binary," *Texas Law Review* 75, no. 5 (April 1997):1181–1200.

Chapter 14

Racial Politics in Multiethnic America: Black and Latina/o Identities and Coalitions

Mark Sawyer

In Little Havana, Miami, a young Afro-Cuban woman went into a "Cuban" hair salon seeking to make an appointment. She politely asked in Spanish how she might make an appointment to have her hair done. The proprietor of the salon snapped back in English, "We don't work on Black hair here—you will have to go somewhere else." The women in the salon then went back to conversing in Spanish and the Afro-Cuban woman left dejected.

The vignette is more than a story about rude treatment by a business owner. It is a case of race making in which the Afro-Cuban woman seeking to reaffirm her "Cubanness" was being cast out of being Cuban within the United States and told to seek her fortune with African Americans. The story serves as a sign for how the unresolved issue of racism within Latina/o communities toward Latinas/os of darker hues might contribute to prevent interethnic alliances with African Americans. However, this essay not only looks at this side of the equation of Black-Latino relations but addresses how the unwillingness of African Americans to recognize experiences of racial groups other than the U.S.-born Black experience also contributes to problems in coalitions.

In this essay I explore how conflicts among Blacks and Latinas/os have been nurtured both by the unresolved racism within Latina/o communities that has its origins in their respective countries of origin and by the frequently parochial way in which African Americans privilege the U.S.-born Black experience and fail to recognize the struggles of immigrants of all colors. These narrow definitions of social, cultural, and political identity prevent interethnic alliances and foment ethnic conflict among groups who share substantial political interests and issue concerns. However, there have been notable points of cooperation among Blacks and Latina/os. Ultimately, if we exclude ideologically conservative Cuban Americans from the analysis, it becomes easier to find meaningful patterns of both convergence and difference of interests on political issues. Further, by engaging common and bridging identities like Afro-Latinas/os, it is possible to forge a progressive politics that includes the concerns of both groups and challenges the sharp distinctions between Black and Latina/o that many commentators currently attempt to highlight.

Electoral Politics

As José Cruz (2000) notes, there has not been a consistent pattern of U.S. Black and Latina/o political interaction. Patterns of cooperation, conflict, and ambivalence have been hallmarks of Black/Latina/o relations. However, there is a growing literature by commentators, such as the legal scholar Nicolás Vaca (2004), who emphasize difference and conflict. They point to a variety of cases without reference to the more mixed record.

For instance, in the last ten years Blacks in California voted for Proposition 187 (54 percent to 46 percent), supported by Governor Pete Wilson, that would have denied services to undocumented immigrants. However, that figure is far below the 65 percent of whites that supported Proposition 187. While 187 was explicitly anti-Latina/o, the rhetoric surrounding 209, the anti–affirmative action initiative, supported by Governor Wilson, was more explicitly anti-Black (Santa Ana, 2002). Though 209 passed, a solid majority of African Americans and Latinas/os in California voted against the initiative. Black and Latina/o voters seemingly learned from the rotating-target politics of the California initiative process and voted against the antibilingual initiative 227. However, the case that looms large for Vaca and others is the defeat of Antonio Villaraigosa's bid to become the first Latino mayor of Los Angeles. Villaraigosa lost because of lower than necessary Latina/o voter turnout and because 80 percent of Black votes were cast for James Hahn, a white candidate (Vaca, 2004). While Hahn had significant support among the Black leadership due to his father's legacy of representing the African American community, he ran a campaign largely aimed at garnering conservative white voters in the San Fernando Valley by using the crime issue. Hahn used racist advertisements targeting Villaraigosa that were reminiscent of the Willie Horton advertisements from the Bush-Dukakis campaign.

Nicolás Vaca argues that the vote for Hahn was an anti-Latina/o vote among Blacks despite evidence that Black voters and the older Black leadership joined Hahn out of support for Black police chief Bernard Parks and allegiance to Hahn's deceased father who represented South Los Angeles for many years (Vaca, 2004). Hahn was the only candidate to commit to keeping Chief Parks, while the other candidates, including Villaraigosa, did not show strong support for him. Still, despite very little racialized campaign rhetoric by Black leaders or in the public discourse, Vaca concludes that Villaraigosa was defeated by "unspoken" racial antagonism against Latina/os.

While Vaca's own interviews and evidence themselves tend to support the argument that it was a pro-Hahn vote rather than an anti-Villaraigosa vote, he nonetheless uses unseen evidence to conclude that the election results point to racial and ethnic conflict. For Vaca the lack of evidence speaks to the need for his book, since there is a conspiracy of silence about Black and Latina/o conflict in U.S. society. Thus, he selects cases across the United States, including Houston and Compton where, he argues, there was unmitigated "Black/brown" conflict in elections. He even suggests this conflict was visible in the defeat of Fernando Ferrer in the New York mayoral election, despite Ferrer's receiving over 70 percent of the African American vote (Vaca, 2004). Nicolás Vaca also fails to recognize that the subsequent firing of African American police chief Bernard Parks by Mayor James Hahn raises serious questions as to whether the African American community would again give Hahn its overwhelming support. This is not the kind of question that those who continue to write doomsday tales of Black and Latina/o political coalitions care to answer. However, there have been no shortage of articles that emphasize Black and Latina/o competition for jobs and in electoral districts, yet Vaca, like other writers, simply uncritically joins the drumbeat as a self-styled racial maverick and continually ignores evidence that does not prove his thesis.

While Vaca points to some disappointing results, there are equally encouraging examples of African American–Latina/o coalitions around the country. For example, in the California recall election, Lieutenant Governor Cruz Bustamante received a higher percentage of Black votes than Latina/o votes in his losing effort (Baretto and Ramírez, 2004). However, it was the defection of white democrats to Schwarzenegger after attacking Bustamante on racialized issues like Indian gaming and driver's licenses for undocumented immigrants that cost Bustamante the governor's mansion. Still, Latina/o and Black coalitions do not always spell defeat. In Chicago, Harold Washington was elected in 1983 and 1987 from a progressive coalition that included Mexicans, Puerto Ricans, Blacks, gays, and lesbians of all colors and reform-minded whites. Washington reformed city government and gained control of the city council in his second term only by expanding and supporting Latina/o insurgent city council candidates against ethnic whites. He also pushed legislation that allowed undocumented immigrants to vote in local school council elections. The Washington coalition set the conditions for the creation of the first Latina/o majority congressional seat now held by Luis Gutiérrez, a former Washington ally. Gains for Mexicans and Puerto Ricans in Chicago synergistically aided Black political power (Pinderhughes, 1997). Similarly, in Georgia in 2003, Sam Zamarippa was elected to the Georgia House of Representatives in an overwhelmingly Black district of Atlanta that includes the Martin Luther King Jr. Center and Ebenezer Baptist Church. In Texas, Black voters supported the election of Henry Cisneros who became the first Latina/o mayor of San Antonio. In another case, Black and Latina/o voters came together in Denver to help elect first Frederico Peña and later African American Wellington Webb as mayors. There is also a mixed record in the area of public opinion (Hero, 1997).

Public Opinion

Traditionally, public opinion research about race has focused predominantly on white attitudes about Blacks. Only recently have studies begun to challenge this approach and to search for alternative paradigms to describe minority attitudes as well as interminority relations (Oliver and Wong, 2003; Fu, 2003; Kaufmann, 2003). While this research is in its infancy, it is clear that paradigms used to explain white attitudes about Blacks also serve to frame the attitudes of Latinas/os and Blacks about each other. Yet, for the most part, Blacks and Latinas/os share support for affirmative action and generally support a social democratic agenda in government and spending much more than do whites or Asians (Fu, 2003). Unlike white Americans, an overwhelming majority of Blacks and a large number of Latinas/os opposed the U.S. invasion of Iraq in 2003.[1] Despite Vaca's argument that whites have more in common with Blacks than with Latinas/os, public opinion data show that Blacks and Latinas/os are far closer on most issues than either are to whites (Oliver and Wong, 2003; Fu, 2003). But what about the question of competition? While Nicolás Vaca allows for some ideological convergence in his work, he asserts that, on a microlevel, there are simply different "interests" (Vaca, 2004).

Though Blacks see some decline in their political power as a result of growing numbers of Latinas/os, they largely see these gains as "fair" (McClain et al., 2003). Many Blacks recognize that growing Latina/o political power may result in less power for African Americans, but they also do not believe Latinas/os are sufficiently represented in local government (McClain et al., 2003). These nuances lead to facile misinterpretations of conflict among Blacks and Latinas/os. For example, in their book *Black Pride, Black Prejudice*, Paul Sniderman and Thomas Piazza (2003) interpret as "anti-immigrant" the fact that a majority of Blacks believe that growing numbers of immigrants in their community will necessitate more taxes and spending on public services. However, since most Blacks generally support social spending, it is difficult to assume that this is not merely a factual account of how rising populations will necessitate more services. In fact, in many cities where populations would have fallen without the presence of immigrants, it can be argued that immigration has preserved middle-class jobs for many Black service providers. Black social workers, teachers, bus drivers, postal workers, and the like have benefited from the expansion and maintenance of city services driven by immigration.

While there is some perception of job competition among Blacks and Latinas/os, as well as anti-Black attitudes on the part of Latinas/os and anti-Latina/o attitudes among Blacks, these attitudes never rise to the levels of those held by whites who are not involved in similar neighborhood competition (Oliver and Wong, 2003). In fact, for Blacks and Latinas/os it appears that social contact in neighborhoods reduces rather than exacerbates tensions (Oliver and Wong, 2003). Thus, public opinion matches the mixed picture of the electoral process, with no clear conclusion to be drawn about the prospects of Black and Latina/o relations (García and Duerst-Lahti, 2004).

Why Now?

Since the empirical picture is so mixed, it is important to ask: What is behind the emphasis on conflict among Blacks and Latinas/os? Clearly, one cannot excuse the white power structure. From this point of view, an emphasis on Black-Latina/o competition and conflict is an effort to discipline Latina/o ideology and political behavior and prevent Black and Latina/o political alliances. However, although one could describe it as a simple divide-and-conquer strategy, doing so would ignore the significant role that Black and Latina/o agents play in creating and maintaining conflict. Indeed, the agents of this process are numerous. They include the white left which has grown weary of "identity politics" on behalf of Blacks and others; right-wing politicians who seek to isolate Blacks and incorporate Latinas/os into the right; and African American political agents who, in the wake of the erosion of gains acquired during the civil rights era, want to hold on to Black status as the most important minority. Other agents are xenopho-. bic whites who are uncomfortable with the changing racial character of U.S. society; and finally Latinas/os who feel the route to social mobility is through emphasizing their difference from Blacks who have traditionally been at the bottom of the racial hierarchy in the United States (Vaca, 2004; Rodríguez, 2003; Chávez, 1998).

Two popular and intellectual perspectives that on the surface seem quite different, I argue, are related to each other. These are Samuel Huntington's essay "The Hispanic Challenge," excerpted from his forthcoming book, *Who We Are* (2004), and Vaca's *Presumed Alliance* discussed above. Huntington's essay is a standard xenophobic rant that homogenizes Latinas/os and argues that they (1) are not assimilating; (2) do not respect or conform to Anglo-Saxon values; (3) are threatening democracy through their large numbers and unwillingness to assimilate; and (4) are depressing wages and benefits for working-class whites.[2] In fact, Huntington relies on Carol-Swain's *The New White Nationalism in America* (2003) to argue that Latino immigrants are *creating* racism by coming to the United States in large numbers and not assimilating once here. It is important to note that while Huntington ignores Blacks, Swain attacks them. She argues that Black on white crime, affirmative action, and other presumably unreasonable demands are similarly causing the rise of vicious racism that threatens U.S. democracy. The anti-Black politics of Huntington's article, like that of Propositions 187 and 209, is prefigured by his citation of Swain. Swain and Huntington are part of a generalized attack on multiculturalism, which targets Asians, Arabs, African Americans, and Latinas/os. Both adopt a politics of attacking the "other" in defense of "American" values. These attacks have intensified in the post-9/11 world of American patriotic nationalism, the PATRIOT Act, and declining employment.

The Latina/o response to these attacks has often been disappointing. After all, the attacks are meant to reify racism against Blacks and to discipline future Latina/o politics. In many cases, the response of many Latina/o commentators has not been to question the supremacy of Anglo-Saxon culture or the ethics of forced assimilation, but rather to say "Yes, we are American" (Navarette, 2004). These responses ignore the fact that as a racialized minority Blacks have never been *allowed* to assimilate into the American mainstream. However, by clearly emphasizing their difference from Blacks and their closeness to whites and "mainstream values," many Latina/o commentators suggest that growing numbers of Latinas/os should not be a source of concern for white America, and consequently end up denigrating the Black experience in the United States. This perspective does not challenge the terms of the debate set by white racists but argues that Latinas/os can fit into narrow definitions of Americanness that exclude Blacks. Music critic Ed Morales calls these commentators "Brownologists"

(Morales, 2004) and included Richard Rodríguez and Nicolás Vaca among them. Morales contends that they emphasize the closer nature of Latinas/os to whites while ignoring the very existence of Afro-Latinas/os. For example, Morales quotes Jack Miles's *Atlantic Monthly* article: "Latino immigrants generally do not instill the same fear among whites that blacks can. The social distance between brown and white has never been as great as that between white and black" (Morales, 2004). The emphasis on this closeness and on Latinas/os as representative of a new mixed-race America is meant to distance Latinas/os from Blacks and to redefine race in U.S. society as a concept not so very different from the Latin American myth of racial democracy, which effectively denies racism by emphasizing miscegenation. In addition, this perspective seeks to protect Latinas/os from the racialization that comes with critical engagement with U.S. identity, and is itself a critique of U.S. social and economic institutions that have been the hallmark of African American politics since the birth of the nation. By criticizing or ignoring African Americans and emphasizing brownness in contrast to blackness, writers such as Rodríguez and Vaca seek to answer racists like Huntington by simply opting out of oppositional racial politics. There are those like Patrick Buchanan (2002) who suggest that there is a reconquest in progress, and another group that seeks to colonize Latinas/os by offering them a taste of conditional whiteness.[3] These discourses are attempts to make sense of a United States in the coming century that will not be majority white but that aims to maintain white power and privilege. These works overemphasize differences between Latinas/os and African Americans and ignore political and ideological convergences. Hence, for example, "Brownologists" like Vaca have tended to overemphasize conflict in service of an assimilationist political agenda. These commentators also fail to recognize that the United States is no longer a place with caste differences but one where race matters as one of multiple vectors of disadvantage. Yet it is important not to overlook the problem areas. Hence, in the following pages, I interrogate both Black and Latina/o identities to examine the sources of real conflict and potential solutions.

The Limits of Black Politics

In the current political climate, in which the gains of the civil rights struggle are under attack and the left and right have both largely turned against African American political concerns in support of a "color-blind" politics, it is not surprising that African Americans would retrench and defend their ethnic interests. The advocacy of color-blind politics comes at a time when affirmative action and African American voting rights are under attack. Furthermore, the mainstream Democratic Party has grown indifferent to African American concerns, focusing instead on attracting middle-class suburban white voters. Thus, so-called progressives like the editorial board of *Mother Jones* magazine have concluded that issues of race and in particular African American "identity politics" distance the left from their historical constituency of white working-class men and suburbanites (Frymer, 1999). This is an unfortunate reversal, given that many of these battles were fought in the 1960s, a time when the idea of a left without an explicit demand for racial justice was anathema.

In the wake of this retreat things have not gotten better for African Americans. Mass imprisonment and racial profiling have become features of the new reality for Blacks as well as for Latinas/os—a reality that flies in the face of the idea that the United States is now becoming color-blind. In response to this marginalization, African Americans have sought to renew demands including reparations and other concerns that assert the particularity of the Black experience within the United States (Dawson and Popoff, 2004).

This response by African Americans has often been accompanied by an essentialist view of Black identity. African Americans have in some ways come to attack other expressions of "difference" as a way to protect the particularity of the African American predicament and its consequences. Hence, gender, sexual orientation, and in some cases class have today fallen prey to a construction of a "universal" but narrow Black identity (Cohen, 1999). Much like women and gays and lesbians, Black immigrants from Africa, Latin America, or the Caribbean must choose to either be Black or assert their ethnic identity as if the two were mutually exclusive. Cathy Cohen calls this process secondary marginalization (Cohen, 1999). Hence, the multiplicity of Black experiences outside and within the United States have not come together to form a broader, more inclusive dialogue (Rogers, 2000).

The inability to see the Black experience in broader diasporic terms prevents the development of a new Black politics that incorporates issues of immigration and citizenship along with traditional Black concerns that might provide a bridge of interests between African Americans and Latinas/os. In addition, the consistent place of African Americans at or near the bottom of the American racial hierarchy creates suspicion about joint struggles with other racial ethnic groups who may after some limited gains leave behind the African American community. In this case, Afro-Latinas/os or Latinas/os with significant levels of African ancestry do not become bridges between the communities but rather become examples of how no one wants to be Black in the United States. The Latina/o history of denying the very existence of Black heritage along with the sociocultural practice of whitening only further damages the possibility of interethnic cooperation.

The Race of Latina/o Politics

In this conservative era, pundits have sought to suggest that Latinas/os may have a broader set of political options than Blacks. In an attempt to reverse consistent patterns of alienating Latinas/os through anti-immigrant legislation, President George W. Bush has reached out symbolically to Latina/o voters by appointing Latinas/os to hold key positions in his administration and emphasizing the "ethnics" within the otherwise WASP Bush family.

The message in popular culture is confusing. Latinas/os are both potentially whites and "others." For instance, the construction of Jennifer Lopez (J-Lo) as exotic other who, when necessary, plays the role of an Italian woman shows the schizophrenia that greets U.S. Latinas/os. J-Lo is interesting because the media tried very hard to make her white and to emphasize Black and Latina/o differences through her.

Her use of the dreaded word "nigger" in her performance with rapper Ja Rule, for example, was discussed in the media as if it had been said by a white woman instead of a Latina. In this case, J-Lo was able to traverse the difficult racial boundaries by reemphasizing her relationship with Puff Daddy (now P-Diddy) and her connection to Bronx street culture. J-Lo represents an often-suppressed history of hip-hop culture that in its inception was as much Jamaican and Puerto Rican as African American (Flores, 2000). However, this controversy and Hollywood portrayals of J-Lo emphasize the attempt to portray Latinas/os as "potential whites."

The intraracial politics in Latina/o communities actually supports this approach to their race. Concepts of whitening within Latina/o culture have existed since the advent of Latin American nations (Stepan, 1991; Nobles, 2000). Active attempts to create "white" and modern nations were explicitly connected with ideas that racial mixture would eliminate the negative racial influences of Blacks and indigenous peoples. As national myths grew that all were mixed and moving toward white, discussions of racism that assumed that Blacks damaged the national character disappeared, as did assertions of the unique experience of Afro-Latinas/os (Sawyer, 2004; Sidanius et al., 2001). The construction of national identities around mestizo/white somatic norms denied the existence of racism and Black populations more generally (Hanchard, 1994; Sawyer, 2004). It should therefore be no surprise that upon arriving in the United States, Latinas/os are slow to identify with Blacks. After all, not only are Blacks at the bottom of the racial hierarchy but Latin Americans and U.S. Latinas/os have consistently denied the problems of racism and the existence of blackness in their home countries and in their communities (Sawyer, 2004; Peña et al., 2004).

In this case the identity of Latina/o as being exclusive of Black forces Afro-Latinas/os to choose either to be Black or to be Latina/o. The denial of blackness can be so intense that it is both sad and comical. Dominicans have taken it so far that they have resurrected a myth of indigenous heritage in order to explain their dark skin (Torres-Saillant, 1998). The obviously Black baseball star of the Chicago Cubs, Sammy Sosa, for instance, becomes an "indio" (Indian) rather than a Black, since according to this national myth and tradition Dominicans "cannot be Black."[4] The same goes for figures like pitcher Pedro Martínez of the Boston Red Sox. However, Dominicans are not the only examples of this, and many of them after years in the United States identify as Black (Torres-Saillant and Hernández, 1998). In Central American countries, such as Mexico, Honduras, and El Salvador, blackness has literally been erased from the national history and consciousness. Despite their nappy hair, full lips, and dark skin many Central Americans find it impossible to think that African heritage plays a significant role in their racial makeup. This denial extends to myths that slavery never existed in their countries and Blacks never set foot on the land.

Given these facts, it is no secret that politics in the western United States with its high concentrations of Central Americans and Mexicans frequently involve less inter-ethnic cooperation than places in the East. It is also not surprising that the Cuban American community that once enforced racial segregation while in control of Cuba has frequently been anti-Black in its political activities in the U.S. context (Croucher, 1997; Sawyer, 2003). Any study of Latina/o politics that does not represent the diversity of the Latina/o experience in terms of race, gender, sexual identities, and ideology erases blackness from the Latina/o experience and ends up presenting Latinas/os as "ethnics" who are closer to whites. Yet it is through recognizing the diversity of Latinas/os that the possibilities for a truly progressive politics arise. Moreover, it is the unresolved issue and invisibility of blackness within Latino communities that prevent bridges and encourage antagonism with African Americans.

Thus, a broad and multispectrum "Latina/o" identity that recognizes diversity is important. Public opinion evidence points to the fact that those who have such a pan-Latina/o identity or who identify as Blacks feel closer and more willing to enter into coalitions with African Americans (Kaufmann, 2003). Thus, when pan-Latina/o identity accommodates and recognizes the diversity of the Latina/o experience, it becomes a progressive alternative to identities that emphasize brownness as an alternative to blackness or country-specific identities. Latinas/os who speak English and have either been born in or lived in the United States for many years are more likely to feel closer to Blacks. Thus, we can say that negative notions about blackness from their countries of origin play a substantial role in Latina/o attitudes about Blacks (Kaufmann, 2003). It is also notable that Puerto Ricans and Dominicans feel more commonality with Blacks than with whites. A full 50 percent of Puerto Ricans feel they have a lot in common with Blacks, while 44 percent feel they have a lot in common with whites. Further, even Salvadorans feel they have slightly more in common with Blacks than with whites, but the numbers may fall within the margin of error (Kaufmann, 2003). These numbers speak to the necessity to research Black experiences in countries of origin and to interrogate anti-Black racism in Latin America. Since Mexicans are the largest group, there is a need for studies that address the problem of race in Mexican history, politics, and culture.

The Primacy of Diaspora Research and Consciousness

So far it might seem that a color-blind point of view could represent the best alternative to the problem of identity politics. However, the Latin American myth of racial democracy alerts us to the danger of emphasizing color-blind alternatives without having first achieved racial equality. It silences those who want to articulate their experiences of exclusion based upon race and legitimizes a de facto "mainstream color" that ultimately comes to be accepted as the society's norm. In the United States this impulse is likely to erase African Americans from the political landscape, ignore Afro-Latinas/os, as well as Latinas/os with indigenous features, and finally offer conditional acceptance into the mainstream solely to light-skinned Latinas/os. In this context, what are the alternatives?

The concept of diaspora presents an interesting alternative to this political problem. It is not only analytically correct to understand that the experience of African people cannot be confined within the boundaries of the nation-state. In the case of Blacks and Latinas/os, it becomes a political necessity. By examining the overlapping experiences and cultures of people of African descent both within and outside of the United States, we can create a discussion about racism in Caribbean and Latin American countries as well as reveal connections and a sense of shared struggle among people of African descent. Rather than creating divisions, diaspora research presents opportunities to understand the interesting alternative of how Black identities can be thought of in more flexible terms and how Black culture can be integrated into national cultures (Dzidzienyo, 1995; Rout, 1976; Fontaine, 1982; do Nascimento and Larkin Nascimento, 1992; Hanchard, 2004). This integration and struggle better approximate the problem of race in the post–civil rights era and can be instructive for African Americans in terms of understanding barriers to political mobilization.

While culture is an important element of diasporic inquiry, it is not the end of the rainbow. Diaspora research challenges notions of culture as commodity, set forth by Adolph Reed (1999), for it emphasizes the power and interconnected nature of "local" cultures and folkways without the intervention of global capital. Further, culture is not the only diasporic connection and, in fact, may be the weakest one—although it is important to note that it may be the only option available to most Afro–Latin American groups until recently. The interactions between political elites and members of grassroots political movements are perhaps the most effective ways to reveal diaspora. Here we are not creating new connections but merely unearthing moments when political actors conceived of them and their work as transnational in scope (Robinson, 2000). Political actors in the United States in the 1980s, for example, who protested South African apartheid and the Reagan administration's Central American politics form an important bridge in understanding historical convergence between antiracist politics in the United States and the struggle for social justice and popular sovereignty in Latin America (Perla, 2004). In both cases diasporic populations in the United States played a critical role in challenging destructive U.S. policy toward their brethren and formed alliances across organizational and ethnic lines.

However, diasporic consciousness is not a panacea. It can only be an effective tool in the U.S. context if connected to expanding integration of African American and Latina/o interests through expanded labor organizing and an emphasis on core issues such as access to education, housing, health care, and police reform. These issues, together with cultural factors and research challenging the parochial nature of both Black and Latina/o politics, can create grassroots visionary leadership that establishes lasting bonds rather than the limited patterns of convergence, ambivalence, and conflict that have plagued Black-brown relations to date. In many ways, Afro-Latinas/os become a metaphor. They are both Black and Latina/o, though not quite completely accepted as either. The struggle for citizenship, the fractal patterns of racial exclusion within U.S. society and the Latina/o community, and the substantial ambivalence of the African American community are further complications, which position Afro-Latinas/os at a point on the crossroads of political identities that represents a space for greater cross-cultural understanding or the tragedy of missed opportunity.

Politics on the Ground

Culture and diasporic research do have their limits. Close attention to emergent coalitions among Blacks and Latinas/os can shed light on issues related to Blacks and Latinas/os and help to formulate a progressive political agenda for the twenty-first century. Such a politics must be locally and internationally grounded and cover issues that are of paramount concern to both groups: a living wage, health care, globalization, education, human rights, U.S. foreign policy.

On the issue of immigration, Blacks must recognize that they have no interest in defending nativist and racist policies driven by white conservatives that only benefit business elites. Although such a recognition is already evident, it has not been acknowledged by critics like Vaca. The response of Black leaders and groups to the Immigrant Workers Freedom Ride of 2003 was a step in the right direction. Groups like the NAACP and the Urban League, along with individuals like Jesse Jackson and Congressman John Lewis, joined with labor organizations and African American freedom riders to support the cause of human rights for immigrants.[5] The rides drew an important symbolic connection between the African American struggle for human rights in this country and the struggle for Latina/o immigrant rights. As with the freedom rides, labor organizations must emphasize that legalization and unionization for immigrants and African American workers, rather than nativist policies, are the solution to downwardly spiraling wages and benefits. In *The New White Nationalism in America*, Carol Swain (2003) shows the discursive relationship between anti-Black and anti-Latina/o politics. The struggle against white racism is one that African Americans and Latinas/os share. Similarly, fair trade policy that emphasizes labor and environmental agreements can benefit African American and Latina/o workers in the United States as well as workers in Latin America and Africa.

While economic issues are critical, other foreign policy concerns are also important rallying points for coalition building. While many among the African American and Latina/o communities alike may have opposed the war in Iraq, members of both disproportionately serve in the military for economic reasons. U.S. policy toward the island of Vieques in Puerto Rico drew protests from Latinas/os as well as prominent African Americans such as the Reverend Al Sharpton who was arrested and jailed for three months. Ongoing struggles for freedom and sovereignty throughout the region also may galvanize African Americans and Latinas/os. The Bush administration's aid in overthrowing President Jean-Bertrand Aristide in Haiti in March 2004 parallels its support of regime instability in Venezuela. As more countries respond to the pain of neoliberalism, it is incumbent upon Blacks and Latinas/os in the United States to encourage respect for democracy. In terms of international politics, the recent move by the Congressional Black Caucus and Congressional Hispanic Caucus, led by Congressman Charles Rangel, to recognize the situation and concerns of Afro-Latinas/os in the context of major transformations in Latin American economics and politics is a powerful first step. It is both symbolically and substantively important. However, much of politics is still local, and local coalitions must form.

The mass incarceration of African American and Latina/o youth and adults is an issue that has not been given enough attention. Both communities share this burden equally and have strikingly similar interests in seeing a criminal justice system that is fair and focused on rehabilitation. Improving urban schools and increasing affordability and access to higher education are also issues that bring Latinas/os and African Americans together. On these issues there is no divergence of interests. Similarly, supportive minority set-aside programs and protecting living-wage jobs are issues that bond Latinas/os and African Americans, and must be emphasized. These issues cut across class and ethnic lines in both communities. Latinas/os and African Americans share support for affirmative action, and its defense must be cast in multi-ethnic terms. African Americans should not and cannot fight the battle for affirmative action alone nor can they rhetorically exclude Latinas/os from the struggle.

The two communities must be willing to support politicians who are sensitive to substantive issues that are of importance to both. The recent election of Karen Bass to the Fourteenth District Assembly in California was another step toward a new generation of Black leadership in Los Angeles that had no previous ties to James Hahn or the white power structure. With the support of former mayoral candidate and city councilman Antonio Villaraigosa, Los Angeles County Labor Council president Miguel Contreras, and other prominent Latinas/os and rising star African American politicians, Bass, a community activist, defeated City Councilman Nate Holden, a representative of the old guard of Black politics. The victory party featured speeches in English and Spanish, and the volunteers represented a rainbow of grassroots community groups and labor organizations that worked across ethnic lines on common issues to usher in a new leadership and coalition. In an impassioned speech in Spanish, State Senator Richard Alarcon emphasized that African Americans understand the critical issues that matter to Latina/o communities and share critical beliefs about fairness and justice. If one were to accept the anti-Latina/o bias in Black communities that Vaca sees, these coalitions would be neither possible nor successful. We must remember that Martin Luther King Jr. and Cesar Chavez supported and respected each other. The struggle for justice and civil rights for farmworkers included a substantial Black presence and solidarity. No single group owns the movement or concerns for justice, and in this era of neoliberalism and right-wing activism, no group can advance on its own. Coalitions are the only way and road to progressive politics.

Conclusion

The problem of building Black and Latina/o political coalitions rests upon the development of mutual understanding and building bridges across political interests. Through diaspora research we can understand the political conundrums that draw Blacks and Latinas/os together and challenge the parochial nature of the way in which political, social, and cultural identities are conceived. Rather than being an essentialist formulation, diaspora studies represent a way to expand identities and create new political possibilities.

Furthermore, a focus on the practical issues that bond Latinas/os and African Americans to a common political agenda, mediated through labor organizations and other community groups, needs to be emphasized. Issues of race and culture need to be confronted by both groups. While we cannot ignore that popular perceptions are politically significant, it is also important to keep in mind, contrary to Vaca's assertions, that the argument that Latinas/os take jobs from African Americans has never actually been proven in the context of social science research, and widespread African

American antipathy toward Latinas/os or immigrants has also never been proven. We cannot let the assumptions of these conflicts go unchecked or be discussed in simplistic terms, nor can we allow repetition of these assumptions in the media to make them true. At the same time, the above proposal of research and politics sets out a progressive intellectual and political agenda that ultimately raises significant issues and concerns for both groups. A focus on social justice, human rights, and cultural recognition and respect challenges and undercuts conflict and forms the foundation for coalition politics.

Notes

1. Pew Hispanic Center poll, February 18, 2003: "Survey of Latino Attitudes on a Possible War with Iraq."
2. It is interesting to note that Samuel Huntington, an expert on civil-military relations (see *Soldier and the State: The Theory and Politics of Civil-Military Relations* [1957]) ignores the disproportionate participation of Latinas/os in the U.S. military and, in particular, those who have been called green-card soldiers who see military participation as a pathway to citizenship. For a more expansive treatment of the relationship between race, military service, and citizenship, see Christopher Parker (2001).
3. Ironically, for these commentators white Americans are now the true "natives" of America, and with no regard for manifest destiny or their own conquest of both the West and land previously held by Mexico, they speak of a "reconquest," positioning white Americans as the historical victims of conquest.
4. It is interesting to note that following the Sammy Sosa corked-bat scandal, African American callers to sports radio in Chicago supported Sammy Sosa and charged that the attack by the league, white sports writers, and callers was "racist."
5. For an account of the Immigrant Workers Freedom Ride of 2003 and a list of the many organizations that supported it, see www.iwfr.org.

References

Baretto, Matt A., and Ricardo Ramírez. 2004. Minority participation and the California recall: Latino, Black, and Asian voting trends, 1990–2003. *PS: Political Science & Politics* 37(1): 11–14.

Buchanan, Patrick. 2002. *The Death of the West: How Dying Populations and Immigrant Invasions Imperil Our Country and Civilization*. New York: St. Martin's Press.

Chávez, Lydia. 1998. *The Color Bind: The Campaign to End Affirmative Action*. Berkeley: University of California Press.

Cohen, Cathy. 1999. *The Boundaries of Blackness: AIDS and the Breakdown of Black Politics*. Chicago: University of Chicago Press.

Croucher, S. L. 1997. *Imagining Miami: Ethnic Politics in a Postmodern World*. Charlottesville: University Press of Virginia.

Cruz, Jose. 2000. Interminority relations in urban settings: Lessons from the Black-Puerto Rican experience. In *Black and Multiracial Politics in America*, ed. Yvette M. Alex-Assensho and Lawrence J. Hanks. New York: New York University Press.

Dawson, Michael, and Rovana Popoff. 2004. Reparations: Justice and greed in black and white. *DuBois Review* 1 (1):47–91.

Dzidzienyo, Anani. 1995. Conclusions. In *No Longer Invisible: Afro-Latin Americans Today*, ed. Minority Rights Group, 345–358. London: Minority Rights Publications.

do Nascimento, Abdias, and Elisa Larkin Nascimento. 1992. *Africans in Brazil: A Pan-African Perspective*. Trenton, NJ: Africa World Press.

Flores, Juan. 2000. *From Bomba to Hip-Hop*. New York: Columbia University Press.

Fontaine, Pierre-Michel, ed. 1982. *Race, Class, and Power in Brazil.* Los Angeles: UCLA Press.

Frymer, Paul. 1999. *Uneasy Alliances: Race and Party Competition in America.* Princeton, NJ: Princeton University Press.

Fu, Mingying, 2003. Opposing affirmative action: Self-interest, principles, or racism. Paper presented at the Midwestern Political Science association's annual conference, April 3–6, Chicago, Illinois.

García, Wellinthon, and Duerst-Lahti, Georgia, 2004. Entering the agenda: Framing Dominican Americans in politics. Paper presented at the annual meeting of the Western Political Science Association, March, Portland, Oregon.

Hanchard, M. G. 1994. *Orpheus and Power: The Movimento Negro of Rio de Janeiro and São Paulo, Brazil, 1945–1988.* Princeton, NJ: Princeton University Press.

———. 2004. Acts of misrecognition: Transnational Black politics, anti-imperialism, and the ethnocentrisms of Pierre Bourdieu and Loic Wacquant. *Theory, Culture, and Society* 20 (4):5–29.

Helg, A. 1990. Race in Argentina and Cuba, 1880–1930: Theory, policy, and popular reaction. In *The Idea of Race in Latin America 1870–1940*, ed. Richard Graham. Austin: University of Texas Press.

Hero, Rodney E. 1997. Latinos and politics in Denver and Pueblo, Colorado: Differences, explanations, and the "steady-state" of the struggle for equality. In *Racial Politics in American Cities*, ed. Rufus Browning, Dale Marshall, and David Tabb. New York: Longman.

Huntington, Samuel. 2004. The Hispanic challenge. *Foreign Policy.* March–April 2004, 30–46.

Jones-Correa, Michael. 2000. Immigrants, Blacks, and cities. In *Black and Multiracial Politics in America*, ed. Yvette M. Alex-Assensho and Lawrence J. Hanks. New York: New York University Press.

Kaufmann, Karen M. 2003. Cracks in the rainbow: Group commonality as a basis for Latino and African-American political coalitions. *Political Research Quarterly* 56 (2):199–210.

McClain, Paula, Niambi Carter, Victoria DeFrancesco, J. Kendrick, Monique Lyle, Shayla Nunnally, Thomas Scotto, Jeffrey Grynaviski, and Jason Johnson. 2003. What's new about the New South?: Race, immigration, and intergroup relations in a southern city. Paper presented at the annual meeting of the American Political Science Association, Philadelphia, August 27.

Morales, Ed. 2004. Brown like me? *The Nation.* February 19.

Navarette, Ruben. 2004. It's not the immigrants that America should worry about. *Oakland Tribune*, March 3.

Nobles, Melissa. 2000. *Shades of Citizenship: Race and the Census in Modern Politics.* Stanford, CA: Stanford University Press.

Oliver, J. Eric, and Janelle Wong. 2003. Intergroup prejudice in multiethnic settings. *American Journal of Political Science* 47 (4):567–582.

Parker, Christopher. 2001. War, what is it good for?: Race, military service, and social change, 1945–1995. Ph.D. diss., University of Chicago.

Peña, Yesilernis, James Sidanius, and Mark Sawyer. 2004. Racial democracy in the Americas: A Latin and U.S. comparison. *Journal of Cross-Cultural Psychology* 35 (November):749–762.

Perla, Hector. 2004. Challenging Reagan: The Central American Peace and Solidarity Movement as a transnational social movement. Paper presented at the annual meeting of the Western Political Science Association, March, Portland, Oregon.

Pinderhughes, Dianne. 1997. An examination of Chicago politics for evidence of political incorporation and representation. In *Racial Politics in American Cities*, ed. Rufus Browning, Dale Marshall, and David Tabb. New York: Longman.

Reed, Adolph. 1999. *Stirrings in the Jug: Black Politics in the Post-Segregation Era.* Minneapolis: University of Minnesota Press.

Robinson, Cedric. 2000. *Black Marxism: The Making of the Black Radical Tradition.* Chapel Hill: University of North Carolina Press.

Rodríguez, Richard. 2003. *Brown: The Last Discovery of America.* New York: Penguin Press.

Rogers, Reuel. 2000. Afro-Caribbean immigrants, African Americans, and the politics of group identity. In *Black and Multiracial Politics in America*, ed. Yvette M. Alex-Assensho and Lawrence J. Hanks. New York: New York University Press.

Rout, Leslie B., Jr. 1976. *The African Experience in Spanish America, 1502 to the Present Day.* New York: Cambridge University Press.

Santa Ana, Otto. 2002. *Brown Tide Rising: Metaphors of Latinos in Contemporary American Public Discourse.* Austin: University of Texas Press.

Sawyer, Mark Q. 2003. What we can learn from Cuba: Comparative perspectives on the African American experience. *Souls* 5 (2).

———. 2004. Cuban exceptionalism: Group-based hierarchy and the dynamics of patriotism in Puerto Rico, the Dominican Republic, and Cuba. *DuBois Review* 1 (1):93–113.

Sidanius, J., Y. Peña, and M. Sawyer. 2001. Inclusionary discrimination: Pigmentocracy and patriotism in the Dominican Republic. *Political Psychology* 22:827–851.

Sniderman, Paul, and Thomas Piazza. 2003. *Black Pride, Black Prejudice.* Princeton, NJ: Princeton University Press.

Stepan, N. L. 1991. *The Hour of Eugenics: Race, Gender, and Nation in Latin America.* Ithaca, NY: Cornell University Press.

Swain, Carol. 2003. *The New White Nationalism in America: Its Challenge to Integration.* New York: Cambridge University Press.

Torres-Saillant, S. 1998. The Dominican Republic. In *No Longer Invisible: Afro-Latin Americans Today,* ed. Minority Rights Group, 109–138. London: Minority Rights Publications.

Torres-Saillant, S., and Ramona Hernández, 1998. *The Dominican Americans.* New York: Greenwood Publishing Group.

Vaca, Nicolás. 2004. *The Presumed Alliance: The Unspoken Conflict Between Latinos and Blacks and What It Means for America.* New York: Rayo.

Chapter 15

Racism in the Americas and the Latino Scholar

Silvio Torres-Saillant

The Presence of the Past

Citizens become most deserving of the name when they recognize themselves as agents of change responsible for making society more truly human. In that respect, the burden of citizenship usually weighs heavier for members of diasporic communities than for the regular citizenry, since they have more than one society to improve. Among ethnic minorities in the United States, Latinos face this civil overload with distinct acuity. I can think of at least two reasons for this. First, Latinos for the most part still retain meaningful ties to their ancestral homelands. This is true whether their insertion into the U.S. population resulted from an act of American imperial conquest such as those of 1848 and 1898 or from the massive migratory flows that poured in from Latin America beginning in the first half of the twentieth century. Second, most Latin American societies have in recent decades made seductive advances to their respective emigré communities to secure the continued flow of remittances that have become practically indispensable to the region's economies. These advances include dual citizenship and voting rights abroad, initiatives whereby Latin American state authorities have sought to formalize legislatively their ties to their diasporic communities. Given this scenario, Latinos can feel authorized to intervene on behalf of the downtrodden in their ancestral homelands without concern for the predictable charge that in seeking to influence Latin American societies from their location in the North they might perpetuate the ethnocentric assumptions of American cultural imperialism in the region. It will become clear in the pages ahead that Latino spokespersons derive their moral ascendancy from a long record of subversion against hegemonic paradigms in American society, where they inhabit the margin rather than the center. Besides, the social inequities that they would set out to challenge in Latin America have been perpetrated almost invariably by U.S.-backed regimes. In other words, the oppressors have strong allies in the North. There is hardly any sound reason to wish for the oppressed to fend for themselves. Latinos are historically poised, therefore, to exercise their civil intervention simultaneously in the United States and in their Latin American countries of origin. Finally, only to the extent to which they uphold salutary positions regarding racial oppression in their respective homelands will Latino scholars activate the moral vision and the political alertness necessary for effectively addressing the tensions that often mar the rapport among racially distinct segments of the U.S. Hispanic population as well as the Latino community's interaction with African Americans.

For a long time Mexican-American, Puerto Rican, and other U.S. Hispanic communities have accrued an estimable record of struggle for justice and equality, greatly contributing to the large social movement that has brought American society closer to living up to the true meaning of its creed. In light of that legacy, I would like in the pages that follow to explore whether Latinos might also commit themselves to the equally necessary struggle against racial and ethnic prejudice in Latin America and the Caribbean. I refer here to a prejudice that has a harsh correspondence in hurtful policies and practices in an area where over 146 million indigenous and African-descended people suffer "poverty, stigmatization, and exclusion," as a result of "structural" impediments bequeathed by a history of what Roberto Marquez has called the "Society of Race and racial castes" in the Americas (ECLAC, 2000; Marquez, 2000:20). Alvaro Bello and Marta Rangel's recent study, *Ethnicity, "Race," and Equity in Latin America and the Caribbean,* finds that "integration of indigenous and African-American people" in the region has remained "symbolic and discursive in nature, while in practice it has been denied" (cited in ECLAC, 2000:6). I would like to stress the role that U.S.-based Hispanic scholars can play in helping lessen the misery endured by disempowered ethnically differentiated constituencies south of the Rio Grande. As this opening suggests, I believe that academics, intellectuals, and cultural workers can make a difference in the possible amelioration of real-life conditions especially when the existing injustices have come about through the involvement of the wielders of ideas. The Hispanic intelligentsia has a service to render to help dismantle the intellectual paradigms that have historically condoned oppression against specific groups in the region. This proposition has particular significance at the present juncture. Now, perhaps more than ever before, an international climate seems to exist that encourages people to remain vigilant about contemporary injustices committed abroad as well as at home, and the sense prevails that we in the present have a position to take regarding the atrocities perpetrated against our fellow human beings in the past. The resilient belief that construes any recollection of past conflicts as a source of disruption, echoed by President William Jefferson Clinton at the closing of his last State of the Union address to the United States Congress in January 2000, appears at present to be outmatched by several persuasive pronouncements that urge us to confront the wrongs of previous generations so we can start the clock on the process of healing that must precede any effort to achieve unity and harmony.

Two recent gestures concerning the atrocities of former generations bear mentioning here for their unique value as illustrations of the prevailing tendency of contemporary society to assume responsibility for the evil of our elders. The first refers to the recommendation made in February 2000 by a state commission of the Oklahoma House of Representatives to pay reparations to the survivors or descendants of the victims of the white mob that on May 31, 1921, rampaged through Greenwood, Tulsa's Black residential business district, leaving a toll of some 3,000 people dead and reducing to ashes the thousands of homes and hundreds of businesses that had made the district one of the most prosperous in the city. The Tulsa Race Riot Commission, which the Oklahoma legislature had appointed to study the case, reported prelimi- nary research findings that incriminated the government. The report stated that "city officials not only failed to protect the lives of black residents but also contributed to the riot by deputizing many members of the white mob that attacked Greenwood . . . many of whom were members of the Ku Klux Klan" (Yardley, 2000). The study, in short, implicated the local, state, and federal governments whose laws tolerated racial hatred and whose law enforcement personnel facilitated the violence perpetrated against the Black victims (Ruble, 2000). In recommending reparations on behalf of the victims of the Tulsa district once known as the "Negro Wall Street of America," the commission cited the precedent of a 1994 provision by the Florida legislature that had allocated $2 million to compensate survivors of a smaller race riot in 1923, when whites destroyed the small town of Rosewood, killing at least six of its Black residents (Brand-Williams, 2000).

The other gesture concerns the "Declaration of Repentance of the Church of France" issued by the French bishops in Drancy on September 30, 1997. Through this pronouncement, the Catholic hierarchy admitted its fault for remaining indifferent to the plight of the Jews, 40,000 of whom found themselves in French internment camps by February 1941 during the Vichy government. A few months before, on October 3, 1940, the French government, then led by Philippe Pétain, had issued its first anti- Jewish statutes, and the church of France did not react. Before the very eyes of the Catholic Church, the Jews suffered the onslaught of a series of anti-Semitic legislation which deprived them of French citizenship, relegating them to the most inferior status in the nation, and subjected them to the horrors of the concentration camps. Starting from the realization that "no society, nor for that matter any individual, can live in peace with itself if it has a history of repression and deceit," the French prelacy announced that "the time has come" for the church "to submit her very own history to a critical reading, without hesitating to recognize the sins committed by her sons, and to demand pardon from God and man" (L. Thomas, 1997). The clergymen said: "we are forced to acknowledge that the Bishops of France did not express publicly their outrage, acquiescing by their silence to the flagrant violations of the rights of man, allowing open season to a most deadly system" (ibid.). Their document laments the fact that while the Nazi crimes were taking place, "the hierarchy of the Church consid- ered its first obligation to be that of insuring the practice of Catholicism, the promo- tion of its institutions, and the protection of her faithful" (ibid.). Such an institutional priority, which could only be effectively pursued by adherence to a code of behavior that the vicious regime found palatable, had the inescapable consequence of making the church complicit in the genocide that the Third Reich was perpetrating.

Consistent with the climate illustrated by these two gestures, Pope John Paul II spoke out in a March 12, 2000, statement beseeching forgiveness for the sins of Catholics and Catholicism over the centuries, noting especially sins committed against the Jewish people. The pope further decried "the crimes of the past" during his trip to Israel and the Middle East later in March. Speaking at the Holocaust Museum in Jerusalem, he said, "I assure the Jewish people that the Catholic Church . . . is deeply saddened by the hatred, acts of persecution and displays of anti-Semitism directed against the Jews by Christians at any time and in any place. The Church rejects racism in any form as a denial of the image of the Creator inherent in every human" (cited by Griffin-Nolan, 2000:1). The foregoing positions, corresponding to the widespread demand on today's conscience to take a stand on past evils, were predicated on the realization that the present bears responsibility for the past as much as it does for the future. "This act of remembrance," said the bishops of France, "calls us ever the more to a vigilance with regard to humanity both now and in the future." If our memories of pain inflicted years ago on large numbers of people of an ethnicity other than ours fail to move us to righteous indignation, I seriously doubt whether we could muster the empathy necessary to feel emotionally and morally affected by the grief of the victims should the atrocity occur in our own time and place.

The Morality of Scholarship

As we tackle the thorny question of race and ethnicity in Latin America and the Caribbean, it behooves us to consider whether we might arrive at a stage in our academic conversations where we transcend the civil routine of respectable scholarly work in order to confront head-on the horrors of our own past. We might wish to dare entertain some harsh, theoretically uncouth questions regarding our own relationship to the racial crimes that have been and continue to be committed by Latin American and Caribbean states against differentiated subsections of their respective populations. Too often in the academy we circumscribe our social interventions to producing "objective" (i.e., advocacy-free) discourse as the most suitable to the realm of the lecture hall or the scholarly monograph, while failing to interrogate the human value of the knowledge that we in our research and writing purport to create. Trained as we are in the humanities and the social sciences to increase the level of sophistication of our queries rather than to attempt to discern possible answers to the problems that complicate the lives of the people we study, we content ourselves with merely expanding the intellectual horizons of our own fields. The typical scholarly paper on the human sciences, even when dealing with life-and-death topics such as racial oppression or interethnic conflict in this or that country of the hemisphere, normally closes with a sedate paragraph in which the scholar points to pertinent questions that call for further exploration or to additional areas of research evinced by the findings of the present project. The purpose of research in the end becomes to formulate questions for additional research. One gets credit for having made contributions to the discipline by merely increasing the number of research questions in one's field, leaving as legacy a cycle that is vicious in more than one way. Careers are thus built, grants awarded, and brilliant reputations earned, even as the trail of tears that may have served as our subject matter remains unabated and the oppressive structures that may have fueled our research continue patiently to await redressing.

I would propose that we too often have done an insufficient job of articulating for ourselves a position whereby we first recognize ourselves as implicated in the depravity of the state in our respective homelands and then take the appropriate steps to separate ourselves from the infamy of the society in question. Latinos trace their origins back to countries that have bought into visions of progress and modernization that depend on the devastation of countless habitats, where animals, plants, and people have their dwelling. The Guarani in northern Argentina, the Yuquí in Bolivia, the Cofán in the Ecuadorian Amazon, the Kuna Indians of eastern Panama, among other endangered peoples in the vanishing forests of Latin America, bear the brunt of a Faustian bargain between the developing nations of the hemisphere and the developed world. These nations have embraced a model of development that involves attracting investment from the United States, Europe, and Japan, as well as borrowing millions of dollars from foreign banks, which in the end have the result of cutting the lifeline of indigenous communities. Alan Weisman and Sandy Tolan (1993) traveled through fifteen countries of the hemisphere to document a "swift, often irreversible destruction." They attested to a Guarani village "burned to make way for yet another hotel. The next Indian village to the south is also gone, swallowed by the waters of a new reservoir" (221). From a government contract in the 1970s that turned the Ecuadorian Amazon over to Texaco to build an oil industry, to the ancient hardwood rainforests on Tierra del Fuego that in the 1990s Canadian and Japanese companies would turn into fax paper, these development strategies have seemed less horrific than they are because their devastating impact has fallen most directly on the lives and lands of indigenous communities. It is no secret that the Indians occupy the bottom rung—even as compared with Blacks—of the socioeconomic ladder in the hemisphere (Ferguson, 1961:75).

The ethnic distance that might separate us from the immediate victims of the ecological genocide that modernization has brought about in Latin America may have made the calamity more tolerable than it ought to be. Perhaps to help us overcome the insufficient solidarity that ethnic difference stimulates in us, we might wish to pay heed to the suggestion of Marguerite Duras, referring to the Nazi horror, that we "turn it into a crime committed by all humanity," that we see ourselves implicated in it, that we "share the crime" (Duras, 1993:83). We need this mental exercise so that our proximity to both the victims and the perpetrators may become apparent. Once we can feel the evil closer to our own skin, we will then be in a position to come to terms with our level of involvement and genuinely take a stand on it. We need, in effect, a soul-searching maneuver that will produce the effect that Pablo Neruda's "Ode to Paul Robeson" credits to the great African American singer. The Chilean poet evokes Robeson's undaunted devotion to the cause of human justice in these lines: "Your voice/separated us from crime/once more/it rescued the light from the darkness" [Tu voz/nos separó del crimen/una vez más/apartó/la luz de las tinieblas] (Neruda, 1962:1232–1233). I would say that especially when we study the history and the permanence of racial oppression in Latin America and the Caribbean, we tread a delicate moral ground if we do not make enough of an effort to separate ourselves from the crimes that our research activities bring us into contact with.

Urgent Words, Compulsory Silences

Latino and U.S.-based Latin American scholars who have chosen the study of their people as fields of academic inquiry share membership in a community of knowledge with undeniable political privileges irrespective of the challenges they might face as a result of their relative marginality in American institutions of higher education. In many respects, that uneasy location between privilege and marginality constitutes the greatest asset that emigré and diasporic communities can boast. Working mostly from our intellectual trenches at university-based ethnic studies or area studies units, we enjoy the creative tension of inhabiting a space marked by challenge as much as by potential. We enjoy the dual perspective of the incurable outsider who has accessed significant degrees of insiderness. We have succeeded at gaining entrance into an industry that permits us to make a living by participating in thought production. No one can deny the considerable empowerment involved in the act of making a living by wielding the weapons of discourse. Yet, given our marginality relative to the mainstream bodies of knowledge that the academy values most, we achieve a problematic insertion. That mediated access encourages in us a perspective that enables us to look critically at American society's questionable record of racial disharmony and its economic and political implications. By the same token, we achieve as members of emigré or diasporic communities a critical distance from our homelands or the homelands of our elders that makes it possible for us to become demanding, even judgmental, regarding questions of equality and social justice in the old countries. Elsewhere I have sought to demonstrate the extent to which in the case of U.S. Dominicans one can speak of an "alternative epistemic community" vis-à-vis the schemes of thought that prevail in standard definitions of nation in the Dominican Republic, describing the "diasporic perspective" typically deployed in the emigré community's critical assessment of cultural myths and political behavior "back home" (Torres-Saillant, 1999:37, 393–404).

A Puerto Rican illustration of the same phenomenon appears in Edgardo Rodríguez-Julia's *Las tribulaciones de Jonás* (1981), where the author recollects an eventful visit paid in 1978 by him, his wife, a guide, and his friend Roberto Márquez, "a Puerto Rican brought up in New York," to the house of the elder statesman and living political legend Luis Muñoz Marín (Rodríguez-Julia, 1981:22). From the author's mere description of Márquez's gait as they approached the patriarch's house ("with a self-assurance possible only for someone who learned about him from afar"), it seems clear that the Nuyorican in the group was freer than the other guests from the spell of meek obsequiousness that the presence of the ruling class can cast on the members of the citizenry in the homeland (22). Muñoz Marín was "a true prince of the Creole ruling caste," but Márquez, unlike the other visitors, refrains from using the respectful form "Don Luis" when addressing him (25, 31). As their jovial conversation proceeds, the most disquieting of the topics covered and the questions formulated invariably come from the lips of Márquez, "the black Puerto Rican brought up in a New York ghetto, one of the 'oppressed' [by Muñoz?] children of the emigrants" (30). Indeed, from Márquez, and from nobody else, came the million-dollar question posed on that day to the champion of Operation Bootstrap, the famed development initiative that led to the massive exodus of Puerto Ricans from their homeland in the 1940s. Márquez asked the former governor of Puerto Rico, "What was the Partido Popular's policy on emigration," to which the old Partido Popular leader answered: "We figured: After two generations the problem of the Puerto Ricans in New York would no longer exist, simply because by then they would no longer be Puerto Ricans" (39). The response contained a greater degree of honesty than Márquez had probably expected, but it most likely merely confirmed a truth he had intuited and resented, hence his less obeisant demeanor in the rapport with "Don Luis." I would contend that, whatever its degree of articulateness, this justifiable resentment toward the ruling elites of Latin America often appears in the pronouncements of Latino voices in the diaspora, sharpening our critical edge. Though it entails a measure of trauma, that situation, born of the uprooting that begets diasporic identity, has the advantage that it can turn us into hyperconscious citizens, that is, people with an acute awareness of the terms and the implications of their rapport with a particular state. Given their characteristic alertness vis-à-vis the polity of their affiliation, one could think of hyperconscious citizens as less susceptible than regular citizens to state-induced social, political, and cultural deception.

Furthermore, U.S.-based Hispanic scholars have the not-so-negligible advantage that they live and work—they exist intellectually—outside the reach of the Latin American and Caribbean thought police. Speaking and writing in the United States, they enjoy the freedom to expose the iniquities of presidents, cardinals, generals, legislators, and magnates in the home countries without risk of facing consequences as serious as those one would have to face if launching one's critiques in situ. This is hardly the place to recount the history of intellectuals who suffered harm for voicing unflattering though truthful indictments of the actions of those in power in the countries of the region. The possibility of suffering physical injury or even "disappearing" still exists. On April 28, 1998, Monsignor Juan Gerardi Conedera met his death at the hands of hit men two days after he, as head of the Guatemalan Archbishop's Human Rights Office, made public a report that summarized three decades of violence and human rights violation mostly by the military (Hayner, 1998:32).

Given the foregoing scenario, one can hardly expect scholars in Latin America to be at the forefront of the struggle for equality and social justice. The 1990s witnessed a climate in which societies in the region committed themselves to effectuating a transition to democratic practices while remaining acutely aware of the need to make flattering concessions to the old guard of authoritative, corrupt, and murderous regimes. The intelligentsia had to learn to cope with an amoral political climate in which the likes of Joaquín Balaguer and Augusto Pinochet dictated the logic that would inform the narration of the immediate past. They passively stomached the deliberations among the multipartisan legislature that, in 1998 in Chile, conferred upon General Pinochet the near sacred rank of senator-for-life and that, in 1997 in the Dominican Republic, anointed Balaguer with the title of Gran Propulsor de la Democracia Dominicana (Torres-Saillant, 1999:72). In that climate, insisting on unofficial, unregulated forms of remembering, dwelling on the need to narrate the immediate past in a way that would do justice to the human dignity of the thousands of Chileans and Dominicans who lost their lives or their well-being when the violence of Pinochet's and Balaguer's governments ran rampant, might be dismissed as an old-fashioned intellectual nuisance. Worse still, such insistence entails the risk of causing the disfavor of entrenched power sectors. One could lose one's job and the use of the established venues for the intellectual exchange of ideas. Though less likely, the possibility of suffering bodily harm on account of one's ideas is not inconceivable. But the social ostracism, which inevitably translates into lack of access to necessary resources, including funding, would seem to suffice to scare Latin American intellectuals into compliance with the behavior desired by the political forces currently in place in the region.

In light of this background one can appropriately affirm that Latino and Latin American scholars in the United States have discernible advantages in comparison with their counterparts in the countries of the region. They enjoy freedom from the pressures exerted on their colleagues in Latin America by politicians, the military, the church, and the other sectors of the power structure. As a tenured faculty member in the City University of New York, for instance, a colleague could in the year 2001 conceivably dare to publish an essay that provokes the discomfort of Mayor Rudolph Giuliani, Governor George Pataki, and President George W. Bush without suffering direct punishment or losing the job. Our colleagues in universities from Argentina to Uruguay cannot boast a comparable freedom. This discursive advantage of ours must be kept firmly in mind when we speak of racial inequality in the hemisphere. That advantage would even seem to impose an inescapable responsibility, since we might see it as our moral obligation to use our relative safety and freedom to articulate the critiques that our counterparts in the home countries can simply not afford to voice. The fact that we can easily say the things about which they, out of understandable fear, must keep silent almost imposes on us the duty of saying them. The silences they leave, we have the power to fill.

Latinos and Racism: A Model for Coherence

We have another, perhaps more powerful reason for feeling an obligation to pronounce ourselves on racial injustices in Latin America and the Caribbean: to avoid moral and political incoherence. Given the peculiar racial history of the United States and the circumstances under which nonwhite ethnic minorities gained access to the corridors of the academy, Latino scholars, like their African American, Native American, and Asian American colleagues, have become quite adept at detecting racially based privilege and exclusion. We have sharpened our instincts to recognize inequality when we see it and quickly to stand up for racial rightness. We stand out as natural advocates of diversity, inclusion, and appropriate representation in public spaces, the job market, and the academy. In light of that aptitude we might wish to take appropriate measures to ensure our coherence. We can begin by asking ourselves whether, for instance, our Mexican American colleagues, as forceful and articulate as they have been since the advent of the Chicano movement in demanding social equity and respect for difference on this side of the Rio Grande, have spoken up loudly and consistently enough on behalf of the oppressed indigenous populations of the supremely *guerocentric* Republic of Mexico. I made a memorable visit to Guadalajara during the meeting of the Latin American Studies Association there in the spring of 1997. During each of the three days of the conference I bought a copy of the newspaper *El Exelsior* and two other of the major dailies expressly to examine the phenotype of the people shown in the photographs that illustrated their pages. I went through hundreds of newspaper pages a day looking specifically for indigenous-looking faces, to no avail.

Latinos have persuasively laid their claim to a social space in which the rest of the U.S. population recognizes the community's "cultural citizenship." Renato Rosaldo and William Flores (1997) define the concept of cultural citizenship as "the right to be different (in terms of race, ethnicity, or native language) with respect to the norms of the dominant national community, without compromising one's right to belong, in the sense of participating in the nation-state's democratic processes" (57). But one wonders if we have allowed ourselves a sort of double standard when it comes to witnessing denials of full citizenship to ethnically differentiated groups in our countries of origin. One could ask whether Chicano spokespersons have effectively challenged *guero* society in Mexico in a way that accords with their inestimable trajectory in the struggle for equality in the United States for more than four decades. Ironically, one observes instead a tendency among Latinos to speak up stridently about issues of equality and diversity in American society while proceeding leniently when their countries of origin overtly practice racially and ethnically based exclusions. When U.S. Puerto Ricans and Dominicans travel back to the lands of their elders, they seldom analyze the quality of life on those islands with the same zealous political urgency that they normally display in their examination of U.S. society. Perhaps the numbing of one's political edge when looking at the ancestral land has a psychological explanation.

One could conjecture that uprooting oneself from the original homeland to settle in the United States, where one has constantly had to negotiate ethnic antipathy by remaining politically on guard, has made for a tiring process. Perhaps this condition of incessant ideological belligerence makes us yearn for a comfort zone where we psychologically might rest awhile. The original abode then becomes a source of spiritual strength that confirms our cultural identity. In effect, we conjure our Aztlan as a near transcendental realm where history gives way to myth. When we travel, we experience an existential homecoming that permits us to reconnect with the food, the music, the landscape, the family. Even a writer as radical as Cherrie Moraga, who owes her celebrity to her defiance of all oppressive structures, including normative heterosexuality, reveals a soft ideological spot when describing her frequent travel to Mexico. In her deconstruction of androcentric Latino culture, she does not spare her own "Chicana mother" whom she places in the Mexican "wifely" tradition, going back to Malinche's mother, of betraying her daughter by "putting the male first" (Moraga, 1999:152). Yet she does not glance at the interior of Mexican society—the internal injustices that people in every country perpetrate against their compatriots—with politically activated eyes, limiting her critique to the geopolitical concern over

"the colonial relationship between the United States and Mexico." In a recent interview she has said: "The land, that is the best! That is the reason I like to go there,
especially the southern part. I've visited the pyramids, the ruinas. I have also studied
a lot of Mesoamerican, pre-Columbian history. It is always very relaxing for me, and
it also affects my work as you have seen. . . . There is no home for me in Mexico,
except the land. The desert. I spent time in Sonora and Chihuahua a couple of
summers ago. It's the land. These are my raices. My family is from Sonora. The land
calms me down, opens me up. I feel it is a rich resource in my writing. I experience
a quietness there that is difficult to conjure in this country" (Moraga, 2000:108).
Regarding the likelihood of ever residing in Mexico, Moraga has said, "I hope to do
that for periods of time. Particularly when you have a kid, your priorities change. I
feel like I want to give my kid what I did not get: a direct sense of Mexican culture
and some spots of land without gringo interference" (ibid.).

Moraga's testimony illustrates a process whereby through contact with the ancestral land we undergo a cultural refill, a social renewal that energizes us, enhancing our
ability to confront the challenges of living as part of a disempowered ethnic minority upon our return to the United States. The danger, of course, lies in that deacti-
vating the political eye when looking at the native land during our restorative trips
entails a measure of self-deception that carries serious moral implications. For, in fact,
we shield ourselves psychologically to remain unmoved by the injustices we see
happening over there. We go to Guadalajara or Mexico City, rely on the invaluable
services of Indian-looking people—from the porter in the baggage claim area of the
airport, to the cleaning lady in the hotel or residence, to the taxi driver who brings
us back to catch the return flight; but then, except in the most unflattering circumstances, we do not see them when we watch Mexico on TV or read about Mexican
society in the paper. We go to the Dominican Republic, stay at a hotel or in a relative's house in the city of Santo Domingo, and see Blacks and mulattos everywhere,
as well we should, for they constitute nearly 90 percent of the country's population.
The African presence in the hemisphere was first evident in this city in 1502. This
land also witnessed the first Black slave insurrection registered in the history of the
Americas, in 1522, and certain neighborhoods such as San Carlos de los Minas—
initially known as San Carlos de los Negros—began as townships populated specifically by residents of African descent. Yet blackness magically disappears when one
watches the Dominican family as represented in TV commercials or the visage of the
Dominican nation as reflected in the society pages and the supplements of the major
dailies. If we find nothing disturbingly wrong with that picture, one could argue that
we have learned to tolerate in the native land the same social ills that we purport to
wish to correct in American society. We have become morally dual, and our apparent
indifference to the pain endured by the sectors of the population that suffer exclusion
turns us into accomplices in oppressions that we know much about because we make
our living studying them in the United States.

As we reflect on issues related to race and ethnicity in Latin America and the
Caribbean, then, it pays to examine the privilege of our positionality as U.S.-based
Hispanic scholars. We must not forget that in exploring the issues in question we will

inevitably discern serious crimes, and we cannot get around the need to take a stand vis-à-vis the crimes that our research brings into visibility for us. We can recognize the crimes easily because of their pervasiveness. They stem almost invariably from particular formulations of a notion of national identity that, for the most part, not only fails to account for the racial and ethnic diversity of most Latin American and Caribbean populations but also tends to embrace definitions of nationhood that reek of antipathy toward ethnically differentiated components of those populations. Formal European colonialism in the Americas began to recede in the mid-1800s, with abolition coming soon thereafter. During the 1880s Cuba and Brazil freed their slaves, putting an end to the "peculiar institution" in the Americas. Yet, as Peter Winn has noted, slavery's "legacies—racism, poverty, inequality—remain, a burden that the region's one hundred million people of African descent still bear today" (1999:279). Needless to say, the legacy of colonial oppression still harms the lives of millions of Indians also. When independence came and the Latin American creole elites founded their sovereign nations, little changed for the Indians.

Perhaps one needn't be shocked by this outcome, since the builders of nations in the region happened to be the political and cultural heirs of the Spanish conquerors who had robbed the Indians of their lands and massacred their ancestors during the colonial transaction centuries before. Ironically, the advent of independence brought "increasing encroachments on communal lands by a creole and mestizo elite freed from imperial constraints" (Winn, 1999:250). The peasant uprising in the region around Cayambe, Ecuador, led by the Confederation of Indigenous Nationalities of Ecuador (CONANE) in June 1990, responded to the hopeless disempowerment to which Indians in Ecuador, as well as in Peru and Bolivia, had been subjected since the conquest. Excluded from power, deprived of their abodes, and deemed irrelevant in the land of their ancestors, they reasonably lost patience, much to the chagrin of the government that chastised the "agitators" who led the movement for their lack of "a sense of nationality" and their desire "to divide the country" (262). In Guatemala during the counterinsurgency years of 1978–1985 the armed forces destroyed over 400 communities and took the lives of some 200,000 people, mostly "unarmed Indians," and little doubt exists in the minds of the victims of the violence that their ethnicity made them easy targets, the army certain that no retaliation would come, since they were "just Indians" (266). And despite the renown of a Guatemalan Maya activist of the caliber of Rigoberta Menchu, who won the 1992 Nobel Peace Prize for her defense of the human rights of indigenous people, a constitutional reform that would acknowledge Guatemala as a "multiethnic, multicultural, multilingual society" did not get the necessary votes in a May 1999 referendum (269).

Racial Fictions, Fictional Harmony, and Genocide

I would argue that the conceptual manipulations implicit in the intelligentsia's construction of the idea of nation in Latin America discussion. In keeping with the foregoing stemmed automatically from the Eurocentric and white supremacist paradigms that the region's thinkers embraced rather than from discernibly malicious conspiratorial design. The same applies to the intellectual tradition that disputes the significance of race in social interactions and historical phenomena in the Americas. Many would earnestly subscribe to what Anani Dzidzienyo describes as the "much admired non-contentiousness" of race relations patterns (1995:345). Elsewhere Dzidzienyo mentions the leading example of Edson Arantes do Nascimento, the former Brazilian minister for sport better known as the great soccer player Pelé. He recalls, "the 'King of Football' was an invaluable ally of the Brazilian authorities, constantly used to demonstrate the validity of their 'racial democracy.' " Pelé himself claimed, "there is no racism in Brazil" (cited by Vieira, 1995:39). The fact that a Black Brazilian should fail to see racism in his country has to do not only with the fact that his superior talents as a sportsman elevated him socially above the level of everyday ethnic vulnerability but also with the success of the narrative of racial noncontentiousness in the case of Brazil. Abdias do Nascimento has stated in no uncertain terms that the Brazilian "Black movement expends enormous energies trying to 'prove' to its own people that their situation is due to race" (1995:106). Similarly, the Dominican case, which I have examined elsewhere, points to the possibility that discrete historical developments can lead to the emergence among people of African descent of a "deracialized consciousness" with the power to preclude the rise of "a discourse of black affirmation," keeping the community from wielding the appropriate intellectual tools to counterbalance de facto negrophobia (Torres-Saillant, 1998:136). Deracialization may also come from a particular state-sponsored ideology, as Carlos Moore argues was the case in Cuba with the advent of a Marxist revolution which advocated the "non-racial" identity of Cubans and warned against the dangers of Black self-affirmation (1995:219, 225).

Even more pernicious than the myth of noncontentiousness is the tradition that would have us believe in a harmonious process of miscegenation triggered by the colonial transaction following the conquest of the Americas. The standard wisdom, variously pastoralizing the emergence of the mestizo or the mulatto, posits that miscegenation led to a state of pervasive hybridity devoid of racial tensions. That tradition incorporates among its conceptual features elements born of the "white legend" that Spanish thinkers promoted to counterattack the "Black legend" that spokespersons for competing European empires had deployed during the great intercolonial clashes of times past. Unlike their Dutch, French, and English counterparts, the Spanish, so the argument goes, thought nothing of the racial difference of the peoples they conquered. They intermingled carnally with their ethnic other and produced well-liked mestizo or mulatto offspring. The distinguished Spanish essayist and physician Gregorio Marañón adhered fervently to that interpretation of things in a prologue he wrote in the mid-twentieth century for a book on the mestizos of Spanish America by José Pérez de Barradas. In an evidently self-congratulatory tone he boasts as follows: "If there is one thing that Hispanic peoples can undeniably feel proud of it is not having ever assigned undue importance to the question of race" (Marañón, 1948:iii). But we cannot credit the Spanish with the sole ownership of the tradition that presents miscegenation as a normal, concordant feature of the Latin American experience. Creole voices, even if occasionally harboring hostile feelings toward Spain, often needed to embrace pastoral visions of *mestizaje* from the early days of the independence movement in order to foster notions of national unity in the face of the empirically observable ethnic heterogeneity. Addressing the second National Congress of Venezuela in Angostura on February 15, 1819, the liberator Simon Bolivar tackled the political challenge posed by diversity: "We do not retain the vestiges of our original being. We are not Europeans; we are not Indians; we are but a mixed species of aborigines and Spaniards. Americans by birth and Europeans by law, we find ourselves engaged in a dual conflict: we are disputing with the natives for titles of ownership, and at the same time we are struggling to maintain ourselves in the country that gave us birth against the opposition of the invaders" (Bolivar, 1951:175–176). But his candid recognition of the complexity did not deter his prescribing a clear solution: "Unity, unity, unity must be our motto in all things. The blood of our citizens is varied: let it be mixed for the sake of unity" (191).

Bolivar expressed his view of *mestizaje* as a desideratum and a sine qua non for national unity. Subsequent voices have purported to describe it as having existed all along. The Spanish liberal Salvador de Madariaga evoked a historical process whereby the diverse ethnic contingents of the region, including Blacks, have communally blended into a well-integrated hybrid. "Whatever statistics might say," he confidently affirms, "the soul of the Americas is, in effect, an essentially mestizo soul" (cited by Mörner, 1961:11). The smooth fusion of different races as a fait accompli naturally leads to the claim that recognizable racial distinctions have disappeared in Latin America. As Bollinger and Lund have argued, the idea upheld by intellectuals during the first half of the twentieth century that no racial problem per se existed in the region, and their assumption that the great degree of miscegenation occurring there diminished the racial dimension of human interaction, have actually presented a serious obstacle to the development of a theory of Latin American racism (1994:228). Under the prevailing interpretation the sources of conflict and intergroup tensions in the region point to other causes. One is class difference, which would normally merit a lengthy discussion in its own right, but which I would simply address here by posing rhetorical questions regarding, for instance, the implications of the fact that in Honduras 99 percent of the Garifuna communities in the mid-1990s had "no postal service, telegraph or radio" and, where available, some of these services were either unreliable or difficult to come by, just as the majority of Garifuna settlements had "no water, electricity or latrine services" and lacked basic transportation (Guevara Arzu, 1995:243). One would have a hard time showing the absence of a link between the Garifunas' destitution—their class oppression—and their ethnic difference vis-à-vis non-Black Hondurans. Or can one possibly deracialize the denial of citizenship rights to the Dominican-born children of Haitian immigrants by the Dominican government at the very end of the twentieth century (López and Azcona, 1999:1)?

But perhaps the most resilient disclaimer of the significance of race in Latin America has been the contention that as a result of miscegenation racial distinctions vanished, having become subsumed under the more powerful unifying mantle of culture. Pedro Henríquez Ureña articulated this position most succinctly when he deployed his peculiar definition of Spanish America as constituting the location of a unified race despite "the multicolor multiplicity of peoples speaking our language in the world." He put it thus: "What unites and unifies this race, not so much a real as an ideal race, is its community of culture, which is predicated, mainly, on its linguistic commonality" (Henríquez Ureña, 1978:12–13). Race and ethnicity, then, evaporate into the vaster ether of culture and language. As the eminent philologist himself suggested, the evaporation would not occur haphazardly. He did not have in mind a symmetrical fusion of ethnicities. The West—not Africa, Indo-America, or even the East—would provide the structure into which the various ethnicities would fuse. Henríquez Ureña had no qualms about tracing the cultural roots of Hispanic America to the Roman Empire, as Sarmiento had suggested (13). His model presupposed the belief held by José Ingenieros that the European race that came to the Americas during the colonial transaction represented a higher stage in the evolution of the human species than that of the Indians and Blacks. Henríquez Ureña did not overtly echo the pronouncements of the likes of Carlos O. Bunge, who proclaimed the lesser capacity of Blacks to think and work at the quality level of Europeans, and who charged Ibero-American Creoles with "impairing their own stock" by intermingling with Blacks and Indians. Yet he did go to considerable lengths in chapter 7 of his monograph *El español en Santo Domingo* to deny that his country had had an African presence prior to 1916, when the United States invaded the Dominican Republic and promoted the flow of workers from Haiti (Henríquez Ureña, 1982:130, 134). As a mulatto, he himself had encountered negrophobic hostility in Mexico and in the United States, yet this did not seem to discourage his view of race in his country (Díaz Quiñones, 1994:69). Interestingly, the negroid features of his mother, which he visibly inherited, and the embarrassment they caused to the family in late-nineteenth-century Santo Domingo, as well as to him and his sister Camila in early twentieth-century Minnesota, appear as a leit motif in the history-based novel *In the Name of Salomé* by the notable Dominican American writer Julia Alvarez (2000).

The ideologues of *mestizaje* as the historical outcome that suspended racial tensions would have been hard put to explain a series of episodes in the countries of Iberian America that have displayed all the trappings of downright racial clashes and racial oppression. It was a realization of the racial nature of their subjection that led to the 1912 insurrection of Black Cubans in Oriente Province led by Evarito Esteñoz and Pedro Ivonet during the Gomez administration. Some 300 Blacks met their deaths when the government troops responded, decisively crushing the insurgents (Levine, 1980:3). Nor has the discourse of noncontentious hybridity provided reasoning that would explain away the virulent antipathy that the region's indigenous peoples have endured. We know the verbal violence in Domingo Faustino Sarmiento's dismissal of the Indian as a possible source of any cultural asset for Argentinian society, and we know that the Creoles did not limit themselves to rhetorical aggression. The 1819 speech at Angostura by Bolivar refers in passing to the nation's disputes "with the natives for the titles of ownership," a candid reminder that the nations of the Americas were built on territories previously occupied by indigenous peoples. To build a country, the Creoles often had to begin by clearing the ground of its native inhabitants. Obviously, then, a nation that needed to remove the Indian in order to come into being could not be expected to exhibit much affection for the surviving indigenous communities. Typically, in 1868 the Bolivian government declared Indians to be an impediment to the development and stability of the nation and promoted the outright spoliation of their lands. Referring to the Quechua and Aymará peoples, Bolivian policy makers spoke of "the hopelessness of trying to civilize" the Indian "through education and training in our institutions" (cited by Calderon G., 1977:197). Given that portrayal of the natives, it seemed logical to regard the communities in question as unfit to own and manage any property associated with development; hence this declaration: "to remove these lands from the hands of the ignorant and backward Indians is to achieve the most salutary transformation in the social and economic order of Bolivia" (197). In keeping with that syllogistic line of reasoning, the government of General Mariano Melgarejo in 1868 declared "the lands hitherto possessed by the Indians" to be the sovereign property of the Bolivian state. The government would then sell the lands in question "by public auction and the proceeds" collected would go "to cover the internal debt and public service expenditure" (198). There should be no doubt that the atrocities that ensued in this and other similar instances, the further reduction of the indigenous peoples of Latin America, though carried out by generals and soldiers bearing firearms, derived their legitimacy and their justification from ideological formulations devised and made current by intellectuals wielding the pen. The intelligentsia created the conceptual paradigms that facilitated the crimes. They provided definitions of national identity that rendered specific ethnically differentiated subsections of the existing population of the region inimical to the very constitution of the nation. They gave intellectual respectability to racial oppression and to ethnic exclusion. The effects of that opprobrious legacy have hardly died out. They run rampant at the beginning of the twenty-first century.

Latino Racial Proficiency and White Supremacy's Ubiquity

Latino and U.S.-based Hispanic scholars writing and speaking from American university settings about race and ethnicity in Latin America and the Caribbean have some serious issues to contend with. South of the Rio Grande the intelligentsia has collaborated in grievous crimes against humanity, and we, working in the North, have the moral imperative to take a stand with respect to that legacy. If we are to deserve a hearing when we speak out against racism in the United States, we have to reveal ourselves devoid of double standards. We have to show moral consistency as manifested in the willingness to oppose racism wherever it occurs. There is absolutely nothing that makes the ideas of a negrophobic, anti-immigrant Anglo in the Northeast significantly worse than those of an anti-Indian, white-supremacist journalist or statesman in the Rio de la Plata region. If we somehow find something more palatable in the one than in the other, we must admit to a defective function in our moral radar. The theory of *mestizaje* can indeed play tricks on the mind, but once we detect the racism inherent in the formulation of the advantages of miscegenation, the moral alarm should go off immediately. José Vasconcelos posited in *La raza cósmica*

(1925) a potentially admirable view of hybridity leading up to a "synthetic race," which he called the "fifth universal race," but he made himself objectionable as soon as he showed he accepted the existing ideology of superior and inferior races. His prediction of "the cosmic race" depended on the absorption of "the inferior races" by "the superior," with Blacks, for example, becoming "redeemed, step by step, by voluntary extinction" (Vasconcelos, 1997:32). Ultimately, he assigns to whites, with their beauty and their intelligence, the power to correct the defects of the colored races. One wonders, therefore, where exactly the celebrated "Chicana tejana-lesbian-feminist" poet and fiction writer Gloria Anzaldúa actually stands in terms of racial ideology when she uncritically upholds Vasconcelos as an advocate of "inclusivity" whose ideas present an antidote to the "racial purity that white America practices" (Anzaldúa, 1999:99). The schemes of thought behind *mestizaje* can have profoundly racist roots. Abdias do Nascimento has reacted precisely to this awareness in his assessment of the "Luso-Tropicalism" of Brazilian writers like Gilberto Freyre and Jorge Amado. He has decried their mystification of race mixture as a conceptual strategy that has done much to consolidate the misleading idea of racial democracy in Brazil. Freyre's model of *metarracial brunettism* insists on the extent to which Indian and African women, by becoming the domestics, concubines, and occasionally wives of the white masters, contributed meaningfully to the social democratization of Brazil, while Amado produces a scenario wherein the hypersexualized Black complements the reserved and rational white psyche (Nascimento, 1995:112, 113, 114).

Ultimately, the celebration of miscegenation as a harmonious blending of disparate ethnic elements that fuse into a new transracial Iberian American being underscores the assurance that the Caucasian ideal will continue to predominate and to regulate the place accorded to each of the constituent parts of the resulting aggregate entity. The mestizo model allows for the persistence of normative whiteness. The Caucasian ideal and an unbendingly Eurocentric definition of culture conceptually prevail in the configuration of the nation in public discourse. The prevalence of this scheme encounters little opposition in light of the "deeply-ingrained belief" among people of all colors in the region "that whites are naturally superior to all other races" (Moore, 1995:210). The rise of the mestizo as a conceptual paradigm creates an optical illusion that tricks nonwhite ethnic minorities into compliance with the white norm. Mestizo identity allows for acknowledgment of difference in theory while circumventing the need to practice de facto inclusion. Theoretical inclusion breeds tolerance for practical exclusion. With that mental scenario in place, Venezuelan society can admit to the racial heterogeneity of its population without necessarily discontinuing the practice of representing the visage of the nation through the homogeneously white women it sends to compete in the Miss Universe beauty pageant every year. Colombia, for its part, can celebrate diversity while continuing to render the Indian and Black segments of the population invisible, even after the 1991 constitution that took the radical step of recognizing that different ethnic groups actually existed in the country (Arocha, 1998:71). And the guardians of official Dominican culture can continue to prefer the 10 percent white over the 90 percent

Black and mulatto portion of the population to display the nation's face on the international stage.

Parting with Crime

We owe to our rootedness in American society, the arena par excellence of the struggle for multicultural inclusion and racial equality, that we possess what I would call a hyperethnicified perception that disposes us quickly to react to the deception inherent in the Latin American scenario just described. Nonwhite ethnic minorities in the United States have had to fight fiercely for the share of access or the level of empowerment they may now enjoy. That race is a social construction offers them no consolation. The truth of race for them, then, is concrete. Its implications impinge on their life chances and on the possibility of aspiring to a condition of prosperity. Our partaking in American society's overt racial contentiousness—affirmative action and the other compensatory measures inserted in the Civil Rights Act couldn't have more categorically admitted to the reality of that contentiousness—has sharpened our perception to the point that we can now look at Latin American social interactions and easily recognize the violence that the harmony posited by official discourse conceals. I do not refer here only to the moral violence sustained by large portions of the population that have to coexist in society with white supremacist configurations that systematically exclude their faces from visual representations of the nation. I refer also, and more importantly, to the economic, political, and, in not so few cases, genocidal violence that white supremacist formulations might encourage. Eurocentric and negrophobic definitions of Dominican national identity made it expedient for the Trujillo dictatorship in the fall of 1937 to murder several thousand unarmed, peaceful Haitian immigrants and their Dominican-born offspring in an effort to extirpate an unwanted ethnic element and strengthen the Dominicanness of the cities exposed to Haitian influence in the border zone (Vega, 1998:390–392).

A quarter of a century later, during a government led by civilians, Dominican society again witnessed the massacre of several thousand peasants in the village of Palma Sola, a section of San Juan de la Maguana, on December 28, 1962, again on account of safeguarding the "Christian values" and the economic, political, and cultural mores of the modern Dominican nation (Ferreras, 1983:318–320, 328, 332). The people slaughtered in Palma Sola were predominantly African-descended Dominicans, and their deaths did not provoke widespread indignation against the government for its evil, just as the living accomplices of Trujillo in the genocide of 1937, such as Balaguer, suffered no repudiation for their crime against humanity. Nor did the government led between 1996 and 2000 by Leonel Fernández Reyna of the Partido de la Liberación Dominicana, a party formerly known for its left-wing leanings, have to contend with collective reproach for the illegal and cruel practice of denying a birth certificate to the Dominican-born children of Haitian immigrants in order to keep them from effectively claiming Dominican citizenship, which the country's constitution, in keeping with the principle of jus soli, would automatically grant them. The Inter-American Commission on Human Rights of the Organization of

American States (1999:82), in an October 1999 report, expressed concern for the denial of "fundamental rights, such as the right to nationality of the country of birth, access to health care, and access to education," to "numerous children of Haitian origin." But instead the government took offense and proceeded to retaliate by deporting thousands of Haitians, and Cardinal Nicolás de Jesús López Rodríguez, the influential vicar of Christ in the land, came out in defense of the inhumane government. The vociferous archbishop of Santo Domingo declared, among other things, "We are a nation, and we have a Dominican identity, and we have a flag . . . we are Dominican and we wish to remain being that" (Feliz, 1999:1, 6). He added that all countries have "their own territory, their own citizenship, their own culture, their own language," and he decried what he believed to be a practice of Haitian women: near parturition they come to the Dominican Republic in order to give birth there and claim Dominican citizenship for their children (Figueroa, 1999).

When we think of the stateless, helpless, disempowered children of Haitians in Dominican society, lacking the birth certificate that would certify that they exist, and when we reflect on the plight of numerous other ethnically differentiated communities suffering unjust destitution throughout the countries of Latin America and the Caribbean, it behooves us to decide what to do. As U.S.-based scholars with a connection to the societies that perpetrate the atrocities in question, we have compelling reasons to care. White supremacy has been the conceptual glue that holds together the cultural logic of spoliation, discrimination, compulsory invisibility, and genocide in the hemisphere. Whether by preserving the exclusionary discourse of monoethnicity in the face of observable ethnic diversity or by paying lip service to pluralism while promoting a homogeneous picture of the visage of the nation, Eurocentric formulations of national culture and the seduction of the Caucasian ideal have given currency to schemes of thought that endanger the mental and physical well-being of distinct groups among the peoples of Latin America and the Caribbean. As a result of their adherence to ideologies that allow ethnic antipathy to creep into definitions of the nation, the region's intelligentsia became an accessory to serious crimes against Indians and Blacks. We must have that background firmly in mind when we undertake to tackle the issue of race and ethnicity in the Americas. We cannot allow the concern to remain strictly academic. We are inescapably involved in the subject of our inquiry. At the very least, we ought to explore the ways in which our efforts, our intellectual labor, could help to dismantle the pervasive schemes of thought that have made us permissive of the harm done to minorities in our ancestral lands. Lest we risk the sin of complicity, we should do the best we can to separate ourselves from racial crime.

Afro-Latinos and the Future

But let us not fall into the temptation of thinking that what's at stake in our confronting the legacy of Latin American racism is a purely moral imperative. We have equally powerful motivations associated with convenience and self-interest, with serious implications for the U.S. Hispanic population's own ability to achieve appropriate levels of economic and political empowerment. Racial tensions can obstruct the ability of nonwhite ethnic minorities with common needs to present a united front in their pursuit of shared goals in the United States. Frank Bonilla recently reminded us of the seriousness of interethnic distrust between Blacks and Latinos by pointing to the failure in the 1930s of the political leadership in both communities to seize control of the assembly seat in Manhattan's 17th District, even though Black and Latino voters outnumbered whites (Bonilla, 1995). Similarly, Suzanne Oboler has pointed to a comparable tension that in the Southwest during the 1960s may have prevented the likes of Chicano grassroots leader Reies López Tijerina, head of the Alianza Movement, from forging effective alliances with such African American activists as Martin Luther King Jr., leader of the civil rights movement (Oboler, 1995:63). Again, New York City in the 1990s witnessed the breakdown of communication between the political voices of the two communities, which no doubt contributed to the defeat of the first Black mayor in the history of the city, David N. Dinkins, in his bid for reelection and the rise of Rudolph Giuliani whose eight-year regime proved atrocious for Hispanic communities.

But beyond the question of impairing the ability of Latinos to forge salutary alliances with other ethnic groups, the issue of racial animosity has serious consequences for the various U.S. Hispanic communities to achieve intraethnic unity so as better to advance their common interests and increase their levels of empowerment in American society. I believe that our failure to look closely at the racial divide within the Latino population can have a grave debilitating impact on the political and economic initiatives that are predicated on the notion that Latinos constitute one community sharing a common sense of identity. Evelio Grillo's *Black Cuban, Black American: A Memoir* (2000), which narrates the author's experiences as a U.S.-born Black Cuban growing up in Tampa, Florida, in the 1930s, gives us an inkling of the white supremacist imaginary in the Latino community. For Grillo, the whites whose clubs he could not enter in the Jim Crow South all had Spanish surnames and Cuban ancestry. The Smith College sociologist Ginetta E. B. Candelario has unearthed an important chapter in the history of Dominican migration to the United States, shedding meaningful light on a rift that caused dark-skinned Dominicans who, having come to Washington, DC, in the 1940s as domestic servants to light-skinned diplomats and their families, embraced African American identity practices and segregated themselves from their elite compatriots (Candelario, 2000). Candelario cites Mariela Medina, a Black Dominican who, having attended Harvard University, became an articulate spokesperson for the concerns of her community. Medina understood that to insert oneself in civil rights agendas as a non–Puerto Rican or non–Mexican American Hispanic, a dark-skinned Dominican in Washington had to use the African American route (25).

Down These Mean Streets (1967), the harrowing autobiographical account of Piri Thomas's descent into and eventual escape from social hell, attests to the agony that some Black Puerto Ricans endured in New York and other cities after the great migration that followed the implementation of Operation Bootstrap in the island's economy. Poverty leads the young Piri to become involved in violence, theft, the perils of street gang life, and addictive drugs, but the most traumatic of the challenges he has to face is no doubt the internal turmoil that stems from his pronounced blackness, which sets him noticeably apart from his Caucasian-looking sibling, making it imperative for him to seek desperately for an identity comfort zone wherein to situate himself existentially. After a series of traumatic episodes in which Piri's Afrocentric self-assertion leads to his parting with the family, his brother José movingly voices his farewell saying, "Piri, I can't help what I am, or what I look like, or how I feel, any more than you can. You wanna be Black. You wanna find out if you can fit better. That's you. You're still my brother, if you can overlook my color. That's me" (P. Thomas, 1997:151). We no longer live in the world of rigid racial segregation evoked by Piri Thomas. Decades of struggle for racial justice in and outside the civil rights movement have not happened in vain. But dark-skinned Latinos in the United States still have to deal with a greater share of social impediments than their light-skinned counterparts. For, while most Hispanics typically have to contend with the structural barriers erected by mainstream American society, Black Latinos need to wrestle with additional obstacles born of the enduring legacy of Hispanic negrophobia.

I have elsewhere noted that anyone watching Hispanic TV in the United States will easily recognize the white supremacist value system that governs the way mass media corporations imagine the collective visage of the Latino community (Torres-Saillant, 2002:444–447). The *Washington Post* journalist Michael A. Fletcher has reported on "the rigid racial hierarchy" that controls "Spanish-language television in the United States," pointing to the "almost exclusively Caucasian face" that the industry puts forward (Fletcher, 2000). His article features the testimony of popular Spanish-language radio personality Malín Falu, a black-skinned Puerto Rican talk-show host who has repeatedly failed to land a job on Hispanic TV. The exclusion that Black Latinos have historically suffered—exception being made of course for the entertainment fields of boxing, baseball, some pop music forms, and other manifestations of what I would generically describe as the gladiator's arena—has resulted in the gradual development among dark-skinned Hispanics of a sense of self-recognition in their otherness vis-à-vis light-skinned Hispanics. As a result, in the 1990s we witnessed the emergence of the term *Afro-Latino* to designate a new category in the conceptual paradigms brandished by U.S. Hispanics to articulate their identity. The celebration in the fall of 1999 of distinctly Afro-Latino events in Washington, DC, at the Smithsonian Institution's National Portrait Gallery and at the White House speaks to the growing visibility of African-descended Latinos as a differentiated constituency in American society.

A persuasive indication that Latinos have a very real possibility of overturning the nefarious legacy of negrophobia that they inherit from their ancestral Latin American homelands, which they supplement with the white supremacist heritage indigenous to Anglo-American society, is the way U.S. Dominicans interact with Haitians in New York and other American cities where the two communities share space. The history of the animosity between the two nations that occupy the island of Hispaniola, the Republic of Haiti and the Dominican Republic, has been competently evoked in journalist Michelle Wucker's *Why the Cocks Fight* (1999). But the shared marginality that Haitians and Dominicans endure in the United States seems to awaken both groups to the realization of their commonality. At least the young in colleges and universities throughout the Northeast and in New York community organizations have given compelling evidence of a radically new understanding of Haitian-Dominican rapport. At City College of the City University of New York, for instance, the Haitian and Dominican student associations shared the same office space and supported each other's activities throughout the 1980s. In the fall of 1997 Haitian and Dominican students at Cornell University joined in an effort to celebrate their heritage, featuring, among the highlights, readings by Haitian American best-selling author Edwidge Danticat and her Dominican American counterpart Junot Diaz. I served as keynote speaker in fall 1998 during the fifth anniversary of the joint gala organized by the Haitian-American Students Association and Casa Dominicana at the University of Massachusetts–Amherst. More strikingly still, in February 1999, the members of the Manhattan-based Dominican organization Centro Cultural Orlando Martínez brought together Haitian writers, speakers, and performers for a joint commemoration of the 155th anniversary of Dominican independence. Since Dominicans founded their sovereign state by separating themselves from Haitian rule, one can imagine the many ideological hurdles the organizers had to overcome in the process of conceiving a way of commemorating Dominican independence that steered clear of antipathy toward their nation's political other.

I am convinced that U.S. Dominicans' more humanized rapport with Haitians, breaking with their ancestral homeland's inimical construction of their neighbors, has to do in large measure with their enhanced appreciation of the African heritage that connects them to the people of Haiti. The racial history of this country soon awakens Dominicans to their marginality with respect to mainstream society, making it untenable for them to engage in strategies of othering toward other African-descended communities. They also recognize their relative marginality with respect to the larger segments of the U.S. Hispanic population, namely Mexican Americans, Cubans, and Puerto Ricans who tend to be lighter-skinned. In other words, their self-recognition as Afro-Latinos contributes to their greater solidarity with the Haitian community. By the same token, a comparable dynamic could contribute to bridging the communication gap between U.S. Hispanics and African Americans in the public sphere. The emergence of the self-recognition of Afro-Latinos as members of a differentiated ethnoracial constituency places them in an ideal position to mediate with the Black community. Their negroid phenotype can open them to doors of communication with African Americans. The mediating role of Afro-Latinos, coupled with the persuasive espousal of Black symbols and urban youth culture within the Hispanic population, may very well hold the key to a salutary future in the relationship between Latinos and African Americans. By looking closely at the specific experience of Afro-Latinos and drawing the lessons contained therein, the Latino scholar will contribute to shedding light on one of the most serious impediments to the community's collective advancement: namely, intra-Latino racism. Without an understanding of that unsavory phenomenon, Latinos have a very slim chance of making a meaningful contribution to social justice either in the United States or in their ancestral Latin American homelands, with the result that their protesting any instances of exclusion from participation in the benefits of full citizenship will have trouble commanding credibility.

References

Alvarez, Julia. 2000. *In the Name of Salomé: A Novel*. Chapel Hill, NC: Algonquin Books of Chapel Hill.

Anzaldúa, Gloria. 1999. *Borderlands/La Frontera: "The New Mestiza."* 2nd ed. San Francisco: Aunt Lute Books.

Arocha, Jaime. 1998. Inclusion of Afro-Colombians: Unreachable national goal. *Latin American Perspectives* 25 (3):70–89.

Bolivar, Simon. 1951. *Selected Writings of Bolivar*. Vol. 1. Ed. Harold A. Bierck and trans. Lewis Bertrand. New York: Colonial Press.

Bollinger, William, and Daniel Manny Lund. 1994. Minority oppression: Toward analyses that clarify and strategies that liberate. In *Race and Ethnicity in Latin America*, ed. Jorge I. Domínguez, 218–244. New York: Garland Publishing.

Brand-Williams, Oralandar. 2000. Oklahoma raises hopes for slavery reparations. *Detroit News*, February 6.

Bonilla, Frank. 1995. Urban challenges for Blacks and Latinos in the 1990s: Strategies of contention and collaboration. Paper presented at Collaboration and Contentions Among African Americans and Latinos: A Working Conference, Center for Urban Economic Development, University of Illinois at Chicago, September 7–9.

Calderón G., Fernando. 1977. The Quechua and Aymará peoples in the formation and development of Bolivian society. In *Race and Class in Post-Colonial Society*, ed. UNESCO. Paris: UNESCO.

Candelario, Gineta E. B. 2000. Situating ambiguity: Dominican identity formations. Ph.D. diss., City University of New York.

Díaz Quiñones, Arcadio. 1984. Pedro Henríquez Ureña: Modernidad, diáspora y construcción de identidades. In *Modernización e identidades sociales*, ed. Gilberto Giménez and Ricardo Pozas H., 59–117. Mexico: Universidad Autónoma de Mexico.

Duras, Marguerite. 1993. We must share the crime. Trans. D. G. Luthinger. In *On Prejudice: A Global Perspective*, ed. Daniela Gioseffi, 83. New York: Anchor Books.

Dzidzienyo, Anani. 1995. Conclusions. In *No Longer Invisible: Afro-Latin Americans Today*, ed. Minority Rights Group, 345–358. London: Minority Rights Publications.

ECLAC. 2000. Indigenous and Afro-American people live in Poverty. *ECLAC Notes* (newsletter of the United Nations Economic Commission for Latin America and the Caribbean) 13 (November):1, 6.

Feliz, Raysa. 1999. Cardenal pide Gobierno no tema a EEUU. *Hoy*, November 1.

Ferguson, J. Halcro. 1961. *Latin America: The Balance of Race Redressed*. London: Oxford University Press.

Ferreras, Ramón Alberto. 1983. *Negros*. Vol. 4. Serie Media Isla. Santo Domingo: Editorial del Nordeste.

Figueroa, Manuel. 1999. Dijo que le gustaría que la propuesta de la OEA. *El Siglo*, November 1.

Fletcher, Michael A. 2000. Latino actors cite color barrier in U.S. *Boston Sunday Globe*, August 6.

Griffin-Nolan, Ed. 2000. The long hard road. *IRC News* (newsletter of the InterReligious Council of Central New York), May, 1, 7.

Grillo, Evelio. 2000. *Black Cuban, Black American: A Memoir*. Ed. Kenya Dworkin y Mendez. Houston: Arte Público Press.

Guevara Arzu, Roy. 1995. The Garifunas in Honduras. In *African Presence in the Americas*, ed. Carlos Moore, Tanya Sanders, and Shawna Moore, 241–248. Trenton, NJ: Africa World Press.

Hayner, Priscilla. 1998. Truth commissions: Exhuming the past. *NACLA Report on the Americas* 32 (2):30–32.

Henríquez Ureña, Pedro. 1978. *La utopía de América*, ed. Angel Rama and Rafael Gutiérrez Girardot. Caracas: Biblioteca Ayacucho.

————. 1982. *El español en Santo Domingo*. 4th ed. Santo Domingo: Editora Taller.

Inter-American Commission on Human Rights. 1999. *Report on the Situation of Human Rights in the Dominican Republic*. Washington, DC: Organization of American States.

Levine, Robert M. 1980. *Race and Ethnic Relations in Latin America and the Caribbean: An Historical Dictionary and Bibliography*. Metuchen, NJ: Scarecrow Press.

López, Kleiner, and Manuel Azcona. 1999. López Rodríguez: Los hijos de haitianos son haitianos. *Listín Diario*, November 8, A1, 4.

Marañón, Gregorio. 1948. Prólogo. In *Los mestizos de América*, by José Pérez de Barradas, i–v. Madrid: Cultura Clásica y Moderna.

Marquez, Roberto. 2000. Raza, racismo, e historia: "Are all my bones from there?" Keynote address, Symposium on Afro-Latinos and the Issue of Race in the New Millennium, Brooklyn College, City University of New York, October 21.

Martínez-Echazábal, Lourdes. 1998. *Mestizaje* and the discourse of national/cultural identity in Latin America, 1845–1959. *Latin American Perspectives* 25 (3):21–42.

Moore, Carlos. 1995. Afro-Cubans and the Communist revolution. In *African Presence in the Americas*, ed. Carlos Moore, Tanya R. Sanders, and Shawna Moore, 199–239. Trenton, NJ: Africa World Press.

Moraga, Cherrie. 2000. City of desire: An interview with Cherrie Moraga. In *Latina Self-Portraits: Interviews with Contemporary Women Writers*, ed. Bridget Kevane and Juanita Heredia, 97–108. Albuquerque: University of New Mexico Press

————. 1999. A long line of vendidas. In *Border Texts: Cultural Readings for Contemporary Writers*, ed. Randall Bass, 144–160. Boston and New York: Houghton Mifflin Company.

Mörner, Magnus. 1961. *El mestizaje en la historia de Ibero-América*. Comisión de Historia. Mexico, D.F.: Instituto Panamericano de Historia y Geografía.

Nascimento, Abdias do. 1995. The African experience in Brazil. In *African Presence in the Americas*, ed. Carlos Moore, Tanya R. Sanders, and Shawna Moore, 97–117. Trenton, NJ: Africa World Press.

Neruda, Pablo. 1962. Oda a Paul Robeson. In *Obras completas*, 1230–1238. 2nd ed. Buenos Aires: Editorial Losada.

Oboler, Suzanne. 1995. *Ethnic Labels, Latino Lives: Identity and the Politics of (Re)Presentation in the United States*. Minneapolis and London: University of Minnesota Press.

Rodríguez-Julia, Edgardo. 1981. *Las tribulaciones de Jonás*. San Juan: Ediciones Huracán.

Rosaldo, Renato, and William V. Flores. 1997. Identity, conflict, and evolving Latino communities: Cultural citizenship in San Jose, California. In *Latino Cultural Citizenship: Claiming Identity, Space, and Rights*, ed. William V. Flores and Rina Benmayor, 57–59. Boston: Beacon Press.

Ruble, Renee. 2000. Victims of America's worst race riot to be compensated: Up to 300 killed in 1921 rampage in Tulsa, Oklahoma. *Ottawa Citizen*, February 5.

Thomas, Laurence, trans. 1997. The declaration of repentance of the Church of France [La 'déclaration de repentance' de l'Eglise de France], *Le Monde*, October 1.

Thomas, Piri. 1997. *Down These Mean Streets*. New York: Vintage Books.

Torres-Saillant, Silvio. 2002. Problematic paradigms: Racial diversity and corporate identity in the Latino community. In *Latinos: Remaking America*, ed. Marcelo M. Suárez-Orozco and Mariela Paez, 435–455. Berkeley, Los Angeles, and London: University of California Press and David Rockefeller Center for Latin American Studies/Harvard.

————. 1999. *El retorno de las yolas: Ensayos sobre diaspora, democracia y dominicanidad*. Santo Domingo: Ediciones Librería La Trinitaria & Editora Manatí.

————. 1998. The tribulations of blackness: Stages in Dominican racial identity. *Latin American Perspectives* 25 (3):126–146.

Vasconcelos, José. 1997. *The Cosmic Race/La raza cósmica*, ed. and trans. Didier T. Jaén. Afterword by Joseba Gabilondo. Baltimore and London: Johns Hopkins University Press.

Vega, Bernardo. 1998. *Trujillo y Haiti (1930–1937)*. Vol. 1. Santo Domingo: Fundación Cultural Dominicana.

Vieira, Rosángela Maria. 1995. Brazil. In *No Longer Invisible: Afro-Latin Americans Today*, ed. Minority Rights Group, 19–46. London: Minority Rights Publications.

Weisman, Alan, and Sandy Tolan. 1993. Central America: Vanishing forests, endangered peoples. In *On Prejudice: A Global Perspective*, ed. Daniela Gioseffi, 221–225. New York: Anchor Books.

Winn, Peter. 1999. *Americas: The Changing Face of Latin America and the Caribbean*. Berkeley: University of California Press.

Wucker, Michelle. 1999. *Why the Cocks Fight: Dominicans, Haitians, and the Struggle for Hispaniola*. New York: Hill and Wang.

Yardley, Jim. 2000. Panel recommends reparations in long-ignored Tulsa race riot. *New York Times*, February 5.

Appendix

Witnessing History: An Octogenarian Reflects on Fifty Years of African American–Latino Relations

Nelson Peery

The people, the masses, are the foundation of democracy. Our people—Black, brown, and white—have a history of struggling for unity and democracy. It is much more than a moral question. They understand that if they are to achieve the necessities of a decent life, they must unite and struggle together. This history is often overlooked in favor of the more dramatic instances of disunity. In fact, in my experience and direct involvement in Black-Latino relations across the country, I have found that it is only the fear of being marginalized by the other group that compels African Americans and Latinos alike to band together on the basis of color or language in defense of their particular interests and to the exclusion of the other group. This disunity is the firmest foundation of an exploitative system that is crushing them both.

My introduction to African American–Latino relations was violent and ugly. In 1949 Cleveland's ghetto was bursting at the seams. Natural barriers such as railroad tracks and industrial belts prevented its expansion to the west. The city center was to the north. The more affluent Blacks were slowly pushing south as the adjacent Jewish community sold out and moved to the suburbs. To the east, across wide Carnegie Avenue, was a working-class community of Appalachian whites and Puerto Ricans. It was the natural direction for the crowded Blacks to expand.

Before World War II Puerto Rican migration to the mainland United States was discouraged if not forbidden. During the war Cleveland's steel mills, desperate for labor, sent recruiters to the island colony. They brought back only the most light-skinned Puerto Ricans, who were told they were white and who acted accordingly in relation to Black people.

Before migrants and immigrants learn the Pledge of Allegiance they learn that the African American is at the bottom of the social and economic ladder in the United States. If they wanted to become an American and not join African Americans at the bottom, then they had to join in the oppression of Blacks. The Appalachians and Puerto Ricans united against the Blacks.

There were violent clashes when African Americans crossed Carnegie looking for a decent place to live. Toward the end of summer a Black man was killed. As the news reached the tavern where I was having an evening beer, the pent-up frustrations exploded. The tavern emptied into a growing crowd running across Carnegie where the group of murderers stood celebrating their kill. For five or six brutal hate-filled minutes we beat and cursed and stomped them. As the police approached we fled back to the safety of the ghetto. Like most African Americans, I had no idea where Puerto Rico was or who lived there. Whoever they were, I placed them alongside the rest of the immigrant poor who hated us more than they loved democracy.

A few years later I left the Midwest and went to Dunkirk, New York, to work on a construction project. An agricultural town dependent on migrant labor, Dunkirk was rigidly segregated. The Puerto Rican and Black workers were restricted to a large rooming house, which had a tavern and restaurant on the first floor. The menu included arroz con pollo and collard greens with smoked pig knuckles. The jukebox alternately blared Chuck Berry and Puerto Rican music. At the bar a brown-skinned young man introduced himself as Arturo, a student from Puerto Rico. After explaining that he worked in the fields every year in order to continue his education, he proposed to teach me Spanish if I would help him with his English.

I learned a lot more than Spanish from Arturo. When the job was done and I returned to Cleveland, I had reformulated my favorite slogan to "When the workers have nothing to lose but their chains, they can unite."

There are issues that bring African Americans together with Latinos, just as some issues create obstacles to alliances. The issues that bring Latinos and African Americans together arise not only from discrimination based on color but also from economic status: they constitute such a large part of the lowest economic class. Their concrete problems cannot be solved on the basis of nationality or color alone, or on the basis of class alone. When agents of the ruling class skillfully counterpoise class with nationality, very little, with and often nothing, is won. For example, I remember my pre–World War II experiences as an agricultural worker. Whites, Mexicans, and Blacks seldom worked together. The whites got the best jobs, such as working with the peaches or oranges; Mexicans got the lettuce and such. The African Americans got the cotton and the very hard labor associated with preparing for the next planting.

But jobs, education, housing, health care, police brutality, and the justice system are common concerns for African Americans and Latinos. These concerns in and of themselves cannot bring the groups together. They will come together only when leaders make the necessary effort to bring them together.

I

During the 1950s anyone who fought for interracial unity along class lines was automatically branded a Communist—and with good reason. The Communist Party was effective because, almost alone, it could and did raise the demand for racial equality within all the races and nationality groups. By 1958 the international movement was in disarray. The American Communist Party split into contending factions. One of the largest, which contained most of the Black and Latino comrades, was called the Provisional Organizing Committee—the POC. When differences within the party became irreconcilable, the POC walked out with the intention of forming a new Communist party. A few months later, during an acrimonious meeting of the POC, most of the Blacks and Puerto Ricans aligned themselves on one side and most of the whites on the other. The POC split when almost all the white comrades walked out of the meeting. Since they had been functionaries with years of experience in running a party, the clear message was that contrary to their nonwhite comrades, they were the ones who understood organization. There was a moment of confused silence as our hopes and dreams shattered. Armando Román, a former officer in the Communist Party and the only remaining elected official of the POC, slowly got up and went to the podium. Staring through his thick glasses, he said, "I don't see anything here but niggers and spics. Do you think we can build a Communist Party?" The shocked silence gave way to an excited, adrenal-pumping cheer. Yes! We who were the demonstrators, the leaflet passers. Yes! We who were used to having the educated white comrades explain everything to us. Yes! We who filled the jails. Yes! We who fought the cops and the scabs. Yes! We who can't speak English or butchered it with our "dis" and "dat." Yes! We can build a party that will liberate our peoples and bring peace on earth. It was the most exciting moment of my life as we cheered and pounded one another on the back. It was the first time that such a section of the working class had made such an effort.

This unity of Blacks and Latinos manifested itself in several ways. We produced a paper to fight those at home and abroad who betrayed the revolution. We organized ourselves to learn Marxism. What we lacked in formal education we made up for in effort. After work, before going home, my group would meet to make sure we understood the lesson to be discussed that night. There was Curo, the old Basque who was still fighting Franco's fascists; there was José, the carpenter, and Harold who shoveled shit at the city sanitation department. There was Lucy who pounded a typewriter somewhere. Anabelle lived to see Haiti free, and Sandy who, totally blacklisted, eked out a living selling newspapers. Undaunted, we opened *Capital* and grappled with Marx's weaver and tailor until we understood surplus value. On Saturday afternoons we put up our soapbox in Spanish Harlem, and Black revolutionaries talked to, and answered the questions of, the Puerto Rican people. In the evening we moved to 125th and Lenox and Puerto Rican revolutionaries talked to the Black folk of Harlem. Malcolm X came and listened for a while and the next week the Black Muslims set up their soapbox. We moved down the street to avoid any friction.

II

Coming home from work, I would exit the subway station at 137th and enter the Siboney Café for one of their delicious blender-made drinks. The café was always full of young people engaged in earnest discussion. When the waiter asked what type of drink I wanted, I told him the only tropical fruit I could think of: "I'll take papaya." There were snickers and muffled laughter. I looked around wondering what I had said wrong. One of the young women leaned out of her booth and, accompanied by the laughter of the rest, explained in a heavy Dominican accent why I could not say papaya, I had to say *fruta bomba* in public. I turned to the waiter: "I like papaya. Bring me papaya." When the laughter died down, we all exchanged names and shook hands. Cubans, Dominicans, Puerto Ricans, they were all with the 26th of July Movement. After a few months they insisted that I join them. I did.

When Fidel came to address the United Nations, he moved into the Hotel Theresa at 125th Street, thwarting the government's attempt to isolate him. Fidel knew that unity with the African Americans was the most reliable base of support for revolutionary Cuba. At the Siboney we made plans to demonstrate. After a few phone calls a conga line of perhaps fifty people formed on 138th and Broadway. Turning and dancing, singing "Cuba, sí, Cuba, sí, Cuba, sí, sí, sí-sí-sí!" my black-skinned Dominican comrade Alias from the POC led the line. Down Broadway we danced, picking up Latinos at every corner. Then east on 125th and the line grew longer and blacker. African Americans were already milling around the hotel as the conga line of several hundred arrived. Shouts of "Lumumba! Lumumba!" merged with "Fidel! Fidel!" Someone began to beat on a set of conga drums. Blacks and Latinos shimmied and danced and hugged. Fidel opened a window, waved, and threw us kisses. It was pandemonium! Even the cops seemed to be doing the conga as they gently urged us to disperse and open 125th Street to traffic.

The newspapers showed pictures of Fidel and his group in Harlem, bringing into full view a historic event which transcended Black-Latino relations.

The old Puerto Rican independence movement had a firm grip on the politics of Spanish Harlem. The POC played an important role in breaking that isolation and making common cause with the African Americans. In hindsight, I believe that this was the key, decades later, to the election of David Dinkins, New York's first Black mayor. It was a time when Black and Latino political cooperation bore fruit and concretized efforts that came from a long and complicated history.

As sometimes happens in the revolutionary movement, Armando Román became a counterrevolutionary and POC disintegrated. Sometimes the good that men do lives after them, and the years of POC proved that with vision, with lofty goals, with cadres firmly planted in both arenas, it is possible to bridge the problems of language and culture. My time in New York convinced me that the people want to unite. They want to dance together in the streets.

III

The 1965 uprising in Watts, California, was the beginning of a new era for the various minorities. What, then, is the historical significance of Watts? Before Watts there was no great class differentiation in the African American community, at least in California. Twenty-seven years before Watts, 98 percent of African Americans lived in official poverty. The African American people were "led" by the politically compromised, dependent "Black bourgeoisie." This tiny class dominated the Black mass organizations and, having close ties with the power structure, expressed its social and political perspectives. By 1965 economic, political, and social forces had combined to make this old way of governing untenable. The mechanization of southern agriculture and the consequent demographic shifting of the African Americans from scattered rural groups to concentrations in the northern inner cities demanded a new method of control. More importantly, politicized by the independence of African countries, the war in Vietnam, the cold war rhetoric about freedom and human rights, and the freedom struggles in the South, the African Americans would no longer accept the old way of being governed.

I lived in the heart of Watts, across the street from the Jordan Downs housing project. I belonged to a revolutionary organization, the Provisional Organizing Committee, made up primarily of Black and Puerto Rican revolutionaries. At that time we were the only active entity based in Watts. The influence of the NAACP, the Urban League, and even the L.A. police and fire departments stopped at the boundaries of Watts. Therefore, as the fighting broke out, leadership slipped momentarily into the hands of the Black proletariat. As they had no channels of communication with the power structure, their only tactic was to meet violence with violence. At its most intense point some seventy thousand people were in the streets. It took the equivalent of three army infantry divisions to contain them. The cost in lives, property destruction, and damage to U.S. prestige in the middle of the cold war was enormous.

The U.S. economy was no longer dependent on serflike agricultural manual labor, or on the social order (segregation, discrimination, and lynch law) that it had created. The government attempted to maintain control in two ways. On the one hand, it tried to politically weaken and disorient the newly self-conscious Black proletariat. On the other, through government programs, it attempted to expand and strengthen the tiny, but vocal Black petite bourgeoisie, who established a political and economic base reinforced by cultural nationalism. This nationalism separated them from their immediate and most important ally—the Latino population.

Something new was happening in the United States. Millions of people—not just African Americans—were struggling against the inequalities and injustices of the system. The Watts rebellion galvanized them into a different level of activity. New cultural nationalist movements—Chicano, Native American, Puerto Rican—new forms of the youth movement, such as Students for a Democractic Society, the Black Panthers, the Young Lords, and the Brown Berets, and a new women's movement developed. We tried hard to develop that unity. But the government had other ideas and the resources to implement them. Suddenly huge amounts of money were up for grabs. Who was going to get it? The Blacks could get it if they prevented the Latinos from getting it and vice versa. Suddenly there were fortunes to be made fighting poverty and racism. The secret was not to let it become a class fight. The old ideological nationalism was revived.

IV

In 1974 I moved to Chicago, which, in my view, is the most working-class of American cities. It was a prime target of Black migration and the number two destination for immigrant Mexicans. If there could ever be unity between Latinos and Blacks it would happen here. As we got into that struggle, we learned two things right away. First, there were murderous criminal elements embedded in Chicago politics and nothing less than a mass movement could challenge them. Second, standing in the way of creating that mass movement were the Black and Latino political gangs that were part of Mayor Richard Daley's machine. Their access to the pork barrel depended upon the two groups being permanently kept apart and competing with each other. This way, the need for forging a united front against their common oppression, would not arise.

A series of events, beginning with the death of Mayor Daley, made it possible for Harold Washington to run for mayor of the city. Harold was a respected, seasoned politician. As a councilman he fought for unity and had a base in both communities. He was more than a familiar figure in the Mexican neighborhood of Pilsen or on the streets of historically Black South Chicago. Harold presented a vision of a new Chicago to the people, one that was free of the corruption and race hatred that so disfigure our city. This vision made the rallies, the wine and cheese parties, and the neighborhood get-togethers places where the Latinos and Blacks mingled easily, smiled, and shook hands. The events around Harold Washington's campaign and election show that the people are more ready to sacrifice for vision than for personal gain.

The Mexican American activist Rudy Lozano, at thirty-five, was already an important leader in this fight. In an effort to thwart this vision, this unity that might have changed Chicago, gun-wielding thugs broke into Lozano's home and murdered him in front of his family. The community held firm in its desire for unity, and Harold was elected.

V

African American and Latino relations do not exist in a vacuum. These relations are affected by events in the Caribbean and in Central and South America. The African Americans judge international events by the same yardstick they use to judge local politicians and events: Have they helped the Black people achieve equality? The outstanding example in this respect was the Cuban Revolution. Some Black nationalists launched a campaign (with, perhaps, official U.S. help) to discredit the revolution because it could not overcome the legacy of slavery immediately. The declaration by President Castro that Cuba was not only Latin but also African (i.e., Black) resonated among African Americans and created Black support for Cuba.

What we witnessed in the 1960s and 1980s is perhaps being played out anew as we contemplate events related to Hugo Chavez and the Bolivarian revolution in Venezuela today. Relatively few Blacks knew anything about the Venezuelan social struggles until the press carried an article about the establishment of an African Venezuelan university. Suddenly sectors of Black America discovered the large African Venezuelan minority, and several delegations have gone to Venezuela, met with President Chavez, and returned with glowing accounts of progress. The fact that the opposition has referred to Chavez as "the nigger" has, of course, galvanized African American support.

This yardstick also applies to the situation in Brazil. African Americans have long considered Brazil the "best" country in the Americas. The election of Lula, his inclusive policies, and his resistance to American diktat have made even broader sections of the African Americans aware of and sympathetic to Latin America as a whole. This was also shown when Cuahtemoc Cárdenas visited Chicago before his first presidential campaign. Cárdenas shrewdly made a point of visiting the African American community and colleges with large Black student bodies. I was happy to give what assistance I could. I was subsequently invited to the First Congress of the Revolutionary Democratic Party (PDR). At the congress I was treated with a courtesy that I could not imagine receiving in the United States. Cárdenas took a few moments from his busy schedule to chat with me. My picture with him is one of my most treasured mementos.

VI

The leveling effects of poverty, combined with the activities of visionary leaders on both sides, have created some historic examples of Blacks and Latinos' fight for unity. The cross-county march of the Texas Farm Workers Union is a prime example of the way that struggles for unity consistently remain unpublicized. During the 1970s Antonio Orendain, the Texas director of the United Farm Workers (UFW), defended and wanted to organize undocumented Mexican workers. The UFW leadership opposed him. A bitter struggle ensued; and the Texas Farm Workers left the UFW and formed a separate union. In 1977, in an effort to call attention to their serflike conditions, the TFW organized a march from Austin, Texas, to Washington, DC. Orendain, who militantly believed in interracial unity among the farmworkers, purposely took a route through the heart of the Black Belt of the South. Along that 1,600-mile route the marchers were befriended, fed, sheltered, and assisted by the impoverished Black sharecroppers and farm laborers in Louisiana, Mississippi, Georgia, and the Carolinas. Wherever they stopped, Black ministers would go ahead to the next town and arrange food, shelter, and protection from the Klan, which threatened them all along the way. The press, in favor of publicizing some gang fight, ignored such unity by "men of the soil."

Today, relations between African Americans and Latinos are approaching a critical moment. The rapid growth of the Latino minority presents us with a two-edged sword. There is a tendency for the Latino nationalists to feel strong enough to "go it alone." Conversely, the Black nationalists are putting out feelers to see if they can maintain their traditional status by becoming a counterbalance to the growing political and economic clout of the Mexican minority in particular. This was clearly shown in the Los Angeles elections when the African American political structure in South Central joined with reactionary whites to defeat the mayoral candidacy of the Mexican American politician Villaraigosa.

I believe that there is a natural class instinct to unite. But instinct is not enough, for the omnipresent system stands against it. There must be organizations based on the interests of the class to which most Blacks and Latinos belong. The Latino and African

American minorities make up the core of a new and decisive class, which is working at part-time, contingency, and minimum-wage jobs. They are poor and getting poorer. They cannot make demands exclusively for Latinos or Blacks. Their every demand is in the interests of their entire class. Conversely, that class cannot unite without struggling to resolve the particular problems of each of these minorities. To a great extent the future of our country rests on concretizing this unity.

NOTES ON THE CONTRIBUTORS

Mark Anderson is Assistant Professor of Anthropology at the University of California Santa Cruz. He received his Ph.D. at the University of Texas and held a Harper Fellowship at the University of Chicago. His research examines the intersection between identity politics within nation-states and transnational processes of cultural exchange and racial identification. He is currently working on a manuscript tentatively titled *Indigenous Rights and African Diasporas: The Politics of Identity among Garifuna in Honduras*. He is also developing a comparative analysis of the relations between Afro-Latino and indigenous social movements in Honduras and other Latin American countries.

John J. Betancur teaches urban planning and policy at the University of Illinois at Chicago (UIC). Previously he worked at universities in Colombia, Latino nonprofits in Chicago, and UIC's Center for Urban Economic Development. His research moved from squatter settlements and strategies of reproduction of the urban poor through community economic development, to, most recently, the impact of globalization and gentrification on underrepresented groups and Black-Latino relations. He coedited *The Collaborative City: Opportunities and Struggles for Blacks and Latinos in U.S. Cities* (Garland, 2000). He has published in multiple journals and edited books in Latin America and the United States.

José E. Cruz is Associate Professor of Political Science at the University at Albany, State University of New York. He is the author of *Identity and Power: Puerto Rican Politics and the Challenge of Ethnicity* (Temple University Press, 1998) and, with Edna Acosta-Belén et al., of *Adiós Borinquen Querida: The Puerto Rican Diaspora, Its History and Contributions* (CELAC, 2000). His book on Puerto Rican politics in New York City from 1960 to 1990 will be published by University Press of Florida in 2005.

Carlos de la Torre is Associate Professor of Sociology at Northeastern University and Profesor-Investigador at FLACSO-Ecuador. His research has focused on racism in *Latin America* and on populism. His latest publications are *Afroquiteños: Ciudadanía y Racismo (CAAP, 2002), Populist Seduction in Latin America* (Ohio University Press, 2000), and *El Racismo en Ecuador: Experiencias de los Indios de Clase Media* (CAAP, 1996).

Jorge Duany is Professor of Anthropology at the University of Puerto Rico in Río Piedras. He previously served as Director of *Revista de Ciencias Sociales* and as Visiting Professor of Latino Studies at the University of Michigan. He earned his Ph.D. in Latin American Studies, specializing in anthropology, at the University of California, Berkeley. He has published extensively on Caribbean migration, ethnic identity, and popular culture in Puerto Rico, the United States, Europe, Latin America, and the Caribbean. His most recent book is *The Puerto Rican Nation on the Move: Identities on the Island and in the United States* (2002).

Ariel Dulitzky is Senior Human Rights Specialist at the Inter-American Commission on Human Rights of the Organization of American States. Previously Mr. Dulitzky was the Latin America Program Director at the International Human Rights Law Group where he designed and implemented a program on racial discrimination in Brazil and promoted the participation of Afro–Latin American organizations in the Third World Conference against Racism. Mr. Dulitzky received his law degree from the University of Buenos Aires in 1990 and an L.L.M. from Harvard Law School in 1999. He has published extensively on human rights and racial discrimination in Latin America.

Anani Dzidzienyo is Associate Professor of Africana Studies and Portuguese and Brazilian Studies at Brown University. His publications include *The Position of Blacks in Brazilian Society* (1979); "Activity and Inactivity in the Politics of Afro-Latin America" (1978); "The African Connection and Afro-Brazilian Social Mobility," in P. M. Fontaine, ed., *Race, Class, and Power in Brazil* (1985); "Os Brasileiros no Contexto Nacional e Internacional," in *Desigualdades Raciais no Brasil Contemporaneo* (1992), edited by Peggy Lovell; "Brazilian Race Relations: Old Problems/New Ideas?" (1993); the conclusion to *No Longer Invisible: Blacks in Latin America* (1995); and "Ex Africa Semper Aliquid Novi" in *Black Culture in Brazil*, edited by Randall Johnson and Larry Crook (1999).

Kevin R. Johnson is Associate Dean for Academic Affairs and Professor of Law and Chicana/o Studies at the University of California at Davis. He has published extensively on immigration law and policy, racial identity, and civil rights. His book *How Did You Get to Be Mexican? A White/Brown Man's Search for Identity* was published in 1999 and was nominated for the 2000 Robert F. Kennedy Book Award. He also has published *Race, Civil Rights, and American Law: A Multiracial Approach and Mixed Race America and the Law: A Reader*. His latest book, *The "Huddled Masses" Myth: Immigration and Civil Rights*, was published early this year. A graduate of Harvard Law School, he clerked for the Honorable Stephen Reinhardt of the U.S. Court of Appeals for the Ninth Circuit.

Louis Herns Marcelin is Director of Research, Family and Youth Community Research Center, Inc. He is on the Research Faculty of the Department of Anthropology and Department of Epidemiology and Public Health at the University of Miami.

Nancy Raquel Mirabal is Associate Professor of Raza Studies at San Francisco State University. She has published articles on the early history of Afro-Cuban diasporic communities in the United States and on the production and uses of blackness and Latinidad. She is currently coediting a volume on Latina/o theoretical reformulations, entitled *Techn/futuros: Genealogy, Power, and Desire*, and directing, with Richard Candida Smith, a collaborative community oral history of gentrification in the Mission District.

Suzanne Oboler is Associate Professor of Latin American and Latino Studies at the University of Illinois at Chicago. Her current research focuses on racism, citizenship, and national belonging in the Americas, and on the transnational experience of first- and second-generation South Americans and other Latinos in the United States. She is the founding editor of the international academic journal *Latino Studies* (Palgrave Press) and coeditor, with Deena González, of the forthcoming four-volume *Encyclopedia on Latinos and Latinas in the United States*. Her publications include *Ethnic Labels, Latino Lives: Identity and the Politics of (Re)Presentation* and *Changing Citizenship: Latinos in U.S. Society Today* (forthcoming).

Nelson Peery is author of the award-winning memoir *Black Fire: The Making of an American Revolutionary*. The book describes his years growing up in rural Minnesota as the son of a postal worker in the only African American family in the town, and his years in the U.S. Army. He wrote *Black Fire* because no one had told the story of the Black soldier during World War II and he wanted to set the record straight. He also wanted to show how a person becomes a revolutionary from life experience. Since his youth in Minnesota, Mr. Peery has not been a stranger to fighting for social change, justice, and equality. His initiation into the struggle came through the defense of the Scottsboro boys. Throughout his life, he has come to know America—his hobo days took him to every back country road of this country, while his years as a bricklayer took him to major cities such as New York, Los Angeles, Ohio, and Chicago, where he built their skyscrapers. While he is a proud union cardholder, his life has been dedicated to making real change in America. He is a founding member of the League of Revolutionaries for a New America. His other books include *The Future Is Up to Us* and *Moving Onward: From Racial Division to Class Unity*. He has published numerous essays and articles on African American liberation, the global economy, and a vision of a new cooperative America. His articles appear in the *People's Tribune/Tribuno del Pueblo* newspaper.

Mark Sawyer holds appointments as Assistant Professor in the Department of Political Science and the Ralph J. Bunche Institute for African American Studies at UCLA. He is currently on leave until 2005 as a postdoctoral fellow in the Robert Wood Johnson Foundation Scholars in Health Policy Program at the University of California at Berkeley. He has published articles and reviews in, among others, the *Journal of Political Psychology*, *Perspectives on Politics*, *Palara*, and *Souls*. He is completing a book manuscript entitled "Black and Red: Racial Politics in Post-Revolutionary Cuba." Additionally he is beginning work on a project that will examine health, immigration, race, and citizenship.

Silvio Torres-Saillant, Associate Professor of English and Director of the Latino–Latin American Studies Program at Syracuse University, is the founder and former director of the CUNY Dominican Studies Institute at the City College of New York. He is a senior editor for the forth-coming *Encyclopedia of Latinos and Latinas in the United States* (coedited with Suzanne Oboler and Deena González and associate editor of *Latino Studies*. He serves on the Board of Directors of the New York Council for the Humanities, the University of Houston's Recovering the U.S. Hispanic Literary Heritage Project, and the MLA Committee on the Literatures of People of Color in the United States and Canada. His book-length publications include *Caribbean Poetics* (1997), *El retorno de las yolas* (1999), and *The Dominican Americans* (1998), coauthored with Ramona Hernández. He has coedited volume 4 of *Recovering the U.S. Hispanic Literary Heritage* (with José Aranda) and *Desde la Orilla: Hacia una nacionalidad sin desalojos* (with Ramona Hernández).

Bobby Vaughn is Assistant Professor of Anthropology at Notre Dame de Namur University in Belmont, California. His current research interests began with a year of ethnographic research in Mexico as a Fulbright scholar in 1993–1994. In 2001 he earned his doctorate in anthropology from Stanford University; his dissertation is entitled Race and Nation: A Study of Blackness in Mexico. In 2002–2003 he was Visiting Assistant Professor of Anthropology and African American Studies at Colby College. Vaughn's Website is www.afromexico.com.

INDEX

Printed in the United States
68757LVS00001B/91-498